THE PIMLICO COMPANION TO FASHION

Colin McDowell is an internationally recognised fashion historian who has been involved with fashion for almost thirty years, as a designer, commentator and critic. Among his many books on fashion are *McDowell's Directory of Twentieth-Century Fashion*; *The Designer Scam*; *Dressed to Kill: Sex, Power and Clothes*; *Hats: Status, Style and Glamour* – published in the UK, the USA and France; and *Shoes: Fashion and Fantasy* – published in the UK, the USA, France, Germany, Italy and China.

Colin McDowell has written for numerous newspapers and magazines, including *Vogue*, *Elle*, *Marie Claire* and *Women's Journal*. He is a regular contributor to the Style Section of the *Sunday Times*. He appears frequently on radio and television, and wrote and presented *J'accuse* on Channel 4 on the subject of Christian Dior. He has written two successful popular novels set in the world of Italian fashion, and is at work on a third. He lives near Folkstone in Kent.

THE PIMLICO
COMPANION TO
FASHION

A Literary Anthology

EDITED BY
COLIN McDOWELL

PIMLICO

For Mary Witt

Published by Pimlico 1998

2 4 6 8 10 9 7 5 3 1

Copyright in the compilation and editorial matter © Colin McDowell 1995

Colin McDowell has asserted his right
under the Copyright, Designs and Patents Act 1988
to be identified as the author of this work

Permission to reproduce copyright material in this anthology is
acknowledged between pages 429-32 of this edition

First published by Sinclair-Stevenson as
The Literary Companion to Fashion in 1995
Pimlico edition 1998

Pimlico
Random House, 20 Vauxhall Bridge Road,
London SW1V 2SA

Random House Australia (Pty) Limited
20 Alfred Street, Milsons Point, Sydney,
New South Wales 2061, Australia

Random House New Zealand Limited
18 Poland Road, Glenfield,
Auckland 10, New Zealand

Random House South Africa (Pty) Limited
Endulini, 5A Jubilee Road, Parktown 2193, South Africa

Random House UK Limited Reg. No. 954009

A CIP catalogue record for this book
is available from the British Library

ISBN 0-7126-6609-5

Papers used by Random House UK Limited are natural,
recyclable products made from wood grown in sustainable forests.
The manufacturing processes conform to the environmental
regulations of the country of origin

Printed and bound in Great Britain by
Mackays of Chatham PLC

One had as good be out of the world,
as out of the fashion.

Colley Cibber, *Love's Last Shift*

CONTENTS

PREFACE

FASHION IS A nebulous affair, more a state of mind than anything else. And yet it has fascinated intelligent men and women for centuries. It has also irritated quite a lot of them. Fashion suffers by being very much more interesting than those who follow it. The slavish fashion freak who will accept anything, no matter how extreme, provided it is à la mode, has long been a stock character in the literature of Western civilization. Fops, dandies, ladies of fashion – especially when ageing – all have had the satirist's knife taken to their affectations and pretensions. Restoration comedy, Oscar Wilde, Nancy Mitford, Armistead Maupin . . . writers have had much fun at fashion's expense and I hope they'll continue to do so. Conversely we have had much fun out of the moralists and sourpusses who exhibit their fear of fashion by the virulence of their attacks on it: from Stubbes to Carlyle and a thousand scribblers beyond. We know why they are afraid. Fashion is potent because it is the outward and visible sign of emotions many of us prefer to keep hidden. Vanity, jealousy and lust are all part of the fashion equation. But fashion has a broader significance than the merely personal. Clothes articulate society in the most direct and revealing of ways. It has taken social scientists and scholars of history a very long time to realise this. Their tardiness has resulted in much valuable information being swept away or ignored. But, if the artefacts have gone, at least the literature remains.

This is my tenth book and I have enjoyed it more than any other – not least because it has permitted me to sit down in the middle of the morning and read novels, knowing that it was work. I hope that *The Literary Companion to Fashion* gives you as much pleasure as it has given me.

I have used 'fashion' as a catch-all word to cover many attitudes to dress far removed from the couturiers' perfumed salons. It isn't only the rich and grand who feel the pull of finery. I hope the extracts I have chosen demonstrate the extent to which concern over dress penetrates all classes and areas of society, including the poorest. If Shaw was right to suggest in *St Joan* that 'all dress is fancy dress, is it not, except our natural skins', then it must affect us all.

Because I am interested in ideas on fashion which cross the boundaries of 'set' time periods, I have not arranged the extracts chronologically. A piece from the sixteenth century may be followed by one from the twentieth, but I hope that the broad subject grouping and the placing within each group will fulfil my intention to show periods illuminated by the attitudes and views of other times. I have dated extracts, wherever possible, where it seemed to me that the writer might not be known to the general reader. There is little here earlier than the fifteenth century because I feel that the few references to clothes that there are from previous periods are of scant interest to the non-specialists. I would like to make clear that this book is the work of an enthusiast, not a specialist. I am sure that costume historians will be surprised by some omissions. I hope that they occur by intent and not from ignorance. Certainly, anything which I felt might not hold the interest of the general reader was avoided, even though I personally might have liked it.

When I started to compile *The Literary Companion to Fashion* I felt a compulsion to try to include everything I could which referred to the subject of dress. The result was a series of bulging folders which, unedited, would have filled a book three times the size of this volume. It would have been extremely boring and repetitive for all but the most dedicated and enthusiastic specialist costume historian. In weeding out pieces, my criteria were simple: anything worthy of inclusion had to be interesting, amusing or surprising – just as clothes are. The choice is a personal one: what I find entertaining will not necessarily have the same effect on everyone. But I hope it does.

Compiling an anthology which includes the work of writers still in copyright – by far the majority in the twentieth century – is a costly business. For that reason, there are examples from some writers which I have not been able to afford and I regret that they are missing. I am especially sorry to lose Edith Sitwell's *Façade*, but the price demanded for 67 lines was truly extortionate. Nevertheless, the anthology is 99 per cent as I had hoped it would be. Readers will soon become aware of my personal favourites, *Cranford, Vanity Fair* and *The Old Wives' Tale* amongst them – why no one has snapped up Arnold Bennett's most inexplicably neglected novel for film or television is a mystery. Favourite writers include Nancy Mitford and Armistead Maupin; Zola and Colette; Osbert Sitwell and Angus Wilson: all write with acuity about the social importance of clothes. Angela Carter's *Wise Children* and Beryl Bainbridge's *The Dressmaker* should be read by anyone with even a passing interest in the importance of dress in everyday life.

I have had a great deal of help with this anthology, especially from enthusiasts and friends who have reminded me of passages I had forgotten and have told me of many of which I was unaware.

Although the final choice is mine, I am happy to acknowledge all the suggestions I've received for authors I might otherwise have missed. In particular, I wish to record the generosity of a fellow author, Christina Walkely, whose books I have long admired but whom I had not met until two years ago. A mutual friend introduced us and I went down to visit Christina in Devon. After a delightful lunch, kept very lively by her sons, she produced a folder of items for an anthology on which she had been working for ten years. 'Take it,' she said. 'Use whatever you like.' If this anthology has any richness or claim to distinction, the part played by Christina's amazingly generous act must be acknowledged. Her reading had covered many different areas from mine and, alongside mutual favourites, she introduced me to several writers of whom I had never heard.

Others who gave me help are Jenny de Gex, Celia Gregory, Madeleine Ginsburgh, Sarah Harmer, Valerie Mansfield, Pat Murgatroyd and Mary Witt. I was given generous access to the Cunnington archives at the Gallery of English Costume, Platt Hall, in Manchester, and to the Mansfield Collection in Essex. Various members of the Costume Society and the Costume Society of America responded to my requests for help. Penny Hoare, my editor at Sinclair-Stevenson, shared my enthusiasm to a gratifying degree and made sure that I had the back-up help I needed. I must especially thank my desk editor, Katie Green, for her calm approach to problems which to me seemed intractable, and Simon Denis and Clare Naylor for help with chasing up permissions. Thanks to Vivienne Phillips for her invaluable work in finding who was published by whom – ground-breaking work on the back-breaking job of getting permissions – and to Christine Motley, who finished off the task for me. Finally, warm thanks to those publishers and agents who allowed me to quote from works for which they were responsible.

1

Advice, Opinion, Theory

Clothes are *inevitable*. They are nothing less than the furniture of the mind made visible, the very mirror of an epoch's soul.

James Laver, *Style in Costume*

Unto Adam also and to his wife did the LORD God make coats of skins, and clothed them.

Genesis (III, 21)

The best dressed of every age have always been the worst men and women.

The Habits of Good Society (Anon, 1859)

Fashion: A word which knaves and fools may use
Their knavery and folly to excuse.

Charles Churchill, *The Rosciad* (1761)

To a woman the consciousness of being well dressed gives a sense of tranquility which religion fails to bestow.

Helen Olcott Bell (1876)

. . . she had a womanly instinct that clothes possess an influence more powerful over many than the worth of character or the magic of manners.

Louisa M. Alcott, *Little Women*

And he said unto his disciples, Therefore I say unto you, Take no thought for your life, what ye shall eat; neither for the body, what ye shall put on . . . Consider the lilies how they grow: they toil not, they spin not; and yet I say unto you, that Solomon in all his glory was not arrayed like one of these.

St Luke (XII, 22 and 27)

I do not think the state of womanhood is quite so pitiable, now that it is the fashion to walk the streets in black cloth gaiters; they are the comfort of my life.

The Early Married Life of Maria Josepha, Lady Stanley (1899)

It's a funny thing to be educated – but nothing compared to the dizzying experience of owning six new dresses.

Jean Webster, *Daddy-long-legs*

It's wonderful what us bits of women do with a string of beads, but they don't go far with a gentleman.

Ronald Firbank, *Concerning the Eccentricities of Cardinal Pirelli* (1926)

Fashion is the abortive issue of vain ostentation and exclusive egotism: it is haughty, trifling, affected, servile, despotic, mean and ambitious, precise and fantastical, all in a breath – tied to no rule, and bound to conform to every whim of the minute.

William Hazlitt, *On Fashion*

Clothes. Dress as you do in a country house. Never wear a tweed coat and flannel trousers – always a suit. And go to a London tailor; you get better cut and longer credit

Evelyn Waugh, *Brideshead Revisited*

There's something sensible about a real, unadulterated top-coat.

Cuthbert Bede (Edward Bradley), *Adventures of Mr Verdant Green* (1853)

Singularity in dress shows something wrong in the mind.

Samuel Richardson, *A Collection of the Moral and Instructive Sentiments*

Gervaise

There was a young belle of old Natchez
Whose garments were always in patchez.
When comment arose
On the state of her clothes,
She drawled, When Ah itchez, Ah scratchez!

                                                    Ogden Nash

Nothing els is garish apparraile, but Prydes ulcer broken forth.

                        Thomas Nashe, *The Anatomie of Absurditie* (1589)

It is the extremities of fashion that distort good taste.

                                    Marcel Vertes, *Art and Fashion*

On Traditional Dress

The costume elastic, the dresses gymnastic,
The wonderful suits for the tricycle-ess –
Though skirts be divided, I'm clearly decided,
It isn't my notion of Rational Dress!

See gowns hygienic, and frocks calisthenic,
And dresses quite worthy of modern burlesque;
With garments for walking, and tennis, and talking,
All terribly manful and too trouseresque!

And habits for riding, for skating, or sliding,
With 'rational' features they claim to possess;
The thought I can't banish, they're somewhat *too* mannish,
And not quite the thing for a Rational Dress!

Note robes there for rinking, and gowns for tea-drinking,
For yachting, for climbing, for cricketing too;
The dresses for boating, the new petticoating,
The tunics in brown and the trousers in blue.

The fabrics for frockings, the shoes and the stockings,
And corsets that ne'er will the figure compress:
But in the whole placeful there's little that's graceful
And girlish enough for a Rational Dress!

'Tis hardy and boyish, not girlful and coyish –
We think, as we stroll round the gaily-dight room –
A masculine coldness, a brusqueness, a boldness,
Appears to pervade all this novel costume!

In ribbons and laces, and feminine graces,
And soft flowing robes, there's a charm more or less –
I don't think I'll venture on dual garmenture,
I fancy my own is the Rational Dress!

Punch (1895)

If men were really what they profess to be they would not compel women to dress so that the facilities for vice would always be so easy.

Mary Walker, *Saturday Review* (1935)

If a woman really repents, she has to go to a bad dressmaker, otherwise no one believes in her.

Oscar Wilde, *Lady Windermere's Fan*

Too great attention to nicety in dress, is undoubtedly a proof of a little mind; and, notwithstanding the compliment paid by Cicero to the talents and understanding of Hortensius, it is difficult not to consider him a very weak or very litigious man, when he summoned a person before the judges, because he had accidentally ruffled the order and plaits of his gown. Macrobius, however, seems sensible of this frivolity in Hortensius, whom he thus describes. 'Hortensius was professedly soft and effeminate, and made all decency to consist in outward show. He was vastly finical in his dress, and to adjust it the better, he employed a looking glass, by the assistance of which he so disposed his gown, that the plaits did not fall at random, but were arranged very carefully by means of a knot, and the fold or lappet falling or flowing down, with art went round the knot at his side.' It was for deranging this elaborate dress, that an unconscious colleague was summoned before a Roman tribunal.

Percy Anecdotes (1832)

People who study Greek must take pains with their dress.

Henry Adams

One may become rich but one is born elegant.

Honoré de Balzac, *Traite de la Vie Elégante*

ST CYPRIAN
From A Treatise on the Dress of Virgins

GOD NEITHER MADE the sheep scarlet nor purple, nor taught the juices of herbs and shell fish to dye and colour wool, nor arranged necklaces with stones set in gold, and with pearls distributed in a woven series or numerous cluster, wherewith you would hide the neck which he made; that what God formed in man may be covered, and that may be seen upon it which the devil has invented in addition. Has God willed that wounds should be made in the ears, wherewith infancy as yet innocent, and unconscious of worldly evil, may be put to pain, that subsequently from the scars and holes of the ears precious beads may hang, heavy, if not by their weight, still by the amount of their cost? All which things sinning and apostate angels put forth by their arts, when, lowered to the contagious earth, they forsook their heavenly vigour. They taught them also to paint the eyes with blackness drawn round them in a circle, and to stain the cheeks with a deceitful red, and to change the hair with false colours, and to drive out all truth, both of face and head, by the assault of their own corruption . . .

Are you not afraid, I entreat you, being such as you are, that when the day of resurrection comes, your maker may not recognise you again – and say, 'This is not my work, nor is this our image. You have polluted your skin with a false medicant, you have changed your hair with an adulterous colour, your face is violently taken possession of by a lie, your figure is corrupted, your countenance is another's. You cannot see God, since your eyes are not those which God made, but those which the devil has spoiled. You have followed him, you have imitated the red and painted eyes of a serpent. As you are adorned in the fashion of your enemy, with him also you shall burn by and by.'

JOHN LANGDON-DAVIES
From The Future of Nakedness

IT IS NOT at all hard to see what interests a tailor most about nakedness; it is the same thing that interests an old cab horse about a taxi, or an archer about a musketeer, or a sheep about roast mutton; at least it is if the tailor chances to be a prophetic tailor. Most tailors, of course, have minds no better than Wordsworth's when he wrote about our arrival on this planet not having been in a state of complete amnesia, 'nor yet in utter nakedness, but trailing clouds of glory'. But a prophetic tailor sees that the day may come when, to speak metaphorically, the glory may be on the other leg, when men may prefer the nakedness, in fact, to the inconvenient trailing garment which pleased Wordsworth.

But it is not only in their genesis that clothes are seen to be used for purposes of sexual attraction, and here is an interesting example of the effect of their sudden or sporadic introduction into a naked society to-day. The men of Pongo in Northern Nigeria use natural and sometimes manufactured clothing, but they refuse to allow their women to affect any kind of clothing at all, and they give as their reason for this refusal that if the women wore clothes they would become beautiful and be desired by men of foreign villages. Moreover, the first gown introduced among the Waja was worn to shreds, owing to its being constantly used by young men in their quest for wives. The authority for this valuable evidence is a government official of unimpeachable scientific ability; and his evidence can be rounded off by a quotation from one of the greatest of French novels of manners: readers of *Les Liaison Dangereuses* will remember that the Marquise de Merteuil wrote to the Vicomte de Valmont as follows: 'at last when I was alone with "the faithful servant!" I dressed myself as a waiting woman while she disguised herself as a lackey. She then brought a cab to my garden gates and off we went. When we reached the Temple of Love, I chose the most seductive dishabille. It was really delicious; it is my own invention; it lets nothing be seen and yet allows everything to be guessed at. I promise you a pattern for your Madame de Tourvel when you have rendered her worthy of wearing it.' Evidently Pongo and Paris are in one mind on the uses of concealment.

Thus we can sum up the situation by saying that humanity is afraid to take off its clothes because it is afraid of catching cold, afraid of magical forces harming its physical weak spots, afraid of being less attractive to the opposite sex, and afraid of being a worse Don Juan than it is. The first fear is genuine but temporary. Bodies used to do without clothes without suffering from heat or cold; if necessary they will learn to do so again; they have indeed already learned at Leysin. The second fear is surely obsolete in Regent Street. The third fear is the most important, and characteristically enough we are not even consciously aware that it exists. It is the true fear; the rest are phobias. The last fear is utterly groundless. Adam was not even a monogamist before he assumed the fig leaf.

The ascent to healthful nakedness is then not hopeless; we shall all learn in the school of necessity to take off our clothes.

(1929)

MRS M.R. HAWEIS
From The Art of Dress

COSTUME VIBRATES PERPETUALLY in our country between the need of being seen and the need of being covered. Now one bit of the body's beauty is displayed, and the rest is sacrified and covered up; it is invariably felt to be an incomplete experiment, and thrown over. Another scrap of arm or shoulder has its day, and gives way to the foot, or the waist, or something else.

The real truth would seem to be, although we do not like to confess it, that the human creature, by nature not a clothed animal, but a naked animal, is ever reverting by bits to its original state. Never can it attain to it, in the temperate zone, under whatsoever revolution of feeling, health, or morals. Clothed it must be; and yet is impelled dimly to be at once clothed and unclothed.

There is no part of the frame which has not at some time been *in fashion*. The arm, the bust, the back, the whole outline, has in turn been fully acknowledged. The Englishwoman has indeed for many generations refused to confess to legs, but she has 'come to'; not as wisely as the Turkish woman, but as well – too well. We shrink from no inconsistency. However cold, however clogged and impeded by ill-shapen gowns, we all go on bearing the nuisance with indomitable heroism. However comfortable in wraps of fur, or easy skirts, not long we brook 'the restless, dissatisfied longing', and arm, foot, or shoulder shakes itself free of comfort.

(1879)

Do not conceive that fine clothes make fine men any more than fine feathers make fine birds. A plain genteel dress is more admired and obtains more credit than lace and embroidery in the eyes of the sensible.

George Washington, letter to his nephew, Bushrod Washington, 15 January 1783

Too rich a dress may sometimes check desire.

Ovid, quoted in Beau Brummell, *Male and Female Costume*

A really well made button hole is the only link between Art and Nature.

Oscar Wilde, *Chameleon*

JEAN COCTEAU
From Past Tense

IT WOULD BE curious to make a study of the Incroyables, the Mérveilleuses, the Zazous, the Existentialists, and their ancestors. Including Alcibiadism, Dandyism, etc. The amazing hairstyles with sideburns of the male Zazous. The females like Thomas Diafoirus (Molière) for the hair and a little Breton cross around the neck. The tiny beard and the tight jeans of the male existentialist. His checked shirt. His loafers. The careful slovenliness of the existentialist female, her hair hanging down to her shoulders in long, limp locks. The black turtleneck. The vast scorn of everything that doesn't belong to this race. The racism of fashion.

Diary, June 1953

Everything a man of fashion puts on his body must be broken in. Nothing should appear new.

August Kotzebue, *Souvenirs of Paris* (1804)

Crime committed in evening dress is what most appeals to popular imagination.

Anatole France, *A Literary Life* (1888–92)

THOMAS CARLYLE
From Sartor Resartus

STRANGE ENOUGH, IT strikes me, is this same fact of there being Tailors and Tailored. The Horse I ride has his own whole fell: strip him of the girths and flaps and extraneous tags I have fastened round him, and the noble creature is his own sempster and weaver and spinner; nay his own boot-maker, jeweller, and man-milliner; he bounds free through the valleys, with a perennial rainproof court-suit on his body; wherein warmth and easiness of fit have reached perfection; nay, the graces also have been considered, and frills and fringes, with gay variety of colour, featly appended, and ever in the right place, are not wanting. While I – good Heaven! – have thatched myself over with the dead fleeces of sheep, the bark of vegetables, the entrails of worms, the hides of oxen or seals, the felt of furred beasts; the walk around a moving Ragscreen, overheaped with shreds and tatters raked from the Charnel-house of Nature, where they would have rotted, to rot on me more slowly! Day after day, I must thatch myself anew; day after day, this despicable thatch must lose some film of its thickness; some film of it, frayed away by tear and wear, must be brushed-off into the Ashpit, into the Laystall; till by degrees the whole has been brushed thither, and I, the dust-making, patent Rag-grinder, get new material to grind down. O subterbrutish! vile! most vile! For have not I too a compact all-enclosing Skin, whiter or dingier? Am I a botched mass of tailors' and cobblers' shred, then; or a tightly-articulated, homogeneous little Figure, automatic, nay alive?

MRS ERIC PRITCHARD
From The Cult of Chiffon

CHIC IS INIMITABLE, so we have been told by fashion writers. But I am not so sure that they are entirely right, for some of us have acquired it without being born with it. Very few Englishwomen, in fact, possess this quality as a birthright. They may boast of their style, but their style differs from *chic* as widely as the scent of patchouli from the aroma of old rose leaves. *Chic*, indeed, is that subtle and indefinable air of good taste that only the best bred can attain to. It is a quality so impalpable and subtle that the ordinary British woman neither understands nor desires it. But she makes the greatest mistake, for with *chic* the ugliest woman can be made not only presentable but irresistible, while the professional beauty, with all her style, may be unattractive without *chic*.

(1902)

ERIC GILL

From Trousers and the Most Precious Ornament

IN COUNTRIES CIVILIZED according to the current industrial commercial idea of civilization, while women flaunt their sexual attractiveness on all occasions, men do exactly the opposite. Sex in civilized man is signified solely by a certain kind of clothes, and he does his best to suppress all appearance of his maleness of body. Men's clothes are simply a more or less convenient covering, convenient for the job of being a clerk in an office, a covering to obscure all his animal nature – there is no use for such in the city. But sex in civilized women is not signified simply by clothes of a conventional kind. We do not say: Look, there goes a woman; you can tell by her skirt. We know her for a woman by the shape of her legs, the roundness of her croup and by the protuberance of her bosom. A woman dressed in men's clothes has no such opportunities for exposition, and a man in his own clothes is as much sexless as possble. He shaves his face so that, if he be young & fair, you'd not know but that he might be a girl, and any protuberance by which his sex might be known is carefully and shamefully suppressed. It is an organ of drainage and not of sex. It is tucked away and all sideways, dishon-oured, neglected, ridiculed and ridiculous – no longer the virile member and man's most precious ornament, but the comic member, a thing for girls to gig-gle about – comic and, to nursemaids, dirty – 'You dirty little boy, put it away'. . .

This matter is not only to be seen with eyes fixed on England; it has world-wide importance. In England we are told that, in spite of the fact that more boys are born than girls, there are a million or so more women than men of mar-riageable age; and doubtless, whether they are aware of it or not, this fact, this condition, has something to do with the present exhibitionism of women of all classes. A million or more of them cannot possibly marry – as marriage is under-stood in our erstwhile christian and still largely christianesque society. They must do something about it. The wiles, the not very wiley wiles, of the professional prostitute must be used – scents, paint, closely clothed hips and croups, a sway-ing walk, immense care of the face and hair, short skirts in the street, diaphanous clinging drapes in the evening, bare backs and chests.

Hence it is that in a world devoted to commerce, trading, shop-keeping, money-making, the male creature is under eclipse. He is not wanted, and a pre-mium is put upon the rabbit type, the kind that sees nothing wrong in travelling in a tube to and from the city where, cooped up in burrows, they scuffle and scoop and nibble and grab for little profits and 'quick returns', where the high-est ambition is to make lots of money. . . No wonder they dress him in trousers and tie up his maleness all crushed and sideways and tell him it's dirty. . .

I am not arguing that women should hide their bodies and men expose them, rather I am arguing that both men and women should regain their human dignity and dress accordingly. Today, it would seem that we only think of ourselves as a kind of superior animal. We say how convenient such and such clothes are, or how inconvenient, how comfortable or how uncomfortable, healthy or unhealthy. We never say how appropriate or inappropriate, suitable or unsuitable; at any rate such considerations are very much in the background and the chief thing in the minds of those who would reform modern dress are hygiene and functional convenience. The idea that man is a being having intrinsic dignity (child of God, 'and if child, heir also') is forgotten. We dress either as fashion demands or imposes (which is largely a matter of salesmanship and advertisement exploiting human vanity) or we dress simply for convenience; as when we wear shorts for cycling, slips for swimming and, strange as it may seem, 'plus fours' for golfing. And if I have been at considerable pains to throw contumely upon man's modern dress and to sneer at its sexlessness, it is not because I wish men to flaunt their maleness as women flaunt their femaleness, but because I consider such clothes unworthy of human beings and derogatory to their male & female natures. The highlander in his kilt (beneath which he is normally naked) is not exposing his sex, but, on the other hand, neither is he dishonouring it.

FYNES MORYSON

From An Itinerary

ENGLAND – BESIDES THE famous Broad cloth, it yields for clothing many Stuffes, whereof great quantitie is also imported. And I will not omit, that howsoever it hath silke from forraigne parts, yet the English silke stockings are much to be preferred before those of Italy, Spaine, or any part of the World.

The wives of Merchants, though little yielding to others in pride or expence, yet have long used, and still retaine a decent attire, with little or no inconstancy in the fashion. They weare a gowne of some light stuffe or silke, gathered in the backe, and girded to the body with a girdle, and decked with many gardes at the skirt, with which they weare an apron before them, as some silke or stuffe, or fine linnen. They weare upon their heads a coyfe of fine linnen, with their haire raised a little at the forehead, and a cap of silke, or a little hat of beaver, yet without fit difference of estate or condition, and some weare light French chaines and necklaces of pearle.... Husbandmen weare garments of course cloth, made at home, and their wives weare gownes of the same cloth, kirtles of some light stuffe, with linnen aprons, and cover their heads with a linnen coyfe, and a high felt hat, and in generall their linnen is course, and made at home.

Gentlewomen virgins weare gownes close to the body and aprons of fine linnen and goe bareheaded, with their haire curiously knotted, and raised at the
forehead, but, many against the cold (as they say) weare caps of haire that is not
their owne, decking their heads with buttons of gold, pearles, and flowers of silke,
or knots of ribbon. They weare fine linnen, and commonly falling bands, and
often ruffles, both starched, and chaines of pearle about the necke, with their
breasts naked. The graver sort of married women used to cover their head with
a French hood of Velvet, set with a border of gold buttons and pearles: but this
fashion is now left, and they most commonly weare a coyfe of linnen, and a little hat of beaver or felt, with their haire somewhat raised at the forehead. Young
married women sometime goe bare headed, as virgins, decking their haire with
Jewels, and silke ribbens, and more commonly they use the foresaid linnen coyfe
and hats. All in generall weare gownes hanging loose at the backe, with a kirtle
and close upper-body of silke or light stuffe, but have lately left the French sleeves
borne out with hoopes of whalebone, and the young married Gentlewomen, no
lesse than the Virgins shew their breasts naked.

France – Frenchwomen weare very light gownes, commonly blacke, and hanging loose at the backe, and under it an upper-body close at the breast, with a kirtle
of a mixed or light colour, and of some light stuffe, laid with many gardes, in
which sort the women are generally attired. They weare sleeves to their gownes
borne out with whalebones, and of a differing colour from the gowne, which
besides hath other loose hanging sleeves cast backward, and aswel the upper-
bodies, as the kirtles, differ from the gowne in colour and stuffe. And they say,
that the sleeves borne up with whale-bones, were first invented, to avoid mens
familiar touching of their armes... In France as well men as women, use richly
to be adorned with Jewels... The Ladies weare their Jewels commonly at the
breast, or upon the left arme, and many other waies, for who can containe the
mutable French in one and the same fashion.

(1617)

If you rebel against high-heeled shoes, take care to do so in a very smart hat.

George Bernard Shaw

It is astonishing how resolutely the advanced professors of medicine . . . have
denounced the practice of compressing the body in the stages of its growth. . .

It is equally astonishing how resolutely the votaries of fashion have resisted the teaching of the learned.

Dr Richardson in *The Gentleman's Magazine* (1880)

The following recipe for a lady's dress occurs where one would least expect it, in the works of Tertullian: 'Let simplicity be your white, chastity your vermillion; dress your eye-brows with modesty, and your lips with reservedness. Let instruction be your ear-rings, and a ruby cross the front pin in your head. Submission to your husband, is your best ornament. Employ your hands in housewifery, and keep your feet within your own doors.'

Percy Anecdotes (1823)

No dress can be good which is not useful and adapted to practical necessities, nor can any dress be perfect into which the element of individuality does not enter.

Mrs Oliphant, *Dress* (1878)

We would have the skirt reaching down to a little below the knee, and not made quite so full as is the present fashion. Underneath this skirt, trousers made moderately full, in fair mild weather, coming down to the ankle (not instep) and there gathered in with an elastic band, or, what we think decidedly prettier, gathered three or four times, half an inch apart, and drawn up to just sufficient width to permit the foot to pass through. The shoes or slippers to suit the occasion. For winter or wet weather, the trousers also full, but coming down into a boot, which should rise at least three or four inches above the ankle. This boot should be gracefully sloped at the upper edge and trimmed with fur, or fancifully embroidered, according to the taste of the wearer. The material might be cloth, morocco, mooseskin, and so forth, and made waterproof if desirable.

Amelia Bloomer describing the Bloomer Costume in *The Lily* (1850)

Elegance is refusal.

Diana Vreeland

The reason the Frenchwoman is so well dressed as a rule is that she is immensely critical of her appearance.

Jean-Philippe Worth, *A Century of Fashion* (1928)

I suppose this is the time I should give you advice. I never had any myself except once from your cousin Alfred. Do you know, in the summer before I was going up, your cousin Alfred rode over to Boughton especially to give me a piece of advice? And do you know what that advice was? 'Ned,' he said, 'there's one thing I must beg of you. *Always* wear a tall hat on Sundays during term. It is by that, more than anything, that a man is judged.'

Evelyn Waugh, *Brideshead Revisited*

Fashion is like God, man cannot see it in its holy of holies and live. And it is, like God, increate, springing out of nothing, yet the maker of all things – ever changing yet the same yesterday, to-day and for ever.

Samuel Butler, *Notebooks*

One should never give a woman anything she can't wear in the evening.

Oscar Wilde, *An Ideal Husband*

Don't ever wear artistic jewellery; it wrecks a woman's reputation.

Colette

Sir, – May I be allowed in your columns to ask why the British public is so horrified at the idea of women dressing in trousers, seeing that they have for many years tolerated a number of men from the North of the Tweed in wearing petticoats, and shockingly short petticoats too?

Amelia Bloomer, in *The Daily News* (1854)

Modern costume is made not to reveal beauty but to conceal defects.

Alma Tadema (1836–1912)

LORD CHESTERFIELD
From Letters to his Son

DRESS IS A very foolish thing; and yet it is a very foolish thing for a man not to be well dressed, according to his rank and way of life; and it is so far from being a disparagement to any man's understanding, that it is rather a proof of it, to be as well dressed as those whom he lives with: the difference in this case, between a man of sense and a fop, is, that the fop values himself upon his dress; and the man of sense laughs at it, at the same time that he knows that he must not neglect it: there are a thousand foolish customs of this kind, which, not being criminal, must be complied with, and even cheerfully, by men of sense. Diogenes the Cynic was a wise man for despising them, but a fool for showing it.

Dress is the great secret of address. Clothes and confidence will set anybody up.

William Hazlitt, *On Fashion*

Fine clothes are good only as they supply the want of other means of procuring respect.

Samuel Johnson

Rich apparel has strange virtues: it makes him that hath it without means, esteemed for an excellent wit; he that enjoys it with means, puts the world in remembrance of his means; it helps the deformities of nature, gives lustre to her beauties, and makes continual holiday where it shines.

Ben Jonson

Dress consists not so much in the garment as in the way it is worn.

Honoré de Balzac, *Traite de la Vie Elégante*

About clothes, it's awful. Everything makes you want pretty clothes like hell. People laugh at girls who are badly dressed. Jaw, jaw, jaw... 'Beautifully dressed woman...' As if it isn't enough that you want to be beautiful, that you want to have pretty clothes, that you want it like hell. As if that isn't enough. But no, it's jaw, jaw and sneer, sneer all the time. And the shop-windows sneering and smiling in your face. And then you look at the skirt of your costume, all crumpled at the back. And your hideous underclothes. You look at your hideous underclothes and you think, 'All right, I'll do anything for good clothes. Anything – anything for clothes.'

Jean Rhys, *Voyage in the Dark*

Dress, like writing, should never appear the effect of too much study and application.

William Shenstone (1764)

STEPHEN POTTER
From Gamesmanship
The Second Rule of Gamesmanship

IF THE OPPONENT WEARS, OR ATTEMPTS TO WEAR, CLOTHES CORRECT AND SUITABLE FOR THE GAME, BY AS MUCH AS HIS CLOTHES SUCCEED IN THIS FUNCTION, BY SO MUCH SHOULD THE GAMESMAN'S CLOTHES FAIL.

Corollary: Conversely, if the opponent wears the wrong clothes, the games-man should wear the right.

'If you can't volley, wear velvet socks,' we Old Gamesmen used to say. The good-looking young athlete, perfectly dressed, is made to feel a fool if his bad shot is returned by a man who looks as if he has never been on a tennis-court before. His good clothes become a handicap by virtue of their very suitability.

It is true that against the new golf-club member, inclined to be modest and nervous, a professional turn-out can be effective. A well-worn but well-cut golf jacket and a good pair of mackintosh trousers can, in this situation, be of real value. (My own tip here is to take an ordinary left-hand glove, cut the thumb off, make a diamond-shaped hole on the back, and say, 'Henry Cotton made this for me – he never plays with any other.')

If the wench wants a good gown, don't give her a fine smelling bottle because it is more delicate.

Samuel Johnson

JANE AUSTEN
From Northanger Abbey

DRESS IS AT all times a frivolous distinction, and excessive solicitude about it often destroys its own aim. Catherine knew this very well; her great aunt had read her a lecture on the subject only the Christmas before; and yet she lay awake ten minutes on Wednesday night debating between her spotted and her tamboured muslin, and nothing but the shortness of the time prevented her buying a new one for the evening. This would have been an error of judgement, great though not uncommon, from which one of the other sex rather than her own, a brother rather than a great aunt might have warned her, for man only can be aware of the insensibility of man towards a new gown. It would be mortifying to the feelings of many ladies, could they be made to understand how little the heart of man is affected by what is costly or new in their attire; how little it is biassed by the texture of their muslin, and how unsusceptible of peculiar tenderness towards the spotted, the sprigged, the mull or the jackonet. Woman is fine for her own satisfaction alone. No man will admire her the more, no woman will like her the better for it. Neatness and fashion are enough for the former, and a something of shabbiness or impropriety will be most endearing to the latter.

Fashions, after all, are only induced epidemics, proving that epidemics can be induced by tradesmen.

George Bernard Shaw, Preface to *The Doctor's Dilemma* (1906)

MRS GASKELL
From Cranford

THE CRANFORD LADIES have only an occasional little quarrel, spirted out in a few peppery words and angry jerks of the head; just enough to prevent the even tenor of their lives from becoming too flat. Their dress is very independent of fashion; as they observe, 'What does it signify how we dress here at

Cranford, where everybody knows us?' And if they go from home, their reason is equally cogent: 'What does it signify how we dress here, where nobody knows us?' The materials of their clothes are, in general, good and plain, and most of them are nearly as scrupulous as Miss Tyler, of cleanly memory; but I will answer for it, the last gigot, the last tight and scanty petticoat in wear in England, was seen in Cranford – and seen without a smile.

EDWARD BULWER-LYTTON

From Pelham, or The Adventures of a Gentleman

KEEP YOUR MIND free from all violent affectations at the hour of the toilet. A philosophical serenity is perfectly necessary to success. Helvetius says, justly, that our errors arise from our passions.

Remember that none but those whose courage is unquestionable can venture to be effeminate. It was only in the field that the Spartans were accustomed to use perfumes and curl their hair.

The handsome may be showy in dress, the plain should study to be unexceptionable; just as in great men we look for something to admire – in ordinary men we ask for nothing to forgive.

There may be more pathos in the fall of a collar, or the curl of a lock, than the shallow think for.

There is an indifference to please in a stocking down at heel – but there may be malevolence in a diamond ring.

(1828)

I never saw so many shocking bad hats in my life.

The Duke of Wellington on the First Reform Parliament (1831)

LORD CHESTERFIELD
From Letters to his Son

WHEN YOU COME to Paris, you must take care to be extremely well dressed, that is, as the fashionable people are. This does by no means consist in the finery, but in the taste, fitness, and manner of wearing your clothes; a fine suit ill-made, and slatternly or stiffly worn, far from adorning, only exposes the awkwardness of the wearer. Get the best French tailor to make your clothes, whatever they are, in the fashion, and to fit you, and then wear them; button them or unbutton them, as the genteelest people you see do. Let your man learn of the best *friseur* to do your hair well, for that is a very material part of your dress. Take care to have your stockings well gartered up, and your shoes well buckled; for nothing gives a more slovenly air to a man than ill-dressed legs.

Nowe my deare hearte let me parlye a little with thee about trifles, for when I am present with thee, my speeche is preiudiced by thy presence which drawes my mind from itselfe; I suppose now, upon thy unkles cominge there will be advisinge & counsellinge of all hands; and amongst many I know there will be some, that will be provokinge thee, in these indifferent things, as matter of apparell, fashions and other circumstances; I hould it a rule of Christian wisdome in all things to follow the soberest examples; I confesse that there be some ornaments which for Virgins and Knights Daughters &c may be comly and tollerable wch yet in soe great a change as thine is, may well admitt a change allso; I will medle with noe particulars neither doe I thinke it shall be needfull; thine own wisdome and godliness shall teach thee sufficiently what to doe in such things. I knowe thou wilt not grieve me for trifles. Let me intreate thee (my sweet Love) to take all in good part.

John Winthrop to Margaret Tyndale (1616)

ROBERT HERRICK
Leprosie in Cloathes

When flowing garments I behold
Enspir'd with *Purple, Pearle*, and *Gold*;
I think no other but I see
In them a glorious leprosie

That do's infect, and make the rent
More mortall in the vestiment.
As flowrie vestures doe descrie
The wearers rich immodestie;
So plaine and simple clothes doe show
Where vertue walkes, not those that flow.

From *Hesperides* (1648)

All high and more than human Sciences are decked and enrobed with
Poeticall stile. Even as women . . . make trunk-sleeves of wyre, and whalebone bodices, backes of lathes, and stiffe bumbasted verdugals, and, to the
open-view of all men, paint and embellish themselves with counterfeit and
borrowed beauties, so doth learning.

Michel de Montaigne, *Essayes . . . now done into English by John Florio*

Husband: Really, Laura, if these skirts get any shorter they'll be hardly decent.
Wife: My dear man, don't you understand? All skirts are decent, but not all legs.

Punch (1920s)

From 'The Unhappy Consequences of Women's Love of Finery'

THE PEARL NECKLACE, the flowered stomacher, the artificial nosegay, and
shaded furbelow, may be of use to attract the eye of the beholder, and turn
it from the imperfections of her features and shape. But if ladies will take my
word for it, and as they dress to please men they ought to consult our fancy rather
than their own in this particular, I can assure them there is nothing touches our
imagination so much as a beautiful woman in a plain dress. There might be more
agreeable ornaments found in our own manufacture than any that rise out of the
looms of Persia.

This, I know, is a very harsh doctrine to womankind, who are carried away
with everything that is showy, and with what delights the eye, more than any one
species of living creatures whatsoever...

Many a lady has fetched a sigh at the toss of a wig, and been ruined by the tapping of a snuff-box. It is impossible to describe all the execution that was done by the shoulder-knot while that fashion prevailed, or to reckon up all the virgins that have fallen a sacrifice to a pair of fringed gloves. A sincere heart has not made half so many conquests as an open waistcoat; and I should be glad to see an able head make so good a figure in a woman's company as a pair of red heels.

The Tatler, c. 1710

Go where you will, and you will see French fashions but only in Paris do you see how they should be worn.

Mrs Frances Trollope (1835)

> Costly apparel let the fair one fly,
> Enrich'd with gold, or with the Tyrian dye,
> What folly must in such expense appear,
> When more becoming colours are less dear!

Ovid, quoted by Beau Brummell in *Male and Female Costume*

No dress can be beautiful that is stiff. Drapery is essential

William Morris (1834–96)

What's the Use?

> Sure, deck your lower limbs in pants;
> Yours are the limbs, my sweeting.
> You look divine as you advance –
> Have you seen yourself retreating?

Ogden Nash, *The Face is Familiar*

The fashionable woman has long legs and aristocratic ankles but no knees. She has thin, veiled arms and fluttering hands but no elbows.

Kennedy Fraser, *The Fashionable Mind* (1981)

About White Spats

IHAVE BEEN TRYING to find out why men wear white spats. Nobody seems to know, or at any rate to admit, the reason.

My own theory has always been that white spats were originally devised to protect the trousers against the shoe-blacking; but an examination of my trousers, both where they fall on to the shoe and where the shoe falls on to them in one of my favourite attitudes of repose, reveals the fact that modern blacking (anyhow the brand my boot-boy uses) does not make a mess of my trousers.

There are only two good reasons that I can think of for wearing white spats. One, because your socks are of an unsightly design or sag at the ankle or, in rather extreme cases, are odd; and two, because you are wearing turned-down trousers which catch in the back of your shoes.

In well-regulated families, of course, the first necessity does not arise; but the second one is a good and sufficient cause why white spats should be included in every man's wardrobe. Occasions are bound to arise when one likes to affect turned-down trousers – weddings, garden-parties, business luncheons and so forth; and there is nothing which fills a man with such self-contempt as the knowledge that he is going about with his trousers caught up in the back of his shoes.

Some men, it is true, wear white spats because of their power to arrest attention; and it must be confessed that they have a certain usefulness in this respect. White spats draw the eye of an observer down to the feet, and, though feet are seldom much of an attraction in themselves, there is undoubtedly a type of man whose feet are less trying to the eye than his upper parts.

It will be seen then that the true function of the white spat is purely defensive. It creates nothing, builds nothing; it merely corrects and covers up. The argument that white spats are cooling in hot weather holds no water. It is a hygiological fact (I expect) that the more things you put round a thing the hotter it gets; so spats, unless you wear them in lieu of socks, can have no possible effect other than to make the feet hotter. And that other argument too, that white spats give an impression of affluence and so carry a man higher up the social ladder, has gone by the board in an age when the top of the ladder is held by poor people. Ostentation of wealth is nowadays a distinct barrier to social advancement; therefore wear your white spats only when need be.

Taken all round, it is a pity about the white spat. It is a tricky garment. One of the chief disadvantages about it is that you cannot leave the bottom button undone, as you do with a waistcoat. You must do up this button at all costs; and there is no button in the world so hard to do up as the bottom button of a spat.

If you have chosen your spat to fit you neatly round the thin end of the calf, this button won't do up; if you have chosen your spat because the bottom button will do up, your leg will fit into it something like the toothpick into the top of a bottle of angostura. You must be careful of these points when you are buying your white spats; spat sellers mostly don't mind about them.

Then too white spats cramp your style. It is a *sine qua non* about them that they should be white, just as it is with dress-shirts; but they are much harder to keep white because they are worn so much closer to the ground. And there are your feet. The natural place for one's feet when one is in a comfortable sitting posture is on top of one another, or at any rate rubbing up against one another. With white spats this won't do. You must think of each foot separately. Your right foot must know all the time what your left foot is doing; it must treat it as if it were a complete stranger, as if it were somebody else's foot. White spats make you foot-conscious; they are unnatural things. They spoil your day. They spoilt my Ascot.

Thank goodness one could do Wimbledon in turned-up trousers.

Punch (1920s)

ALEXANDER PICCOLOMINI

From Raffaella: A dialogue of the fair perfectioning of ladies

Margaret   I would wish, Mistress Raffaella, to hear somewhat more of you in the matter of dress.

Raffaella   I would that a young lady every few days should change her dress and never lay aside a fashion which is good, and if her judgment suffices her to find out fashions new and fair, it would be most suitable for her often to put forward some one of them; but should her judgment not suffice, she should cleave to those of other ladies which are the better thought of.

Margaret   What property should a fashion have to be called good?

Raffaella   I would that a fashion should be rich and handsome.

Margaret   In what lies this being rich?...

Raffaella   I say then that the richness of dress lies for great part in the seeking out with care that the stuffs, the cloths, the serges or other tissues should be of the finest and best that may be found; because the dressing in thick cloths as, to give an instance, Mistress Lorenza does, who for her fashion has made her a frock almost like a friar's, calls for a 'slender fashion'.

Margaret   How 'almost'? It is like a friar's, most friar-like.

Raffaella   So much the worse! I would that garments furthermore were ample and abundant but not so far as to leave the body too incommoded. And this full-ness is of great import, because there is nothing worse than when we see some of our gentlewomen, who go about Siena in little dresses of a sort which contain less than sixteen ells of cloth; and for their short capes which reach not to their tails by a span, they twist one part of them round their necks and hold a flap in their hand, and so they go masked down the street; and with their other hand lifting up the dresses lest they wear out by trailing the ground, down the street they go as if possessed, with a clitter-clatter of pattens as though the Devil had got between their legs. And perhaps they lift up the dresses so as to show a pretty foot, with some part of the leg all tiffed up. But all they show are their broad ugly feet, ill shod with some slippers all out at seam for very age . . . I would also that these garments, be they ample as I tell thee, should be full of guards, of cuts, of slash-es, of broderies and other such things; some another time should be quite plain, since this varietie of dressing shows great sumptuousness and much good lies therein . . .

Raffaella   In fine, in what I say, I intend that expense should accord with what is possible. She who cannot do all, let her do the most that is possible, even constraining herself a little.

Margaret   Continue then.

Raffaella   Returning to my theme I say it is a most ill-favoured thing to wear one and the same dress for a long time, and worst of all when others may per-ceive that of one dress another has been made, by dyeing it or turning it inside out or otherhow, as did the wife of a gentleman who is now one of our Lords. Nay, having made herself, when she was a bride, a garment of white damask, and worn it for some years after till it became very filthy, she turned it, putting the inside without, and so went on wearing it for five years more, Sunday after Sunday. But then, when it was rending, she had it dyed in gingerline colour, or Lion-tawny as we like to call it, so that she might seem to have changed her dress, and also because in this colour it was harder to perceive the rents than in the white; besides this, also, because at her age it was no longer seemly for her to wear white. Then, when after a year or two the dress began to burst asunder most blithely, she determined for all that to despoil it, and made for herself of one part fringes for a sort of purple frock, and of the rest some cuffs, which soon resolv-ing themselves into bare threads, she then covered over with linen cutwork, and so they are today. We shall see what will happen next; my thought is that, before the poor damask finds peace in its grave, it will go on still atoning for its sins, in other forms, for some years yet.

(1538)

Virtue is like a rich stone, best plain set.

Francis Bacon, *Essays*

Why not be oneself? That is the whole secret of a successful appearance. If one is a greyhound, why try to look like a Pekingese?

Dame Edith Sitwell

Those who make their dress a principal part of themselves, will, in general, become of no more value than their dress.

William Hazlitt, *On Dress*

Pink is the navy blue of India.

Diana Vreeland

A sincere heart has not made half so many conquests as an open waistcoat.

The Levellers: A Dialogue, *Harleian Miscellany* (1744–6)

Fashion, like fossils, reveals the habits of extinct beings.

C. Willett Cunnington, *English Women's Clothing in the Nineteenth Century*

It is the bourgeoisie, the respectable people, who finally decide what a fashion shall be, although they very rarely inaugurate it.

James Laver, *Taste and Fashion*

2

Childhood –
Memories and Misery

John had
Great Big
Waterproof
Boots on;
John had a
Great Big
Waterproof
Hat;
John had a
Great Big
Waterproof
Mackintosh –
and that
(said John)
Is
That.

A.A. Milne, 'Happiness'

What the Earl saw was a graceful childish figure in a black velvet suit, with a lace collar, and with lovelocks waving about the handsome, manly little face, whose eyes met his with a look of innocent good-fellowship.

Frances Hodgson Burnett, *Little Lord Fauntleroy*

CHARLES AND MARY LAMB
Going into Breeches

Joy to Philip, he this day
Has his long coats cast away,
And (the childish season gone)
Put the manly breeches on.
Officer on gay parade,
Red-coat in his first cockade,
Bridegroom in his wedding-trim,
Birthday bean surpassing him,
Never did with conscious gait
Strut about in half the state,
Or the pride (yet free from sin)
Of my little MANIKIN:
Never was there pride, or bliss,
Half so rationed as his.
Sashes, frocks, to those that need 'em!
Philip's limbs have got their freedom:
He can run, or he can ride,
And do twenty things beside
Which his petticoats forbad:
Is he not a happy lad?

Auntie's Skirts

Whenever Auntie moves around.
Her dresses make a curious sound;
They trail behind her up the floor,
And trundle after through the door

Robert Louis Stevenson, from *A Child's Garden of Verses*

Every night we were wrap'd up like Pomatum sticks in greasy brown paper, our hands, faces and chests were completely covered with tallow and brown paper made into various sorts of ointments; our arms were suspended in the air by strong ropes fastened to the tester of the bed, our feet tied to the valence to stretch our legs and make us grow tall.

Retrospections of Dorothea Herbert (1770–89)

WILLIAM MAKEPEACE THACKERAY
From Vanity Fair

SOMETIMES – ONCE OR twice in a week – that lady visited the upper regions in which the child lived. She came like a vivified figure out of the *Magasin des Modes* – blandly smiling in the most beautiful new clothes and little gloves and boots. Wonderful scarfs, laces, and jewels glittered about her. She had always a new bonnet on, and flowers bloomed perpetually in it; or else magnificent curling ostrich feathers, soft and snowy as camellias. She nodded twice or thrice patronizingly to the little boy, who looked up from his dinner or from the pictures of soldiers he was painting. When she left the room, an odour of rose, or some other magical fragrance, lingered about the nursery. She was an unearthly being in his eyes, superior to his father – to all the world; to be worshipped and admired at a distance. To drive with that lady in the carriage was an awful rite: he sate up in the back seat, and did not dare to speak; he gazed with all his eyes at the beautifully dressed princess opposite to him. Gentlemen on splendid prancing horses came up, and smiled and talked with her. How her eyes beamed upon all of them! Her hand used to quiver and wave gracefully as they passed. When he went out with her, he had his new red dress on. His old brown holland was good enough when he stayed at home. Sometimes, when she was away and

Dolly his maid was making his bed, he came into his mother's room. It was as the abode of a fairy to him – a mystic chamber of splendour and delights. There in the wardrobe hung those wonderful robes – pink and blue and many-tinted. There was the jewel-case, silver-clasped; and the wondrous bronze hand on the dressing-table, glistening all over with a hundred rings. There was the cheval-glass, that miracle of art, in which he could just see his own wondering head, and the reflection of Dolly (queerly distorted, and as if up in the ceiling), plumping and patting the pillows of the bed. O thou poor lonely little benighted boy! Mother is the name for God in the lips and hearts of little children, and here was one who was worshipping a stone!

W. SOMERSET MAUGHAM
From Of Human Bondage

OUTSIDE THE DOOR of his mother's bedroom he stopped and listened. Though no one had told him not to go in, he had a feeling that it would be wrong to do so; he was a little frightened, and his heart beat uncomfortably; but at the same time something impelled him to turn the handle. He turned it very gently, as if to prevent anyone within from hearing, and then slowly pushed the door open. He stood on the threshold for a moment before he had the courage to enter. He was not frightened now, but it seemed strange. He closed the door behind him. The blinds were drawn, and the room, in the cold light of a January afternoon, was dark. On the dressing-table were Mrs Carey's brushes and the hand mirror. In a little tray were hairpins. There was a photograph of himself on the chimney-piece and one of his father. He had often been in the room when his mother was not in it, but now it seemed different. There was something curious in the look of the chairs. The bed was made as though someone were going to sleep in it that night, and in a case on the pillow was a night-dress.

Philip opened a large cupboard filled with dresses and, stepping in, took as many of them as he could in his arms and buried his face in them. They smelt of the scent his mother used. Then he pulled open the drawers, filled with his mother's things, and looked at them: there were lavender bags among the linen; and their scent was fresh and pleasant. The strangeness of the room left it, and it seemed to him that his mother had just gone out for a walk. She would be in presently and would come upstairs to have nursery tea with him. And he seemed to feel her kiss on his lips.

It was not true that he would never see her again. It was not true simply because it was impossible. He climbed up on the bed and put his head on the pillow. He lay there quite still.

V.S. PRITCHETT

From A Cab at the Door

MOTHER HAD A hard time making both ends meet and, on a day like this, wanted us to be dressed in something respectable.

The day before, she put the sewing-machine on the dining-room table, took out a paper pattern and set about making me some trousers.

She made many of her own dresses and a lot of our clothes; indeed, if she was making a dress for herself or my sister, I was often the model. I had to stand up while she pinned patterns all over me.

She was often puzzled by the strips of pattern that were left over. If only she had her Cousin Louie, the dressmaker, she would say; for it was a fate with her often to cut out, say, two left sleeves, or to be short of a quarter of a yard on the length. She knitted our stockings and never learned how to turn a heel, so that a double heel often hung over the backs of our boots: jerseys for us she never finished; but for herself – for she did not want to make victims of us – she would knit recklessly on while I read the instructions for her, and turn out narrow tubes of wool that would stretch, laughing till she cried, to her knees. She had to pay for the material for her dressmaking out of the housekeeping money and she would raid any free material in sight.

I have described her attacks on our curtains. Her own bloomers were a byword: for in gay moments she would haul up her long skirts above her knees and show my father – who was always shocked – what could be done with a chair cover or something robust of that kind.

'You want me in the business instead of "that woman",' she'd say.

For she had a vengeful streak in her, and looking at our father, the impressive Managing Director, and counting his suits and knowing how she couldn't get a penny out of him for our clothes, she attacked his wardrobe. She found a pair of striped trousers of the kind worn with morning dress. Just the thing for me. Out came the scissors. Slicing the enormous trousers roughly at the knees she saw that my brother and I could get into them both at once. She was upset by our laughter.

She now slashed at the trousers again and narrowed them to my size.

The insoluble difficulty was the fly buttons; these she pulled round to the side of the leg; cutting and then tacking her way up the middle while they were on me at the final try-on, she sewed me up totally in front. 'I won't be able to *go*, Mum,' I said.

She was flabbergasted, but in her careless way, she snipped a couple of stitches in her tacking.

These were the trousers I was wearing as I stood before Mr Timms, very pleased by father's fashionable stripes and willing to show any boy who was interested in the original touch of having Savile Row fly buttons down the side of one leg. What I feared was happening: the hole was lengthening in front, I could feel an alarming draught.

I dared not look down, as my mother chatted on and on about our family. Nothing happened. I went to my class-room; at playtime I dared not run, for fear the tacking would go. When I pulled the thread to tighten it I was left with a length of thread hanging down from the vulnerable part.

When I went home after school the thread went altogether and I had to cover myself with my hand. So my first day at Rosendale School began.

RICHARD LLEWELLYN

From How Green Was My Valley

THE FIRST TIME I went in there was with my father to have my measures taken so that he would know how much tweed to buy from the mill. Two and a half yards.

Down we went to the mill inside the yard, and through the low doorway into the weaving-room. There is a lovely smell with tweed. Good it is, and honest, of the earth and of humankind, and a pleasure to wear, and always your friend to you.

I had a brown tweed, the colour of a ploughed field in the pebbly soil, when leaf has been put down about three months before, and grass is just poking through, barely to be seen, but there.

That, and a grey, the colour of spring rain, and almost as soft to the touch. My father bought a bolt of it for my mother and sisters, and black for himself and my brothers, and we watched a piece come from the loom in green, and that my father took for Olwen and Gareth to have little cloaks.

We went from there like journeymen loaded for a trip to the Indies, and by the time we got to Hwfa Williamson's I was ready to drop, so heavy was my share.

'Long trews or short, Mr Morgan?' Hwfa asked my father, and his eyes smiling and shining at me like little blue shoe-buttons. 'Shall he be a man or stay a boy?'

'O, Dada,' I said, 'long, is it?' My father looked at me, and turned to look through the window that was covered with pictures of elegant gentlemen with narrow waists and trews tight at the ankles, with capes, and canes with tassels. I was aching all over and shouting at him in my mind for him to say yes.

And Hwfa rubbed his thimble along his bottom lip and his blue shoe-buttons went first to me and then to my father.

'Very well, Huw, my little one,' my father said, and I could have swung on the beams, 'long trews. You are grown, now, of course.'

'Four button front, do up the top,' said Hwfa, and coming very practical. 'Front pocket trews; collar to waistcoat. Flaps to top waistcoat pockets?' And the shoe-buttons went again to my father, and my father looked at me.

'Yes, Dada, please,' I said.

'Yes,' said my father, and looking through the window again.

'Fitting for Master Huw Morgan. Thursday next, five of the evening,' said Hwfa, all business now, and speaking to old Twm, who kept the writings and the patterns, and put braid on coats and sewed buttonholes. 'Right, you,' said old Twm, with needles sticking from the side of his mouth and all over his waist-coat. 'And Nan Mardy coming in at half-past the hour for a three-quarter coat and a rain-coat with black braid and pocket both sides.'

'Never mind to talk of Nan Mardy, man,' Hwfa said. 'Master Huw Morgan, I said.' 'Well, only saying I was,' old Twm said, with impatience, 'in case.'

'In case, in case,' Hwfa said, and the shoe-buttons flying everywhere. 'What, in case, for the dear love of God, you old fool, you?'

'In case he do have his trews about his boottops and the shirt tails above his chin, man,' old Twm shouted, out of temper. 'O, to hell with you,' Hwfa shouted back. 'Mind your own shirt tails and let everybody else mind his and devil fly off with old Nan. A good look at a shirt tail would put life in her.'

'Come you,' said my father. 'Mr Williams, please to guard your tongue while this boy is near you.'

'The boy will learn quick enough,' Hwfa said. 'Five on the evening of Thursday, and to hell with Nan Mardy and this old fool by here, is it?' 'Good afternoon now,' said my father, and I pulled the door harder to have more noise from the bell. Hwfa was still shouting and old Twm was swearing back at him when we were two houses away, and my father looked at me and smiled.

'Why will a good look at a shirt tail put life in Nan Mardy, Dada?' I asked him.

'Mind your business,' said my father, 'then Nan shall mind hers, and we shall all be happy.'

WINIFRED FOLEY

From A Child in the Forest

MAM WAS ALL but defeated by the problem of keeping her brood clothed. She was thankful for any garment that anyone would give her for us, regardless of fit or suitability. I kept a piece of string permanently round my mid-dle to hold up the odd assortment of drawers I had to wear. The boys at school used to chant:

> Sing, sing
> What shall I sing?
> Poll Mason's britches
> Be tied up with string!

A stout middle-aged neighbour once produced a pair of her faded blue fleecy-lined bloomers for me. My piece of string kept them up, more or less, but the crutch came down to my knees, the bottoms almost to my ankles. 'Thee'st look like one o' they sultanas from a harem,' said my eldest sister, Bess. I crept unwillingly to school, well behind everyone else. Before I got there I hid in the ferns, took off the bloomers, and chewed a hole each side of the waist. I put my arms through the holes, and wore them like a pair of combinations.

ALISON UTTLEY

From The Country Child

SHE HAD BEEN taught to read, she was familiar with the Bible, and had read *Pilgrim's Progress*, and many religious stories and poems with morals attached. She was quick at figures and she had already made a sampler with cross-stitch men and trees. Susan looked forward to being someone of importance, when her mother took her to see the headmistress, but her hopes were soon dashed to the ground. Mrs Garland had found in an oak chest a dress which had belonged to a girl of a bygone age. It lay among blue silk-fringed crinolines and soft coloured Paisley shawls: a brown checked woollen frock with *ruches* of cut material trimming the tight bodice, and edging the high neck and the flounced skirt. It was buttoned from chin to foot with large cream bone buttons with steel centres. It was a godsend to Mrs Garland, warm as a blanket, strong as a horse-cloth, and thick. With a little alteration it made a new frock. Susan protested in vain, she wept, she hated its ugliness and the horrible buttons. So, a quaint old-fashioned little figure, her feet peeping out of the bottom frill which went nearly to her ankles, her chin almost lost in the top, she went for a first day at school.

Her short hair was strained back from her forehead and threaded through a round black comb which encircled her head like a coronet, with the hairs sticking up in a fringe at the back, 'being trained'.

She kept near her mother whilst she explained her hopes and fears for Susan to the sharp-eyed, thin-faced headmistress, and watched with alarm the horde of children playing round the big door. Then Mrs Garland smiled benignly at all the little ruffians, kissed Susan 'God bless you, child,' and left her.

The village children laughed and pointed at her.

'What's your name?' they shouted.

'Susanna Catherine Mary Garland,' replied Susan, with her dark eyes wide and startled . . .

'Where do you come from?' they jeered . . .

'From Windystone Hall, near Marlow,' she replied with a shy pride . . .

'Windystone, ruin stone, who went down the lane alone?' mocked a wit, and the children shook back their hair and yelled with glee.

'Aye. What a figure of fun. Where did you get that frock?' they gibed.

She had loathed her dress, but now she held it tightly with one hand. It came from her own home, and was part of her. She had been called 'a figure of fun'. She stood with her back against the wall and a crowd of jeering girls jostled her. One pulled her hair with a mischievous tug, one opened her satchel and looked at her sandwiches, and one, the most shameless, put her tongue out at her. A little boy her own age ran up rudely and kissed her. He rushed away screaming with laughter, and Susan took out her handkerchief and rubbed her cheek as the cries and jibes rose higher. She stood like a frightened rabbit, her face white, her eyes big with horror. 'Mother,' she whispered to her heart, and the school bell rang.

EILEEN ELIAS

From Straw Hats and Serge Bloomers

NEW, LIKE THE panama hats now we were Big Girls, were the blazers. Blazers – glorious word! We all longed for one, though as yet they were optional wear; the authorities were still wondering whether blazers were altogether too masculine, too sporty, to be ladylike. We had no such doubts. In a blazer you could feel just like your brother or the boy across the road, swaggering round with your hands in your pockets – strictly forbidden, of course; no nice girl walked like that – and your chin in the air. Blazers were to us the symbol of the really emancipated schoolgirl. Add a hockey-stick and you had achieved the lot.

MARK TWAIN

From The Adventures of Tom Sawyer

MARY TOOK HIM in hand, and when she was done with him he was a man and a brother, without distinction of colour, and his saturated hair was neatly brushed, and its short curls wrought into a dainty and symmetrical general effect. (He privately smoothed out the curls, with labour and difficulty, and plastered his hair close down to his head; for he held curls to be effeminate, and his own filled his life with bitterness.) Then Mary got out a suit of his clothing that had been used only on Sundays during two years – they were simply called his 'other clothes' – and so by that we know the size of his wardrobe. The girl 'put him to rights' after he had dressed himself; she buttoned his round-about up to his chin, turned his vast shirt-collar down over his shoulders, brushed him off and crowned him with his speckled straw hat. He now looked exceedingly improved and uncomfortable; and he was fully as uncomfortable as he looked; for there was a restraint about whole clothes and cleanliness that galled him. He hoped that Mary would forget his shoes, but the hope was blighted; she coated them thoroughly with tallow, as was the custom, and brought them out. He lost his temper, and said he was always being made to do everything he didn't want to do, but Mary said persuasively:

'Please, Tom – that's a good boy.'

So he got into his shoes, snarling. Mary was soon ready, and the three children set out for Sunday-school, a place that Tom hated with his whole heart; but Sid and Mary were fond of it.

WILLIAM MAKEPEACE THACKERAY

From Vanity Fair

A FAMOUS TAILOR FROM the West End of the town – Mr Osborne would have none of your City or Holborn bunglers, he said, for the boy (though a City tailor was good enough for *him*) – was summoned to ornament little George's person, and was told to spare no expense in so doing. So, Mr Woolsey, of Conduit Street, gave a loose to his imagination, and sent the child home fancy trousers, fancy waistcoats, and fancy jackets enough to furnish a school of little dandies. Georgy had little white waistcoats for evening parties, and little cut velvet waistcoats for dinners, and a dear little darling shawl dressing-gown, for all the world like a little man. He dressed for dinner every day, 'like a regular West End swell,' as his grandfather remarked. One of the domestics was affected to his special service, attended him at his toilette, answered his bell, and brought him his letters always on a silver tray.

ALISON UTTLEY
From Ambush of Young Days

M Y FATHER'S CLOTHES were made by the tailor, chosen from the very best cloth, cut and fitted with as much care as if they were the Squire's.

The trousers were made in the style of the 1860s, a fashion he would not have changed. He always chose finely striped greys and with the suits he wore spotted blue satin cravats which the tailor made for him.

The material never wore out, and many years later one saw these clothes on old men who had once worked for us. He had many pockets in the large loosely fitting coat, and the waistcoat, too, had odd extra pockets for secret things. These pockets were a source of wonder to me, for he put his hand in one, and then another, bringing out strange things, especially after he had driven to the town. Out would come sausages, sweets, cartridges, a toy trumpet, a doll, a musical box, a bottle of liniment, a box of pills, a new pair of spectacles, a bag of rosy pears, more and more things, till one stared as if he were a conjuror, and my mother protested that he would spoil the shape of his coat. 'What are pockets for if you can't fill them?' he would ask, and I wished I had more than my solitary pocket, which hung at that time, like Lucy Locket's, dangling from my waistband, a gathered bag.

CHARLOTTE BRONTË
From Villette

O N AWAKING WITH daylight, a trickling of water caught my ear. Behold! there she was risen and mounted on a stool near the washstand, with pains and difficulty inclining the ewer (which she could not lift) so as to pour its contents into the basin. It was curious to watch her as she washed and dressed, so small, busy, and noiseless. Evidently she was little accustomed to perform her own toilet; and the buttons, strings, hooks and eyes, offered difficulties which she encountered with a perseverance good to witness. She folded her nightdress, she smoothed the drapery of her couch quite neatly; withdrawing into a corner, where the sweep of the white curtain concealed her, she became still. I half rose, and advanced my head to see how she was occupied. On her knees, with her forehead bent on her hands, I perceived that she was praying.

Her nurse tapped at the door. She started up.

'I am dressed, Harriet,' said she: 'I have dressed myself, but I do not feel neat. Make me neat!'

'Why did you dress yourself, missy?'

'Hush! speak low, Harriet, for fear of waking *the girl* (meaning me, who now lay with my eyes shut). 'I dressed myself to learn, against the time you leave me.'

'Do you want me to go?'

'When you are cross, I have many a time wanted you to go, but not now. Tie my sash straight; make my hair smooth, please.'

'Your sash is straight enough. What a particular little body you are!'

'It must be tied again. Please to tie it.'

'There, then. When I am gone you must get that young lady to dress you.'

'On no account.'

'Why? She is a very nice young lady. I hope you mean to behave prettily to her, missy, and not show your airs.'

'She shall dress me on no account.'

'Comical little thing!'

'You are not passing the comb straight through my hair, Harriet; the line will be crooked.'

'Ay, you are ill to please. Does that suit?'

'Pretty well. Where should I go now that I am dressed?'

'I will take you into the breakfast-room.'

'Come then.'

They proceeded to the door. She stopped.

'Oh! Harriet, I wish this was papa's house! I don't know these people.'

'Be a good child, missy.'

'I am good, but I ache here;' putting her hand to her heart, and moaning while she reiterated 'Papa! papa!'

I roused myself and started up, to check this scene while it was yet within bounds.

E. NESBIT

From Long Ago When I Was Young

MARGUERITE, THROUGHOUT MY illness, behaved like an angel. I only remember one occasion on which I quarrelled with her – it was on the subject of dress. We were going to a children's party and my best blue silk was put out for me to wear.

'I wish you wouldn't wear that,' said Marguerite hesitatingly, 'it makes my grey cashmere look so old.'

Now I had nothing else to wear but a brown frock which I hated. 'Never mind,' I said hypocritically, 'it's better to be good than smart, everybody says so,' and I put on my blue silk.

When I was dressed, I pranced off to the kitchen to show my finery to the cook, and under admiring eyes executed my best curtsey. It began, of course, by drawing the right foot back; it ended in a tub of clothes and water that was standing just behind me. I floundered out somehow, and my first thought was how funny I must have looked, and in another moment I should have burst out laughing but as I scrambled out, I saw Marguerite in the doorway, smiling triumphantly, and heard her thin little voice say, 'The blue silk can't mock the poor grey cashmere now!'

An impulse of blind fury came upon me. I caught Marguerite by her little shoulders, and before the cook could interfere I had ducked her head-first into the tub of linen. Madame Lourdes behaved beautifully; she appeared on the scene at this moment, and impartial as ever, she slapped us both, but when she heard from the cook the rights of the story, my sentence was 'bed'.

'But Marguerite,' said her mother, 'has been punished enough for an unkind word.' And Marguerite was indeed sobbing bitterly, while I was dry-eyed and still furious. 'She can't go,' I cried, 'she hasn't got a dress!' 'You have spoilt her dress,' said Madame Lourdes cooly, 'the least you can do is to lend her your brown one.' And that excellent woman actually had the courage to send her own daughter to a party in my dress, an exquisite punishment to us both.

Marguerite came to my bedside that night; she had taken off the brown dress and wore her little flannel dressing-gown.

'You're not cross now, are you?' she said. 'I did beg mother to let you come, and I've not enjoyed myself a bit, and I've brought you this from the party.'

It was a beautiful little model of a coffee-mill made of sugar. My resentment could not withstand this peace-offering. I never quarrelled with Marguerite again, and when my mother sent for me to join her at Bagneres I wept as bitterly at leaving Madame Lourdes as I had done at being left with her.

ELEANOR FARJEON

From A Nursery in the Nineties

THE DRESS WAS a salmon-pink surah silk, with cream silk trimmings. There was another in blue silk, pretty, but not *so* pretty, and a half a sovereign cheaper. I tried both on, while Mama and the shop assistant twitched the dress about, and told me to stand still and not fidget, and to hold my shoulders straight, and walk away a little and turn my back. I was sure it would be the blue one. When Mama said, 'Now try the pink one again,' my heart leapt, and when she smiled into my excited eyes and said, 'We'll have this one,' I could have hugged her.

The salmon-pink surah was ordered to be sent, and I went home full of hopes for the best. The frock arrived next day, and wasn't taken out of its tissue paper till the evening of Mrs Labouchere's party, when my stomach was behaving worse than usual. It was some comfort to slip the pretty dress on over the stiff, scratchy petticoats that were one of the minor tortures of my life. So was the hat elastic, which left a red mark under my chin, and when slipped behind my ears for relief, made my head ache. So were the tight little kid gloves worked down my fingers till I could get my thumb in. So were the bronze boots now being buttoned over two pairs of stockings, Cashmere underneath and silk on top, so that I shouldn't take cold; because of this my insteps were pinched, and my feet were icy. But the new dress *did* look nice, and my uncle in America had sent me for Christmas a tiny gold ring with three real garnets in it. So I hoped that, in spite of my plain, straight hair and spectacles, I might pass among the gay little girls as though I were one of themselves.

MARY CLIVE

From Christmas with the Savages

THE NEXT DISTURBANCE came when we were getting ready to go downstairs. It was Betty being tiresome, and she choose to do it with her bedroom door open so as to attract as much attention as possible.

This was rather a way of hers and was considered very unsporting by the others. Betty and Rosamund always wore either pink or blue sashes on their white frocks, and Rosamund had dressed first and had put on the pink sash which had been laid ready for her. Suddenly Betty said that she couldn't wear pink, she wouldn't wear pink, nothing in the world would make her wear pink. Nana Savage would probably have given in, only Rosamund would not, of course, change to blue, and if they had gone downstairs with different sashes awkward questions would have been asked. Besides, Betty was shouting so loudly that everyone was hearing about it. 'Oh, very well,' said Nana Savage, 'go down and ask your mother if you need wear pink.' Bold as brass, Betty stumped off downstairs, followed by the rest of us longing to see what would happen. The library looked even grander than before, the grown-ups round the fire seemed even older and more remote.

However, Betty walked down the middle of the room in a very don't-care way and, when she got to the circle of elders, said in the coarse voice which she used when she wanted to assert herself:

'Need I wear a pink sash? I 'ates pink.'

Her mother, who was among the group of ladies, said:

'Oh, Betty! Don't talk like a fish-wife.'

Betty put on an aggrieved whine.

'But I don't know what a fish-wife talks *like*.'

There was a sort of rustle among the ladies, but Betty's mother said seriously: 'Why don't you like pink?'

'Because,' replied Betty, frowning at her angrily, 'it upsets my apple-cart.'

At this there was a loud roar – a roar of laughter really, only Betty took it to be a roar of rage. She thought she must have gone too far this time and have said something really terrible. Suddenly losing her nerve, she turned and bolted out of the library.

When she returned later on it was with a very red face and a pink sash.

NICHOLETTE DEVAS
From Two Flamboyant Fathers

THE OLDER BOYS went to a local school dressed in long belted smocks over corduroy trousers and their hair in long bobs. These clothes set them apart and in self-defence they became a gang of John boys against all comers. Eccentric their clothes might be, but Augustus's sons had inherited strong bodies and fighting instincts; at school they repelled insults with bloody noses . . .

Augustus found the fashions of the day unpaintable, and his household dressed to suit his painting. Dodo and Edie were skilled dressmakers and evolved the long flowing skirts gathered at the waist, and the loose smock top with the sleeves cut in one. In the drawings and paintings these clothes follow the movement of the figure like timeless, classic draperies. The materials used were those beloved by the artists through the ages; cotton velveteen for the quality of the drapery, and the highlights on the ridge of the fold, the depth of colour in the crease. Shantung was another favourite material; it came in clean bright dyes and the shimmering surfaces described the body beneath.

Some years later when Augustus and Dodo and assorted children were in France, they asked for rooms at the posh Carlton Hotel in Cannes. As they were all dressed in their bright and original clothes, the manager of the hotel took them for gipsies and refused to admit them until Augustus had shown the money bag and found someone to vouch for him.

With his furniture, William Morris started the fundamental simplicity idea on which the John clothes were based. The cry was, back to the early craftsmanship where the construction and joins, either nails or seams, were an integral part of the design. This was a reaction from the Industrial Revolution with its shoddy decoration. In dressmaking it meant that all the seams must be saddle stitched by hand on the outside of the garment, using contrasting coloured silk; orange silk on blue shantung for instance.

The John clothes did not stop at dresses, but probed deeper to underclothes. The girls suffered bitterly from the cold. For not only were stockings and closed knickers banished, but wool vests or combinations too. I shall never forget the horrible chilliness of draughty linen against the skin. And if that was not enough, there was the new health fad for fresh air. Open windows. We lived with a permanent wind blowing up our legs.

From Joyce Grenfell Requests the Pleasure

HERE IS A little snob story. My mother went to a party in one of her home-made dresses and Queen Marie of Roumania was there and liked the dress so much that she invited her to come and see her next day at Buckingham Palace where she was visiting her cousin King George V and Queen Mary; my mother was to bring material and cut out a dress for Queen Marie. As I have said, my mama was slight with a small waist: Queen Marie of Roumania was a fine figure of a woman, but waistless. My mother could not do sums any more than she could spell, but something told her that what hung freely on her to be gathered into a wide sash was going to be more exact on the Queen and would not leave any fullness to be gathered and held in anywhere by anything. She felt she had bitten off more than she could chew, but it was exciting to be going to the Palace, and later she was going to have tea with the King and Queen. It was a sharp spring day and, like me, my mother hated being cold, so she had put on a cosy little old white woolly spencer under her light spring coat, planning to take it off before she saw the royals and leave it with the footman. He was understanding and said he would keep it safely for her until the time came for her to leave. All went well with the cutting out of the dress. My mother had never seen a queen in her petticoat before and enjoyed the experience but wished the lady's maid hadn't looked so superior when she put the material on the floor to cut it out. There were, as my mama feared, not many folds when Queen Marie tried the dress on, but she liked herself in it and it was handed to the lady's maid to seam and hem.

Tea with Queen Mary and King George was interesting and jollier than she had expected . . . and she was a success and stayed late. The Prince of Wales, whom she already knew, went down with her in the lift to see her into her taxi. My mother didn't want to lose her little old cosy white woolly spencer, for she was fond of it, but she didn't feel she could ask the footman to give it back and help her into it in front of the Prince. The footman had no intention that she should; he indicated that he had the whole thing under control and gave her a meaningful wink. She took this to mean he would keep the woolly spencer until she could collect it quietly on another occasion. And that is what she did.

LADY CLODAGH ANSON
From Victorian Days

WE WERE VERY badly dressed always, and I must say my mother was not very dressy herself, one reason being that she spent all her allowance on helping people who were down on their luck, and the other that her usual reason for going to any dressmaker at all was the fact that the latter was starving, probably because she was so bad that no one else would go to her. My father declared that the first time he saw my mother, he remarked to someone that she was a nice girl but badly dressed. She had on a white muslin frock with a pink sash, and was very much excited at the thought of seeing this young man, so she dressed up, very smartly as she thought, but was rather dashed by her old nurse saying dryly, 'Well, no one can say you aren't clean,' as she started to go downstairs.

LAURA INGALLS WILDER
From Little Town on the Prarie

'WELL,' LAURA BEGAN; then she stopped and spun round and round, for the strong wind blowing against her always made the wires of her hoop skirt creep slowly upward under her skirts until they bunched around her knees. Then she must whirl around and around until the wires shook loose and spiralled down to the bottom of her skirts where they should be.

As she and Carrie hurried on she began again. 'I think it was silly, the way they dressed when Ma was a girl, don't you? Drat this wind!' she exclaimed as the hoops began creeping upward again.

Quietly Carrie stood while Laura whirled, 'I'm glad I'm not old enough to have to wear hoops,' she said. 'They'd make me dizzy.'

'They are rather a nuisance,' Laura admitted. 'But they are stylish, and when you're my age you'll want to be in style.'

GWEN RAVERAT
From Period Piece

CLOTHES WERE A major cause of rows, naughtiness, misery and all unpleasantness, right through my whole youth. The difficulties were caused, not only by best clothes, but by practically everything we wore.

In her own way my mother took a good deal of trouble about dress, not only about her own, but about ours, too. She used to spend hours and hours super-intending a humble daily dressmaker in cutting old dresses to pieces, and putting them together again in new permutations and combinations; for that marble-hearted fiend Economy, who was her evil angel, was always putting in his spoke and preventing her from having things made at a good shop. Sometimes the results of this home manufacture were rather clumsy; but as far as my mother was concerned it really did not matter much, as she always managed to look attractive, even if it were in spite of, rather than because of, her dress. For one thing she had a very fair idea of what became her; she never wore those dread-ful hard boater hats, when they were so fashionable; and she knew that soft floppy things suited her better than tailor-made suits. She was in her glory in a 'tea-gown'; or in a summer dress, with a feather boa, ostrich-plume hat and parasol.

My share of the dressmaking industry was the unpicking of the old dresses, which I did most unwillingly. Sometimes, when it went on for too long, Good God, there was such a scene! But even that was not so bad as when I had to try on a new frock myself. It seemed to me then that I was kept standing on the table for whole days at a time (I suppose it may have been about twenty minutes), while she and the dressmaker fumbled about, with their mouths full of pins; cutting with ice-cold scissors against my bare neck, and constantly saying: 'Now *please* stand up straight for a minute'; or 'For Goodness' sake do keep still'; until at last there was a real explosion.

For, in spite of my mother's efforts, I thought all my clothes horrible.

EILEEN ELIAS

From On Sundays We Wore White

THE FIRST TWO years of my school life were made miserable by those button boots. They were the fashion at the time, and Mother and Aunt Jane didn't have to do them up. I longed in silence for any other kind of footwear but button boots.

The buttonholes, when the boots were new, were so hard and slit-like that they hurt your fingers, and you didn't always have a button-hook. Even if you had, it invariably hooked the wrong button into the hole. I would sit on the wooden lock-er in the cloakroom at school long after all the other children had gone home, wrestling with my button boots and choking back tears. Getting them off was easy. You just ripped gloriously and they were undone. But getting them on! As often as not, I would be forced to walk out into the road with the buttons half undone, and pretend not to notice the grins and glances of my schoolmates out-side. Some of the girls wore fashionable button boots that came right up to the knee; but then they knew how to manage them. Mine were the unfashionable sort, coming half way up the calf; but that was bad enough. I prayed and prayed for the fashion of button boots to go out, and for some easier form of shoe to come in. Who could understand the vagaries of fashion? Certainly not a little girl. And every time we went to Jones and Higgins to buy a new pair, I would throw out desperate hints, only half hoping they would be taken up. 'Strap shoes are pretty,' I would suggest, gazing at a pair in the showcase. But nobody would even hear my remark. 'Or what about those?' as some luckier child proudly walked out of the Boot and Shoe department in a pair of laced brown shoes.

At any rate you could learn how to do up laces; but buttonholes seemed to have a life of their own that defied anyone's expertise.

Mother and Aunt Jane firmly stuck to the button boots, and it wasn't till years later that the fashion changed and 'went out' as mysteriously as it had come in. I was profoundly thankful.

DIANA HOLMAN-HUNT
From My Grandmothers and I

WAITING FOR BREAKFAST on Friday morning, Grand studied the invitations round the looking-glass over the fireplace . . . She turned round; her eyes were shining. 'I've kept my surprise until now, a surprise for you, my pet.'

My hopes rose. Could it be a kipper?

She went to a drawer and pulled out something that looked like a choir boy's surplus. Helen came in with the tray. The egg had been fried.

'Diana's classical dress,' cried Grand, 'it's fit for a Goddess!' She shook out the stuff and displayed it over the sofa. The egg on the tray was congealing.

'The hours, the golden hours I've spent on the embroidery! I know I shouldn't boast, dear Holman was so admirably modest, but look at the crescent moon, Diana's symbol, made of silver beads! They were so fine I couldn't thread them on a needle. I used my own hair and a magnifying glass, stitching under the lamp, night after night, longing for your visit. As I worked I recalled the charming brown wedding dress Holman designed for pretty Ellen Terry when she married Mr Watts and I remembered the exquisite embroidery he worked on the sleeves of – was it Orlando's blouse? No, he wore the armour which was lent by Mr Frith. The maid said, "There's a tin weskit and trousers in the hall . . ." '

It dawned on me slowly that I was to wear this horrible garment at the party. 'But I have a nice dress. It isn't unpacked. Red velvet, and Fowler says the collar is Brussels lace – it's in points like this.' I traced a zig-zag on the table. 'I've got a white fur coat with cord frogging – the lining is satin – and black kid shoes with silver buckles and white silk socks. Everything's there in my hamper. Helen, I mean someone, should have steamed the velvet; Fowler gets so cross if anything is creased.'

'But of course you must wear this dress and be a little Goddess. Hop out of bed and let me hold it against you.' It had no shape and hung in limp folds from my shoulders to the ground.

It looked like a curtain. 'Please Grand,' I pleaded, 'don't make me wear it!'....

'Youth is cruel,' she whispered sadly, picking up the dress and sinking on the sofa. We sat panting and staring at each other. Her eyes were wet with disappointment, and I felt defeated. Tears rolled slowly down her face. 'It's all right, Grand,' I seized her skinny wrist, 'don't you worry, I'll wear it.' . . . After all it wasn't asking much; I might have had to drown a kitten.

LOUISA M. ALCOTT

From Little Women

'MADEMOISELLE IS CHARMANTE, *très jolie*, is she not?' cried Hortense, clasping her hand in an affected rapture.

'Come and show yourself,' said Miss Belle, leading the way to the room where the others were waiting.

As Meg went rustling after her, with her long skirts trailing, her earrings tinkling, her curls waving, and her heart beating, she felt as if her 'fun' had really begun at last, for the mirror had plainly told her that she *was* 'a little beauty'. Her friend repeated the pleasing phrase enthusiastically; and for several minutes she stood, like the jackdaw in the fable, enjoying her borrowed plumes, while the rest chattered like a party of magpies . . .

The 'queer feeling' did not pass away, but she imagined herself acting the new part of a fine lady, and so got on pretty well, though the tight dress gave her a side-ache, the train kept getting under her feet, and she was in constant fear lest her earrings should fly off, and get lost or broken. She was flirting her fan, and laughing at the feeble jokes of a young gentleman who tried to be witty, when she suddenly stopped laughing, and looked confused; for just opposite she saw Laurie. He was staring at her with undisguised surprise, and disapproval also, she thought, for, though he bowed and smiled, yet something in his honest eyes made her blush, and wish she had her old dress on....

He glanced at her frizzled head, bare shoulders, and fantastically trimmed dress, with an expression that abashed her more than his answer, which had not a particle of his usual politeness about it.

'I don't like fuss and feathers.'

GWEN RAVERAT
From Period Piece

I REMEMBER, WHEN I was at school in 1902, walking at the back of our Sunday crocodile, and seeing all the girls in front of me, very smart and Sundayfied, going down the hill to church. And I thought (I am afraid, with a touch of superiority): 'How frightful they all look, and what a lot of trouble they have taken to make themselves still more frightful. I am sure I look every bit as hideous, but at any rate I haven't taken any trouble about it at all.' I thought them much 'the worse for dress', as Uncle Lenny once said of an over-dressed lady of his acquaintance. The thought comes back to me perfectly clear, every time I get a whiff of something which reminds me of the empty, damp, suburban, Sunday-morning smell of Wimbledon Common; and then I see again their beribboned top-heavy hats, stuck on to the top of the hair they had spent so long in frizzling and puffing out; and their tightly corseted, bell-shaped figures wobbling down the hill, as they chattered their way to church.

VERA BRITAIN
From Testament of Youth

A LL GIRLS' CLOTHING of the period appeared to be designed by their elders on the assumption that decency consisted in leaving exposed to the sun and air no part of the human body that could possibly be covered with flannel. In these later days, when I lie lazily sunning myself in a mere gesture of a bathing-suit on the gay *plage* of some Riviera town – or even, during a clement summer, on the ultra-respectable shores of southern England – and watch the lean brown bodies of girl-children, almost naked and completely unashamed, leaping in and out of the water, I am seized with an angry resentment against the conventions of twenty years ago, which wrapped up my comely adolescent body in woollen combinations, black cashmere stockings, 'liberty' bodice, dark stockinette knickers, flannel petticoat and often, in addition, a long-sleeved, high-necked, knitted woollen 'spencer'.

At school, on the top of this conglomeration of drapery, we wore green flannel blouses in the winter and white flannel blouses in the summer, with long navy-blue skirts, linked to the blouses by elastic belts which continually slipped up or down, leaving exposed an unsightly hiatus of blouse-tape or safety-pinned shirt-band. Green and white blouses alike had long sleeves ending in buttoned cuffs at the wrist, and high collars covering the neck almost to the chin, and fastening tightly at the throat with stiff green ties. For cricket and tennis match-es, even in the baking summer of 1911, we still wore the flowing skirts and high-necked blouses, with our heavy hair braided into pigtails; it was not until after the war that the school went into sleeveless white linen for summer games.

L.M. MONTGOMERY
From Anne of Green Gables

CHRISTMAS MORNING BROKE on a beautiful white world . . . Anne ran down-stairs singing until her voice re-echoed through Green Gables.

'Merry Christmas, Marilla! Merry Christmas, Matthew! Isn't it a lovely Christmas? . . . Why – why – Matthew, is that for me? Oh, Matthew!'

Matthew had sheepishly unfolded the dress from its paper swathings and held it out with a deprecatory glance at Marilla, who feigned to be contemptuously filling the teapot, but nevertheless watched the scene out of the corner of her eye with a rather interested air.

Anne took the dress and looked at it in reverent silence. Oh, how pretty it was – a lovely soft brown gloria with all the gloss of silk; a skirt with dainty frills and shirrings; a waist elaborately pin-tucked in the most fashionable way, with a lit-tle ruffle of filmy lace at the neck. But the sleeves – they were the crowning glory! Long elbow cuffs and above them two beautiful puffs divided by rows of shirring and bows of brown silk ribbon.

'That's a Christmas present for you, Anne,' said Matthew shyly. 'Why – why – Anne, don't you like it? Well now – well now.'

For Anne's eyes had suddenly filled with tears.

'*Like* it! Oh, Matthew!' Anne laid the dress over a chair and clasped her hands. 'Matthew, it's perfectly exquisite. Oh, I can never thank you enough. Look at those sleeves! Oh, it seems to me this must be a happy dream.'

OUIDA
From Moths

'MAY I SWIM here?' asked Vere.

'Of course; it's the thing to do. Can you dive?'

'Oh yes! I am used to the water.'

'Very well, then. But wait; you can't have any bathing-dress?'

'Yes. I brought it. Would you wish to see it? Keziah – '

Keziah was bidden to seek for and bring out the bathing-dress, and after a little delay did so.

Lady Dolly looked. Gradually an expression of horror, such as is depicted on the faces of those who are supposed to see ghosts, spread itself over her countenance and seemed to change it to stone.

'That thing!' she gasped.

What she saw was the long indigo–coloured linen gown – nigh to the throat and down to the feet – of the uneducated British bather, whose mind has not been opened by the sweetness and light of continental shores.

'That thing!' gasped Lady Dolly.

'What is the matter with it?' said Vere, timidly and perplexed.

'Matter? It is indecent!'

'Indecent?' Vere coloured all over the white rose-leaf beauty of her face.

'Indecent,' reiterated Lady Dolly. 'If it isn't worse! Good gracious! It must have been worn at the deluge. The very children would stone you! Of course I knew you couldn't have any decent dress. You shall have one like mine made to-morrow, and then you can kick about as you like. Blue and white or blue and pink. You shall see mine.'

She rang, and sent one of her maids for one of her bathing costumes, which were many and of all hues.

Vere looked at the brilliant object when it arrived, puzzled and troubled by it. She could not understand it. It appeared to be cut off at the shoulders and the knees.

'It is like what the circus-riders wear,' she said, with a deep breath.

'Well, it is, now you name it,' said Lady Dolly amused. 'You shall have one to-morrow.'

Vere's face crimsoned.

'But what covers one's legs and arms?'

'Nothing! What a little silly you are! I suppose you have nothing the matter with them, have you? No mark, or twist, or anything? I don't remember any when you were little. You were thought an extraordinarily well-made baby.'

Might one then go naked provided only one had no mark or twist? Vere wondered, and wondered at the world into which she had strayed.

'I would never wear a costume like that,' she said quietly, after a little pause.

'You will wear what I tell you,' said her sweet little mother sharply; 'and for goodness' sake, child, don't be a prude whatever you are. Prudes belong to Noah's Ark, like your bathing-gown.'

Vere was silent.

MARK TWAIN

From The Adventures of Tom Sawyer

THE SUMMER EVENINGS were long. It was not dark yet. Presently Tom checked his whistle. A stranger was before him; a boy a shade larger than himself. A newcomer of any age or either sex was an impressive curiosity in the poor little village of St Petersburg. This boy was well dressed, too – well dressed on a week-day. This was simply astounding. His cap was a dainty thing, his close-buttoned blue cloth roundabout was new and natty, and so were his pantaloons. He had shoes on, and yet it was only Friday. He even wore a neck-tie, a bright bit of ribbon. He had a citified air about him that ate into Tom's vitals. The more Tom stared at the splendid marvel, the higher he turned up his nose at his finery, and the shabbier and shabbier his own outfit seemed to him to grow. Neither boy spoke. If one moved the other moved – but only sidewise, in a circle. They kept face to face and eye to eye all the time. Finally, Tom said:

'I can lick you!'

SUE TOWNSEND

From The Secret Diary of Adrian Mole Aged 13¾

Thursday June 4th

Doreen answered the phone to my mother first thing this morning. My mother asked to speak to me. She demanded to know what Doreen was doing in the house. I told her that my father was having a breakdown and that Doreen Slater was looking after him. I told her about his redundancy. I said he was drinking heavily, smoking too much and generally letting himself go. Then I went to school. I was feeling rebellious, so I wore red socks. It is strictly forbidden but I don't care any more.

Friday June 5th

Miss Sproxton spotted my red socks in assembly! The old bag reported me to pop-eyed Scruton. He had me in his office and gave me a lecture on the dangers of being a nonconformist. Then he sent me home to change into regulation black socks. My father was in bed when I got home; he was having his impotence cured. I watched Play School with Maxwell until he came downstairs. I told him about the sock saga.

He instantly turned into a raving loonie! He phoned the school and dragged

Scruton out of a caretakers' strike-meeting. He kept shouting down the phone; he said, 'My wife's left me, I've been made redundant, I'm in charge of an idiot boy,' – Maxwell, I presume – 'and you're victimizing my son because of the colour of his socks!' Scruton said if I came to school in black socks everything would be forgotten but my father said I would wear whatever colour socks I liked. Scruton said he was anxious to maintain standards. My father said that the England World Cup team in 1966 did not wear black socks, nor did Sir Edmund Hillary in 1953. Scruton seemed to go quiet then. My father put the phone down. He said, 'Round one to me'.

This could well get into the papers: 'Black socks row at school'. My mother might read about it and come home.

Saturday June 6th

Oh Joy! Oh Rapture! Pandora is organizing a sock protest! She came round to my house today! Yes! She actually stood on our front porch and told me that she admired the stand I was taking! I would have asked her in, but the house is in a squalid state so I didn't. She is going round the school with a petition on Monday morning. She said I was a freedom fighter for the rights of the individual. She wants me to go round to her house tomorrow morning. A committee is being set up, and I am the principal speaker! She wanted to see the red socks but I told her they were in the wash.

Doreen Slater and Maxwell went home today. My grandma is coming round tonight, so all traces of them have got to be wiped out.

Sunday June 7th
WHIT SUNDAY

Grandma found Maxwell's dummy in my father's bed. I lied and said that the dog must have brought it in off the street. It was a nasty moment. I am not a good liar, my face goes bright red and my grandma has got eyes like Superman's, they seem to bore right through you. To divert her I told her about the red-sock row, but she said rules were made to be kept.

Pandora and the committee were waiting for me in the big lounge of her house. Pandora is Chairperson, Nigel is Secretary and Pandora's friend Clair Neilson is Treasurer. Craig Thomas and his brother Brett are just ordinary supporters. I am not allowed to hold high office because I am the victim.

Pandora's parents were in the wooden kitchen doing *The Sunday Times* crossword. They seem to get on quite well together.

They brought a tray of coffee and health biscuits into the lounge for us. Pandora introduced me to her parents. They said they admired the stand that I was taking. They were both members of the Labour Party and they went on about the Tolpuddle Martyrs. They asked me if the fact that I had chosen to protest in *red* socks had any significance. I lied and said I had chosen red because it was a symbol of revolution, then I blushed revolutionary red. I am turning into quite a liar recently.

Pandora's mother said I could call her Tania. Surely that is a Russian name? Her father said I could call him Ivan. He is very nice, he gave me a book to read; it is called *The Ragged Trousered Philanthropists*. I haven't looked through it yet but I'm quite interested in stamp collecting so I will read it tonight.

Washed red socks, put them on radiator to dry ready for the morning.

Monday June 8th

Woke up, dressed, put red socks on before underpants or vest. Father stood at the door and wished me luck. Felt like a hero. Met Pandora and rest of committee at corner of our road; all of us were wearing red socks. Pandora's were lurex. She has certainly got guts! We sang 'We shall not be moved' all the way to school. I felt a bit scared when we went through the gates but Pandora rallied us with shouts of encouragement.

Pop-eyed Scruton must have been tipped off because he was waiting in the fourth-year cloakroom. He was standing very still with his arms folded, staring with poached egg eyes. He didn't speak, he just nodded upstairs. All the red socks trooped upstairs. My heart was beating dead loud. He went silently into his office and sat at his desk and started tapping his teeth with a school pen. We just stood there.

He smiled in a horrible way then rang the bell on his desk. His secretary came in, he said, 'Sit down and take a letter, Mrs Claricoates'. The letter was to our parents, it said:

> Dear Mr and Mrs ....,
> It is my sad duty to inform you that your son/daughter has deliberately flaunted one of the rules of this school. I take an extremely serious view of this contravention. I am therefore suspending your son/daughter for a period of one week. Young people today often lack sufficient moral guidance in the home, therefore I feel that it is my duty to take a firm stand in my school. If you wish to discuss the matter further with me do not hesitate to ring my secretary for an appointment.
>> Yours faithfully,
>> R. G. Scruton
>> Headmaster

Pandora started to say something about her O levels suffering but Scruton roared at her to shut up! Even Mrs Claricoates jumped. Scruton said that we could wait until the letters had been typed, duplicated and signed and then we had better 'hot foot it out of school'. We waited outside Scruton's office. Pandora was crying (because she was angry and frustrated, she said). I put my arm round her a bit. Mrs Claricoates gave us our letters. She smiled very kindly, it can't be very easy working for a despot.

We went round to Pandora's house but it was locked, so I said everyone could come round to my house. It was quite tidy for once, apart from the dog hairs. My father raged about the letter. He is supposed to be a Conservative but he is not being very conservative at the moment.

I can't help wishing that I had worn black socks on Friday.

LORD BERNERS
From First Childhood

DEBARRED, AS SHE was, from participation in any wider form of social entertainment, she retained nevertheless a passion for clothes. She would spend as long a time as she was able – before exhaustion compelled her to stop – in front of her mirror, rather pathetically trying on new dresses and hats that were sent to her from Paris and London. She often allowed me to help her to undo the parcels that arrived from the dressmakers and, with an almost equal delight, we would examine the delicate fabrics, the feathers and the artificial flowers as they emerged from their wrappings of tissue-paper. One day she made me a present of a bird of paradise plume which I religiously preserved as though it were a holy relic for many months, until at last it went the way of most of one's childish treasures and mysteriously disappeared. Apart from purely aesthetic reasons I was attracted, I suppose, by this finery because it seemed to afford a glimpse into that glittering realm of festivity I vaguely apprehended from the illustrated papers and from overheard fragments of conversation. Aunt Flora appreciated my admiration, and one evening she put on, for my benefit, a dress she had worn some years previously at Court, before her accident had obliged her to retire from the gay world. As she stood before me in the lamplight with curling ostrich feathers on her head and a long, billowy train of some transparent, silvery material, I felt almost afraid. It was as though she had been transformed into some strange, unearthly being from another world.

NURSERY RHYME

Can you make me a cambric shirt,
Parsley, sage, rosemary, and thyme;
Without any seam or needlework?
And you shall be a true lover of mine.

Can you wash it in yonder well,
Parsley, &c.
Where never sprung water, nor rain ever fell?
And you, &c.

Can you dry it on yonder thorn,
Parsley, &c.
Which never bore blossom since Adam was born?
And you, &c.

Now you have asked me questions three,
Parsley, &c.
I hope you'll answer as many for me,
And you, &c.

ANON

The Modern Hiawatha

When he killed the Mudjokivis,
Of the skin he made him mittens,
Made them with the fur side inside,
Made them with the skin side outside,
He, to get the warm side inside,
Put the inside skin side outside;
He, to get the cold side outside,
Put the warm side fur side inside,
That's why he put fur side inside,
Why he put the skin side outside,
Why he turned them inside outside.

3

Youth –
Joys and Uncertainties

She wore her evening dress, all her dresses, like sports clothes – there was a jauntiness about her movements as if she had first learned to walk upon golf courses on clean, crisp mornings.

F. Scott Fitzgerald, *The Great Gatsby*

ROBERT HERRICK
Upon Julia's Clothes

Whenas in silks my Julia goes,
Then, then (me thinks) how sweetly flowes
That liquefaction of her clothes.

Next, when I cast mine eyes and see
That brave Vibration each way free;
O how that glittering taketh me!

From Hesperides (1648)

MAX BEERBHOM
From Zuleika Dobson

'SHE DID NOT look like an orphan,' said the wife of the Oriel don, subsequently, on the way home. The criticism was a just one. Zuleika would have looked singular in one of those lowly double-files of straw-bonnets and drab cloaks which are so steadying a feature of our social system. Tall and lissom, she was sheathed from the bosom downwards in flamingo silk, and she was liberally festooned with emeralds. Her dark hair was not even strained back from her forehead and behind her ears, as an orphan's should be. Parted somewhere at the side, it fell in an avalanche of curls upon one eyebrow. From her right ear drooped heavily a black pearl, from her left a pink; and their difference gave an odd, bewildering witchery to the little face between.

ROSAMUND LEHMANN

From Invitation to the Waltz

N OW FOR THE dress.

After all, I shall probably enjoy the dance frightfully.

Quarter of an hour passed.

Kate put her head round the door.

'Ready?'

Olivia was standing still, with leaden stillness, before the glass. One glance, and Kate had spotted disaster.

'Here. You've got it twisted.' She gave a few sharp twitches to the waist and skirt. After a pause she said with restraint, 'It looks all right. Very nice.'

But it was not so. In the silence the truth weighed, became a stone that could not be rolled away.

Uneven hem; armhole, too tight; and the draping – when Olivia looked at the clumsy lumpish pointless draping a terrible boiling-up, a painful constriction from chest to forehead started to scorch and suffocate her.

'It simply doesn't fit anywhere . . .' The words burst from her chokingly. 'It's the most ghastly – It's no good. I won't go looking like a freak. I must simply *rip* it off and burn it and not go to the dance, that's all.' She clutched wildly at the bodice, as if to wrench it from her.

Kate cried suddenly.

'You've got it on back to front!'

Olivia's hands dropped.

'Have I?' she said meekly.

'You would.' With the asperity of relief Kate seized and reversed her hurriedly, plunged her once more through the armholes. 'Now let's see you. Hm. It drops at the back now, of course.'

Olivia turned away from the glass while Kate hooked, tweaked, patted her into shape. It was a comfort to look into space for a little while before having to face once more the now irrevocable and perhaps scarcely improved image.

'The arms seem to catch a bit.' She crossed her elbows, strained at the seams and heard them crack with satisfaction.

'You're *not* to do that, Livia. You'll just have to bear it. Why on earth couldn't you *force* her to cut them properly? It's always the same with your clothes. You never could control her.'

'I know. I seem to make her feel so cheerful.'

Olivia sighed, thinking how at each fitting Miss Robinson had become increasingly volatile – her scissors more profuse and inconsequent, her piano-playing more frequent.

'She's loopy,' said Kate vigorously; adding, as she gave the skirt a final tweak: 'And I really believe you are too. Not to know your back from your front. How'll you ever get on in the world? Mm? . . . There.'

Now I must look.

She looked.

It was not so bad. It dipped at the back; and there was a queer place in the waist where, owing to a mistake in the cutting, Miss Robinson had had, in her own words, to contrive it. But still, but still . . . if one didn't look too closely, it was all right. Certainly the colour was becoming.

Delivered from despair, once more a young girl dressed for her first dance – not a caricature of one – able again to compete with and appreciate others, she saw Kate suddenly with seeing eyes and cried enthusiastically.

'Oh! You look simply topping!'

The airy apple-green frock which Kate had made for herself flared out below her hips and clung lightly to waist and breast. A little floating cape was attached just over each flat delicately moulded shoulder-blade by a band of minute flowers, buds, leaves of all colours. She wore green stockings and silver shoes. Against the green, her skin looked white as coral, and her hair had a green-blonde gleam.

'You look like the girl on the cover of a Special Spring Number.'

Twisting to look at her cape, Kate said placidly:

'I just took it straight from *Vogue*.'

Side by side they stood and looked at their reflections. After a bit Kate said: 'Thank heaven, anyway, we don't look alike.'

JOHN BUCHAN
From The Dancing Floor

IN HER HUNTING-KIT she had looked handsome in an outlandish way, but as she swept down – without any apology – on our hungry mob there was no question of her beauty. For one thing she walked superbly. Few women can walk, and the trouble about the new fashion in clothes is that it emphasizes ugly movement. She wore a gown of a shade of green which would have ruined most people's looks, but she managed to carry it off, and something more. For a young girl she was far too heavily made up, but that too she forced one to accept. I suddenly had a new view of her, and realized that there was quality here, a masterfulness which might charm, an arrogance which perhaps was not *blasé* but virginal.

HENRY JAMES
From The Wings of the Dove

M RS STRINGHAM WAS never to forget . . . her own first sight of the striking apparition, then unheralded and unexplained: the slim, constantly pale, delicately haggard, anomalously, agreeably angular person, of not more than two-and-twenty summers . . . whose hair was somehow exceptionally red even for the real thing . . . and whose clothes were remarkably black even for robes of mourning . . . it was New York mourning, it was New York hair, it was a New York history.

ZELDA FITZGERALD
From A Millionaire's Girl

T WILIGHTS WERE WONDERFUL just after the war. They hung above New York like indigo wash, forming themselves from asphalt dust and sooty shadows under the cornices and limp gusts of air exhaled from closing windows, to hang above the streets with all the mystery of white fog rising off a swamp. The far-away lights from buildings high in the sky burned hazily through the blue, like golden objects lost in deep grass, and the noise of hurrying streets took on that hushed quality of many footfalls in a huge stone square. Through the gloom people went to tea. On all the corners around the Plaza Hotel, girls in short squirrel coats and long flowing skirts and hats like babies' velvet bathtubs waited for the changing traffic to be suctioned up by the revolving doors of the fashionable grill. Under the scalloped portico of the Ritz, girls in short ermine coats and fluffy, swirling dresses and hats the size of manholes passed from the nickel glitter of traffic to the crystal glitter of the lobby.

In front of the Lorraine and the St Regis, and swarming about the mad-hatter doorman under the warm orange lights of the Biltmore façade were hundreds of girls with Marcel waves, with colored shoes and orchids, girls with pretty faces, dangling powder boxes and bracelets and lank young men from their wrists – all on their way to tea. At that time, tea was a public levee. There were tea personalities – young leaders who, though having no claim to any particular social or artistic distinction, swung after them long strings of contemporary silhouettes like a game of crack-the-whip. Under the sombre, ironic parrots of the Biltmore the halo of golden bobs absorbed the light from heavy chandeliers, dark heads lost themselves in corner shadows, leaving only the rim of young faces against the winter windows – all of them scurrying along the trail of one or two dynamic youngsters.

Caroline was one of these. She was then about sixteen, and dressed herself always in black dresses – dozens of them – falling away from her slim, perfect body like strips of clay from a sculptor's thumb.

SAMUEL RICHARDSON
From Clarissa

HER HEAD-DRESS was a Brussels lace mob, peculiarly adapted to the charming air and turn of her features. The sky-blue ribbon illustrated that. But although the weather was somewhat sharp, she had not on either hat or hood; for, besides that she loves to use herself hardily (by which means, and by a temperance truly exemplary, she is allowed to have given high health and vigour to an originally tender constitution), she seems to have intended to show me that she was determined not to stand to her appointment. O Jack! that such a sweet girl should be a rogue!

Her morning gown was a pale primrose-coloured paduasoy: the cuffs and robings curiously embroidered by the fingers of this ever-charming Arachne, in a running pattern of violets and their leaves; the light in the flowers silver; gold in the leaves. A pair of diamond snaps in her ears. A white handkerchief, wrought by the same inimitable fingers, concealed – O Bedford! what still more inimitable beauties did not conceal! (by its throbbing motions I saw it!) dancing beneath the charming umbrage.

Her ruffles were the same as her mob. Her apron a flowered lawn. Her coat white satin, quilted: blue satin her shoes, braided with the same colour, without lace; for what need has the prettiest foot in the world of ornament? Neat buckles in them: and on her charming arms a pair of black velvet glove-like muffs of her own invention; for she makes and gives fashions as she pleases. Her hands, velvet of themselves, thus uncovered the freer to be grasped by those of her adorer.

Young girls at a dancing class

Our entry was like a west wind blowing over a hill covered with lilies, orange-blossoms, jasmine and white roses and causing them to sway gently; for they all rose and bowed, were all dressed in white, and only their unpowdered brown hair and green, red, blue and violet girdles cast a kind of shadow and broke the brilliance; the light, white caps lay in neat, almost fantastic folds, quite artlessly tied, and the curls in rolls on the prettiest of necks; angel visions wherever our gaze roved, and the beauty of the pretty creatures was surprising, ranging from six to sixteen years of age.

From the diary of Sophie V. La Roche

WILLIAM GERHARDIE
From Of Mortal Love

WALTER THOUGHT THE ball to which he was taking Dinah was to be a grand affair, just the kind of thing Dinah missed so sorely in her life because, being beautiful, she would have liked to shine at these parties where other women, less pleasing to the eye, were photographed for the illustrated weeklies. Dinah had shown great enthusiasm for this party, and weeks ahead she bought the material and made her own dress. When she arrived at his flat it was nearly midnight and, as he was short of money as usual, he rather stressed that there was no sense in dining first at a restaurant, seeing that they would be sure to have supper the moment they arrived at the ball. Dinah had had great trouble with her dress, altering it at the last moment. 'Just fasten my dress at the back, if you can.' She was counting on Walter's admiration, since he had never seen her in gala dress. But he thought that her back was cut much too low, and that the material, modern, as Dinah had explained, was rather too much like a towel. Nor did he like the colour, beige and blue; though he was loud in his praise of the cut. She was certainly very clever to be able to cut her own dress and give it that look of a Paris model. But Dinah resented his qualified praise, where she had expected a burst of admiration. She felt cold and hungry in the taxi, and though Walter said they would have supper the moment they got there, Dinah looked sulky.

But when they arrived, there was only a buffet with sandwiches, no champagne or wine, only coffee and tea and lemonade, and the party was commonplace and dull in the extreme – not a face you had ever seen anywhere before. There was a long narrow room with chairs round it. They danced and, alternately, sat out.

'But this isn't at all a smart party,' she complained as they sat together by the door and watched the dancing couples turn past them.

ENID BAGNOLD

From Autobiography

I WAS STILL ON my seventy-five a year, and I had been to Reveille's in Hanover Square because they had a sale of hats. No one would serve me with a hat. They were clustered round a fur-coat clientele buying mink. Or if it wasn't mink in those days it was musquash. Defiant, I picked up a three-quarter-length coat and tried it on. I saw I looked a smasher in it and I wondered what it cost. With more dash than the days of the gull hat in Bond Street I 'sent for' Mr Reveille. He came: he couldn't know I wasn't a millionaire. I explained to him that I couldn't pay for the coat whatever it cost. In time, yes. But not yet.

'It's eighty pounds,' he said. (More than a year's allowance). 'Wait there while I talk to my accountant.'

I sat in the cubicle looking at myself in the coat. He came back and said: 'You can have the coat on a down-payment of five pounds if, on your marriage, you promise to get your trousseau from me.'

'I'm not going to be married.'

'Not engaged?'

'No.'

He laughed. 'With that coat you'll be engaged in a month!'

VERA BRITTAIN

From Testament of Youth

A S I FOLLOWED the scout across the garden, the Principal got up to greet me. Her immensely tall, angular figure seemed to go on unfolding for several minutes before my apprehensive eyes, and the vast gulf of lawn between us made me even more conscious than usual of my insignificant stature. Being quite ignorant of the plain-Jane-and-no-nonsense conventions of Oxford women dons, I had carefully changed, in accordance with the sartorial habits of Buxton, into evening dress, and was wearing a flimsy lace frock under a pale blue and grey reversible satin cloak, and an insubstantial little pair of high-heeled white suede shoes. So unlike the customary felt hat and mackintosh of the average 1913 woman student was this provincially modish attire, that the Principal actually referred to it when she interviewed me during the Scholarship Examinations in the following March. 'I remember you,' she said immediately, 'you're the girl who came across the lawn in a blue evening cloak.'

ANNE DOUGLAS SEDGWICK

From The Little French Girl

THEY HELPED GILES with his books and pictures next morning, and in the afternoon he said he must show her Oxford while his mother shopped. It was raining. Giles had on a rain-coat turned up about his ears, and so had she. She had never seen so many bicycles, and from under a dripping umbrella, after one had dodged them, she found the Gothic quadrangle and deep emerald gardens, the meditative swans gliding, at Worcester, on the water, and the mist-washed vistas of the High, all triste . . .

'All the women wear velour hats of the same shape,' she observed as they made their way along the High. 'All turn up behind and down in front. Now I would turn mine down behind and up in front – with a very slight curve to the side; the line is better. And for *costumes tailleurs* it is so needful that the skirt should hang evenly.'

'Is it?' said Giles with a gloomy grin. 'I'm showing you the architecture, not the clothes of Oxford.'

'Are they all the wives of philosophers?' Alix inquired, and the question indubitably interested her more than the architecture.

'A good many of them are, no doubt,' laughed Giles. 'Do you wonder if my wife will look like that?'

Alix had a sudden vision of Toppie in the rainy High Street. Yes, even dear Toppie would sink, she felt, into the fatal sameness, embody the type. She could see her, slender, in her wet grey tweed, speeding on a bicycle in just such a velour hat. They, too, were perhaps Toppies if one could have a careful look at them.

MARGARET DRABBLE

From The Radiant Way

ALIX WAS MOUSY, square faced, healthy of complexion, and, even then, extraordinarily pleasant of expression, with a pleasantness that was at times radiant, and almost always irrefutable: she was wearing, as girls who had them did for their Oxbridge interviews in those days, a two-piece middle-aged suit of an oatmeal mix, with square shoulders and a straight skirt. Esther was small, neat, brown of skin, smooth, tidy, even (almost) elegant, yet somehow at the same time pugnacious of aspect, subversive, aggressive, commanding, Napoleonic of manner. She was wearing a severe school uniform, olive green, from an expensive private school. It looked ironic, satiric, suggestive on her small frame.

Flora Piercy was wearing black velvet trousers, and a large white cable-knit sweater. Her eyelids were painted blue with a blue greasy paste called eye-shadow. Alix bought some the next day, on her free half day in Cambridge before she took the Bletchley route to her Oxford interview (for she was a clever girl, Alix) – but she never dared to apply it, save in the privacy of her own room, until she went to Cambridge herself as a bona fide student the following autumn.

RUMER GODDEN

From The Greengage Summer

'I SHALL GO TO this party,' said Joss, 'and I shall wear Sin.'
It was called Sin because she had had no right to buy it. A year before Uncle William had given Joss money to buy a new raincoat: her old one was up to her knees and showed inches of wrist, but she had gone into a dress shop and bought a dress. That was in the sales too, 'and it had been marked down from ten guineas,' said Joss.

'Ten guineas for a dress!' That seemed fabulous to us – except Willmouse.

'A dress can cost a hundred pounds,' said Willmouse.

'But . . . when will you wear it?' Mother had asked, bewildered.

'Perhaps never,' said Joss, 'but I had to have it.' It was ivory silk, stamped with roses. 'Not many roses,' Hester had said critically, 'and not much silk.' There did not seem much of anything to cost all that money; it left Joss's neck and arms bare and the skirt was narrow. 'It's the cut,' Willmouse had explained and examined it carefully. 'It is influenced by the Chinese,' he pronounced, 'which is why it suits her.'

For a year it had hung in Joss's cupboard. Now, after she had washed her face and brushed her hair, she took it out of the wardrobe. I had opened the door into my room to let the others in and we watched while she put it on.

Beside Sin our seersuckers looked very ordinary and home-made, and . . . the old envy came back. 'It's too tight,' I said spitefully. 'You *show*.'

Joss looked at herself in the looking-glass and smiled. 'All the better,' she said and laughed at my scandalised face.

HELEN B. MATHERS
From Comin' Thro' the Rye

STEPS COME DOWN the corridor; no mincing feminine ones this time, but a man's bold decided tread. I lay down my stitching to listen. The door opens, a head is popped in. 'Cricket?' says a loud clear voice, the door is shut again, and down go work and thimbles, a Babel of delighted cries bursts forth, and in thirty seconds the room is cleared, and we are all upstairs, pulling off ribbons, gowns, crinolines, all our feminine belongings, and pulling on knickerbockers and blouses. Yes, *knickerbockers*! Let no one blush or look shocked, for they are long and ample, and tied modestly in at the ankle; and as to the blouse, which descends below the knee, and is trimly belted in at the waist, it is as decent and uncompromising as that worn by Dr Mary Walker; our costume being, in short, nothing more or less than that which is designated by the somewhat opprobrious title of 'Bloomer'. The knickerbockers bring comfort, the tunic confers respectability. It is a lovely thought that I can kick up my heels to my heart's content, and yet preserve decorum. As to what manner of female I look, I care nothing; my sensations are all I think about, and they are blissful. I feel as light as a feather, and equal to Jack at running, vaulting or hurdle jumping.

On my way downstairs I fall in with the girls – shrunken, insignificant creatures, measured by the standard of half an hour ago, when they boasted a circumference of from four to five yards of petticoat. They even look meek; for it is a fact that a large proportion of a woman's assurance lies in her tail. Shear her of that and she is no way superior to man. Out in the cricket field I scan the assembly critically, and nothing but the consciousness of looking a greater guy than any one present prevents me from going off into a fit of convulsive laughter. If only Charles Lovelace, George Tempest, or Jack could see us!

We have roly-poly girls and bean-stalk girls, little girls, big girls, long girls, short girls; girls whose plump proportions fit their garments as closely as a kernel fits a shell; girls whose garments hang upon them loose, as did the armour on Don Quixote's gaunt form; girls who waddle, amble, jig, trot, hurry, and stride – their action plainly shown in the narrow, straight costume. Can an English girl walk? I trow not. It is a pity the time spent in needlework is not used in drilling. Conspicuous, even among this remarkable throng, is the German governess, short, square, stout, not over young, with a large flat face, enormous feet and hands, and that general look of a Dutch doll that usually marks her stolid race. She wears the regulation trousers and blouse; but whether under an impression that she is not sufficiently clad, or whether she wishes to give a full dress air to a somewhat severe costume I know not; at any rate she has over and above arrayed herself in a very large, ample, white muslin jacket, profusely frilled and starched, and tightly belted in at the waist, and these frills set straight out from her sturdy form in a fashion that would bring a smile to the face of a crocodile.

(1875)

LOELIA, DUCHESS OF WESTMINSTER
From Grace and Favour

UNDERCLOTHES WE DID not bother about, but evening shoes were a horrible expense. We danced so much and in such congested rooms that our brocaded shoes (laced at the ankle with satin ribbons, like ballet dancers') wore out quickly, and I remember re-covering a pair myself, a feat I should now consider impossible. I dipped the heels in red ink and laboriously stitched black satin neatly above the soles. Getting round the toe was so difficult that I nearly gave up, but I persevered and in the end produced a pair of shoes that passed muster in a crowd. Another unavoidable expense was long white kid gloves. They had to be cleaned every time they were worn and as the Season advanced they refused to yield up their stains, becoming stiff as parchment and giving off an unpleasant chemical smell; however we (and our partners who all also wore gloves) had to put up with that, as few girls could afford to replace them until they actually split. Gloves were worn at every dance, but my mother went further and asserted that they should be taken down at dinner at large week-end parties in the country; the first time we went on a visit together she insisted that I should do so. Little as I knew about the world and much as I respected my mother, I realized that this was an out of date piece of etiquette and I managed to shove them behind a large silver-framed photograph of Royalty as soon as we entered the drawing-room. I felt I had scored off my mother but later I had the agonizing shame of having to reclaim them, as even to keep up face, I could not bear to lose my new pair of 'sixteen buttons'. (They hadn't really sixteen buttons – it was just the shop name for them. 'Twenty buttons' were longer still and reached up to your arm-pits.)

WILLIAM HICKEY

From Memoirs

UPON ENTERING THE sitting-room, the first object that met my eyes was Mr John Rider, so metamorphosed that, until he spoke, I knew him not. He had returned from his French excursion about an hour before we arrived. Instead of the plain brown cloth suit we had last seen him in, with unpowdered hair and a single curl, we now beheld a furiously powdered and pomatumed head with six curls on each side, a little skimming dish of a hat, the brim not four inches deep – two of which were covered with silver lace – and immensely wide in front. His coat was of a thick silk, the colour sky blue, and lined with crimson satin, the waistcoat and breeches also of crimson satin, coat and waistcoat being bedizened with a tawdry spangle lace. The cut, too, was entirely different from anything we had seen, having a remarkable long waist to the coat with scarce any skirts. He was a little fat squab of a man, which made his appearance the more extraordinary. Altogether, so grotesque a figure I never beheld, and we had a hearty laugh at him. This suit he assured us was the latest and veritable Parisian fashion; he had it made up during the few hours he remained at Boulogne. The hat he purchased at Calais where they put in, and where his head was made *à la regle*. The hat was said to have been introduced by the Duc de Nivernois, French Ambassador at the British court, and was therefore distinguished by the name of '*Chapeau Nivernois*'. I thought his habiliments preposterous and ugly, except the hat, which appeared becoming, and I gave that as my opinion; whereupon he (John Rider) told me the master of the vessel had purchased some of them upon speculation, and if I chose it he would purchase one for me. This I requested him to do, and I thus obtained a '*Nivernois*' even more *outré* than Rider's, and which was afterwards the cause of great mirth at Madras. Mr Jacob Rider was quite delighted with the whole of the French dress, telling his brother that he must let him have it to make the people stare in Bengal; and he actually made John strip, and had the suit put into his own trunk, the height and form of the two brothers being exactly similar.

OUIDA

From Under Two Flags

LIFE PETTED HIM, pampered him, caressed him, gifted him, though of half his gifts he never made use; lodged him like a prince, dined him like a king, and never recalled to him by a single privation or a single sensation that he was not as rich a man as his brother-in-arms, the Seraph, future Duke of Lyonnesse. How could he then bring himself to understand, as nothing less than truth, the grim and cruel insult his father had flung at him in that brutally bitter phrase – 'A Pauper and a Guardsman'? If he had ever been near a comprehension of it, which he never was, he must have ceased to realize it when – pressed to dine with Lord Guenevere near whose house the last fox had been killed, while a groom dashed over to Royallieu for his change of clothes – he caught a glimpse, as they passed through the hall, of the ladies taking their preprandial cups of tea in the library, an enchanting group of lace and silks, of delicate hue and scented hair, of blonde cheeks and brunette tresses, of dark velvets and gossamer tissue; and when he had changed the scarlet for dinner-dress, went down among them to be the darling of that charmed circle, to be smiled on and coquetted with by those soft, languid aristocrats, to be challenged by the lustrous eyes of his châtelaine and chère amie, to be spoiled as women will spoil the privileged pet of their drawing-rooms whom they have made 'free of the guild', and endowed with flirting commission, and acquitted of anything 'serious'.

He was the recognized darling, and permitted property, of the young married beauties, the unwedded knew he was hopeless for *them*, and tacitly left him to the more attractive conquerors, who hardly prized the Seraph so much as they did Bertie, to sit in their barouches and opera boxes, ride and drive and yacht with them, conduct a Boccaccio intrigue through the height of the season, and make them really believe themselves actually in love while they were at the moors or down the Nile, and would have given their diamonds to get a new distraction.

OSBERT SITWELL

From Great Morning!

MUCH RITUAL EXISTED, however, in other directions and at other times. The newly-joined ensign was instructed not only in the general and accepted code, but, if he were not already aware of it, was advised on what constituted for him the right kind of shoes, collars, shirts and suits to wear, being given pieces of precise information; such as, for example, that when leave was granted to him, he should never spend a day of it in London, and that he must, when not in uniform – which he only wore, of course, on duty – always, if the King was in London, wear a morning suit and top-hat.

In those days – and probably until the beginning of the 1939 war the habit continued – the Adjutant would attend the first fittings of each young officer, surveying with a practised eye the whole effect, and scrutinising minutely the cut of the tunic of scarlet Melton cloth, the smoothness of shoulders and waist. Above all, there must be no wrinkling. And this constituted, withal, an important question, both for the young man and his parents, since the uniform cost several hundreds of pounds. The review-belt alone, made of scarlet and gold, cost thirty-six pounds, I remember, and I only had occasion to wear it once; then there was the bearskin, as well, to be fitted and tried on, and the perfection of this proved to be of so esoteric a kind that no-one new to the matter would be able to tell a good from a bad, and, myself, I never contrived to master the principles that governed the choice. The bearskin had, of course – for it must measure some one and a half foot to one foot and ten inches high – to be sufficiently well-balanced and well-fitting to enable the ensign to carry it on his head, and the Colour in front of him, in a gale, without mishap – and this, even with the best constructed bearskin, was not easy: because the Fore Court of Buckingham Palace gives ample space for the east wind, which the front faces, to play, while the weight of the Colour, although the butt of it is supported most of the time in a pipe-clayed belt, is considerable, and the left arm, to balance, and also for the sake of smart appearance, must swing free. In addition, however, to these necessary qualities, I may place it on record for those in the future of an enquiring disposition, that the good bearskin should possess an interior curl and a special gloss, at once perceptible to the expert.

The fitting of headgear and uniform and belts constituted something of an ordeal. Not only did it without exception occupy a full hour – and by nature I have always been too impatient either to deserve or to obtain perfectly fitting clothes – but, while the young officer, prodded from time to time with questing fingers, as if he were a prize bull at a show, stood in the centre of a small closet, full of mirrors, set at different angles, so as to reflect him in his half-finished scarlet tunic, and every detail of his dress, with a kind of dull but yet varied repetition that recalled delirium, during all these minutes, a highly technical conversation was taking place between the Adjutant and the tailor. After they had debated some particularly enthralling point, the tailor would call in the cutter and ask for his view on it: but the cutter, partially blind from his work, would pretend to be deaf also. This, I think, he did as some personal form of subservience combined with defiance, that he had worked out for himself – but at any rate, every question would have to be put at least three times before he would answer. 'The best cutter in London, now that the ladies have taken all the others', the tailor would say of him, adding, 'But he's a very difficult man to deal with, must be given his head.' Occasionally, the tailor himself would dart at my shoulder or waist, and rip the seam open, so that the grey padding stood exposed beneath the vermilion stuff. It was true that one felt oneself to be the most important person there – as the prize bull must feel himself; the very centre of the debate. Yet, too, one felt at the same time curiously left out of things: for neither Adjutant, tailor nor cutter seemed to see the man who wore the uniform, only the uniform itself. The tunic glowed, ember-like, in the misty and pocked mirrors, and the cutter peered through spectacles that magnified his eyes to the size of a god's: he jabbed and snipped, but never spoke.

MABEL BARNES GRUNDY
From The Vacillations of Hazel

AUNT MENELOPHE SIMPLY snorted.
'Checks were an invention – not of the devil – but of some grasping, economical cloth manufacturer who wanted to use up his odds and ends of wool. He should have been strung up. Imagine a woman in ancient Greece wearing a check chess-board robe with a girdle round it! And people say we have progressed! No, never wear checks if you desire to be known as a well-dressed woman. Cultivate flowing lines, simplicity in form, and really good colours. Don't *heap* things on your person; don't look like an escaped bazaar. When I see women dangling chains and trinkets and chatelaines and ribbons and velvets, and dabbing rosettes and bows and ruchings on every spare place, I yearn to pluck them as you would a fowl. And when you get to my age wear soft tones of grey. Grey blends and harmonises with faded faces and eyes. It softens the lines and gives an effect of mellowness. Whatever women may say to you, don't pass your entire existence in black. Black should be an elderly woman's bugbear. It accentuates wrinkles and sallowness and flabby chins. It shows up sunken cheeks and knobbly jaw-bones, and forms a striking background for the stout chin of the three-decker character. But put her in soft mauves and greys with rich, old, champagne-coloured lace at her throat, and you will forget she is old. Her younger women friends will be bound to say she dresses in much too juvenile a style and is aping to be young. There has scarcely been a woman in this world who has not said that some other woman dresses too young. It is a way she has.'

Then Aunt Menelophe floated in an atmosphere of soft, grey cloth and chinchilla and velvet, crowned by her lovely grey hair, to the waiting cab, and as she said 'The station, driver,' I felt proud to belong to her.

ELINOR GLYN
From The Vicissitudes of Evangeline

I COULD SEE THEIR eyes often straying to my night-gown and dressing-gown, laid out on a chair beside the fire.

'Oh, Lady Katherine, I am afraid you are wondering at my having pink silk,' I said, apologetically, 'as I am in mourning, but I have not had time to get a white dressing-gown yet.'

'It is not that, dear,' said Lady Katherine, in a grave duty voice. 'I – I – do not think such a night-gown is suitable for a girl.'

'Oh! but I am very strong,' I said. 'I never catch cold.'

Mary Mackintosh held it up, with a face of stern disapproval. Of course it has short sleeves ruffled with Valenciennes, and is fine linen cambric nicely embroidered. Mrs Carruthers was always very particular about them, and chose them herself at Doucet's. She said one never could know when places might catch on fire.

'Evangeline, dear, you are very young, so you probably cannot understand,' Mary said, 'but I consider this garment not in any way fit for a girl – or for any good woman for that matter. Mother, I hope my sisters have not seen it!!'

I looked so puzzled.

She examined the stuff, one could see the chair through it, beyond.

'What *would* Alexander say if I were to wear such a thing!'

This thought seemed almost to suffocate them both, they looked genuinely pained and shocked.

'Of course it would be too tight for you,' I said, humbly, 'but it is otherwise a very good pattern, and does not tear when one puts up one's arms. Mrs Carruthers made a fuss at Doucet's because my last set tore so soon, and they altered these.'

At the mention of my late adopted mother, both of them pulled themselves up.

'Mrs Carruthers we know had very odd notions,' Lady Katherine said stiffly, 'but I hope, Evangeline, you have sufficient sense to understand now for yourself that such a – a – garment is not at all seemly.'

'Oh! why not, dear Lady Katherine?' I said. 'You don't know how becoming it is.'

'Becoming!' almost screamed Mary Mackintosh. 'But no nice-minded woman wants things to look becoming in bed!'

The whole matter appeared so painful to them I covered up the offending 'nighty' with my dressing-gown, and coughed. It made a break, and they went away, saying good-night frigidly.

And now I am alone. But I do wonder why it is wrong to look pretty in bed, – considering nobody sees one, too!

MOLLY KEANE

From Loving and Giving

EVENING DRESS, TOO, was a matter for Aunt Tossie's close concern and consideration – Dada's pink evening coat, its lining and facings frail and splitting with age, must be handled carefully and aired thoroughly; white tie and waistcoat freshly sparked up, and jewelled cufflinks traced to some forgotten place of retirement.

It was one of Aunt Tossie's more endearing habits to discuss with Nicandra every item in her own wardrobe, and tonight was an occasion for special deliberation. Gigi, no quieter or graver in her advancing years, screamed and flapped, furious at being caged: a necessity, even Aunt Tossie allowed, when velvets, silks, taffetas and bright sequins lay deep on the bed and overflowed the chairs in her bedroom, changes of fashion and flaws of past time limply exposed in the morning light.

'I think I might look quite lovely in *that*,' Aunt Tossie held blue velvet against her tweeds and woollies.

'I like you best in black,' Nicandra said. 'What about your black velvet with the huge skirt? Wear that.'

'Well I don't say yes and I don't say no, I say, well, yes, perhaps,' Aunt Tossie gave the matter further consideration. 'No,' she said at last, 'the lace corsage and the boned neck, a bit ageing, don't you rather think?'

She strained the black velvet across her distinguished breasts, then turned from the looking-glass, 'Nip out all this lace and fuzz and, Bob's your uncle, what do you get? A sweetheart neckline.'

'Oh, you've got a Kestos brassière – *quel* absolute *chic*.' Lally picked the bust-bodice out of the pile of underclothes Lizzie had folded and laid, a picture of precision, on Nicandra's bed. She stretched its modest cups on her hands.

'Aunt Tossie,' Nicandra explained. 'It worries me rather. Still I know she knows.'

'May I try it on?' Without waiting for an answer, Lally stripped off the accepted bandaging of the day. 'Oh, m'dear, too naughty for words.' She screamed with laughter.

Nicandra looked disconcerted and prim before a great light of kindness broke, telling her to spread a little happiness at any cost to herself. 'I'll lend it to you, Lally,' she said, 'just for tonight.'

'Oh, Nico, I wouldn't dream.' Lally fastened a button more securely on its elastic strap. The mild uplift of her breasts was frightening in its unexplored possibilities: 'If you really mean it.' Her acceptance was inevitable, as immediate as her plunge underground of the afternoon. She danced away to her bedroom to dance back a minute later: 'I wasn't going to tell you, but I will.' She had a mystery to share, there was a tinge of the forbidden in her voice. 'It's called "Odor-O-No". Mummie says it could give me cancer, who cares? I'd sooner die than smell, wouldn't you?'

KATHERINE MANSFIELD
From The Garden Party

'**D**ARLING!' MRS SHERIDAN got up and came over to her, carrying the hat. Before Laura could stop her she had popped it on. 'My child!' said her mother, 'the hat is yours. It's made for you. It's much too young for me. I have never seen you look such a picture. Look at yourself!' And she held up her hand-mirror.

'But, mother,' Laura began again. She couldn't look at herself; she turned aside.

This time Mrs Sheridan lost patience just as Jose had done.

'You are being very absurd, Laura,' she said coldly. 'People like that don't expect sacrifices from us. And it's not very sympathetic to spoil everybody's enjoyment as you're doing now.'

'I don't understand,' said Laura, and she walked quickly out of the room into her own bedroom. There, quite by chance, the first thing she saw was this charming girl in the mirror, in her black hat trimmed with gold daisies, and a long black velvet ribbon. Never had she imagined she could look like that . . .

'Laurie!'

'Hallo!' He was half-way upstairs, but when he turned round and saw Laura he suddenly puffed out his cheeks and goggled his eyes at her. 'My word, Laura! You do look stunning,' said Laurie. 'What an absolutely topping hat!'

Laura said faintly 'Is it!' and smiled up at Laurie, and didn't tell him after all.

Soon after that people began coming in streams. The band struck up; the hired waiters ran from the house to the marquee. Wherever you looked there were couples strolling, bending to the flowers, greeting, moving on over the lawn. They were like bright birds that had alighted in the Sheridans' garden for this one afternoon, on their way to – where? Ah, what happiness is to be with people who all are happy, to press hands, press cheeks, smile into eyes.

'Darling Laura, how well you look!'

'What a becoming hat, child!'

'Laura, you look quite Spanish. I've never seen you look so striking.'

And Laura, glowing, answered softly, 'Have you had tea? Won't you have an ice? The passion-fruit ices really are rather special.' She ran to her father and begged him. 'Daddy darling, can't the band have something to drink?'

And the perfect afternoon slowly ripened, slowly faded, slowly its petals closed.

'Never a more delightful garden-party . . .' 'The greatest success . . .' 'Quite the most . . .'

MABEL BARNES GRUNDY

From An Undressed Heroine

SHE DESPISED AND pitied him in the same breath, despised him for his mendacity (if he had truly loved her as he declared he had all these long months, could he have kept away from her?), pitied him for being so poor a thing.

'Do you know,' she queried, and the irony in her voice was very bitter, 'that you are making love to my – clothes?'

He started. 'Your clothes? What do you mean?'

She laughed, and it was a hard little laugh. She was standing in front of him, looking into his eyes, with an amused quizzical expression in her own. 'My frock – how did you call it? – my lovely beetle-wings frock. I am smart to-night, no longer a dowdy thing in – what was it? dingy brown or unbecoming grey? I am in a gown that suits me and that has enhanced what few attractions I may possess. Your eyes are dazzled. What you are asking to be your wife is not *me*, but merely my fine feathers. I myself, beneath them, am just the same as I ever was, except perhaps a little harder, and that self you never really loved, and do not really love now. It's my frock that's bewitched your senses.'

'Stop,' he cried, 'it is not true.'

'It is true, horribly and depressingly true, and hurting to one's pride to know that in so brief a space as a couple of hours a pretty frock has done more to gain what you call love than I could achieve in all the long years, Brian. Do you not realize that it is somebody else who has been busy with the adornment of my person and not I? Neither my gifts nor my interests lie that way. Left to myself,

I should relapse into my old dowdiness. I should fight against it, for I begin to appreciate the fact that the successful dressing of one's body seems to afford great pleasure to those who care for us, but I'm afraid I should not succeed. I should begrudge the time expended, for to be really well turned out, and I know it to my sorrow, means hours spent before a mirror. Do you not realize that if I were so foolish as to believe in you and to marry you, the same old Elfie would inevitably reappear; then where would be your love? In dust and ashes at my unsmart feet?'

BERYL BAINBRIDGE
From The Dressmaker

NELLIE WAS TIRED, but satisfied. She had worked full out on the lovely Valerie's dress. In the afternoon she pressed the skirt and draped the frock over the model. She went down on her hands and knees, crawling round and round the floor to make sure the hem was absolutely even. She had plenty of time. Marge wouldn't be home for a meal – she had gone to her dramatics – and Rita wouldn't want much, not with the poor appetite she had lately. They could have something cold, and she could go round to Valerie's after tea for the final fitting. There was a button not quite in line. She re-sewed it there and then, a little on tip-toe to reach, her eyes screwed up against the light. She sat down to rest and stared critically at the dress. The beauty was in the yards of material in the skirt, the low cut of the bodice. Mrs Mander wanted sequins but Valerie said no, it had to be plain. She saw Valerie whirling round and round like a film star, all her petticoats showing, her plump knees silky in her nylon stockings. She should ask Valerie to get Rita a pair of those nylons. It might cheer her up . . .

Valerie popped in on her way home. Her gloves were real leather. She had a little fur tippet about her neck.

'Oh, it's lovely, Auntie Nellie, it really is.'

She stood in wonder in front of the green taffeta dress, touching the material of the shoulder gently with her fingers.

'The shoulder's alright now,' said Nellie anxiously.

'Oh, it's lovely! I didn't want to crush the skirt.'

'I'll come over after tea for the final fitting.'

CHARLES DICKENS
From Barnaby Rudge

A S TO DOLLY [Varden], there she was again, the very pink and pattern of good looks, in a smart little cherry-coloured mantle, with a hood of the same drawn over her head, and upon the top of that hood, a little straw hat trimmed with cherry-coloured ribbons, and worn the merest trifle on one side – just enough in short to make it the wickedest and most provoking headdress that ever malicious milliner devised. And not to speak of the manner in which these cherry-coloured decorations brightened her eyes, or vied with her lips, or shed a new bloom on her face, she wore such a cruel little muff, and such a heart-rending pair of shoes, and was so surrounded and hemmed in, as it were, by aggravations of all kinds, that when Mr. Tappertit, holding the horse's head, saw her come out of the house alone, such impulses came over him to decoy her into the chaise and drive off like mad, that he would unquestionably have done it, but for certain uneasy doubts besetting him as to the shortest way to Gretna Green; whether it was up the street or down, or up the right-hand turning or the left; and whether, supposing all the turnpikes to be carried by storm, the blacksmith in the end would marry them on credit; which by reason of his clerical office appeared, even to his excited imagination, so unlikely, that he hesitated.

GEORGE ELIOT
From Middlemarch

C ELIA COLOURED, AND looked very grave. 'I think, dear, we are wanting in respect to mamma's memory, to put them by and take no notice of them. And,' she added, after hesitating a little, with a rising sob of mortification, 'necklaces are quite usual now; and Madame Poinçon, who was stricter in some things even than you are, used to wear ornaments. And Christians generally – surely there are women in heaven now who wore jewels.' Celia was conscious of some mental strength when she really applied herself to argument.

'You would like to wear them?' exclaimed Dorothea, an air of astonished discovery animating her whole person with a dramatic action which she had caught from that very Madame Poinçon who wore the ornaments. 'Of course, then, let us have them out. Why did you not tell me before? But the keys, the keys!' She pressed her hands against the sides of her head and seemed to despair of her memory.

'They are here,' said Celia, with whom this explanation had been long meditated and prearranged.

'Pray open the large drawer of the cabinet and get out the jewel-box.'

The casket was soon open before them, and the various jewels spread out, making a bright parterre on the table. It was no great collection, but a few of the ornaments were really of remarkable beauty, the finest that was obvious at first being a necklace of purple amethysts set in exquisite gold-work, and a pearl cross with five brilliants in it. Dorothea immediately took up the necklace and fastened it round her sister's neck, where it fitted almost as closely as a bracelet; but the circle suited the Henrietta-Maria style of Celia's head and neck, and she could see that it did, in the pier-glass opposite.

'There, Celia! you can wear that with your Indian muslin. But this cross you must wear with your dark dresses.'

Celia was trying not to smile with pleasure. 'O Dodo, you must keep the cross yourself.'

'No, no, dear, no,' said Dorothea, putting up her hand with careless deprecation.

'Yes, indeed you must; it would suit you – in your black dress, now,' said Celia, insistingly. 'You *might* wear that.'

'Not for the world, not for the world. A cross is the last thing I would wear as a trinket.' Dorothea shuddered slightly.

'Then you will think it wicked in me to wear it,' said Celia, uneasily.

'No, dear, no,' said Dorothea, stroking her sister's cheek. 'Souls have complexions too: what will suit one will not suit another.'

'But you might like to keep it for mamma's sake.'

'No, I have other things of mamma's – her sandal-wood box, which I am so fond of – plenty of things. In fact, they are all yours, dear. We need discuss them no longer. There – take away your property.'

Celia felt a little hurt. There was a strong assumption of superiority in this Puritanic toleration, hardly less trying to the blond flesh of an unenthusiastic sister than a Puritanic persecution.

'But how can I wear ornaments if you, who are the elder sister, will never wear them?'

'Nay, Celia, that is too much to ask, that I should wear trinkets to keep you in countenance. If I were to put on such a necklace as that, I should feel as if I had been pirouetting. The world would go round with me, and I should not know how to walk.'

Celia had unclasped the necklace and drawn it off. 'It would be a little tight for your neck; something to lie down and hang would suit you better,' she said, with some satisfaction. The complete unfitness of the necklace from all points of view for Dorothea, made Celia happier in taking it. She was opening some ring-boxes, which disclosed a fine emerald with diamonds, and just then the sun passing beyond a cloud sent a bright gleam over the table.

'How very beautiful these gems are!' said Dorothea, under a new current of feeling, as sudden as the gleam. 'It is strange how deeply colours seem to penetrate one, like scent. I suppose that is the reason why gems are used as spiritual emblems in the Revelation of St John. They look like fragments of heaven. I think that emerald is more beautiful than any of them.'

4

The Peacock Male

Without black-velvet breeches, what is Man?

James Bramston, *The Man of Taste* (1733)

WILLIAM SHAKESPEARE
From Henry IV Part One

   Hotspur: My liege, I did deny no prisoners.
But I remember, when the fight was done,
When I was dry with rage and extreme toil,
Breathless and faint, leaning upon my sword,
Came there a certain lord, neat, and trimly
      dress'd,
Fresh as a bridegroom; and his chin new reap'd
Show'd like a stubble-land at harvest-home;
He was perfumed like a milliner;
And 'twixt his finger and his thumb he held
A pouncet-box, which ever and anon
He gave his nose and took't away again;
Who therewith angry, when it next came there,
Took it in snuff; and still he smiled and talk'd,
And as the soldiers bore dead bodies by,
He call'd them untaught knaves, unmannerly,
To bring a slovenly unhandsome corse
Betwixt the wind and his nobility.
With many holiday and lady terms
He question'd me; amongst the rest, demanded
My prisoners in your majesty's behalf.
I then, all smarting with my wounds being cold,
To be so pester'd with a popinjay,
Out of my grief and my impatience,
Answer'd neglectingly I know not what,
He should, or he should not; for he made me
      mad

To see him shine so brisk and smell so sweet
And talk so like a waiting-gentlewoman
Of guns and drums and wounds, – God save the
      mark! –
And telling me the sovereign'st thing on earth
Was parmaceti for an inward bruise;
And that it was great pity, so it was,
This villanous salt-petre should be digg'd
Out of the bowels of the harmless earth,
Which many a good tall fellow had destroy'd
So cowardly; and but for these vile guns,
He would himself have been a soldier.

THOMAS CARLYLE

From Sartor Resartus

First, touching dandies, let us consider, with some scientific strictness, what a Dandy specially is. A Dandy is a Clothes-wearing Man, a Man whose trade, office and existence consists in the wearing of Clothes. Every faculty of his soul, spirit, purse and person is heroically consecrated to this one object, the wearing of Clothes wisely and well: so that as others dress to live, he lives to dress. The all-importance of Clothes, which a German Professor, of unequalled learning and acumen, writes his enormous Volume to demonstrate, has sprung up in the intellect of the Dandy without effort, like an instinct of genius; he is inspired with Cloth, a Poet of Cloth. What Teufelsdröckh would call a 'Divine Idea of Cloth' is born with him; and this, like other such Ideas, will express itself outwardly, or wring his heart asunder with unutterable throes.

But, like a generous, creative enthusiast, he fearlessly makes his Idea an Action; shows himself in peculiar guise to mankind; walks forth, a witness and living Martyr to the eternal worth of Clothes. We call him a Poet: is not his body the (stuffed) parchment-skin whereon he writes, with cunning Huddersfield dyes, a Sonnet to his mistress' eyebrow? Say, rather, an Epos, and *Clotha Virumque cano*, to the whole world, in Macaronic verses, which he that runs may read. Nay, if you grant, what seems to be admissible, that the Dandy has a Thinking-principle in him, and some notions of Time and Space, is there not in this Life-devotedness to Cloth, in this so willing sacrifice of the Immortal to the Perishable, something (though in reverse order) of that blending and identification of Eternity with Time, which, as we have seen, constitutes the Prophetic character?

All Arabia breathes from his scented handkerchief.

Frances Brooke, *The History of Lady Julia Mandeville* (1763)

PIERCE EGAN
From Life in London

THE DANDY WAS got by *Vanity* out of *Affectation* – his dam, *Petit-Maître* or *Macaroni* – his grandam, *Fribble* – his great-grandam, *Bronze* – his great-great-grandam, *Coxcomb* – and his earliest ancestor FOP. His uncle *Impudence* – his three brothers *Trick, Humbug,* and *Fudge!* and allied to the extensive family of the *Shuffletons.*

Indeed, this *Bandbox* sort of creature took so much the lead in the walks of fashion, that the BUCK was totally missing; the BLOOD vanished; the TIPPY is not to be found; the GO out of date; the DASH not to be met with; and the BANG–UP without a leader, at fault, and in the background.

(1821)

Laced up in stays to show his waist,
And highly rouged to show his taste.

Bernard Blackmantle, *The English Spy*, (1825)

MAX BEERBOHM
From 'Dandies and Dandies'

IN ONE WAY dandyism is the least selfish of all the arts. Musicians are seen and, except for a price, not heard. Only for a price may you read what poets have written. All painters are not so generous as Mr Watts. But the dandy presents himself to the nation whenever he sallies from his front door. Princes and peasants alike may gaze upon his masterpieces . . . It is only by the trifling addition or elimination, modification or extension, made by this or that dandy and copied by the rest, that the mode proceeds. The young dandy will find certain laws to which he must conform. If he outrage them he will be hooted by the urchins of the street, not unjustly, for he will have outraged the slowly constructed laws of artists who have preceded him. Let him reflect that fashion is no bondage imposed by alien hands, but the last wisdom of his own kind, and that true dandyism is the result of an artistic temperament working upon a fine body within the wide limits of fashion . . . The dandy is the 'child of his age', and his best work must be produced in accord with the age's natural influence. The true dandy must always love contemporary costume. In this age, as in all precedent ages, it is only the tasteless who cavil, being impotent to win from it fair results. How futile their voices are! The costume of the nineteenth century, as shadowed for us first by Mr Brummell, so quiet, so reasonable, and, I say emphatically, so beautiful; free from folly or affectation, yet susceptible to exquisite ordering; plastic, austere, economical, may not be ignored . . .

Clad according to his convention, the limbs of the weakling escape contempt, and the athlete is unobtrusive, and all is well. But there is also a social reason for the triumph of our costume – the reason of economy. That austerity, which has rejected from its toilet silk and velvet and all but a few jewels, has made more ample the wardrobes of Dives, and sent forth Irus nicely dressed among his fellows . . . Let us be glad that we have so easy, yet so delicate, a mode of expression.

Yes! costume, dandiacal or not, is in the highest degree expressive, nor is there any type it may not express. It enables us to classify any 'professional man' at a glance, be he lawyer, leech or what not. Still more swift and obvious is its revelation of the work and the soul of those who dress, whether naturally or for effect, without reference to convention. The bowler of Mr Jerome K. Jerome is a perfect preface to all his works. The silk hat of Mr Whistler is a real *nocturne*, his linen a symphony *en blanc majeur*. To have seen Mr Hall Caine is to have read his soul. His flowing, formless cloak is as one of his own novels, twenty-five editions latent in the folds of it. Melodrama crouches upon the brim of his *sombrero*. His tie is a Publisher's Announcement. His boots are Copyright. In his hand he holds the staff of *The Family Herald*.

But the dandy, in nowise violating the laws of fashion, can make more subtle symbols of his personality. More subtle these symbols are for the very reason that they are effected within the restrictions which are essential to an art. Chastened of all flamboyance, they are from most men occult, obvious, it may be, only to other artists or even only to him they symbolise.

From *The Works of Max Beerbohm* (1896)

CHARLES BAUDELAIRE
From The Painter of Modern Life

IF I SPEAK of love apropos of dandyism, it is because love is the natural occupation of the idle. But the dandy does not aim at love as a special end. If I have
spoken of money, it is because money is indispensable to people who make a cult
of their passions; but the dandy does not aspire to money as an essential thing;
indefinite credit would do as well for him; he leaves this gross passion to vulgar
mortals. Dandyism is not even, as many rather thoughtless people seem to believe,
an immoderate taste for dress and material elegance. For the perfect dandy these
things are only a perfect symbol of the aristocratic superiority of his spirit. Again,
in his eyes, which are above all smitten with *distinction*, the perfection of dress consists in absolute simplicity, which is, indeed, the best way of achieving distinction.

Transl. P.G. Knody

APHRA BEHN
From The Fair Jilt

AS LOVE IS the most noble and divine passion of the soul, so it is that to which
we may justly attribute all the real satisfactions of life; and without it man is
unfinish'd and unhappy. There are a thousand things to be said of the advantages
this generous passion brings to those, whose hearts are capable of receiving its
soft impressions; for 'tis not every one that can be sensible of its tender touches.
How many examples, from history and observation, could I give of its wondrous
power; nay, even to a degree of transmigration! How many idiots has it made
wise! How many fools eloquent! How many home-bred 'squires accomplish'd!
How many cowards brave! And there is no sort of species of mankind on whom
it cannot work some change and miracle, if it be a noble well-grounded passion,
except on the fop in fashion, the harden'd incorrigible fop; so often wounded,
but never reclaim'd. For still, by a dire mistake, conducted by vast opiniatrety,
and a greater portion of self-love, than the rest of the race of man, be believes
that affectation in his mien and dress, that mathematical movement, that for-
mality in every action, that a face manag'd with care, and soften'd into ridicule,
the languishing turn, the toss, and the back-shake of the periwig, is the direct
way to the heart of the fine person he adores; and instead of curing love in his
soul, serves only to advance his folly; and the more he is enamour'd, the more
industriously he assumes (every hour) the coxcomb. These are love's playthings,

a sort of animals with whom he sports; and whom he never wounds, but when he is in good humour, and always shoots laughing. 'Tis the diversion of the little god, to see what a fluttering and bustle one of these sparks, new-wounded, makes; to what fantastick fooleries he has recourse. The glass is every moment call'd to counsel, the valet consulted and plagu'd for new invention of dress, the footman and scrutore perpetually employed; *billet-doux* and madrigals take up all his mornings, till playtime in dressing, till night in gazing; still, like a sunflower, turned towards the beams of the fair eyes of his Cælia, adjusting himself in the most amorous posture he can assume, his hat under his arm, while the other hand is put carelessly into his bosom, as if laid upon his panting heart; his head a little bent to one side, supported with a world of crevat-string, which he takes mighty care not to put into disorder; as one may guess by a never-failing and horrid stiffness in his neck; and if he had any occasion to look aside, his whole body turns at the same time, for fear the motion of the head alone should incommode the crevat or periwig. And sometimes the glove is well manag'd, and the white hand display'd. Thus, with a thousand other little motions and formalities, all in the common place or road of foppery, he takes infinite pains to shew himself to the pit and boxes, a most accomplish'd ass.

A dandy is now so bolstered up in collars so lost in trousers, so pinched in the middle, that he can neither have bowels of compassion, expansion of heart, nor fair use of his limbs.

The Hermit in London (1819)

VIRGINIA WOOLF
From The Common Reader (Second Series)

HE HAD ONLY a moderate capital of thirty thousand pounds to begin with, and his beauty, of figure rather than of face, was marred by a broken nose. Yet without a single noble, important, or valuable action to his credit he cuts a figure; he stands for a symbol; his ghost walks among us still. The reason for the eminence is now a little difficult to determine. Skill of hand and nicety of judgment were his, of course, otherwise he would not have brought the art of tying neck-cloths to perfection. The story is, perhaps, too well known – how he drew his head far back and sunk his chin slowly down so that the cloth wrinkled in perfect symmetry, or if one wrinkle were too deep or too shallow, the cloth was thrown into a basket and the attempt renewed, while the Prince of Wales sat, hour after hour, watching. Yet skill of hand and nicety of judgment were not enough. Brummell owed his ascendency to some curious combination of wit, of taste, of insolence, of independence – for he was never a toady – which it were too heavy-handed to call a philosophy of life, but served the purpose . . . The grace of his carriage was so astonishing; his bows were so exquisite. Everybody looked overdressed or badly dressed – some, indeed, looked positively dirty – beside him. His clothes seemed to melt into each other with the perfection of their cut and the quiet harmony of their colour. Without a single point of emphasis everything was distinguished – from his bow to the way he opened his snuff-box, with his left hand invariably. He was the personification of freshness and cleanliness and order. One could well believe that he had his chair brought into his dressing-room and was deposited at Almack's without letting a puff of wind disturb his curls or a spot of mud stain his shoes . . .

That 'certain exquisite propriety' which Lord Byron remarked in his dress stamped his whole being, and made him appear cool, refined, and debonair among the gentlemen who talked only of sport, which Brummell detested, and smelt of the stable, which Brummell never visited . . .

Handsome, heartless, and cynical, the Beau seemed invulnerable.

CAPTAIN JESSE
From The Life of George Brummell

HIS VALET WAS coming downstairs one day with a quantity of tumbled neckcloths under his arm, and being interrogated on the subject, solemnly replied: 'Oh, they are our failures.' Practice like this, of course, made him perfect, and his tie soon became a model that was imitated, but never equalled.

The method by which this most important result was attained was communicated to me by a friend of his, who had frequently been an eye-witness of the amusing operation.

The collar, which was always fixed to his shirt, was so large that, before being folded down, it completely hid his head and face, and the white neckcloth was at least a foot in height. The first *coup d'archet* was made with the shirt collar, which he folded down to its proper size; and Brummell then standing before the glass, with his chin poked up to the ceiling, by the gentle and gradual declension of his lower jaw, creased the cravat to reasonable dimensions, the form of each succeeding crease being perfected with the shirt which he had just discarded.

When he first appeared in this stiffened cravat tradition says that the sensation of St James's Street was prodigious; dandies were struck dumb with envy and washerwomen miscarried. No one could conceive how the effect was produced.

> Bernard Blackmantle, *The English Spy* (1825)

'No perfumes,' Brummell used to say, 'but very fine linen, plenty of it, and country washing.'

'If John Bull turns round to look after you, you are not well dressed; but either too stiff, too tight, or too fashionable.'

'Do not ride in ladies' gloves, particularly with leather breeches.'

In short, his maxims on dress were excellent.

> Harriette Wilson, *Memoirs*

Do you call that *thing* a coat?

> Beau Brummell

One day a youthful beau approached Brummell and said, 'Permit me to ask you where you get your blacking?' 'Ah!' replied Brummell, gazing complacently at his boots, 'my blacking positively ruins me. I will tell you in confidence; it is made with the finest champagne!'

> Rees Howell Gronow, *Reminiscences*

RICHARD BRINSLEY SHERIDAN
From A Trip to Scarborough

Lord Foppington: Mr Mendlegs, the calves of these stockings are thicken'd a little too much: they make my legs look like a porter's.

Mendlegs: My lord, methinks they look mighty well.

Lord Foppington: Ay, but you are not so good a judge of these things as I am, I have studied them all my life; therefore, pray let the next be the thickness of a crown piece less.

Mendlegs: My lord, they are the same kind I had the honour to serve your lordship with in town.

Lord Foppington: Very possibly, Mr Mendlegs, but that was the beginning of
the winter, and you should always remember that if you make a nobleman's
spring legs as robust as his autumnal calves, you commit a monstrous
impropriety, and make no allowance for the fatigues of the winter.

GEORGE MEREDITH

From The Egoist

OF THE YOUNG Sir Willoughby, her word was brief; and there was the merit
of it on a day when he was hearing from sunrise to the setting of the moon
salutes in his honour, songs of praise and Ciceronian eulogy. Rich, handsome,
courteous, generous, lord of the Hall, the feast, and the dance, he excited his
guests of both sexes to a holiday of flattery. And, says Mrs Mountstuart, while
grand phrases were mouthing round about him: '*You see he has a leg.*'

That is, the leg of the born cavalier is before you: and obscure it as you will,
dress degenerately, there it is for ladies who have eyes. You *see* it: or, you see *he*
has it. Miss Isabel and Miss Eleanor disputed the incidence of the emphasis, but
surely, though a slight difference of meaning may be heard, either will do: many,
with a good show of reason, throw the accent upon *leg*. And the ladies knew for
a fact that Willoughby's leg was exquisite; he had a cavalier court-suit in his
wardrobe. Mrs Mountstuart signified that the leg was to be seen because it was
a burning leg. There it is, and it *will* shine through! He has the leg of Rochester,
Buckingham, Dorset, Suckling; the leg that smiles, that winks, is obsequious to
you, yet perforce of beauty self-satisfied; that twinkles to a tender midway
between imperiousness and seductiveness, audacity and discretion; between 'you
shall worship me,' and 'I am devoted to you'; is your lord, your slave, alternately and in one. It is a leg of ebb and flow and high-tide ripples. Such a leg, when
it has done with pretending to retire, will walk straight into the hearts of women.
Nothing so fatal to them.

Self-satisfied it must be. Humbleness does not win multitudes or the sex. It
must be vain to have a sheen. Captivating melodies (to prove to you the unavoid-
ableness of self-satisfaction when you know that you have hit perfection), listen
to them closely, have an inner pipe of that conceit almost ludicrous when you
detect the chirp.

And you need not be reminded that he has the leg without the naughtiness.
You see eminent in him what we would fain have brought about in a nation that
has lost its leg in gaining a possibly cleaner morality. And that is often contested;
but there is no doubt of the loss of the leg.

Well, footmen and courtiers and Scottish highlanders, and the corps de ballet, draymen too, have legs, and staring legs, shapely enough. But what are they? not the modulated instrument we mean – simply legs for legwork, dumb as the brutes. Our cavalier's is the poetic leg, a portent, a valiance. He has it as Cicero had a tongue. It is a lute to scatter songs to his mistress; a rapier, is she obdurate. In sooth a leg with brains in it, soul.

He was uncommonly well dressed. What trousers! they stuck so natural to him, he might have been born in them.

Samuel Warren, *Ten Thousand a Year* (1841)

JANE WELSH CARLYLE
From Letter to Dr Russell

YOU WONDER, PERHAPS, what a woman like me had to take up her time with. Here, for example, is one full day's work, not to say two. On the New Year's morning itself, Mr C. 'got up off his wrong side', a by no means uncommon way of getting up for him in these overworked times! And he suddenly discovered that his salvation, here and hereafter, depended on having, 'immediately, without a moment's delay', a beggarly pair of old cloth boots, that the street-sweeper would hardly have thanked him for, 'lined with flannel, and new bound, and repaired generally!' and 'one of my women' – that is, my one woman and a half – was to be set upon the job! Alas! a regular shoemaker would have taken a whole day to do it, and wouldn't have undertaken such a piece of work besides! and Mr C. scouted the idea of employing a shoemaker, as subversive of his authority as master of the house. So, neither my one woman, nor my half one, having any more capability of repairing 'generally' their boots than of repairing the Great Eastern, there was no help for me but to sit down on the New Year's morning, with a great ugly beast of a man's boot in my lap, and scheme, and stitch, and worry over it till night; and next morning begin on the other! There, you see, were my two days eaten up very completely, and unexpectedly; and so it goes on, 'always a something' (as my dear mother used to say).

The right Arm must rise to the Hat with moderate Motion sideways . . . and whilst taking it off, let the Look and Action be complaisantly address'd to the Person to whom the compliment is intended . . . and holding the Glove in an easy, careless manner.

F. Nivelon, The Rudiments of Genteel Behaviour (1737)

JEAN GENET
From Querelle of Brest

NO SOONER HAD he left the house behind him than he was forcibly compelled to satisfy himself by proof positive of his own stature and aura as a member of the Fighting Navy, to touch and feel on and about him the tangible attributes of the uniform he was wearing. First he considered the stiff upturned collar of his oilskin coat, which protected his neck like impenetrable armour-plating. He imagined it as a massive ruff, for inside it he could feel how delicate his neck was despite its being so strong and proud and firm, and he took delight in the delectable hollow where it was joined to his body – the perfect point of vulnerability. He began to flex his knee joints till he could feel the touch of his trouser-legs against them, and very soon he was striding out like a sailor whose one desire is to personify the typical matelot. He adopted a proper rolling gait, inclining now to the right, now to the left, without too obvious a movement of the shoulders. He thought of hitching up his oilskins and thrusting his hands through the slit pockets so that he could feel his naked belly, but he changed his mind and, instead, he put a finger up to his cap and tilted it to the back of his head, almost to the very nape of his neck, in such a way that it rubbed against the edge of his upturned collar. These tangible proofs that he was still a sailor through and through reassured him considerably and had a comforting effect.

Transl. Anthony Blond

JAMES LEO HERLIHY
From Midnight Cowboy

IN HIS NEW boots, Joe Buck was six-foot-one and life was different. As he walked out of that store in Houston something snapped in the whole bottom half of him: A kind of power he never even knew was there had been released in his pelvis and he was able to feel the world through it. Brand-new muscles came into play in his buttocks and in his legs, and he was aware of a totally new attitude toward the sidewalk. The world was down there, and he was way up here, on top of it, and the space between him and it was now commanded by a beautiful strange animal, himself, Joe Buck. He was strong. He was exultant. He was ready.

'I'm ready,' he said to himself, and he wondered what he meant by that . . .

When he arrived at the H tel, a hotel that not only had no name but had lost its O as well, he felt the absurdity of anyone so rich and hard and juicy as himself ever staying in such a nameless, no-account place. He ran up the stairs two at a time, went to the second floor rear and hurried into the closet, emerging seconds later with a large package. He removed the brown paper and placed on the bed a black-and-white horsehide suitcase . . .

Then he took a shower and returned to the room to groom himself for the trip. He shaved with his new electric razor, cleaning it carefully before placing it in the suitcase, splashed his face and armpits and crotch with Florida Water, combed a nickel-sized glob of Brylcreem into his brown hair, making it appear almost black, sweetened his mouth with a fresh stick of Juicy Fruit and spat it out, applied some special leather lotion to his new boots, put on a fresh, seven-dollar shirt (black, decorated with white piping, a shirt that fit his lean, broad-shouldered frame almost as close and neat as his own skin), tied a blue handkerchief at his throat, arranged the cuffs of his tight-thighed whipcord trousers in such a way that, with a kind of stylish untidiness, they were half in and half out of those richly gleaming black boots so you could still see the yellow sunbursts at the ankles, and finally he put on a cream-colored leather sport coat so soft and supple it seemed to be alive.

Now Joe would appraise the finished product. During the grooming process, he seldom looked at his total image. He would allow himself to focus only upon that patch of face being covered by the razor at a given moment, or at the portion of the head through which the comb was travelling, and so on. For he didn't want to wear out his ability to perceive himself as a whole. He was in some ways like a mother preparing her child to meet some important personage whose judgment will decide the child's fate, and so when all was ready and the time had come to assess the total effect, Joe Buck would actually turn his back on the mirror and walk away from it, roll his shoulders to get the kinks out, take a few deep belly breaths and a couple of quick knee bends, and crack his knuckles. Then he would slouch in a way that he thought attractive and that was his habitual stance anyway – most of his weight on one foot – get hold of a certain image in his mind, probably of some pretty, wide-eyed, adoring girl, smile at it with a kind of crooked, indulgent wisdom, light a Camel and stick it into his mouth, and hook one thumb into his low-riding garrison belt. And now, ready for that fresh look at himself, he would swing his eyes back onto the mirror as if some hidden interloper beyond the glass had suddenly called his name: *Joe Buck!*

I was measured, and the young salesman picked off a rack a zoot suit that was just wild: sky-blue pants thirty inches in the knee and ankle narrowed down to twelve inches at the bottom, and a long coat that pinched my waist and flowed out below my knees.

Malcolm X and Alex Haley, *The Autobiography of Malcolm X*

RAYMOND CHANDLER
From The Big Sleep

IT WAS ABOUT eleven o'clock in the morning, mid October, with the sun not shining and a look of hard wet rain in the clearness of the foothills. I was wearing my powder-blue suit, with dark blue shirt, tie and display handkerchief, black brogues, black wool socks with dark blue clocks on them. I was neat, clean, shaved and sober, and I didn't care who knew it. I was everything the well-dressed private detective ought to be. I was calling on four million dollars.

GUY DE MAUPASSANT
From Bel Ami

'MONSIEUR FORESTIER, PLEASE?'
'Third floor – the door on the left.'
The concierge had replied in the cordial tone that indicated her respect for this particular tenant. And Georges Duroy went upstairs.

He felt rather nervous and ill at ease. He was wearing a tail coat for the first time in his life, and his attire as a whole made him uneasy. Every item was, he felt, inadequate; his boots were not of patent leather, though they were quite smart, for he was proud of his feet; his shirt had cost four francs fifty that morning at the Louvre, and its narrow shirt-front had already cracked. All his other shirts, being more or less seriously damaged, were quite unfit for the occasion.

His trousers, which were rather too loose, scarcely showed the outline of his leg, and hung round his calves with the crinkled look of second-hand garments on the limbs they temporarily clothe. The coat alone was passable, being just about his size.

He walked slowly upstairs, his heart throbbing, and much perturbed in mind, harassed in particular by the fear of looking ridiculous. Suddenly he saw before him a gentleman in full evening dress looking straight at him. They were so close to each other that Duroy recoiled, and then stood in amazement; the figure was himself reflected in a tall mirror that provided a vista of the first floor landing. A thrill of joy shot through him, he looked so much more presentable than he could ever have believed.

Transl. Eric Sutton

Not a gentleman; dresses too well.

Bertrand Russell on Anthony Eden

JEAN DE VENETTE
From Chronicles

1365 [THE NOBLES] wore the tightest possible tunics, cut off above the hips and, what was even more monstrous, they affected shoes with very long points in front like horns, which sometimes stretched straight out and sometimes slanted up like the talon on the back of a griffon's foot which it uses in accordance with its nature as a claw. This point or beak is called a *poulairz* in French. It was a truly shameful fashion, in that it went quite contrary to the natural shape of the human foot and thus seemed an abuse of nature. King Charles of France caused heralds to proclaim publicly in Paris that no one, whosoever he might be, should dare to wear them more and that no shoemaker should presume, under threat of heavy penalties, to make or sell pointed shoes or hose. Urban V had in like manner strictly forbidden them in the Roman Curia. Those who deplore such follies hope that by the inspiration of God within a short time scanty robes also and other indecencies of dress worn by men and women alike will be firmly prohibited by prelates and princes, both ecclesiastical and secular, and the whole kingdom will be changed for the better.

FRANÇOIS RABELAIS
From Gargantua

FOR HIS CODPIECE were used sixteen ells and a quarter of the same cloth, and it was fashioned on the top like unto a triumphant arch most gallantly fastened with two enamelled clasps, in each of which was set a great emerald, as big as an orange; for, as says Orpheus, *lib. de lapidibus*, and Plinius, *libro ultimo*, it hath an erective virtue and comfort and comfortative of the natural member. The exiture, out-jecting or out-standing of his codpiece, was of the length of a yard, jagged and pinked, and withal bagging, and strutting out with the blue damask lining, after the manner of his breeches. But had you seen the fair embroidery of the small needle-work pearl, and the curiously interlaced knots, by the gold-smith's art set out and trimmed with rich diamonds, precious rubies, fine torquoises, costly emeralds, and Persian pearls, you would have compared it to a fair Cornucopia, or horn of abundance, such as you see in antiques, or as Rhea gave to the two nymphs, Amalthea and Ida, the nurses of Jupiter.

And, like to that horn of abundance, it was still gallant, succulent, droppy, sappy, pithy, lively, always flourishing, always fructifying, full of juice, full of flower, full of fruit, and all manner of delight. I avow God, it would have done one good to have seen him, but I will tell you more of him in the book which I have made of the dignity of codpieces. One thing I will tell you, that, as it was both long and large, so it was well furnished and victualled within, nothing like unto the hypocritical codpieces of some fond wooers, and wench-courters, which are stuffed only with wind, to the great prejudice of the female sex.

GEOFFREY CHAUCER
From The Parson's Tale

UPON THAT OOTHER side, to speken of the horrible disordinat scantnesse of clothing, as been thise kutted sloppes, or haynselyns, that thurgh hire short-nesse ne covere nat the shameful membres of man, to wikked entente. Allas! somme of hem shewen the boce of hir shap, and the horrible swollen membres, that semeth lik the maladie of hirnia, in the wrappynge of hir hoses; and eek the buttokes of him faren as it were the hyndre part of a she-ape in the fulle of the moone. And mooreover, the wrecched swollen membres that they shewe thurgh disgisynge, in departynge of hire hoses in whit and reed, semeth that half hir shameful privee membres weren flayne. And if so be that they departen hire hoses in othere colours, as it whit and blak, or whit and blew, or blak and reed, and so forth, thanne semeth it, as by variaunce of colour, that half the partie of hire privee membres were corrupt by the fir of seint Antony, or by cancre, or by oother swich meschaunce. Of the hyndre part of hir bottokes, it is ful horrible for to see. For certes, in that partie of hir body ther as they purgen hir stynkynge ordure, that foule partie shewe they to the peple prowdly in despit of honestitee, which honestitee that Jhesu Crist and his freendes observede to shewen in hir lyve.

Now, as of the outrageous array of wommen, God woot that though the visages of somme of hem seme ful chaast, and debonaire, yet notifie they in hire array of atyr likerousnesse and pride.

PHILIP STUBBES
From The Anatomie of Abuses

THEIR DUBLETS ARE no lesse monstrous then the rest; for now the fashion is to haue them hang downe to the middle of their theighes, or at least to their priuie members, being so hard quilted, stuffed, bombasted, and sewed, as they can neither worke, nor yet well playe in them, through the excessiue heate thereof; and therefore are forced to weare them lose about them for the most part, otherwise they could very hardly eyther stoupe or decline to the grounde, so stiffe and sturdy they stand about them. Now, what handsomenesse can be in these dublettes, whiche stand on their bellies, like, or much bigger than a man's codpeece (so as their bellies are thicker than all the bodies beside), let wise men iudge. For my part, handsomnesse in them I see none, and much lesse profite. And, besides, that I see no good end where they serue, except it be to shewe the disposition of the wearer how he is inclined, namely, to gluttonie, gourmandice, riotte, and excesse; for what may be these great bellies signifie els, then that eyther they are such, or els are affected that waye? This is the truest signification that I could euer deuine or presage of them. And this may euery one iudge of them that seeth them; for, certayne I am, there was neuer any kinde of apparell euer inuented that could more disproportion the body of man then these dublettes, with great bellies hanging downe beneath their pudenda (as I haue sayd), and stuffed with foure, fiue, or sixe pound of bombast at the least: I say nothng of what their dubletes be made, some of saten, taffatie, silke, grograine, chamlet, gold, siluer, and what not! slashed, iagged, cut, carued, pincked, and laced with all kinde of costly lace of diuers and sondry colours, for if I shoulde stande vppon these particularities, rather time then matter would be wanting.

(1585)

Field-marshal Count Daun is said to have had a dress for every day in the year; and a volume, in which these magnificent suits, with sword, cane, &c. appendant to each, were beautifully depicted. This book was brought to him every morning, and studied with more attention than any other volume in his immense library.

Percy Anecdotes (1823)

A few minutes before half-past seven, the Duke, arrayed for dinner, passed
leisurely up the High. The arresting feature of his costume was a mulberry-
coloured coat, with brass buttons. This, to anyone versed in Oxford lore,
betokened him a member of the Junta. It is awful to think that a casual
stranger might have mistaken him for a footman. It does not do to think of
such things.

Max Beerbohm, *Zuleika Dobson*

ISAAC BICKERSTAFF
Lionel and Clarissa

A coxcomb, a fop.
A dainty milk-sop;
Who, essenced and dizen'd from bottom to top.
Looks just like a doll for a milliner's shop.
A thing full of prate,
And pride and conceit;
All fashion, no weight;
Who shrugs and takes snuff,
And carries a muff,
A minikin, finiking
French powder-puff.

(1768)

An evening coat is an insane object to look at; it is a garb which art disowns,
and which fancy cannot deign to touch, or allow to be capable of
improvement. But yet most men look their best in this strange confection of
broadcloth, and that is the most telling and effectual of all arguments. The
large expanse of shirt-front, though itself imbecile, and the glossy framework
of black are 'becoming'; they violate every rule of grace, yet they fulfil most of
its conditions.

Mrs Oliphant, *Dress* (1878)

BENJAMIN DISRAELI
From Letters to his family

G IBRALTAR
Tell my mother, that as it is the fashion among the dandies of this place
(that is, the officers, for there are no others) not to wear waistcoats in the morning, her new studs come into fine play and maintain my reputation for being a
great judge of costume, to the admiration and envy of many subalterns. I have
also the fame of being the first who ever passed the Straits with two canes, a
morning and an evening cane. I change my cane on the gun-fire and hope to
carry them both on to Cairo. It is wonderful the effect those magical wands pro-
duce. I owe to them even more attention than to being the supposed author of –
what is it? I forget.

R.S. SURTEES
From Mr Sponge's Sporting Tour

H AVING MENTIONED MR SPONGE'S groomy gait and horsey propensities, it
were almost needless to say that his dress was in the sporting style – you
saw what he was by his clothes. Every article seemed to be made to defy the
utmost rigour of the elements. His hat (Lincoln and Bennett) was hard and heavy.
It sounded upon an entrance-hall table like a drum. A little magical loop in the
lining explained the cause of its weight. Somehow, his hats were never either old
or new – not that he bought them second-hand, but when he got a new one he
took its 'long-coat' off, as he called it, with a singeing lamp, and made it look as
if it had undergone a few probabationary showers.

When a good London hat recedes to a certain point, it gets no worse; it is not
like a country-made thing that keeps going and going until it declines into a thing
with no sort of resemblance to its original self. Barring its weight and hardness,
the Sponge hat had no particular character apart from the Sponge Head. It was
not one of those punty ovals or Cheshire-cheese flats, or curly-sided things that
enables one to say who is in a house and who is not, by a glance at the hats in the
entrance, but it was just a quiet, round hat, without anything remarkable, either
in the binding, the lining, or the band, but still it was a very becoming hat when
Sponge had it on. There is a great deal of character in hats. We have seen hats
that bring the owners to the recollection far more forcibly than the generality of
portraits. But to our hero.

That there may be a dandified simplicity in dress is exemplified every day by our friends the Quakers, who adorn their beautiful brown Saxony coats with little inside velvet collars and fancy silk buttons, and even the severe order of sporting costume adopted by our friend Mr Sponge is not devoid of capability in the way of tasteful adaptation. This Mr Sponge chiefly showed in promoting a resemblance between his neck-cloths and waistcoats. Thus, if he wore a cream-coloured cravat, he would have a buff-coloured waistcoat, if a striped waistcoat, then the starcher would be imbued with somewhat of the same colour and pattern. The ties of these varied with their texture. The silk ones terminated in a sort of coaching fold, and were secured by a golden fox-head pin, while the striped starchers, with the aid of a pin on each side, just made a neat, unpretending tie in the middle, a sort of miniature of the flagrant, flyaway, Mile-End ones of aspiring youth of the present day. His coats were of the single-breasted cut-away order, with pockets outside, and generally either Oxford mixture or some dark colour, that required you to place him in a favourable light to say what it was.

His waistcoats, of course, were of the most correct form and material, generally either pale buff, or buff with a narrow stripe, similar to the undress vests of the servants of the Royal Family, only with the pattern run across instead of lengthways, as those worthies mostly have theirs, and made with good honest step collars, instead of the make-believe roll collars they sometimes convert their upright ones into . . .

In the trouser line he adhered to the close-fitting costume of former days; and many were the trials, the easings, and the alterings, ere he got a pair exactly to his mind. Many were the customers who turned away on seeing his manly figure filling the swing mirror in 'Snip and Sneiders'', a monopoly that some tradesmen might object to, only Mr Sponge's trousers being admitted to be perfect 'triumphs of the art', the more such a walking advertisement was seen in the shop the better. Indeed, we believe it would have been worth Snip and Co.'s while to have let him have them for nothing. They were easy without being tight, or rather they looked tight without being so; there wasn't a bag, a wrinkle, or a crease that there shouldn't be, and strong and storm-defying as they seemed, they were yet as soft and as supple as a lady's glove. They looked more as if his legs had been blown in them than as if such irreproachable garments were the work of a man's hands. Many were the nudges, and many the 'look at this chap's trousers', that were given by ambitious men emulous of his appearance as he passed along, and many were the turnings round to examine their faultless fall upon his radiant boot. The boots, perhaps, might come in for a little of the glory, for they were beautifully soft and cool-looking to the foot, easy without being loose, and he preserved the lustre of their polish, even up to the last moment of his walk. There never was a better man for getting through dirt, either on foot or horseback, than our friend.

(1853)

If you want to understand the individual, look at him in the day-time; see him walking with his hat on. There is a great deal in the build and wearing of hats – a great deal more than at first meets the eye.

William Makepeace Thackeray, *The Book of Snobs*

On being a Swell all Round
I have never in my life succeeded in being this. Sometimes I get a new suit and am tidy for a while in part, meanwhile the hat, tie, boots, gloves and underclothing all clamour for attention and, before I have got them well in hand, the new suit has lost its freshness. Still, if ever I do get any money, I will try and make myself really spruce all round till I find out, as I probably shall in about a week, that if I give my clothes an inch they will take an ell.

Samuel Butler, *Notebooks*

From Holinshed's Chronicles

NEVER WAS IT happier in England than when an Englishman was known abroad by his own cloth; and contented himself at home with his fine russet carsey hosen, and a warm slop; his coat, gown, and cloak of brown, blue or putre, with some pretty furnishings of velvet or fur, and a doublet of sadtawnie or black velvet or comely silk, without such cuts and gawrish colours as are worn in these dayes by those who think themselves the gayest men when they have most diversities of jagges and changes of colours.

(1578)

GEORGE WASHINGTON
From Rules of Courtesy and Decency of Behaviour

IN YOUR APPAREL be modest, and endeavor to accommodate nature rather than procure admiration. Keep to the fashion of your equals, such as are civil and orderly with respect to time and place.

Play not the peacock, looking everywhere about you to see if you be well decked, if your shoes fit well, if your stockings sit neatly, and clothes handsomely.

JOHN GAY
From Trivia

You'll sometimes meet a fop, of nicest tread,
Whose mantling peruke veils his empty head;
At every step he dreads the wall to lose,
And risks, to save a coach, his red-heeled shoes;
Him, like the miller, pass with caution by,
Lest from his shoulder clouds of powder fly.

WILLIAM GILPIN
From his letters and notebooks

GOING TO A Hatter's (Mr Butter at Charing Cross) for a new hat, and having pitched on one, I was to wait 5 minutes to have it dressed. This hat, tho' I saw little it wanted but to be opened or shaped somewhat better to the head, had nevertheless to undergo a great deal of tutoring before it was fit to wear. It was alternately ironed, brushed; plushed, brushed and ironed a dozen times . . . the effects were too small to be discerned by any eye but the Hatter's – I should have been satisfied if he had given me the hat after the iron and brush had passed once round it – but he was not – with him the hat was not compleat till every hair was in its place – At last I received it; but unfortunately as I took it, my arm ran foul of it and discomposed three or four hairs of the crown – this was a sad piece of indecorum, and, not a little disturbed and feeling the hatter – I saw plainly he wished to have it back on the block again . . .

The hat is in all respects a very good hat and I recommend Mr Butter as an excellent hatter to any man that wants one.

From *My Dearest Betsy – a selection from
Gilpin's letters and notebooks*, ed. Peter Benson

THOMAS CORYATE
From Crudities

MANY ITALIANS DO carry other fine things of a far greater price, that will cost at the least a ducat (about seven francs), which they commonly call in the Italian tongue *umbrellaes*, that is, things that minister shadow unto them for shelter against the scorching heat of the sun. These are made of leather, something answerable to the form of a little canopy, and hooped in the inside with divers little wooden hoops, that extend the *umbrella* in a pretty large compass. They are used especially by horsemen, who carry them in their hands when they ride, fastening the end of the handle upon one of their thighs, and they impart so large a shadow unto them that it keepeth the heat of the sun from the upper parts of their body.

(1611)

At Vostitza I found my dearly-beloved Eustathius – ready to follow me not only to England, but to Terra Incognita . . . The next morning I found the dear soul upon horseback clothed very sprucely in Greek Garments, with those ambrosial curls hanging down his amiable back, and to my utter astonishment and the great abomination of Fletcher, a *parasol* in his hand to save his complexion from the heat.

Lord Byron, *Letters*

There is not a man of the nation, no, not even Lord Effingham, who bestows so much time and attempts in rendering the external appearance of his head elegant in the extreme, than the Earl of Scarborough. It is said that his Lordship keeps six French *friseurs*, who have nothing else to do than dress his hair. Lord Effingham keeps only five.

The Morning Post (1798)

He ordered . . . those trifles that rendered men strong and endowed with great charm – a suede belt, soft hat, a checked tie.

Jean Genet, *Our Lady of the Flowers*, transl. Anthony Blond

LESLEY LEWIS

From The Private Life of a Country House

H E HAD A boot cupboard containing about 20 pairs of boots and shoes, all most beautifully made for him by a firm called Taylor. There were black boots with grey cloth tops for formal wear; leather ones for everyday; several pairs of brown shoes of varying weights for country wear; shooting boots – greased instead of polished; white buckskin tennis shoes with rubber soles; and patent-leather pumps for evening dress, with low fronts and little black bows. As time went on, he gave up boots except for shooting but always kept in his room an old pair of gloves to use when putting on and lacing up footwear. Unlike our more ordinary shoes, which were polished by the houseboy with Kiwi or Cherry Blossom in an outside boot hole, my father's were done in the pantry by the butler, with browning or blacking from an earthenware bottle. The syrupy liquid was applied with a stick and then rubbed in and burnished with a stag- or beef-bone to produce a deep gloss which, considering all the work that went into it, was surprisingly vulnerable. Puppies had to be taught very early not to lick it ... it contained some ingredient to which they could become addicted.

(1980)

With an evening coat and a white tie ... anybody, even a stockbroker, can gain a reputation for being civilised.

Oscar Wilde, *The Picture of Dorian Gray*

A swell in London is a swell anywhere.

R.S. Surtees, *Plain or Ringlets?* (1860)

OSBERT SITWELL

From Great Morning!

W HO COULD WONDER that foreigners loved London? Though as different from Vienna or Paris as Peking, it was no less essentially a capital, with all the attractions of the centre of an Empire. It remained unique in being a masculine city, as it had been throughout its history, created to the same degree for men as Paris for women. The luxury shops were unrivalled in their appeal to male tastes, were full of cigarettes, and objects made in leather, glass or silver, better than those to be seen anywhere in foreign capitals; solid, plain, unimaginative, but showing the English feeling for material, the English sobriety. As for suits, shirts, shoes, ties, hats, London was acknowledged, throughout the world, by all races, of all colours, to set the fashion for men. And these years, 1913 and '14, were the last when there was a successor to the long line of fops, macaronis, dandies, beaux, dudes, bucks, blades, bloods, swells and mashers, who for so many centuries had given life to the London world of pleasure. To these was now added the *nut*, or, more jocularly, the k-nut, as personified by a young actor, Mr Basil Hallam, who in this respect both summed up and set the tone, in a song entitled 'Gilbert the Filbert, the Colonel of the Nuts!': the refrain ran –

> I'm Gilbert the Filbert, the Nut with a K,
> The pride of Piccadilly, the blasé roué.
> Oh, Hades, the ladies all leave their wooden huts
> For Gilbert the Filbert, the Colonel of the Nuts.

Dressed in a grey tall-hat and a morning-coat, Hallam gave a rather languid rendering of this song at the Palace Theatre every night in *The Passing Show*, a revue which was running throughout the summer of 1914 and until after the outbreak of war. It was no unusual greeting for a young man, wearing a new suit, to be told, 'What a k-nut you look!' The nut must be thin, clean-shaven except for a small, cut moustache, and have an air of concave and fatigued elegance, in this taking after his Dundreary grandfather rather than his father the swell. On the other hand, he had to dance with vigour and ease, in the new style . . . The nut died fighting in the trenches of 1914, and Mr Basil Hallam, his amiable exemplifier, was killed two years later, in August 1916.

A hole in the trousers may make one as melancholy as Hamlet, and out of bad boots a Timon may be made.

Oscar Wilde, Letter to Frank Harris

NANCY MITFORD
From Love in a Cold Climate

THERE WAS A terrible scene on Oxford platform one day. Cedric went to the bookstall to buy *Vogue*, having mislaid his own copy. Uncle Matthew, who was waiting there for a train, happened to notice that the seams of his coat were piped in a contrasting shade. This was too much for his self-control. He fell upon Cedric and began to shake him like a rat; just then, very fortunately, the train came in, whereupon my uncle, who suffered terribly from train fever, dropped Cedric and rushed to catch it. 'You'd never think', as Cedric said afterwards, 'that buying *Vogue* magazine could be so dangerous. It was well worth it though, lovely Spring modes.'

JANE AUSTEN
From Northanger Abbey

THEY WERE INTERRUPTED by Mrs Allen: 'My dear Catherine,' said she, 'do take this pin out of my sleeve; I am afraid it has torn a hole already; I shall be quite sorry if it has, for this is a favourite gown, though it cost but nine shillings a yard.'

'That is exactly what I should have guessed it, madam,' said Mr Tilney, looking at the muslin.

'Do you understand muslins, sir?'

'Particularly well; I always buy my own cravats, and am allowed to be an excellent judge; and my sister has often trusted me in the choice of a gown. I bought one for her the other day, and it was pronounced to be a prodigious bargain by every lady who saw it. I gave but five shillings a yard for it, and a true Indian muslin.'

Mrs Allen was quite struck by his genius. 'Men commonly take so little notice of those things,' said she: 'I can never get Mr Allen to know one of my gowns from another. You must be a great comfort to your sister, sir.'

'I hope I am, madam.'

'And pray, sir, what do you think of Miss Morland's gown?'

'It is very pretty, madam,' said he, gravely examining it; 'but I do not think it will wash well; I am afraid it will fray.'

'How can you,' said Catherine, laughing, 'be so –' she had almost said, strange.

'I am quite of your opinion, sir,' replied Mrs Allen; 'and so I told Miss Morland when she bought it.'

'But then you know, madam, muslin always turns to some account or other; Miss Morland will get enough out of it for a handkerchief, or a cap, or a cloak. Muslin can never be said to be wasted. I have heard my sister say so forty times, when she has been extravagant in buying more than she wanted, or careless in cutting it to pieces.'

WILLIAM SHAKESPEARE
From Twelfth Night

Malvolio: M, O, A, I; this simulation is not as the former: and yet, to crush this a little, it would bow to me, for every one of these letters are in my name. Soft! here follows prose. [*Reads*] 'If this fall into thy hand, revolve. In my stars I am above thee; but be not afraid of greatness: some are born great, some achieve greatness and some have greatness thrust upon 'em. Thy Fates open their hands; let thy blood and spirit embrace them; and, to inure thyself to what thou art like to be, cast thy humble slough and appear fresh. Be opposite with a kinsman, surly with servants; let thy tongue tang arguments of state; put thyself into the trick of singularity: she thus advises thee that sighs for thee. Remember who commended thy yellow stockings, and wished to see thee ever cross-gartered: I say, remember. Go to, thou art made, if thou desirest to be so; if not, let me see thee a steward still, the fellow of servants, and not worthy to touch Fortune's fingers. Farewell. She that would alter services with thee,

THE FORTUNATE-UNHAPPY'

Daylight and champain discovers not more: this is open. I will be proud, I will read politic authors, I will baffle Sir Toby, I will wash off gross acquaintance, I will be point-devise the very man. I do not now fool myself, to let imagination jade me; for every reason excites to this, that my lady loves me. She did commend my yellow stockings of late, she did praise my leg being cross-gartered; and in this she manifests herself to my love, and with a kind of injunction drives me to these habits of her liking. I thank my stars I am happy. I will be strange, stout, in yellow stockings, and cross-gartered, even with the swiftness of putting on. Jove and my stars be praised!

In the beginning of the present century it was thought proper for a gentleman to change his undergarments three times a day, and the weekly washing bill of a beau comprised twenty shirts, thirty cravats, and pocket-handkerchiefs at discretion.

The Habits of Good Society (1855)

DAVID LODGE

From The British Museum is Falling Down

A DAM CAME TO a halt, and rounded slowly on his wife. 'What are you telling me? D'you mean I haven't got a single pair of underpants to wear?'

'If you changed them more often, this wouldn't happen.'

'That may be so, but I'm not going to argue about personal hygiene at this point. What I want to know is: what am I going to wear under my trousers today?'

'Do you *have* to wear something? Can't you do without for once?'

'Of course I can't "do without"!'

'I don't know why you're making such a fuss. I've gone without pants before.' She looked meaningfully at Adam, who softened at the memory of a certain day by the sea.

'That was different. You know the trousers of my suit are itchy,' he complained in a quieter tone. 'You don't know what it's like, sitting in the Museum all day.'. . .

Barbara was silent for a minute. 'You could wear a pair of mine,' she offered.

'To hell with that! What d'you take me for – a – transvestite? Where are the damp ones?'

'In the kitchen somewhere. They'll take a long time to dry.'

In the passage he nearly tripped over Clare, who was squatting on the floor, dressing a doll.

'What's a transvestite, Daddy?' she inquired.

'Ask your mother,' Adam snorted....

. . . He found a pair of underpants in a tangle of sodden washing in the baby's bath. Improvising brilliantly, he pulled out the grill-pan of the electric stove, wiped the grid clean of grease with a handkerchief, and spread his pants, and turned the switch to high. Fascinated, Dominic stopped tearing up the newspaper and watched the rising steam. Adam stealthily confiscated the remaining portion of the newspaper. The competition again caught his eye . . .

. . .'Dadda, 'ire,' said Dominic, tugging gently at his sleeve. Adam smelled burning cloth, and lunged at the grill. Ire was the word. He stuffed the scorched remains of his underpants into the garbage pail, burning his fingers in the process.

'More, Dadda,' said Dominic.

In the passage Adam met Barbara. 'Where did you say your pants were?' he asked casually.

'In the top left-hand drawer.' She sniffed. 'You've burned something.'

'Nothing much,' he said, and hurried on to the bedroom.

Adam, who had hitherto valued women's underwear on its transparency, now found himself applying quite different standards, and deploring the frivolity of his wife's taste. Eventually he located a pair of panties that were opaque, and a chaste white in hue. Unfortunately they were also trimmed with lace, but that couldn't be helped. As he drew them on, the hairs on his legs crackled with static electricity. The clinging but featherlight touch of the nylon round his haunches was a strange new senstation. He stood thoughtfully before the mirror for a moment, awed by a sudden insight into sexual deviation.

His socks compelled one's attention without losing one's respect.

Saki, *Ministers of Grace*

LAWRENCE DURRELL
From Esprit de Corps

'THEY WERE UNSHAKEN even by his personal appearance ten days later, sitting bolt upright in the back of a Phantom Rolls with the De Mandeville arms stencilled on the doors. He was smoking a cheroot and reading the Racing Calendar with close attention. His chauffeur was unloosing a cataract of white pig-skin suitcases, each with a gold monogram on it. It was quite clear that he was a *parvenu*, old boy. Moreover the two contending odours he gave off were ill-matched – namely gin-fumes and violet-scented hair lotion of obviously Italian origin. He condescendingly waved a ringed hand at me as I introduced myself. It had been, he said, a nerve-racking journey. The Yugoslavs had been so rude at the border that poor Dennis had cried and stamped his foot. Dennis was the chauffeur. "Come over, darling, and be introduced to the Man," he cried. The chauffeur was called Dennis Purfitt-Purfitt. You can imagine my feelings, old man. I felt a pang for poor Polk-Mowbray and not less for Angela who was lying upstairs in the Blue Bedroom sleeping off a hangover. "Dennis is my pianist as well as my chauffeur," said De Mandeville as he dismounted holding what looked like a case of duelling pistols but which later turned out to be his gold-chased flute . . .'

OSBERT SITWELL

From Great Morning!

To one pair Laced Pyjamas £2 : 8 : 4.

THESE GARMENTS, OF a type then almost universal, were frogged across the chest, instead of buttoning in the usual way; and this was what the word *laced* signified technically. My father, however – and nothing would ever subsequently rid him of the idea –, read *laced* as *lace*, and henceforth tenaciously clung to the belief that, arraying myself after the fashion of some of Aubrey Beardsley's figures, I habitually wore pyjamas of *Point de Venise* or *Bruxelles* . . . Very draughty wearing they would have made in the winter climate of the Tower of London, as I told him: but he would not listen, nothing would shake him in his conviction, and for the rest of his life I used to hear him, from time to time, confiding in acquaintances, 'As my son insists on wearing *lace* pyjamas, Lady Ida and myself are obliged to economise . . . It's hard, but young people today seem to think they have a perfect right to everything. I should never have dreamt of wearing lace pyjamas myself at that age!' – as if it constituted one of the comforts of the old.

From James Boswell's Diaries

FROM WHAT MISS Flora Macdonald told me, I have compiled the following: Prince Charles Edward, after the Battle of Culloden, was conveyed to Long Island, where he lay for some time concealed. But intelligence having been obtained where he was, and a number of troops having come in quest of him, it became absolutely necessary for him to quit that country without delay. Miss Flora Macdonald, then a young lady, offered to accompany him in an open boat to Sky, though the coast they had to quit was guarded by ships. He dressed himself in women's clothes, and passed as her supposed maid, by the name of Betty Burke, an Irish girl. They got off undiscovered, though several shots were fired to bring them to, and landed at Mugstot, the seat of Sir Alexander Macdonald. Sir Alexander was then at Fort Augustus, with the Duke of Cumberland; but his lady was at home. Prince Charles took his post upon a hill near the house. Flora Macdonald waited on Lady Margaret, who at once settled that Prince Charles should be conducted to old Rasay, who was himself concealed. The plan was instantly communicated to Kingsburgh who was despatched to the hill to inform the wanderer, and to carry him refreshments. When Kingsburgh approached, he started up, holding a large knotted stick, ready to knock him down, till he said, 'I am Macdonald of Kingsburgh, come to serve your Highness.'

Flora Macdonald dined with Lady Margaret, at whose table there was an officer of the army, stationed here with a party of soldiers, to watch for Prince Charles. She afterwards often laughed with this gentleman on her having so well deceived him.

After dinner, Flora Macdonald on horseback, and her supposed maid and Kingsburgh, with a servant carrying some linen, all on foot, proceeded towards that gentleman's house. Upon the road was a small rivulet which they were obliged to cross. The wanderer, forgetting his assumed sex, that his clothes might not be wet, held them up a great deal too high. Kingsburgh mentioned this to him, observing it might make a discovery. He said he would be more careful for the future. He was as good as his word; for the next brook he crossed, he did not hold up his clothes at all, but let them float upon the water. He was very awkward in female dress. His size was so large, and his strides so great. At Kingsburgh he slept soundly till next day at one o'clock. On the afternoon of that day, the wanderer, still in the same dress, set out for Portree, with Flora Macdonald and a manservant. His shoes being very bad, Kingsburgh provided him with a new pair, and taking up the old ones, said, 'I will faithfully keep them till you are safely settled at St. James's. I will introduce myself by shaking them at you to put you in mind of your night's entertainment and protection under my roof.' He smiled, and said, 'Be as good as your word!'

JAMES PLUMTRE
From Journal of a Tour into Derbyshire

WE HAD THE experience of our former Tour to profit from, and were resolved to make our use of it, not only in respect to more important articles, but also in minutiae, and that as far as concerned our dress and appearance on our journey: this was more material than on our former tour, as we were to travel in a more civilized country, and be at places of greater public resort than any in north Wales. For this purpose we had short blue coats, or rather Jackets, but in other respects made in the fashion; and here, for once, *fashion* coincided with *reason*, the large lapelles being convenient to button over in case of cold or rain; our Breeches were nankeen, with gaters of the same, which came up to them; and, to complete our dress, we had Scotch plaids, which in cold or rain wrapped round us, and in fine weather tucked up and hung at our backs without the least inconvenience. Thus was our dress at once handsome, neat and light; yet serving the double purpose of being airy in fine weather, and a safeguard from cold or wet in more intemperate changes. Our former knapsack was covered with goatskin, for the sake of looking handsome, and contained our usual change of raiment.

(1793)

ARNOLD BENNETT
From The Old Wives' Tale

IN THE YEAR 1893 there was a new and strange man living at No. 4, St Luke's Square. Many people remarked on the phenomenon. Very few of his like had ever been seen in Bursley before. One of the striking things about him was the complex way in which he secured himself by means of glittering chains. A chain stretched across his waistcoat, passing through a special button-hole, without a button, in the middle. To this cable were firmly linked a watch at one end and a pencil-case at the other; the chain also served as a protection against a thief who might attempt to snatch the fancy waistcoat entire. Then there were longer chains, beneath the waistcoat, partly designed, no doubt, to deflect bullets, but serving mainly to enable the owner to haul up penknives, cigarette-cases, match-boxes, and key-rings from the profundities of hip-pockets. An essential portion of the man's braces, visible sometimes when he played at tennis, consisted of chain, and the upper and nether halves of his cuff-links were connected by chains. Occasionally he was to be seen chained to a dog.

SINCLAIR LEWIS
From Babbitt

THE GREY SUIT was well cut, well made, and completely undistinguished. It was a standard suit. White piping on the V of the waistcoat added a flavour of law and learning. His boots were black laced boots, good boots, honest boots, standard boots, extraordinarily uninteresting boots. The only frivolity was in his purple knitted scarf. With considerable comment on the matter to Mrs Babbitt (who, acrobatically fastening the back of her blouse to her skirt with a safety pin, did not hear a word he said), he chose between the purple scarf and a tapestry effect with stringless brown harps among blown palms, and into it he thrust a snake-head pin with opal eyes.

A sensational event was changing from the brown suit to the grey the contents of his pockets. He was earnest about these objects. They were of eternal importance, like baseball or the Republican party. They included a fountain pen and a silver pencil (always lacking a supply of new leads) which belonged in the right-hand upper waistcoat pocket. Without them he would have felt naked. On his watch-chain were a gold penknife, silver cigar-cutter, seven keys (the use of two of which he had forgotten), and, incidentally, a good watch. Depending from the chain was a large, yellowish elk's tooth – proclamation of his membership in the Brotherly and Protective Order of Elks. Most significant of all was his loose-leaf pocket note-book, that modern and efficient note-book which contained the addresses of people whom he had forgotten, prudent memoranda of postal money-orders which had reached their destinations months ago, stamps which had lost their mucilage, clippings of verses by T. Cholmondeley Frink and of the newspaper editorials from which Babbitt got his opinions and his polysyllables, notes to be sure and do things which he did not intend to do, and one curious inscription – D.S.S.D.M.Y.P.D.F.

Diary of a Dandy, Sept. 1818:

S ENT FOR THE tailor and staymaker – ordered a morning demi surtout of the last Parisian cut with the collar à la Guillotine to show the neck behind – a pair of Petersham Pantaloons with striped flounces at bottom – and a pair of Cumberland corsets with a whalebone back. The last pair gave way in stooping to pick up Lady B's glove – the Duke of Clarence vulgar enough to laugh and asked me in the sea slang if I had not missed stays in tacking.

John Ashton, *Social England Under the Regency*

As soon as the English are groomed and are wearing their cravats they seem to grow delicate and warn each other about the danger of catching cold.

Moritz, *Journeys of a German in England*

JOHN EVELYN
From Tyranus, or The Mode

I WOULD CHOOSE THE loose Riding Coat, which is now the *Mode*, and the Hose which his Majesty often wears; or some fashion not so pinching as to need a Shooing-horn with the Dons, nor so exorbitant as the Pantaloons, which are a kind of Hermaphrodite and of neither Sex: and if at any time I fancy'd them wider, or more open at the knees for the Summer, it should be with a mediocrity, and not to set in plaits as if I were supported with a pair of Ionic pillars, or the gatherings of my Grandames loose Gown.

From The Hermit in London

Officer of the Guards to his servant: 'Let me have the last boots which Hoby made me, not the Wellingtons nor the iron-heeled ones but the last ones with copper heels; and be sure to use the blacking which has marasquina in it and oil of lavender . . . and see my regimental jacket is well padded on the breast and well stuffed on the shoulders, and put two handkerchiefs in my regimental jacket, one of cambric and one of my Barcelonas and perfume them well . . . and my gold snuff-box . . . and I'll wear the twenty-guinea gold chain round my neck with the quizzing glass, and bring down my silk nightgown and Turkish embroidered slippers . . . and I must have a cambric chemise with the collar highly starched for dressing time, one of those that look like winkers, and my musical snuff-box for dinner and bring my light morocco boots for dinner with soles as thin as a wafer.'

(1819)

TOBIAS SMOLLETT
From The Adventures of Ferdinand Count Fathom

TAKING HOLD OF a waistcoat that lay upon a chair, 'Sir,' said he, 'give me leave to look at that fringe; I think it is the most elegant knitting I ever saw. I thought plain silk, such as this that I wear, had been the mode, with the pockets very low.'

Before Fathom had time to make any sort of reply he took notice of his hat and pumps; the first of which, he said, was too narrow in the brims, and the last an inch too low in the heels . . . They formed a remarkable contrast with his own, for . . . the brim of his hat if properly spread, would have projected a shade sufficient to shelter a whole file of musketeers . . . and the heels of his shoes were so high as to raise his feet three inches at least.'

A pretty Fellow is known by his dress and behaviour. You may judge of his Intellect by the Powder in his Wig, and his Capacity by the byckling in his shoes.

Grubstreet Journal, 22 May 1735

The 'Spencer'

Few fashions have originated more ridiculously than the spencer, and yet it was so very convenient an article of dress, that it seems remarkable it should have sunk so entirely into disuse. Mr Spencer, a gentleman well known among the men of fashion about the middle of the last reign, and familiarly called 'honest Jack Spencer,' was rather particular in his dress, and had, on more than one occasion, led the way in matters of taste. Being once in company where fashion became the subject of conversation, he remarked that there was nothing so preposterous, but if worn by a person of sufficient consequence, it would be followed. One of the gentlemen doubted this, and offered some arguments to the contrary; when he was interrupted by Mr Spencer, who said, in order to put the question to the test, I will lay you a wager (mentioning the sum) that if I cut off the skirts of my coat, and walk out, with merely the body and sleeves, some person will follow me. 'No doubt of it,' replied one of the gentlemen present, 'for I think, Jack, all the boys in the street will follow you, though it will only be to laugh at you.' Mr Spencer said, he meant that some person would adopt the fashion. The bet was accepted, Mr Spencer's coat 'curtailed of its fair proportion' of skirt, and out he set, first walking down Bond Street, and afterwards passing the shop of a 'man of modes', whom he knew to be always on the watch for novelty. The fashion was soon adopted, and although at first every person acknowledged it to look extremely ridiculous, yet few articles of dress, of a peculiar shape, ever came into more general use. As to Mr Spencer, having set the fashion, he did not long adhere to it, although it still retains his name.

Percy Anecdotes (1823)

'I tossed off the clothes; got softly out of bed; drew on a pair of –'
  'Ladies present, Mr Giles,' murmured the tinker.
  '– of shoes, sir,' said Mr Giles, laying great emphasis on the word.

Charles Dickens, *Oliver Twist*

GEORGE AUGUSTUS SALA
From Twice Round the Clock

IF A MAN wants to be vicious (in the gambling way) now, he must have the *entrée* to the abodes of vice, and a nodding acquaintance with the demon. A neophyte is not allowed to ruin himself how and where he likes. In the days of which I make mention, Regent Street and its purlieus abounded in open gambling houses, and to the skirts of these necessarily hung on a deboshed regiment of rogues, who made their miserable livings as runners, and decoy-ducks, and bravos to these abominable nests. They were called 'Greeks', and two o'clock in the afternoon was their great time for turning out. From what infected holes or pestiferous garrets in Sherrard, or Brewer, or Rupert Street, they came, I know not; but there they were at the appointed hour, skulking with a half sheepish, half defiant stride up and down Regent Street. Miserable dogs mostly, for all their fine clothes – always resplendently, though dirtily, attired. They wore great white coats, shiny hats, and mosaic jewellery, which was just then coming into fashion. There was another fashion, in which they very nearly succeeded, by adopting, to drive out, and make permanently disreputable: that of wearing moustaches. They used to swagger about, all lacquered, pomatumed, bejewelled, and begrimed, till I knew them all by sight and many of them by name and repute.

(1859)

HARRIETTE WILSON
From Paris Lions and London Tigers

CALLAM RETIRED, TO dream of her all night and by ten in the morning behold him, full dressed! He wore, on this grand occasion, a new green coat tinged with yellow hue, a lilac silk under-waistcoat, and his cambric plaited shirt was fastened with a large green emerald pin in the form of a fleur-de-lis; his trousers white with a broad pink stripe, and his upper waistcoat to match. He had been coaxing his hair, ever since he arrived in Paris, to bring it into the true Parisian cut, par devant; and he could now compass something like a ringlet on each temple . . . The back part of his head was scraped tight to the skin, à la Russe; his well-blacked shoes, which only just covered the tips of his toes that his open-work stockings might not be lost to the world, were tied with a very broad black ribbon; his ring was an antique, and his embroidered pocket-handkerchief strongly scented with eau de Portugal. Four French seals dangled from his watch chain which he wore round his neck.

(1825)

Fast talk and slang came in with trousers and turned down collars.

Edward Bulwer-Lytton, *Early Writings* (c. 1825)

ALDOUS HUXLEY
From Crome Yellow

'MY SCHEME FOR dealing with the Church,' Mr Scogar was saying, 'is beautifully simple. At the present time the Anglican clergy wear their collars the wrong way round. I would compel them to wear, not only their collars, but all their clothes, turned back to front – coat, waistcoat, trousers, boots – so that every clergyman should present to the world a smooth façade, unbroken by button or lace. The enforcement of such a livery would act as a wholesome deterrent to those intending to enter the Church.'

GONCOURT BROTHERS
From Letters

De Lurde and Siméon, another important government official, were talking together very seriously. Somebody who had interrupted them said: 'You are busy, I'll leave you.' 'Yes,' he was told. 'We were discussing whether one should wear one's decorations on a visit to a brothel or not. I say one shouldn't; Siméon says one should. He says that if you do, they give you women who haven't got the pox.'

Gentleman shooting in Scotland: 'Might I trouble you to tell my man to get me a new Cumberland corset?'

The Hermit in London (1819)

THOMAS HARDY

A Gentleman's Second-hand Suit

Here it is hanging in the sun
   By the pawn-shop door,
A dress-suit – all its revels done
   Of heretofore.
Long drilled to the waltzers' swing and sway,
   As its tokens show:
What it has seen, what it could say
   If it did not know!

The sleeve bears still a print of powder
   Rubbed from her arms
When she warmed up as the notes swelled louder
   And livened her charms –
Or rather theirs, for beauties many
   Leant there, no doubt,
Leaving these tell-tale traces when he
   Spun them about.

Its cut seems rather in bygone style
   On looking close,
So it mayn't have bent it for some while
   To the dancing pose:
Anyhow, often within its clasp
   Fair partners hung,
Assenting to the wearer's grasp
   With soft sweet tongue.

Where is, alas, the gentleman
   Who wore this suit?
And where are his ladies? Tell none can:
   Gossip is mute.
Some of them may forget him quite
   Who smudged his sleeve,
Some think of a wild and whirling night
   With him, and grieve.

Lord Goring: Yes, father, but I only admit to thirty-two – thirty-one and a half when I have a really good buttonhole. This buttonhole is not (*pause*) trivial enough!

Oscar Wilde, *An Ideal Husband*

There are gentlemen of two sorts; the natural and the tailor-made.

Billy Maguinn, Oliver Yorke of *Fraser's Magazine*

Bodily I may be in 1860, inert, silent, torpid, but in the spirit I am walking about in 1828, let us say – in a blue dress-coat and brass buttons, a sweet figured waistcoat (which I button round a slim waist with perfect ease), looking at beautiful beings with gigot sleeves and tea-tray hats under the golden chestnuts of the Tuileries.

William Makepeace Thackeray, *Roundabout Papers*

Yankee Doodle came to Town
Riding on a Pony
Stuck a Feather in his Cap
And called it Macaroni.

Anon

BRET EASTON ELLIS
From American Psycho

PRICE AND I walk down Hanover Street in the darkest moments of twilight and as if guided by radar move silently toward Harry's. Timothy hasn't said anything since we left P & P. He doesn't even comment on the ugly bum that crouches beneath a Dumpster off Stone Street, though he does manage a grim wolf whistle toward a woman – big tits, blonde, great ass, high heels heading toward Water Street. Price seems nervous and edgy and I have no desire to ask him what's wrong. He's wearing a linen suit by Canali Milano, a cotton shirt by Ike Behar, a silk tie by Bill Blass and cap-toed leather lace-ups from Brooks Brothers. I'm wearing a lightweight linen suit with pleated trousers, a cotton shirt, a dotted silk tie, all by Valentino Couture, and perforated cap-toe leather shoes by Allen-

Edmonds. Once inside Harry's we spot David Van Patten and Craig McDermott at a table up front. Van Patten is wearing a double-breasted wool and silk sport coat, button-fly wool and silk trousers with inverted pleats by Mario Valentino, a cotton shirt by Gitman Brothers, a polka-dot silk tie by Bill Blass and leather shoes from Brooks Brothers. McDermott is wearing a woven-linen suit with pleated trousers, a button-down cotton and linen shirt by Basile, a silk tie by Joseph Abboud and ostrich loafers from Susan Bennis Warren Edwards.

The two are hunched over the table, writing on the backs of paper napkins, a Scotch and a martini placed respectively in front of them. They wave us over. Price throws his Tumi leather attaché case on an empty chair and heads toward the bar. I call out to him for a J&B on the rocks, then sit down with Van Patten and McDermott.

'Hey Bateman,' Craig says in a voice that suggests this is not his first martini. 'Is it proper to wear tasseled loafers with a business suit or not? Don't look at me like *I'm* insane.'

'Oh shit, *don't* ask Bateman,' Van Patten moans, waving a gold Cross pen in front of his face, absently sipping from the martini glass.

'Van Patten?' Craig says.

'Yeah?'

McDermott hesitates, then says 'Shut up' in a flat voice.

'What are you screwballs up to?' I spot Luis Carruthers standing at the bar next to Price, who ignores him utterly. Carruthers is not dressed well: a four-button double-breasted wool suit, I think by Chaps, a striped cotton shirt and a silk bow tie plus horn-rimmed eyeglasses by Oliver Peeples.

'Bateman: we're sending these questions in to *GQ*,' Van Patten begins.

'We have this bet to see which one of us will get in the Question and Answer column first, and so now I expect an answer. *What do you think?*' McDermott demands.

'About *what?*' I ask irritably.

'Tasseled loafers, jerk-*off*,' he says.

'Well, guys . . .' I measure my words carefully. 'The tasseled loafer is traditionally a casual shoe . . .' I glance back at Price, wanting the drink badly. He brushes past Luis, who offers his hand. Price smiles, says something, moves on, strides over to our table. Luis, once more, tries to catch the bartender's attention and once more fails.

'But it's become acceptable just be*cause* it's so popular, right?' Craig asks eagerly.

'Yeah.' I nod. 'As long as it's either black or cordovan it's okay.'

'What about brown?' Van Patten asks suspiciously.

I think about this then say, 'Too sporty for a business suit.'

'What are you fags talking about?' Price asks. He hands me the drink then sits down, crossing his legs.

'Okay, okay, okay,' Van Patten says. 'This is *my* question. A two-parter . . .' He pauses dramatically. 'Now are rounded collars too dressy or too casual? Part two, which tie knot looks best with them?'

A distracted Price, his voice still tense, answers quickly with an exact, clear enunciation that can be heard over the din in Harry's. 'It's a very versatile look and it can go with both suits *and* sport coats. It should be starched for dressy occasions and a collar pin should be worn if it's particularly formal.' He pauses, sighs; it looks as if he's spotted somebody. I turn around to see who it is. Price continues, 'If it's worn with a blazer then the collar should look soft and it can be worn either pinned or unpinned. Since it's a traditional, preppy look it's best if balanced by a relatively small four-in-hand knot.' He sips his martini, recrossing his legs. 'Next question?'

The idea of a man dressing himself in his best clothes to lean against a post all day!

Charles Dickens

CHARLES BURR TODD
From Story of the City of New York

BROADWAY ON A Sabbath morning, as the bells were ringing for Church, must have presented an animated and even brilliant spectacle far exceeding that which modern beaux and belles present. In these days, however, both ladies and gentlemen shone rich as Emperor moths. These worshippers, whom we imagine ourselves watching, come in groups moving down the wide shaded street, some entering Trinity, others turning into Garden Street and passing into the new Dutch Church on that thoroughfare. Both places of worship are equally fashionable. The Dutch Church is the wealthier, but then Trinity has the Governor's pew, and the prestige that comes of State patronage and emolument. Let us describe, as showing the fashions of the day, the dress of this group bearing down abreast of the church yard. They are Nicholas Bayard and Madam Bayard, William Merritt, Alderman and Madam Merritt, and Isaac de Riemer. Bayard, who has been Secretary of the Province, Mayor, and Colonel of the City Militia, wears a cinnamon coloured cloth coat with skirt reaching quite to the knee, embroidered four or five inches deep with silver lace, and lined with sky-blue silk. His waistcoat is of red satin woven in with gold. His breeches, of the same colour and material as his coat, are trimmed with silver at the pockets and knees. Dove coloured silk stockings and low shoes adorned with large silver buckles cover his nether extremities. His hat, of black felt, has a wide flapping brim and is adorned with a band of gold lace.

(1888)

WILLIAM MAKEPEACE THACKERAY
From Vanity Fair

HIS BULK CAUSED Joseph much anxious thought and alarm; now and then he would make a desperate attempt to get rid of his superabundant fat; but his indolence and love of good living speedily got the better of these endeavours at reform, and he found himself again at his three meals a day. He never was well dressed; but he took the hugest pains to adorn his big person, and passed many hours daily in that occupation. His valet made a fortune out of his wardrobe; his toilet-table was covered with as many pomatums and essences as ever were employed by an old beauty; he had tried, in order to give himself a waist, every girth, stay, and waistband then invented. Like most fat men, he *would* have his clothes made too tight, and took care they should be of the most brilliant colours and youthful cut. When dressed at length, in the afternoon, he would issue forth to take a drive with nobody in the Park; and then would come back in order to dress again and go and dine with nobody at the Piazza Coffee-House. He was as vain as a girl; and perhaps his extreme shyness was one of the results of his extreme vanity.

RICHARD STEELE
A Morally Deceased Gentleman's Effects

WHEREAS THE GENTLEMAN that behaved himself in a very disobedient and obstinate manner at his late trial in Sheer Lane on the twentieth instant, and was carried off dead upon taking away of his snuff-box, remains still unburied; the company of upholders, not knowing otherwise how they should be paid, have taken his goods in execution to defray the charge of his funeral. His said effects are to be exposed to sale by auction, at their office in the Haymarket, on the fourth of January next, and are as follows:

A very rich tweezer-case, containing twelve instruments for the use of each hour in the day.

Four pounds of scented snuff, with three gilt snuff-boxes; one of them with an invisible hinge, and a looking-glass in the lid.

Two more of ivory, with the portraitures on their lids of two ladies of the town; the originals to be seen every night in the side-boxes of the playhouse.

A sword with a steel diamond hilt, never drawn but once at Mayfair.

Six clean packs of cards, a quart of orange-flower-water, a pair of French scissors, a toothpick case, and an eyebrow brush.

A large glass case containing the linen and clothes of the deceased; among which are two embroidered suits, a pocket perspective, a dozen pair of red-heeled shoes, three pair of red silk stockings, and an amber-headed cane.

The strong box of the deceased, wherein were found five *billet-doux*, a Bath shilling, a crooked sixpence, a silk garter, a lock of hair, and three broken fans.

A press for books, containing on the upper shelf:

Three bottles of diet-drink.

Two boxes of pills.

A syringe, and other mathematical instruments.

On the second shelf are several miscellaneous works, as:

Lampoons.

Plays.

Tailors' bills.

And an almanac for the year seventeen hundred.

On the third shelf:

A bundle of letters unopened, endorsed, in the hand of the deceased: 'Letters from the old gentleman.'

Lessons for the flute.

Toland's *Christianity not Mysterious*, and a paper filled with patterns of several fashionable stuffs.

On the lowest shelf:

One shoe.

A pair of snuffers.

A French grammar.

A mourning hatband; and half a bottle of usquebaugh.

There will be added to these goods, to make a complete auction, a collection of gold snuff-boxes and clouded canes, which are to continue in fashion for three months after the sale.

The whole are to be set up and priced by Charles Bubbleboy, who is to open the auction with a speech.

From *The Tatler* (c.1710)

RAY BRADBURY
From The Day it Rained Forever

WHISPER RUSTLE . . . THE clean shirt.
        'Ah! . . .'

How clean the new clothes feel, thought Martinez, holding the coat ready. How clean they sound, how clean they smell! Whisper . . . the pants . . . the tie, rustle . . . the braces. Whisper . . . now Martinez let loose the coat which fell in place on flexing shoulders.

'*Ole!*'

Gomez turned like a matador in his wondrous suit-of-lights.

'*Ole*, Gomez, *ole!*'

Gomez bowed and went out the door.

Martinez fixed his eyes to his watch. At ten sharp he heard someone wandering about in the hall as if they had forgotten where to go. Martinez pulled the door open and looked out. Gomez was there, heading for nowhere.

He looks sick, thought Martinez. No, stunned, shook up, surprised, many things.

'Gomez! This is the place!'

Gomez turned around and found his way through the door.

'Oh, friends, friends,' he said. 'Friends, what an experience! This suit! This suit!'

'Tell us, Gomez,' said Martinez.

'I can't, how can I say it!' He gazed at the heavens, arms spread, palms up.

'*Tell* us, Gomez!'

'I have no words, no words. You must see, yourself! Yes, you must see -' And here he lapsed into silence, shaking his head until at last he remembered. They all stood watching him. 'Who's next? Manulo?'

Manulo, stripped to his shorts, leapt forward.

'Ready!'

All laughed, shouted, whistled.

Manulo ready, went out the door. He was gone twenty-nine minutes and thirty seconds. He came back holding to door-knobs, touching the wall, feeling his own elbows, putting the flat of his hand to his face.

'Oh, let me tell you,' he said. '*Compadres*, I went to the bar, eh, to have a drink? But no, I did not go in the bar, do you hear? I did not drink. For as I walked I began to laugh and sing. Why, why? I listened to myself and asked this. Because. The suit made me feel better than wine ever did. The suit made me drunk, drunk! So I went to the *Guadalajara Refriteria* instead and played the guitar and sang four songs, very high! The suit, ah, the suit!'

Dominguez, next to be dressed, moved out through the world, came back from the world.

The black telephone book! thought Martinez. He had it in his hands when he left! Now, he returns, hands empty! What? What? 'On the street,' said Dominguez, seeing it all again, eyes wide, 'on the street I walked, a woman cried, "Dominguez, is that *you*?" Another said, "Dominguez? No, Quetsalcoatl, the Great White God come from the East," do you hear? And suddenly I didn't want to go with six women or eight, no. One, I thought. One! And to this one, who knows *what* I would say? 'Be mine!' or 'Marry me!' *Caramaba*! This suit is dangerous! But I did not care! I live, I live! Gomez, did it happen this way with you?'

Gomez, still dazed by the events of the evening, shook his head. 'No, no talk. It's too much. Later. Villanazul . . . ?'

Villanazul moved shyly forward.

Villanazul went shyly out.

Villanazul came shyly home.

'Picture it,' he said, not looking at them, looking at the floor, talking to the floor. 'The Green Plaza, a group of elderly businessmen gathered under the stars and they are talking, nodding, talking. Now one of them whispers. All turn to stare. They move aside, they make a channel through which a white hot light burns its way as through ice. At the centre of this great light is this person. I take a deep breath. My stomach is jelly. My voice is very small, but it grows louder. And what do I say? I say, 'Friends. Do you know Carlyle's *Sartor Resartus*? In that book we find *his* Philosophy of Suits . . .'

And at last it was time for Martinez to let the suit float him out to haunt the darkness.

Four times he walked around the block. Four times he paused beneath the tenement porches, looking up at the window where the light was lit. A shadow moved, the beautiful girl was there, not there, away and gone, and on the fifth time, there she was, on the porch above, driven out by the summer heat, taking the cooler air. She glanced down. She made a gesture.

At first he thought she was waving to him. He felt like a white explosion that had riveted her attention. But she was not waving. Her head gestured and the next moment a pair of dark-framed glasses sat upon her nose. She gazed at him.

Ah, ah, he thought, so that's it. So! Even the blind may see this suit! He smiled up at her. He did not have to wave. And at least, she smiled back. She did not have to wave either. Then, because he did not know what else to do, and he could not get rid of this smile that had fastened itself to his cheeks, he hurried, almost ran, around the corner, feeling her stare after him. When he looked back, she had taken off her glasses and gazed now with the look of the nearsighted at what, at most, must be a moving blob of light in the great darkness here. Then, for

good measure he went around the block again, through a city so suddenly beautiful he wanted to yell, then laugh, then yell again.

Returning, he drifted, oblivious, eyes half-closed, and seeing him in the door
the others saw not Martinez but themselves come home. In that moment, they
sensed that something had happened to them all.

'You're late!' cried Vanenos, but stopped. The spell could not be broken.

'Somebody tell me,' said Martinez, 'Who am I?'

He moved in a slow circle through the room.

Yes, he thought, yes, it's the suit, yes, it had to do with the suit and them all
together in that store on this fine Saturday night and then here, laughing and
feeling more drunk without drinking, as Manulo said himself, as the night ran
and each slipped on the pants and held, toppling, to the other and, balanced, let
the feeling get bigger and warmer and finer as each man departed and the next
took his place in the suit until now here stood Martinez all splendid and white
as one who gives order and the world grows quiet and moves aside.

'Martinez, we borrowed these mirrors while you were gone. Look!'

The mirrors, set up as in the store, angled to reflect three Martinezes and the
echoes and memories of those who had occupied this suit with him and known
the bright world inside this thread and cloth. Now, in the shimmering mirror,
Martinez saw the enormity of this thing they were living together and his eyes
grew wet. The others blinked. Martinez touched the mirrors. They shifted. He
saw a thousand, a million white-armoured Martinezes march off into eternity,
reflected, reflected, for ever, indomitable, and unending.

F. SCOTT FITZGERALD
From The Great Gatsby

RECOVERING HIMSELF IN a minute he opened for us two hulking patent
cabinets which held his massed suits and dressing-gowns and ties, and his
shirts, piled like bricks in stacks a dozen high.

'I've got a man in England who buys me clothes. He sends over a selection of
things at the beginning of each season, spring and fall.'

He took out a pile of shirts and began throwing them, one by one, before us,
shirts of sheer linen and thick silk and fine flannel, which lost their folds as they
fell and covered the table in many-coloured disarray. While we admired he
brought more and the soft rich heap mounted higher – shirts with stripes and
scrolls and plaids in coral and apple-green and lavender and faint orange, with
monograms of Indian blue. Suddenly, with a strained sound, Daisy beat her head

into the shirts and began to cry stormily.

'They're such beautiful shirts,' she sobbed, her voice muffled in the thick folds. 'It makes me sad because I've never seen such – such beautiful shirts before.'

GUSTAVE FLAUBERT
From Madame Bovary

WHILE MAKING GAME of the Congress, Rodolphe, in order to pass about more freely, showed his blue ticket to the gendarme, and sometimes even stopped before some fine exhibit, which Mme. Bovary would admire but little. He noticed this, and so turned to jesting at the expense of the ladies of Yonville, in point of their dress; then he apologized for the carelessness of his own. The latter had that incoherent blending of common and elegant things, in which the vulgar habitually think to see the revelation of an eccentric existence, the disorders of sentiment, the tyrannies of art, and, always, a certain contempt for social convention which attracts them or exasperates. Thus, his cambric shirt, with pleated wristbands, swelled out at the hazard of the wind in the opening of his waistcoat, which was of gray ticking, and his large-striped trousers disclosed at the ankles his boots of nankeen and patent leather. Their varnish shone so brightly that the grass was reflected in them. He trod down the horse-dung with them as he walked with one hand in his waistcoat pocket, and his straw hat tilted to one side.

'Besides,' he added, 'when one lives in the country . . .'

'All trouble is wasted,' said Emma.

'That is true!' replied Rodolphe. 'To think that not one of these good people is capable of understanding even so much as the cut of a coat!'

Transl. Henry James

JOHN BRAINE
From Life at the Top

THERE WAS A knot of youths by the lamp post at the far end of the Close; I slowed down for a second, wondering whether to turn back. But they were looking towards the jazz club in the basement at Number Seven; someone was trying to cut loose on the trumpet but still was in Leddersford blowing his lungs out on a piece of brass; he hadn't cut loose into pure sound, he hadn't made music, and the grass still grew between the cobblestones and the Close still smelled of cabbage and rancid cooking oil. And the expression of expectancy on the faces of the youths didn't alter it. It was as uniform as their style of dress. Bootlace tie, Slim Jim tie, blue suède shoes with crêpe soles, black leather shoes with brass curb chains, tapered slacks, tight jeans, jackets halfway between raincoat and shirt, jackets with tinsel woven into the fabric – none of them wore the same outfit, but the effect was as if they did. Disquietingly, they all wore crewcuts. They were a gang, they were expecting to enjoy something together.

The English have two possessions of outstanding value: their tweeds and their silences. The silky soft density of the first is only equalled by the noble compactness of the second.

Pierre Daninos, Major Thompson

ISABEL COLGATE
From Statues in a Garden

JAMES HORGAN WAS, as Reggie Mather had reported, an adventurer; but he was not picturesque. He was small and firmly plump, balding, fat-fingered and glossy. His nose was blunt and his eyes, his most attractive feature, round and bright. He wore silk shirts but bought ready-made suits. The trappings of wealth did not appeal to him. He had imagination, but it was all applied to the making and manipulation of money; the spending of it was of no particular interest to him. He merely travelled first-class, stayed at the Savoy, bought silk shirts, and had peaches sent to him from South Africa in the winter. He came from Bradford, but called himself South African. He never thought, walking briskly into the Savoy with a cigar and a camel-hair overcoat, If my mother could only see me now. Not that he had anything against his mother, but he had long ago dismissed her from his mind. He had dismissed a lot of people, and things, from his mind: it gave him his singleness of purpose. He had such a facility for figures as amounted almost to a mental deformity.

HARRIET BEECHER STOWE
From Uncle Tom's Cabin

IT WAS LATE on a drizzly afternoon that a traveler alighted at the door of a small country hotel, in the village of N— , in Kentucky. In the bar-room he found assembled quite a miscellaneous company, whom stress of weather had driven to harbor, and the place presented the usual scenery of such reunions. Great, tall, raw-boned Kentuckians, attired in hunting-shirts, and trailing their loose joints over a vast extent of territory, with the easy lounge peculiar to the race – rifles stacked away in the corner, shot-pouches, game-bags, hunting-dogs, and little negroes, all rolled together in the corners, were the characteristic features in the picture. At each end of the fire-place sat a long-legged gentleman, with his chair tipped back, his hat on his head, and the heels of his muddy boots reposing sublimely on the mantel-piece – a position, we will inform our readers, decidedly favorable to the turn of reflection incident to western taverns where travelers exhibit a decided preference for this particular mode of elevating their understandings.

Mine host, who stood behind the bar, like most of his countrymen, was great of stature, good-natured, and loose jointed with an enormous shock of hair on his head, and a great tall hat on the top of that.

In fact, everybody in the room bore on his head this characteristic emblem of man's sovereignty; whether it were felt-hat, palm-leaf, greasy beaver, or fine new chapeau, there it reposed with true republican independence. In truth, it appeared to be the characteristic mark of every individual. Some wore them tipped rakishly to one side – these were young men of humor, jolly, free-and-easy dogs; some had them jammed independently down over their noses – these were your hard characters, thorough men, who, when they wore their hats, wanted to wear them, and to wear them just as they had a mind to; there were those who had them set far over back – wide awake men, who wanted a clear prospect; while careless men, who did not know, or care, how their hats sat, had them shaking about in all directions. The various hats, in fact, were quite a Shakespearean study.

Divers negroes, in very free-and-easy pantaloons, and with no redundancy in the shirt line, were scuttling about, hither and thither, without bringing to pass any very particular results, except expressing a generic willingness to turn over everything in creation generally for the benefit of master and his guests. Add to this picture a jolly, crackling, rollicking, fire, going rejoicingly up a great wide chimney – the outer door and every window being set wide open, and the calico window-curtain flopping and snapping in a good stiff breeze of damp raw air – and you have an idea of the jollities of a Kentucky tavern.

HARRIETTE WILSON
From Memoirs

I WILL NOT SAY in what particular year of his life the Duke of Argyle succeeded with me. Ladies scorn dates! Dates make ladies nervous and stories dry. Be it only known then, that it was just at the end of his Lorne shifts, and his lawn

shirts. It was at that critical period of his life, when his whole and sole possessions appeared to consist in three dozen of ragged lawn shirts, with embroidered
collars, well fringed in his service; a threadbare suit of snuff colour, a little old
hat with very little binding left, an old horse, an old groom, an old carriage, and
an old château. It was to console himself for all this antiquity, I suppose, that he
fixed upon so very young a mistress as myself.

An Englishman's suit is like a traitor's body that hath been hanged, drawn,
and quartered, and set up in several places: the collar of his doublet and the
belly in France; the wing and narrow sleeves in Italy; the short waste hangs
over a Dutch botcher's stall in Utrich; his huge sloppes speakes Spanish;
Polonia gives him the bootes.

Thomas Dekker, Seven Deadly Sinnes of London (1606)

Portia: He is a proper man's show, but alas who can converse with a dumb
   picture? How oddly he is suited! I think he bought his doublet in Italy, his
   round hose in France, his bonnet in Germany and his behaviour
   everywhere.

William Shakespeare, The Merchant of Venice

Some of the most boring people outside Cheltenham Spa are the wives who
tell you that their husbands can't bear wearing new clothes.

Alison Haig, Night and Day

ANTHONY POWELL

From From a View To a Death

MAJOR FOSDICK FINISHED his second piece of cake. He sat for a few minutes, thinking. Then he got up from his chair and walked slowly out of
the room. He had had enough of his sons for the moment. This was his hour.
The time to please himself. A period of mental relaxation.

He went upstairs to his dressing-room and when he had arrived there he locked
the door. Then he turned to the bottom drawer of his wardrobe, where he kept

all his oldest shooting-suits. He knelt down in front of this and pulled it open. Below the piles of tweed was a piece of brown paper and from under the brown paper he took two parcels tied up with string. Major Fosdick undid the loose knots of the first parcel and took from out of it a large picture-hat that had no doubt been seen at Ascot some twenty years before. The second parcel contained a black sequin evening dress of about the same date. Removing his coat and waistcoat, Major Fosdick slipped the evening dress over his head and, shaking it so that it fell into position, he went to the looking-glass and put on the hat. When he had it arranged at an angle that was to his satisfaction, he lit his pipe and, taking a copy of *Through the Western Highlands with Rod and Gun* from the dressing-table, he sat down. In this costume he read until it was time to change for dinner.

(1933)

Where did you get that hat?
Where did you get that tile?
Isn't it a nobby one
And just the proper style
I should like to have one just the same as that
Where'er I go they'd say, 'Hallo,
Where did you get that hat?'

Popular Song

5

The Power of Clothes

Dress does make a difference, Davy.

Richard Brinsley Sheridan, *The Rivals*

CHARLES READE

From The Course of True Love
Never Did Run Smooth

'CAROLINE,' SAID THE young gentleman gravely.
'Yes Reginald.'

'Dear Caroline do you believe I love you?'

'Better than I deserve, I dare say,' said Caroline.

'No! as you deserve – I will not own my love inferior even to your merit – do you believe that when we are one my life will be devoted to your happiness?'

'I am sometimes – goose enough – to hope so,' murmured Caroline averting her head.

'Shall you then think ill of me if before marriage I ask a favor, perhaps a sacrifice of you? I feel I shall not be ungrateful.'

'There' thought Caroline. 'I am not to wear it – that is plain.' Reginald continued – 'If you wear this dress you will give me pain beyond any pleasure you can derive.'

'Reginald,' said the poor girl, 'I wishes to wear it – now and then; indeed I *had* set my heart on making a *few* – a very few converts to it; see how pretty it is:' – (no answer) – 'but for your sake when I take it off to–night I will give it away, and it shall never, never offend you more.'

Reginald kissed her hand.

There was a pause.

'Caroline,' said he stammering, 'you do not quite understand me; it is to–day I beg you on no account to wear it.'

'Oh! to–day,' said she hastily, 'I have promised to wear it.'

'I entreat you,' said he, 'consider, if you once show yourself to people from every part of New York in this costume, what more remains to be done?'

'Reginald, be reasonable,' said Caroline more coldly. 'I stand engaged to some sixty persons to wear this dress to-night – I have made you a concession, and with pleasure, because I make it to you. It is your turn now – you must think of me as well as of yourself – dear Reginald. I am afraid you must shut your eyes on me for a few hours – that will spoil all my pleasure – or you must fancy as many a lover has been able to do, that I consecrate a dress, not that a dress has power to lower me.'

'Oh! Caroline! do you value my respect?'

'Yes! and therefore I shall keep my word, and so you will feel sure I shall keep my word to you too if ever I promise something about (*blushes and smiles*) love-honour-and obey.'

A battle took place in the young man's mind.

He took several strides backwards and forwards.

At last he burst out, 'There are feelings too strong to be conquered by our wishes. I cannot bear that my wife should do what three-fourths of her sex think indelicate. We never differed in opinion before, we never shall again – if we do, be assured I will bow to you – I would yield here if I could, but I cannot – I think you can – if you can, have pity on me, and add one more claim to my life long gratitude.'

The balance trembled – the tears were in Caroline's eyes – her bosom fluttered – when the Demon of Discord inspired her proud nature with this idea –

'He loves his prejudices better than you,' said Discord 'and this is Tyranny – coaxing Tyranny if you will.'

On this hint spake Caroline.

'I find I have rivals.'

'Rivals?'

'In your prejudices, Reginald. Neither person, nor thing shall ever be my rival. Show me at once which you love with the deeper affection, Mr Seymour's prejudices or Caroline Courtney. I shall wear this dress to-night – only for a few hours: consider! you will be here and keep me in countenance, or you don't love me.'

'No! Caroline,' said Reginald sadly and firmly. 'I have spoken: our future life now rests in your hands – I shall not come – I shall arrange so that if you degrade yourself (I cling to the hope you will not) I shall hear of it and leave the country that minute! Were I to *see* it, by heaven I should leave the world,' he said this in a great heat, but recovering himself said 'Forgive me!' kissed her hand and went despondently away.

(1857)

MARY KINGSLEY
From Travels in West Africa

THE PATH WAS slightly indistinct, but by keeping my eye on it I could see it. Presently I came to a place where it went out, but appeared again the other side of a clump of underbush fairly distinctly. I made a short cut for it and the next news was I was in a heap, on a lot of spikes, some fifteen feet or so below ground level, at the bottom of a bag-shaped game pit.

It is at these times you realize the blessing of a good thick skirt. Had I paid heed to the advice of many people in England, who ought to have known better, and did not do it themselves, and adopted masculine garments, I should have been spiked to the bone and done for. Whereas, save for a good many bruises here was I with the fulness of my skirt tucked under me, sitting on nine ebony spikes some twelve inches long, in comparative comfort, howling lustily to be hauled out.

(1897)

My new French stays . . . are so intolerably wide across the breast, that my arms are absolutely sore with them; and my side so pinched – But it is the 'ton'; and pride feels no pain . . . to be admired, is a sufficient balsam.

Duchess of Devonshire, letter to a friend (1778)

> We sacrifice to dress, till household joys,
> And comforts cease. Dress drains our cellars dry,
> And keeps our larder clean; puts out the fires,
> And introduces hunger, frost, and woe,
> Where peace and hospitality might reign.

William Cowper

JOHN DURANT BREVAL
From Love's Goddess

Love's Goddess now the *Furbeloe* displays,
Invents the *Flounces*, and Reforms the *Stays*;
Her Handmaid Sisters leave their old Abodes,
And make this Town *Metropolis* of Modes.

By Faction guided, Ladies patch the Face,
And to the *Watch* now add the *Twezer Case*.
White Breasts, and Shoulders bare, invade the Eye,
And Legs no more conceal'd, our Jests defy,
Those pretty Legs so Taper, and so Smart,
By which Men guess at ev'ry other *Part*.
The *Petticoat* remain'd a Point in doubt
Till WREN was forc'd to help our Beauties out;
A *Roman Cupola* he show'd in Print,
And thence of *Modern Hoops*, they took the hint;
The vast Circumference gives Air below,
At large they tread, and more Majestick show:
Thro' Lanes of ravish'd Beaus the Wonders pass,
And Names of TOASTS are Cut on conscious Glass.

To you, fair Virgin Throng, With *Myrtle* crown'd
Our Bumpers fill'd with gen'rous Wine go round;
For you, th' *Italian* Worm her Silk prepares,
And distant *India* sends her choicest Wares;
Some Toy from ev'ry Part the Sailor brings,
The Sempstress labours, and the Poet sings.

(1717)

JOHN GAY
The Fan

There stands the toilette, nursery of charms,
Completely furnish'd with bright beauty's arms:
The patch, the powder-box, pulville, perfumes,
Pins, paint a flattering glass, and black-headed combs.
The bosom now its panting beauties shows:
Th' experienc'd eye resistless glances throws:
Now vary'd patches wander o'er the face,
And strike each gazer with a borrow'd grace;
The fickle head-dress sinks, and now aspires
A towery front of lace on branching wires.
How the strait stays the slender waist constrain,
How to adjust the manteau's sweeping train.

(1714)

A-la-Mode

The dress in the year fifty-three that was worn
Is laid in the grave, and new fashions are born;
Then hear what our good correspondents advance,
'Tis the pink of the mode, and 'tis dated from France;
Let your cap be a butterfly, slightly hung on,
Like the shell of a lapwing just hatch'd, on her crown;
Behind, like a coach horse, short dock'd, cut your hair,
Stick a flower before, screw, whiff, with an air:
A Vandyke in frize your neck must surround,
Turn your lawns into gauze, let your Brussels be blond,
Let your stomacher reach from shoulder to shoulder,
And your breast will appear much fairer and bolder;
Wear a gown, or a sacque, as fancies prevail,
But with flounces and furbelows ruffle your tail;
Set your hoop, show your stockings and legs to your knees
And leave men as little as may be to guess:
For other small ornaments do as before,
Wear ribbands a hundred, and ruffles a score;
Let your talk, like your dress, be fantastick and odd,
And you'll shine at the Mall; 'tis taste à-la mode.

Universal Magazine, 1754

Polonius: Costly thy habit as thy purse can buy,
But not expressed in fancy; rich, not gaudy;
For the apparel oft proclaims the man.

William Shakespeare, *Hamlet*

The man is well pleased when his wife is as well dressed as other people's
wives are, and his wife is well pleased when she is well dressed.

Samuel Johnson

Glamour is what makes a man ask for your telephone number. But it is also what makes a woman ask for the name of your dressmaker.

Lilly Daché, *Talking Through My Hats*

Two things I love, two usuall thinges they are:
The Firste, New-fashioned cloaths I love to wear,
Newe Tires, newe Ruffes; aye, and newe Gestures too
In all newe Fashions I do love to goe.
    The Second Thing I love is this, I weene
    To ride aboute to have those Newe Cloaths seene.

At every Gossipping I am at still
And ever wilbe – maye I have my will.
For at ones own Home, praie – who is't can see
How fyne in new-found fashioned Tyres we bee?
Vnless our Husbands – Faith! but very fewe! –
And whoo'd goe gaie, to please a Husband's view?
    Alas! wee wives doe take but small Delight
    If none (besides our husbands) see that Sight.

The Gossipping Wives Complaint (Anon, c. 1611)

Fashion is the expositor, from the standpoint of costume, of our habits and social relations: in a word, of everything pertaining to the charm of life.

M. Augustin Challamel, *The History of Fashion in France*

Berowne: Taffeta phrases, silken terms precise,
    Henceforth my wooing mind shall be express'd
    In russet yeas and honest kersey noes.

William Shakespeare, *Love's Labour's Lost*

I am little given to boasting, but if I may be allowed to say a few words . . . if my dress be extravagant, it is this which supports the working classes . . . In these respects I set, what I think, a laudable example.

Mr Coates, an eighteenth-century actor

MADAME PERRIER
From The Almanac of the Muses

I love the Glove that covers quite
   The rounded arm it rests upon;
I take it off, with what delight!
   With what delight I put it on!
If true it is through mystery,
   A lover's bliss will higher move,
How dear that little hand should be
   Which hides itself beneath a Glove!

But there's another Glove, whose use
   Will every swaggerer displease;
A Glove correcting all abuse,
   Which brings the braggart to his knees;
How many boasting folk I've known,
   Who would, and wisely, rather prove
A flight from out the window thrown,
   Than see before them that same Glove!

The Gloves are useful when we seek
   The fair, the great ones, as we know;
When unto those with Gloves we speak,
   Easy at once their favours grow.
They for intriguers wealth have won,
   No fools their uses are above;
Of what another man has done
   They boast, and give themselves the Glove.

The Gloveless man can ne'er afford
  To dance, no step he makes with grace;
The servant wishes that his lord
  Should put on Gloves in many a case.
When the police are wide awake,
  To cheat those eyes they hardly love,
How many thieves will wisely take
  The greatest care to wear the Glove?

Conseils à Fanny

To rouse the love you'd have us feel,
You choose light stuffs which nought conceal;
The Very finest gauze you take
Our sense of pleasure to awake.
Believe me, what we fail to spy
Inspires still more of ecstasy;
To hide your charms below, above,
Is your true skill to heighten love.

Prévot D'Irai

JOHN GAY
Song from Achilles

Think of Dress in ev'ry Light
'Tis Woman's chiefest Duty;
Neglecting that, our selves we slight
And undervalue Beauty.
That allures the Lover's Eye,
And graces ev'ry Action;
Besides, when not a Creature's by,
'Tis inward Satisfaction.

W. S. GILBERT
From Patience

When I first put this uniform on,
I said, as I looked in the glass,
   'It's one to a million
   That any civilian
My figure and form will surpass.
Gold lace has a charm for the fair,
And I've plenty of that, and to spare,
   While a lover's professions,
   When uttered in Hessians,
Are eloquent everywhere!'
   A fact that I counted upon,
   When I first put this uniform on!

I said, when I first put it on,
'It is plain to the veriest dunce
   That every beauty
   Will feel it her duty
To yield to it, glamour at once.
They will see that I'm freely gold-laced
In a uniform handsome and chaste' -
   But the peripatetics
   Of long-haired aesthetics,
Are very much more to their taste -
   Which I never counted upon
   When I first put this uniform on!

Up to the time I was 29, actually twenty-nine, I was too shabby for any
woman to tolerate me. I stalked about in a decaying green coat, cuffs trimmed
with the scissors, terrible boots, and so on. Then I got a job to do and bought
a suit of clothes with the proceeds. A lady immediately invited me to tea,
threw her arms round me, and said she adored me.

George Bernard Shaw, letter to Ellen Terry (1896)

WILLIAM SHAKESPEARE
From Julius Caesar

Antony: You all do know this mantle: I remember
   The first time ever Cæsar put it on;
   'Twas on a summer's evening, in his tent,
   That day he overcame the Nervii:
   Look, in this place ran Cassius' dagger through:
   See what a rent the envious Casca made:
   Through this the well-beloved Brutus stabb'd;
   And as he pluck'd his cursed steel away,
   Mark how the blood of Cæsar follow'd it,
   As rushing out of doors, to be resolved
   If Brutus so unkindly knock'd, or no;
   For Brutus, as you know, was Cæsar's angel:
   Judge, O you gods, how dearly Cæsar loved him!
   This was the most unkindest cut of all;
   For when the noble Cæsar saw him stab,
   Ingratitude, more strong than traitors' arms,
   Quite vanquish'd him: then burst his mighty heart;
   And, in his mantle muffling up his face,
   Even at the base of Pompey's statue,
   Which all the while ran blood, great Cæsar fell.

HANS CHRISTIAN ANDERSEN
From The Emperor's New Clothes

HE DID NOT care for his soldiers, or for going to the play or for driving in the park except to show his new clothes.

He had a coat for every hour of the day, and just as they say of a king 'He is in his council room,' so they always said of him, 'The Emperor is in his dressing room.'

One day there came two swindlers: they gave out that they were weavers, and said they could weave the finest cloth to be imagined.

They set up two looms, and pretended to be very hard at work, but they had nothing on their looms. They asked for the finest silk and most precious gold: this they put in their own bags, and worked at the empty looms till late into the night . . .

'What is this?' thought the Emperor. 'I do not see anything at all. This is terrible. Am I stupid? Am I unfit to be Emperor? That would indeed be the most dreadful thing that could happen to me.' 'Yes, it is very fine,' said the Emperor. 'It has our highest approval': and, nodding contentedly, he gazed at the empty loom, for he did not like to say that he could see nothing ...

All advised him to wear the new magnificent clothes at a great procession which was soon to take place. All through the night before the procession was due to take place the swindlers were up, and had more than sixteen candles burning. People could see that they were busy getting the Emperor's new clothes ready. They pretended to take the cloth from the loom. They snapped the air with big scissors, they sewed with needles without thread, and said at last: 'Now the Emperor's new clothes are ready.' The Emperor with all his noblest courtiers then came in: and both swindlers held up one arm as if they held something, and said, 'See, here are the trousers', 'Here is the coat!', 'Here is the cloak', and so on. 'They are all as light as cobweb. They make one feel as if one had nothing on at all, but this is just the beauty of it' ... The Emperor took off all his clothes, and the swindlers pretended to put the new clothes upon him, one piece after another: and the Emperor looked at himself in the glass from every side, 'Oh! How well they look!' 'How well they fit!' said all. 'What a pattern!' 'What colours!' 'That is a splendid dress!'

... And so the Emperor marched in the procession under the beautiful canopy, and all who saw him in the street and out of the windows exclaimed: 'How marvellous the Emperor's new suit is!' ... None of the Emperor's clothes had ever been such a success.

'But he has nothing on at all,' said a little child. 'Good heavens! hear what the little innocent says,' said the father, and then each whispered to the other what the child had said. 'He has nothing on – a little child says he has nothing on at all. He has nothing on at all!,' cried all the people at last. And the Emperor too was feeling very worried, for it seemed to him that they were right, but he thought to himself, 'All the same, I must keep the procession going now.'

And he held himself stiffer than ever, and the chamberlains walked on and held up the train which was not there at all.

In Nelson's time, when His Majesty's ships were in harbour, ladies were allowed to sleep on board. The sailors were required to get up at the usual hour, but the ladies might please themselves. A nice problem of discipline thus arose. A solution was found in the fact that the ladies wore their stockings in bed, while the men slept barefooted. If (as usually happened) all the sailors did not appear punctually on deck, it was necessary for the

Boatswain to search for defaulters. He went along the bunks calling out 'Show a leg! show a leg.' The owner of a bare leg was promptly dealt with; but any leg wearing a stocking was allowed to return where it came from, and doubtless the Boatswain would apologize to the lady in nautical terms. Evidently our sailors, being such innocent fellows, never thought of borrowing the ladies' stockings.

Arthur Stanley, *The Bedside Book* (1947)

The greatest motive to love is Dress. I have known a lady at sight fly to a red feather, and readily give her hand to a fringed pair of gloves . . . what moving rhetorick has she often found in the seducing full-bottom? Who can tell the resistless eloquence of the embroidered coat, the gold snuff-box and the amber-headed cane?

The Guardian (1713)

EDWARD MOORE
From The World

From Eve's first fig-leaf to brocade,
All dress was meant for Fancy's aid,
Which evermore delighted dwells
On what the bashful nymph conceals.
When Celia struts in man's attire
She shews too much to raise desire;
But from the hoop's bewitching round
Her very shoe has power to wound.

(1756)

JENNY JOSEPH
Warning

When I am an old woman I shall wear purple
With a red hat which doesn't go, and doesn't suit me.
And I shall spend my pension on brandy and summer gloves
And satin sandals, and say we've no money for butter.
I shall sit down on the pavement when I'm tired

And gobble up samples in shops and press alarm bells
And run my stick along the public railings
And make up for the sobriety of my youth.
I shall go out in my slippers in the rain
And pick the flowers in other people's gardens
And learn to spit.

You can wear terrible shirts and grow more fat
And eat three pounds of sausages at a go
Or only bread and pickle for a week
And hoard pens and pencils and beermats and things in boxes.

But now we must have clothes that keep us dry
And pay our rent and not swear in the street
And set a good example for the children.
We must have friends to dinner and read the papers.

But maybe I ought to practise a little now?
So people who know me are not too shocked and surprised
When suddenly I am old, and start to wear purple.

Instead of home-spun coifs were seen
Good pinners edg'd with colberteen;
Her petticoat, transform'd apace,
Became black sattin flounc'd with lace.
Plain *Goody* would no longer down;
'Twas *Madame*, in the grogram gown.

Jonathan Swift, *Journal of a Modern Lady*

I am not a little surprised to find dress, unless upon public occasions, so little
regarded. The gentlemen are very plainly dressed, and the ladies much less so
than with us. Tis true you must put a hoop on, and have your hair dressed,
but a common straw hat, no cap, only a ribbon upon the crown is thought
dress sufficient to go into company. Muslins are much in taste, but no silks
but lutestrings . . . They paint here nearly as much as in France, but with
more art. The headdress disfigures them in the eye of Americans. I have seen
many ladies but not one elegant one since I came, there is not to see that
neatness in their appearance, which you see in our ladies.

The American ladies are much admired here by the gentlemen, I am told, and in truth I wonder not at it. O my country, my country! preserve, preserve the little purity and simplicity of manners you yet possess. Believe me, they are jewels of inestimable value; the softness peculiarly characteristic of our sex, which is so pleasing to the gentlemen, is wholly laid aside here for the masculine attire and manners of Amazonians!

Abigail Adams, letter from London (1784)

Although Paris may be accounted the soil in which almost every fashion takes its rise, its influence is never so general there as with us. They study there the happy method of uniting grace and fashion, and never excuse a woman for being awkwardly dressed, by saying her clothes are made in the *mode*. A Frenchwoman is a perfect architect in dress.

Anon, *The Bee* (19th century)

Soldier, Won't You Marry Me?

Soldier, soldier, won't you marry me?
　　It's O the fife and drum!
How can I marry such a pretty girl as you
　　When I've got no hat to put on!

Off to the tailor's she did go
　　As fast as she could run,
Brought him back the finest that was there:
　　Now, soldier, put it on!

Soldier, soldier, won't you marry me?
　　It's O the fife and drum!
How can I marry such a pretty girl as you
　　When I've got no coat to put on!

Back to the tailor's she did go
　　As fast as she could run,
Brought him back the finest that was there:
　　Now, soldier, put it on!

Soldier, soldier, won't you marry me?
   It's O the fife and drum!
How can I marry such a pretty girl as you
   When I've got no shoes to put on!

Off to the shoe-shop she did go
   As fast as she could run,
Brought him back the finest that were there:
   Now, soldier, put them on!

Soldier, soldier, won't you marry me?
   It's O the fife and drum!
How can I marry such a pretty girl as you
   When I've a wife and babies at home!

Anon

A strange effeminate age when men strive to imitate women in their apparell . . . On the other side, women would strive to be like men, viz., when they rode on horsback or in coaches weare plush caps like monteros, either full of ribbons or feathers, long periwigs which men used to weare, and riding coate of a red colour all bedaubed with lace which they call vests, and this habit was chiefly used by the ladies and maids of honor belonging to the Queen, brought in fashion about anno 1663, which they weare at this time at their being in Oxon.

The Life and Times of Anthony Wood (1663)

NIKOLAI GOGOL

From The Overcoat

A KAKII AKAKIEVICH WAS still for mending it; but Petrovich would not hear of it, and said, 'I shall certainly make you a new one, and please depend upon it that I shall do my best. It may even be, as the fashion goes, that the collar can be fastened by silver hooks under a flap.'

Then Akakii Akakievich saw that it was impossible to get along without a new overcoat, and his spirit sank utterly. How, in fact, was it to be accomplished? Where was the money to come from? He might, to be sure, depend, in part, upon his present at Christmas; but that money had long been doled out and allotted beforehand. He must have some new trousers, and pay a debt of long standing to the shoemaker for putting new tops to his old boots, and he must order three shirts from the seamstress, and a couple of pieces of linen which it is impolite to mention in print – in a word, all his money must be spent; and even if the director should be so kind as to order forty-five rubles instead of forty, or even fifty, it would be a mere nothing, and a mere drop in the ocean towards the capital necessary for an overcoat: although he knew that Petrovich was wrong-headed enough to blurt out some outrageous price, Satan only knows what, so that his own wife could not refrain from exclaiming, 'Have you lost your senses, you fool?'

At one time he would not work at any price, and now it was quite likely that he had asked a price which it was not worth. Although he knew that Petrovich would undertake to make it for eighty rubles, still, where was he to get the eighty rubles? He might possibly manage half; yes, a half of that might be procured: but where was the other half to come from? But the reader must first be told where the first half came from. Akakii Akakievich had a habit of putting, for every ruble he spent, a groschen into a small box, fastened with lock and key, and with a hole in the top for the reception of money. At the end of each half-year, he counted over the heap of coppers, and changed it into small silver coins. This he continued for a long time; and thus, in the course of some years, the sum proved to amount to over forty rubles.

Thus he had one half on hand; but where to get the other half? Where to get another forty rubles? Akakii Akakievich thought and thought, and decided that it would be necessary to curtail his ordinary expenses, for the space of one year at least – to dispense with tea in the evening; to burn no candles, and, if there was anything which he must do, to go into his landlady's room, and work by her light; when he went into the street, he must walk as lightly as possible, and as cautiously, upon the stones and flagging, almost upon tiptoe, in order not to wear out his heels in too short a time; he must give the laundress as little to wash as possible; and, in order not to wear out his clothes, he must take them off as soon as he got home, and wear only his cotton dressing-gown, which had been long and carefully saved.

To tell the truth, it was a little hard for him at first to accustom himself to these deprivations; but he got used to them at length, after a fashion, and all went smoothly – he even got used to being hungry in the evening; but he made up for it by treating himself in spirit, bearing ever in mind the thought of his future coat. From that time forth, his existence seemed to become, in some way, fuller, as if he were married, as if some friend had consented to go along life's path with him – and the friend was no other than that overcoat, with thick wadding and a strong lining incapable of wearing out. He became more lively, and his character even became firmer, like that of a man who has made up his mind, and set himself a goal. From his face and gait, doubt and indecision – in short, all hesitating and wavering traits – disappeared of themselves.

Fire gleamed in his eyes: occasionally, the boldest and most daring ideas flitted through his mind; why not, in fact, have marten fur on the collar? The thought of this nearly made him absent-minded. Once, in copying a letter, he nearly made a mistake, so that he exclaimed almost aloud, 'Ugh!' and crossed himself. Once in the course of each month, he had a conference with Petrovich on the subject of the coat – where it would be better to buy the cloth, and the color, and the price – and he always returned home satisfied, though troubled, reflecting that the time would come at last when it could all be bought, and then the overcoat could be made.

The matter progressed more briskly than he had expected. Far beyond all his hopes, the director appointed neither forty nor forty-five rubles for Akakii Akakievich's share, but sixty. Did he suspect that Akakii Akakievich needed an overcoat? or did it merely happen so? at all events, twenty extra rubles were by this means provided. This circumstance hastened matters. Only two or three months more of hunger – and Akakii Akakievich had accumulated about eighty rubles. His heart, generally so quiet, began to beat.

On the first possible day, he visited the shops in company with Petrovich. They purchased some very good cloth – and reasonably, for they had been considering the matter for six months, and rarely did a month pass without their visiting the shops to inquire prices; and Petrovich said himself, that no better cloth could be had. For lining, they selected a cotton stuff, but so firm and thick, that Petrovich declared it to be better than silk, and even prettier and more glossy. They did not buy the marten fur, because it was dear, in fact; but in its stead, they picked out the very best of cat-skin which could be found in the shop, and which might be taken for marten at a distance.

Petrovich worked at the coat two whole weeks, for there was a great deal of quilting: otherwise it would have been done sooner. Petrovich charged twelve rubles for his work – it could not possibly be done for less: it was all sewed with silk, in small, double seams; and Petrovich went over each seam afterwards with his own teeth, stamping in various patterns.

It was – it is difficult to say precisely on what day, but it was probably the most glorious day in Akakii Akakievich's life, when Petrovich at length brought home the coat. He brought it in the morning, before the hour when it was necessary to go to the department. Never did a coat arrive so exactly in the nick of time; for the severe cold had set in, and it seemed to threaten increase. Petrovich presented himself with the coat as befits a good tailor. On his countenance was a significant expression, such as Akakii Akakievich had never beheld there. He seemed sensible to the fullest extent that he had done no small deed, and that a gulf had suddenly appeared, separating tailors who only put in linings, and make repairs, from those who make new things.

He took the coat out of the large pocket-handkerchief in which he had brought it. (The handkerchief was fresh from the laundress: he now removed it, and put it in his pocket for use.) Taking out the coat, he gazed proudly at it, held it with both hands, and flung it very skilfully over the shoulders of Akakii Akakievich; then he pulled it and fitted it down behind with his hand; then he draped it around Akakii Akakievich without buttoning it. Akakii Akakievich, as a man advanced in life, wished to try the sleeves. Petrovich helped him on with them, and it turned out that the sleeves were satisfactory also. In short, the coat appeared to be perfect, and just in season.

Petrovich did not neglect this opportunity to observe that it was only because he lived in a narrow street, and had no signboard, and because he had known Akakii Akakievich so long, that he had made it so cheaply; but, if he had been on the Nevsky Prospect, he would have charged seventy-five rubles for the making alone. Akakii Akakievich did not care to argue this point with Petrovich, and he was afraid of the large sums with which Petrovich was fond of raising the dust. He paid him, thanked him, and set out at once in his new coat for the department. Petrovich followed him, and, pausing in the street, gazed long at the coat in the distance, and went to one side expressly to run through a crooked alley, and emerge again into the street to gaze once more upon the coat from another point, namely, directly in front.

Transl. Isabel F. Hapgood

WENDY COPE
Prelude

> It wouldn't be a good idea
> To let him stay.
> When they knew each other better –
> Not today,
> But she put on her new black knickers
> Anyway.

Miriam puts on a garment she privately addresses as *la robe*. Sometimes she paints wearing *la robe*. Sometimes she goes out to the flowers in *la robe* and thinks of Sissinghurst and Vita Sackville-West and her friends wearing those strange clothes they wore. Mainly la robe is a comforter. Larry calls it 'that thing'. 'Why're you in the garden in that thing, Miriam?' 'It's not "that thing",' she wants to say, 'it's la robe.' She loves it. It's loose and full of pockets. She designed it and made it herself with a remnant from Dickins and Jones. She made it for the French holidays, for summer and a terrace. Now she's in it all year till winter.

Rose Tremain, The Swimming Pool Season

Lady Glenmire, now we had time to look at her, proved to be a bright little woman of middle age, who had been very pretty in the days of her youth, and who was even yet very pleasant-looking. I saw Miss Pole appraising her dress in the first five minutes, and I take her word, when she said the next day:

'My dear! ten pounds would have purchased every stitch she had on – lace and all.'

It was pleasant to suspect that a peeress could be poor.

Mrs Gaskell, Cranford

GEORGE AUGUSTUS SALA
From America Revisited

FEMININE FASHIONS IN Baltimore are serious matters. I had been reading that morning in one of the local journals a most portentous column of items, headed 'For the Ladies'. May I venture to hope that some of my lady readers in England may be edified by the announcement that, in the genial city of Maryland, 'hoops threaten to come once more into fashion, and satin cashmere is a new dress material'? Further on I learned that 'the new shade of purple is called "dahlia,"' that 'epingeline' is 'a novel name for uncut velvet', and that 'new plaid stockings have the checks set diagonally'. This I hold to be a decided advantage, since many years ago, when the exuberance of crinoline occasionally led to indiscretions in the revelation of ankles, I remember seeing a lady the rectangular black and white checks on whose hose suggested to an irreverent omnibus conductor in High-street, Knightsbridge, the profane remark to the driver of the vehicle that he would 'werry much like to 'ave a game o' draughts on that gal's legs.' Then, again, I gathered that, 'to be fashionable, one must have a leopard skin muff', and that the 'Derby hat' is very much worn by young coloured girls. Subsequently I came to the mysterious statement that 'an innovation in underwear is seen in the fine pink and blue flannel, beautifully embroidered with flowers in white floss.' 'White skirts,' the oracle went on, 'are no longer worn in the street; black satin or Japanese blue, scarlet or olive green satin or flannel, take their place.' After this I concluded that it was time to retire from the perusal of the column for the ladies. Even the writer seemed to have grown terrified at his own audacity, for after the allusion to the black satin 'underwear', he became slightly trite and jejune, contenting himself with remarking that 'wool plaids in plum-colour, black, and gold are patronised by the most fashionable school-girls', bidding those young ladies 'who have no sealskin sacques cheer up, for the doctors say they are very unhealthy', and drifting at last into the mere platitude of advising girls who wished to have small mouths to repeat, at frequent intervals during the day, 'Fanny Finch Fried Five Floundering Frogs For Francis Fowler's Father.'

(1882)

ANGELA CARTER
From Wise Children

MEANWHILE, MY FRIEND offered me a fur coat. He liked me very much. 'Not a fur, Mr Piano Man, thank you very much,' I said. 'Whatever would Grandma say?' But he wouldn't take no for an answer and a van delivered a big box next morning. In the box, among the tissue paper, a grey squirrel jacket, fingertip length, frail and lovely, 'like her own virtue', as poor old Irish would have put it a year or so hence in another country, but Irish could never afford to give me furs, he taught me to eschew the double negative, instead.

Once that jacket arrived I hadn't the heart to give it back although Grandma cut up something terrible. I've got it still, it's in the big wardrobe in Grandma's room that we don't use any more, wrapped up in a white sheet, there's a ghost of antique Mitsouko clinging to the hairs, mothballs in one pocket, in the other the dehydrated skeleton of a gardenia left where I stuffed it after a Certain Distinguished Person took it out of his buttonhole and slipped it down my cleavage, such as it was, not that Nora and I were ever over-endowed in the bosom department, but, if I'd had a cleavage, that is what his nose would have come up to, he was only a little chap.

Grandma was apoplectic when I got home. The juxtaposition of flora and fauna on my person was too much for her. 'You wouldn't cut off a baby's head and stick it on your best friend's flayed corpse for decoration, would you?' 'I never met a squirrel socially,' I said. I cheeked her. I brazened it out. Perry guffawed but Grandma blew down her nose, huff huff huff, and when she found out who it was that gave me the gardenia, her fury knew no bounds. She had a real down on the Royal Family.

E. M. DELAFIELD

From The Diary of a Provincial Lady

OCTOBER 17TH: Surprising invitation to evening party – Dancing, 9.30 – at Lady B.'s . . .

Decide to get new dress, but must have it made locally, owing to rather sharply worded enquiry from London shop which has the privilege of serving me, as to whether I have not overlooked overdue portion of account? (Far from overlooking it, have actually been kept awake by it at night.) Proceed to Plymouth, and get very attractive black taffeta, with little pink and blue posies scattered over it. Mademoiselle removes, and washes, Honiton lace from old purple velvet everynight tea-gown, and assures me that it will be *gentil à croquer* on new taffeta. Also buy new pair black evening-shoes, but shall wear them every evening for at least an hour in order to ensure reasonable comfort at party . . .

October 19th: Rumour that Lady B.'s party is to be in Fancy Dress throws entire neighbourhood into consternation. Our Vicar's wife comes down on gardener's wife's bicycle – borrowed, she says, for greater speed and urgency – and explains that, in her position, she does not think that fancy dress would do at all – unless perhaps *poudré*, which, she asserts, is different, but takes ages to brush out afterwards. She asks what I am going to do, but am quite unable to enlighten her, as black taffeta already completed. Mademoiselle, at this, intervenes, and declares that black taffeta can be transformed by a touch into Dresden China Shepherdess *à ravir*. Am obliged to beg her not to be ridiculous, nor attempt to make me so, and she then insanely suggests turning black taffeta into costume for (a) Mary Queen of Scots, (b) Mme. de Pompadour, (c) Cleopatra.

I desire her to take Vicky for a walk; she is *blessée*, and much time is spent in restoring her to calm....

October 23rd: Party takes place. Black taffeta and Honiton lace look charming and am not dissatisfied with general appearance, after extracting two quite unmistakable grey hairs. Vicky goes so far as to say that I look Lovely, but enquires shortly afterwards why old people so often wear black – which discourages me.

Received by Lady B. in magnificent Eastern costume, with pearls dripping all over her, and surrounded by bevy of equally bejewelled friends. She smiles graciously and shakes hands without looking at any of us, and strange fancy crosses my mind that it would be agreeable to bestow on her sudden sharp shaking, and thus compel her to recognize existence of at least one of guests invited to her house. Am obliged, however, to curb this unhallowed impulse, and proceed quietly into vast drawing-room, at one end of which band is performing briskly on platform . . .

Lady B.'s house-party, all in expensive disguises and looking highly superior, dance languidly with one another, and no introductions take place.

CHARLOTTE BRONTË
From Villette

I THOUGHT HE HAD nearly done. But no; he sat down that he might go on at his ease.

'While he, M. Paul, was on these painful topics, he would dare my anger for the sake of my good, and would venture to refer to a change he had noticed in my dress. He was free to confess that when he first knew me – or, rather, was in the habit of catching a passing glimpse of me from time to time – I satisfied him on this point. The gravity, the austere simplicity, obvious in this particular were such as to inspire the highest hopes for my best interests. What fatal influence had impelled me lately to introduce flowers under the brim of my bonnet, to wear 'des cols brodés', and even to appear on one occasion in a scarlet gown, he might indeed conjecture, but, for the present, would not openly declare.'

Again I interrupted, and this time not without an accent at once indignant and horror-struck.

'Scarlet, Monsieur Paul? It was not scarlet. It was pink, and pale pink, too; and further subdued by black lace.'

'Pink or scarlet, yellow or crimson, pea-green or sky-blue, it was all one. These were all flaunting, giddy colours; and as to the lace I talked of, *that* was but a "colifichet de plus".' And he sighed over my degeneracy. 'He could not, he was sorry to say, be so particular on this theme as he could wish. Not possessing the exact names of these "babioles", he might run into small verbal errors which would not fail to lay him open to my sarcasm, and excite my unhappily sudden and passionate disposition. He would merely say, in general terms – and in these general terms he knew he was correct – that my costume had of late assumed "des façons mondaines", which it wounded him to see.'

What 'façons mondaines' he discovered in my present winter merino and plain white collar, I own it puzzled me to guess; and when I asked him, he said it was all made with too much attention to effect, and besides, 'had I not a bow of ribbon at my neck?'

'And if you condemn a bow of ribbon for a lady, monsieur, you would necessarily disapprove of a thing like this for a gentleman?' holding up my bright little chainlet of silk and gold. His sole reply was a groan – I suppose over my levity.

After sitting some minutes in silence, and watching the progress of the chain, at which I now wrought more assiduously than ever, he inquired whether what he had just said would have the effect of making me entirely detest him.

I hardly remember what answer I made, or how it came about; I don't think I spoke at all, but I know we managed to bid good night on friendly terms; and, even after M. Paul had reached the door, he turned back just to explain 'that he would not be understood to speak in entire condemnation of the scarlet dress' ('Pink! pink!' I threw in); 'that he had no intention to deny it the merit of looking rather well' (the fact was, M. Emanuel's taste in colours decidedly leaned to the brilliant); 'only he wished to counsel me, whenever I wore it, to do so in the same spirit as if its material were "bure", and its hue "gris de poussière".'

'And the flowers under my bonnet, monsieur?' I asked. 'They are very little ones -'

'Keep them little, then,' said he. 'Permit them not to become full-blown.'

'And the bow, monsieur – the bit of ribbon?'

'Va pour le ruban!' was the propitious answer.

And so we settled it.

JESSICA MITFORD
From Hons and Rebels

H E ARRIVED BACK very late, but victorious.

'Look!' he exulted. 'Only six dollars, waistcoat and all. I got it at a little place on a street called Third Avenue. It's a wonderful place for shopping. The salesman let me have it extra cheap, because the last person who had it had been shot in it, and that's supposed to bring bad luck, so no one else would buy it.'

The tuxedo fitted all right. I looked carefully for the bullet hole, but couldn't find it. The worst part about the suit was the satin lapels, which gleamed and shone like mirrors. I rubbed face powder in them, dimming the lustre somewhat. We debated whether or not to take out the enormous pads in the shoulders, which gave Esmond the appearance of a prize-fighter, but decided against it, for fear it might bring about a total collapse of the coat.

'After all, they'll probably never see you again, so they'll go on thinking those are your normal shoulders,' I said.

Thanks to the power of suggestion, Esmond's tuxedo was a great success. I carefully avoided catching his eye when our host was heard to say: 'There's nothing like English tailoring; they sure know their stuff. Say, that tux is sure a beaut; where did you get it, Savile Row?'

MARY EVELYN

From Mundus Muliebris, or
The Ladies' Dressing Room Unlocked

WHOEVER HAS A MIND to abundance of Trouble,
Let him furni∫h him∫elf with a Ship and a Woman,
For no two things will find you more Employment,
If once you begin to Rig them out with all their Streamers.
Nor are they ever ∫ufficiently adorned,
Or ∫atisfy'd, that you have done enough to ∫et them forth.

He that will needs to *Marry-Land*
Adventure, fir∫t mu∫t under∫tand
For's Bark, what Tackle to prepare,
'Gain∫t Wind and Weather, wear and tare:
Of Point *d'E∫pagne*, a Rich *Cornet*,
Two *Night-Rails*, and a *Scarf* be∫et
With a great Lace, a *Colleret*.
One black Gown of Rich Silk, which odd is
Without one Colour'd, Embroider'd *Bodice*:
Four Petticoats for Page to hold up,
Four ∫hort ones nearer to the Crup:
Three *Manteaus*, nor can Madam le∫s
Provi∫ion have for due undre∫s;
Nor *demy Sultane*, *Spagnolet*,
Nor Fringe to ∫weep the Mall forget,
Of under Bodice three neat pair
Embroider'd, and of Shoos as fair:
Short under Petticoats pure fine,
Some of *Japan* Stuff, forme of *Chine*,
With Knee-high Galoon bottomed,
Another quilted White and Red;
With a broad *Flanders* Lace below:
Four pair of *Bas de ∫oy* ∫hot through
With Silver, Diamond Buckles too,
For Garters, and as Rich for Shoo.
Twice twelve day Smocks of *Holland* fine,
With *Cambric* Sleeves, rich Point to joyn,
(For ∫he de∫pi∫es *Colbertine*.)
Twelve more for night, all *Flanders* lac'd,
Or el∫e ∫he'll think her ∫elf di∫grac'd:

The fame her Night-Gown muſt adorn,
With two Point Waſtcoats for the Morn:
Of Pocket *Mouchoirs* Noſe to drain,
A dozen lac'd, a dozen plain:
Three Night-Gowns of rich *Indian* ſtuff,
Four Cuſhion Cloths are ſcarce enough,
Of Point, and *Flanders*, not forget
Slippers embroidered on Velvet:
A *Manteau* Girdle, Ruby Buckle,
And *Brillant* Diamond Rings for Knuckle
Fans painted, and perfumed three;
Three Muffs of *Sable, Ermine, Grey*;
Nor reckon it among the Baubles,
A *Palatine* alſo of *Sables* . . .
A Saphire Bodkin for the Hair.
Or ſparkling Facet Diamond there:
Then *Turquois, Ruby, Emrauld* Rings
For Fingers, and ſuch petty things;
As Diamond Pendants for the Ears,
Muſt needs be had, or two Pearl Pears,
Pearl Neck-lace, large and Oriental,
And Diamond, and of Amber pale;
For Oranges bears every Buſh,
Nor values ſhe cheap things a ruſh.
Then Bracelets for her Wriſts beſpeak,
(Unleſs her Heart-ſtrings you will break)
With Diamond *Croche* for Breaſt and Bum,
'Till to hang more on there's no room . . .
As Rich and Coſtly as all theſe,
To which a bunch of *Onyxes*,
And many a Golden Seal there dangles,
Myſterious Cyphers, and new fangles.
Gold is her Toothpick, Gold her Watch is,
And Gold is every thing ſhe touches:
But tir'd with numbers I give o're,
Arithmetick can add no more,
Thus Rigg'd the Veſſel, and Equipp'd,
She is for all Adventures Shipp'd,
And Portion e're the year goes round,
Does with her Vanity confound . . .

(1690)

MARGARET MITCHELL
From Gone With The Wind

'I'M NOT PRETTY enough to get him!' she thought, and desperation came back to her. 'I'm thin – oh, I'm terribly thin!'

She patted her cheeks, felt frantically at her collar-bones, feeling them stand out through her basque. And her breasts were so small, almost as small as Melanie's. She'd have to put ruffles in her bosom to make them look larger and she had always had contempt for girls who resorted to such subterfuges. Ruffles! That brought up another thought. Her clothes. She looked down at her dress, spreading its mended folds wide between her hands. Rhett liked women who were well dressed, fashionably dressed. She remembered with longing the flounced green dress she had worn when she first came out of mourning, the dress she wore with the green plumed bonnet he had brought her, and she recalled the approving compliments he had paid her. She remembered, too, with hate sharpened by envy the red plaid dress, the red-topped boots with tassels and the pancake hat of Emmie Slattery. They were gaudy but they were new and fashionable and certainly they caught the eye. And, oh, how she wanted to catch the eye! Especially the eye of Rhett Butler! If he should see her in her old clothes, he'd know everything was wrong at Tara. And he must not know.

What a fool she had been to think she could go to Atlanta and have him for the asking, she with her scrawny neck and hungry cat eyes and raggedy dress! If she hadn't been able to pry a proposal from him at the height of her beauty, when she had her prettiest clothes, how could she expect to get one now when she was ugly and dressed tackily? If Miss Pitty's story was true, he must have more money than anyone in Atlanta and probably had his pick of all the pretty ladies, good and bad. 'Well,' she thought grimly, 'I've got something that most pretty ladies haven't got – and that's a mind that's made up. And if I had just one nice dress—'

There wasn't a nice dress in Tara or a dress which hadn't been turned twice and mended.

'That's that,' she thought, disconsolately looking down at the floor. She saw Ellen's moss-green velvet carpet, now worn and scuffed and torn and spotted from the numberless men who had slept upon it, and the sight depressed her more, for it made her realize that Tara was just as ragged as she. The whole darkening room depressed her and, going to the window, she raised the sash, unlatched the shutters and let the last light of the wintry sunset into the room. She closed the window and leaned her head against the velvet curtains and looked out across the bleak pasture toward the dark cedars of the burying-ground.

The moss-green velvet curtains felt prickly and soft beneath her cheek and she rubbed her face against them gratefully, like a cat. And then suddenly she looked at them.

A minute later, she was dragging a heavy marble-topped table across the floor, its rusty castors screeching in protest. She rolled the table under the window, gathered up her skirts, climbed on it and tiptoed to reach the heavy curtain-pole. It was almost out of her reach and she jerked at it so impatiently the nails came out of the wood, and the curtains, pole and all, fell to the floor with a clatter.

As if by magic, the door of the parlour opened and the wide black face of Mammy appeared, ardent curiosity and deepest suspicion evident in every wrinkle. She looked disapprovingly at Scarlett, poised on the table top, her skirts above her knees, ready to leap to the floor. There was a look of excitement and triumph on her face which brought sudden distrust to Mammy.

'Whut you up to wid Miss Ellen's po'teers?' she demanded.

'What are you up to listening outside doors?' asked Scarlett, leaping nimbly to the floor and gathering up a length of the heavy dusty velvet.

'Dat ain't needer hyah nor dar,' countered Mammy, girding herself for combat. 'You ain't got no bizness wid Miss Ellen's po'teers, juckin' de poles plum outer de wood, an' drappin' dem on de flo' in de dust. Miss Ellen set gret sto' by dem po'teers an' Ah ain' 'tendin' ter have you muss dem up dat way.'

Scarlett turned green eyes on Mammy, eyes which were feverishly gay, eyes which looked like the bad little girl of the good old days Mammy sighed about.

'Scoot up to the attic and get my box of dress patterns, Mammy,' she cried, giving her a slight shove. 'I'm going to have a new dress.'

The person who thinks clothes are simply for modesty will cover himself from head to foot with thick tweeds, but will think nothing wrong in a woman who goes nearly naked to the theatre – provided, of course, she sits in the stalls or boxes, and is protected by a barrier from the poor and needy.

Eric Gill, *Clothes*

JEAN RHYS
Illusion

MISS BRUCE WAS quite an old inhabitant of the Quarter. For seven years she had lived there, in a little studio up five flights of stairs. She had painted portraits, exhibited occasionally at the Salon. She had even sold a picture some-times – a remarkable achievement for Montparnasse, but possible, for I believe she was just clever enough and not too clever, though I am no judge of these matters.

She was a tall, thin woman, with large bones and hands and feet. One thought of her as a shining example of what character and training – British character and training – can do. After seven years in Paris she appeared utterly untouched, utterly unaffected, by anything hectic, slightly exotic or unwholesome. Going on all the time all round her were the cult of beauty and the worship of physical love: she just looked at her surroundings in her healthy, sensible way, and then dismissed them from her thoughts . . . rather like some sturdy rock with impo-tent blue waves washing round it.

When pretty women passed her in the streets or sat near her in restaurants – La Femme, exquisitely perfumed and painted, feline, loved – she would look appraisingly with the artist's eye, and make a suitably critical remark. She exhib-ited no tinge of curiosity or envy. As for the others, the *petites femmes*, anxiously consulting the mirrors of their bags, anxiously and searchingly looking round with darkened eyelids: 'Those unfortunate people!' would say Miss Bruce. Not in a hard way, but broad-mindedly, breezily: indeed with a thoroughly gentle-manly intonation . . . These unfortunate little people!

She always wore a neat serge dress in the summer and a neat tweed costume in the winter, brown shoes with low heels and cotton stockings. When she was going to parties she put on a black gown of crêpe de chine, just well enough cut, not extravagantly pretty.

In fact Miss Bruce was an exceedingly nice woman.

She powdered her nose as a concession to Paris; the rest of her face shone, beautifully washed, in the sunlight or the electric light as the case might be, with here and there a few rather lovable freckles.

She had, of course, like most of the English and American artists in Paris, a private income – a respectably large one, I believe. She knew most people and was intimate with nobody. We had been dining and lunching together, now and then, for two years, yet I only knew the outside of Miss Bruce – the cool, sensible, tidy English outside.

*

Well, we had an appointment on a hot, sunny afternoon, and I arrived to see her about three o'clock. I was met by a very perturbed concierge.

Mademoiselle had been in bed just one day, and, suddenly, last night about eight o'clock the pain had become terrible. The *femme de ménage*, 'Mame' Pichon, who had stayed all day and she, the concierge, had consulted anxiously, had fetched a doctor and, at his recommendation, had had her conveyed to the English Hospital in an ambulance.

'She took nothing with her,' said the *femme de ménage*, a thin and voluble woman. 'Nothing at all, pauvre Mademoiselle.' If Madame – that was me – would give herself the trouble to come up to the studio, here were the keys. I followed Mme. Pichon up the stairs. I must go at once to Miss Bruce and take her some things. She must at least have nightgowns and a comb and brush.

'The keys of the wardrobe of Mademoiselle,' said Mme. Pichon insinuatingly, and with rather a queer sidelong look at me, 'are in this small drawer. Ah, les voila!'

I thanked her with a dismissing manner. Mme. Pichon was not a favourite of mine, and with firmness I watched her walk slowly to the door, try to start a conversation, and then, very reluctantly, disappear. Then I turned to the wardrobe – a big, square, solid piece of old, dark furniture, suited for the square and solid coats and skirts of Miss Bruce. Indeed, most of her furniture was big and square. Some strain in her made her value solidity and worth more than grace or fantasies. It was difficult to turn the large key, but I managed it at last.

'Good Lord!' I remarked out loud. Then, being very much surprised I sat down on a chair and said: 'Well, what a funny girl!'

For Miss Bruce's wardrobe when one opened it was a glow of colour, a riot of soft silks . . . a . . . everything that one did not expect.

In the middle, hanging in the place of honour, was an evening dress of a very beautiful shade of old gold; near it another of flame colour; of two black dresses the one was touched with silver, the other with a jaunty embroidery of emerald and blue; there were – a black and white check with a jaunty belt, a flowered crêpe de chine, positively flowered! – then a carnival costume complete with mask, then a huddle, a positive huddle of all colours, of all stuffs.

For one instant I thought of kleptomania, and dismissed the idea. Dresses for models, then? Absurd! Who would spend thousands of francs on dresses for models . . . No nightgowns here, in any case.

As I looked, hesitating, I saw in the corner a box without a lid. It contained a neat little range of smaller boxes: Rouge Fascination; Rouge Mandarine; Rouge Andalouse; several powders; kohl for the eyelids and paint for the eyelashes – an outfit for a budding Manon Lescaut. Nothing was missing: there were scents too.

I shut the door hastily. I had no business to look or to guess. But I guessed. I knew. Whilst I opened the other half of the wardrobe and searched the shelves for nightgowns I knew it all: Miss Bruce, passing by a shop, with the perpetual hunger to be beautiful and that thirst to be loved which is the real curse of Eve, well hidden under her neat dress, more or less stifled, more or less unrecognized.

Miss Bruce had seen a dress and had suddenly thought: In that dress perhaps . . . And, immediately afterwards: Why not? And had entered the shop, and, blushing slightly, had asked the price. That had been the first time: an accident, an impulse.

The dress must have been disappointing, yet beautiful enough, becoming enough to lure her on. Then must have begun the search for the dress, the perfect Dress, beautiful, beautifying, possible to be worn. And lastly, the search for illusion – a craving, almost a vice, the stolen waters and the bread eaten in secret of Miss Bruce's life.

Wonderful moment! When the new dress would arrive and would emerge smiling and graceful from its tissue paper.

'Wear me, give me life,' it would seem to say to her, 'and I will do my damnedest for you!' And, first, not unskilfully, for was she not a portrait painter? Miss Bruce would put on the powder, the Rouge-Fascination, the rouge for the lips, lastly the dress – and she would gaze into the glass at a transformed self. She would sleep that night with a warm glow at her heart! No impossible thing, beauty and all that beauty brings. There close at hand, to be clutched if one dared. Somehow she never dared, next morning.

I thankfully seized a pile of nightgowns and sat down, rather miserably undecided. I knew she would hate me to have seen those dresses: Mame Pichon would tell her that I had been to the armoire. But she must have her nightgowns. I went to lock the wardrobe doors and felt a sudden, irrational pity for the beautiful things inside. I imagined them, shrugging their silken shoulders, rustling, whispering about the *anglaise* who had dared to buy them in order to condemn them to life in the dark . . . And I opened the door again.

The yellow dress appeared malevolent, slouching on its hanger; the black ones were mournful, only the little chintz frock smiled gaily, waiting for the supple body and limbs that should breathe life into it . . .

When I was allowed to see Miss Bruce a week afterwards I found her lying, clean, calm and sensible in the big ward – an appendicitis patient. They patched her up and two or three weeks later we dined together at our restaurant. At the coffee stage she said suddenly:

'I suppose you noticed my collection of frocks. Why should I not collect frocks? They fascinate me. The colour and all that. Exquisite sometimes!'

'Of course,' she added, carefully staring over my head at what appeared to me to be a very bad picture, 'I should never make such a fool of myself as to wear them . . . They ought to be worn, I suppose.'

A plump, dark girl, near us, gazed into the eyes of her dark, plump escort, and lit a cigarette with the slightly affected movements of the non-smoker.

'Not bad hands and arms, that girl!' said Miss Bruce in her gentlemanly manner.

From *The Left Bank and Other Stories*

JAMES JOYCE
From Ulysses

S AW HIM LOOKING at my frockcoat. Dress does it. Nothing like a dressy appearance. Bowls them over.

—Hello, Simon, Father Cowley said. How are things?

—Hello, Bob, old man, Mr Dedalus answered, stopping.

Mr Kernan halted and preened himself before the sloping mirror of Peter Kennedy, hairdresser. Stylish coat, beyond a doubt. Scott of Dawson street. Well worth the half sovereign I gave Neary for it. Never built under three guineas. Fits me down to the ground. Some Kildare street club toff had it probably. John Mulligan, the manager of the Hibernian bank, gave me a very sharp eye yesterday on Carlisle bridge as if he remembered me.

Aham! Must dress the character for those fellows. Knight of the road. Gentleman. And now, Mr Crimmins, may we have the honour of your custom again, sir. The cup that cheers but not inebriates, as the old saying has it.

GEORGE AND WEEDON GROSSMITH
From The Diary of a Nobody

I was doomed to still further humiliation. I was leaning out of the box, when my tie – a little black bow which fastened on to the stud by means of a new patent – fell into the pit below. A clumsy man not noticing it, had his foot on it for ever so long before he discovered it. He then picked it up and eventually flung it under the next seat in disgust. What with the box incident and the tie, I felt quite miserable. Mr James, of Sutton, was very good. He said: 'Don't worry – no one will notice it with your beard. That is the only advantage of growing one that I can see.' There was no occasion for that remark, for Carrie is very proud of my beard.

To hide the absence of the tie I had to keep my chin down the rest of the evening, which caused a pain at the back of my neck.

She set forth at half-past nine. With extreme care she had preserved an out-of-doors dress into the third summer: it did not look shabby. Her mantle was in its second year only; the original fawn colour had gone to an indeterminate grey. Her hat of brown straw was a possession for ever: it underwent new trimming, at an outlay of a few pence, when that became unavoidable. Yet Virginia could not have been judged anything but a lady. She wore her garments as only a lady can (the position and movement of the arms has much to do with this), and had the step never to be acquired by a person of vulgar instincts.

George Gissing, *The Old Women*

DOROTHY PARKER
The Satin Dress

Needle, needle, dip and dart,
Thrusting up and down.
Where's the man could ease a heart
Like a satin gown?

See the stitches curve and crawl
Round the cunning seams –
Patterns thin and sweet and small
As a lady's dreams.

Wantons go in bright brocade;
Brides in organdie;
Gingham's for the plighted maid;
Satin's for the free!

Wool's to line a miser's chest;
Crape's to calm the old;
Velvet hides an empty breast
Satin's for the bold!

Lawn is for a bishop's yoke;
Linen's for a nun;
Satin is for wiser folk –
Would the dress were done!

Satin glows in candlelight –
Satin's for the proud!
They will say who watch at night,
'What a fine shroud!'

6

Shopping

Things farre-fetched and deare-bought are good for
Ladies.

George Puttenham, *The Arte of English Poesie* (1589)

I had a good deal of employment in choosing patterns for my new clothes. He thought nothing too good; but I thought everything I saw was; and he was so kind to pick out six of the richest, for me to choose three suits, saying we would furnish ourselves with more when in town.

Samuel Richardson, Pamela

'But settling upon new clothes is so trying,' said Lucetta. 'You are that person' (pointing to one of the arrangements), 'or you are that totally different person' (pointing to the other), 'for the whole of the coming spring: and one of the two, you don't know which, may turn out to be very objectionable.'

Thomas Hardy, The Mayor of Caasterbridge

JUNG CHANG
From Wild Swans

ONE DAY MY mother went to the market with Mrs Ting and bought two yards of fine pink flower-patterned cotton from Poland.

She had seen the cotton before, but had not dared to buy it for fear of being criticized for being frivolous.

Soon after she had reached Yibin, she had had to hand in her Army uniform and return to her 'Lenin Suit'. Under that she wore a shapeless, undyed, rough cotton shirt. There was no rule saying it was compulsory to wear this garb, but anyone who did not do the same as everybody else would come in for criticism. My Mother had longed to wear a dash of colour. She and Mrs Ting rushed over to Chang's house with the cloth in a state of high excitement. In no time, four pretty blouses were ready, two for each of them.

Next day they wore them under their Lenin jackets. My Mother turned her pink collar out and spent the whole day feeling terribly excited and nervous. Mrs Ting was even more daring, she not only turned her collar outside her uniform, but rolled up her sleeves so that a broad band of pink showed.

CHARLOTTE BRONTË
From Jane Eyre

THE HOUR SPENT at Millcote was a somewhat harassing one to me. Mr Rochester obliged me to go to a certain silk warehouse: there I was ordered to choose half a dozen dresses. I hated the business, I begged leave to defer it: no – it should be gone through with now. By dint of entreaties expressed in energetic whispers, I reduced the half-dozen to two: these, however, he vowed he would select himself. With anxiety I watched his eye rove over the gay stores: he fixed on a rich silk of the most brilliant amethyst dye, and a superb pink satin. I told him in a new series of whispers, that he might as well buy me a gold gown and a silver bonnet at once: I should certainly never venture to wear his choice. With infinite difficulty, for he was stubborn as a stone, I persuaded him to make an exchange in favour of a sober black satin and pearl-grey silk. 'It might pass for the present,' he said; 'but he would yet see me glittering like a parterre.'

Glad was I to get him out of the silk warehouse, and then out of a jeweller's shop: the more he bought me, the more my cheek burned with a sense of annoyance and degradation. As we re-entered the carriage, and I sat back feverish and fagged, I remembered what in the hurry of events, dark and bright, I had wholly forgotten – the letter of my uncle, John Eyre, to Mrs Reed: his intention to adopt me and make me his legatee. 'It would, indeed, be a relief,' I thought, 'if I had ever so small an independency; I never can bear being dressed like a doll by Mr Rochester, or sitting like a second Danae with the golden shower falling daily round me. I will write to Madeira the moment I get home, and tell my uncle John I am going to be married, and to whom: if I had but a prospect of one day bringing Mr Rochester an accession of fortune, I could better endure to be kept by him now.' And somewhat relieved by this idea (which I failed not to execute that day), I ventured once more to meet my master's and lover's eye; which most pertinaciously sought mine, though I averted both face and gaze. He smiled; and I thought his smile was such as a sultan might, in a blissful and fond moment, bestow on a slave his gold and gems had enriched: I crushed his hand, which was ever hunting mine, vigorously, and thrust it back to him red with the passionate pressure —

'You need not look in that way,' I said: 'if you do, I'll wear nothing but my old Lowood frocks to the end of the chapter. I'll be married in this lilac gingham – you may make a dressing-gown for yourself out of the pearl-grey silk, and an infinite series of waistcoats out of the black satin.'

He chuckled; he rubbed his hands: 'Oh, it is rich to see and hear her!' he exclaimed. 'Is she original? Is she piquant? I would not exchange this one little English girl for the grand Turk's whole seraglio; gazelle-eyes, houri forms, and all!'

The eastern allusion bit me again: 'I'll not stand you an inch in the stead of a seraglio,' I said, 'so don't consider me an equivalent for one; if you have a fancy for anything in that line, away with you, sir, to the bazaars of Stamboul without delay; and lay out in extensive slave-purchases some of that spare cash you seem at a loss to spend satisfactorily here.'

'And what will you do, Janet, while I am bargaining for so many tons of flesh and such an assortment of black eyes?'

'I'll be preparing myself to go out as a missionary to preach liberty to them that are enslaved – your harem inmates among the rest. I'll get admitted there, and I'll stir up mutiny; and you, three-tailed bashaw as you are, sir, shall in a trice find yourself fettered among our hands: nor will I, for one, consent to cut your bonds till you have signed a charter, the most liberal that despot ever yet conferred.'

There are two things which tend to make the ordinary run of Englishwomen dress ill: first that they are never led to seek the relations, the *rapports*, between their outward garb and themselves; and secondly that they are totally devoid of the sense of management. An Englishwoman sets about buying a dress for herself as though she was buying it for somebody else. Dress is, with her, an abstraction.

Mme de Girardin, in a letter (1837)

Shrewsbury tradesman's bill to William Morris, Esq. July 1594: 'with my humble commendations, being glad to hear of your worship's helth but very sorry for the deth of that sweet youth Ellis Morris but we are to praise the Lord for all his works. Sir, your Cosynges gown with petikote and stomacher is redy. I hope you will like very well of them, for the other gownes your measures were so ill taken that the taylor says he cannot tell what to make of them.'

Shropshire Archeological Transcriptions

We saw a west-end tailor's bill the other day in which a plain black coat was made to figure as: 'a superfine black cloth coat, lappels sewn on, cloth collar, cotton sleeve linings, velvet hand-facings, embossed edges and fine wove buttons'. How much? Five pounds, eighteen and sixpence! An article that our own excellent tailor supplies for three pounds fifteen! In a tailor's case a party swore they are to be had for less than four.

R. S. Surtees, *Ask Mama*

The Weaver's Complaint against the Calico Madams

> Every jilt of the town
> Gets a callico gown;
> Our own manufacks out of fashion
> No country of wool was ever so dull:
> Tis a test of the brain of the nation
> To neglect their own works
> Employ pagans and Turks,
> And let foreign trumpery o'er spread 'em.

(Anon, 1719)

MRS GASKELL
From Cranford

I WAS VERY GLAD to accept the invitation from my dear Miss Matty, independently of the conjuror, and most particularly anxious to prevent her from disfiguring her small gentle mousey face with a great Saracen's head turban; and accordingly, I bought her a pretty, neat, middle-aged cap, which, however, was rather a disappointment to her when, on my arrival, she followed me into my bedroom, ostensibly to poke the fire, but in reality, I do believe, to see if the sea-green turban was not inside the cap-box with which I had travelled. It was in vain that I twirled the cap round on my hand to exhibit back and side fronts: her heart had been set upon a turban, and all she could do was to say, with resignation in her look and voice:

'I am sure you did your best, my dear. It is just like the caps all the ladies in Cranford are wearing, and they have had theirs for a year, I dare say. I should have liked something newer, I confess – something more like the turbans Miss Betty Barker tells me Queen Adelaide wears; but it is very pretty, my dear. And

I dare say levender will wear better than sea-green. Well, after all, what is dress, that we should care about it! You'll tell me if you want anything, my dear. Here is the bell. I suppose turbans have not got down to Drumble yet?'

NANCY MITFORD
From Love in a Cold Climate

THE CONVERSATION NOW turned upon the subject of my trousseau, about which Lady Montdore was quite as bossy though less embarrassing. I was not feeling much interest in clothes at that time, all my thoughts being of how to decorate and furnish a charming little old house which Alfred had taken me to see after placing the pigeon's egg on my finger, and which, by a miracle of good luck, was to be let.

'The important thing, dear,' she said, 'is to have a really good fur coat, I mean a proper, dark one.' To Lady Montdore, fur meant mink; she could imagine no other kind except sable, but that would be specified. 'Not only will it make all the rest of your clothes look better than they are but you really needn't bother much about anything else as you need never take it off. Above all, don't go wasting money on underclothes, there is nothing stupider – I always borrow Montdore's myself. Now for evening a diamond brooch is a great help, so long as it has good big stones. Oh, dear, when I think of the diamonds your father gave that woman, it really is too bad. All the same, he can't have got through everything, he was enormously rich when he succeeded, I must write to him. Now, dear, we're going to be very practical. No time like the present.'

Caroline and I went a shopping yesterday, and 'tis a fact that the little white satin quaker bonnets, cap-crowns, are the most fashionable that are worn – lined with pink or blue or white; but I'll not have one, for if any of my old acquaintance should meet me in the street they would laugh, I would if I were them. I mean to send sister Boyd a quaker cap, the first tasty one I see; Caroline's are too plain, but she has promised to get me a more fashionable pattern.

Letter from Elizabeth Southgate Bowne to her sisters in Maine, 1803

PIERRE ERONDELLE
From The French Garden

GOE FETCH MY cloathes: bring my petty-coate bodyes: I meane my damask quilt bodyes with whale bones. What lace doe you give me heere? this lace is too shorte, the tagges are broken, I cannot lace my selfe with it, take it away, I will have that of greene silke: when shall I have my under coate? give me my peti-coate of wrought crimson velvet with a silver fringe ... Give me my whood, for me thinketh it is some-what colde ... Set up my French whood and my Border of Rubies, give me another head attyre; take the key of my closet and goe fetch my long boxe where I set mine Jewels that I used to weare on my head, what is become of my wyer: where is the haire cap, have you any ribans to make knots? where be the laces for to binde my haires? ... Call my Taylor to bring my gowne, not the close one but my open gowne of white Sattin layd on with buttons of Pearle. Shall I not have no vardingale ... You doe playe the foole, doe you not see that I want my buske? what is become of the buske-point ... Let me see that ruffe. How is it that the supporter is so soyled? I knowe not for what you are fit, that you cannot so much as to keep my cloathes cleane, take it away: give me my Rebato of cut-worke edged, is not the wyer after the same sorte as the other? ... Is there no small pinnes for my Cuffes? Looke in the pinne-cushion. Pinne that with a blacke pinne; give me my girdle and see that all the furniture be at it ... Have I a cleane handkercher? I will have no Muffe for it is not colde, but shall I have no gloves? Bring my maske and my fanne. Help me to put on my Chayne of Pearles.

MERCER: Of which would you Madame? plaine Velvet, Rased velvet, pinkt, unwrought velvet, or tufte-taffata, and of what colour would you have?

LADY: I would see some of blacke, of white, of gray, of ash colour, of greene, of red, of yellowe, of crimson, of purple, of tawny, of blewe, of celestial colour, migrene colour, russet colour, Peache colour, strawe colour.

MERCER: Have you no need of any cloath of gold or silver?

LADY: Yes I must have some. What shall I pay you for your cloath of golde, doe not holde it too deere, and I will take some tenne yardes of it.

MERCER: You shall pay foure pounds a yarde.

LADY: It is too much, you are too deere, I will give you fiftie shillings for it.

MERCER: I cannot sell it at that price, it cost me more than you offer me. Take it for three pounds and tenne shillings, and you may say that you have not ill bestowed your money.

(1605)

FANNY BURNEY
From Evelina

M ONDAY.

We are to go this evening to a private ball, given by Mrs Stanley, a very fashionable lady of Mrs Mirvan's acquaintance.

We have been *a shopping*, as Mrs Mirvan calls it, all this morning, to buy silks, caps, gauzes, and so forth.

The shops are really very entertaining, especially the mercers: there seem to be six or seven men belonging to each shop and every one took care, by bowing and smirking, to be noticed; we were conducted from one to another, and carried from room to room, with so much ceremony, that at first I was almost afraid to go on.

I thought I should never have chosen a silk, for they produced so many. I knew not which to fix upon, and they recommended them all so strongly, that I fancy they thought I only wanted persuasion to buy everything they shewed me. And, indeed, they took so much trouble, that I was almost ashamed I could not.

At the milliners, the ladies we met were so much dressed, that I should rather have imagined they were making visits than purchases. But what most diverted (me) was, that we were more frequently served by men than by women; and such men! so finical, so affected! they seemed to understand every part of a woman's dress better than we do ourselves; and they recommended caps and ribbands with an air of so much importance, that I wished to ask them how long they had left off wearing them.

MRS GASKELL
From Cranford

W E BEGAN TO talk of Miss Matty's new silk gown. I discovered that it would be really the first time in her life that she had to choose anything of consequence for herself: for Miss Jenkyns had always been the more decided character, whatever her taste might have been; and it is astonishing how such people carry the world before them by the mere force of will. Miss Matty anticipated the sight of the glossy folds with as much delight as if the five sovereigns, set apart for the purchase, could buy all the silks in the shop; and (remembering my own loss of two hours in a toy-shop before I could tell on what wonder to spend a silver threepence) I was very glad that we were going early, that dear Miss Matty might have leisure for the delights of perplexity.

If a happy sea-green could be met with, the gown was to be sea-green: if not, she inclined to maize, and I to silver grey; and we discussed the requisite number of breadths until we arrived at the shop-door. We were to buy the tea, select the silk, and then clamber up the iron corkscrew stairs that led into what was once a loft, though now a fashion show-room.

The young men at Mr Johnson's had on their best looks, and their best cravats, and pivoted themselves over the counter with surprising activity. They wanted to show us upstairs at once; but on the principle of business first and pleasure afterwards, we stayed to purchase the tea. Here Miss Matty's absence of mind betrayed itself. If she was made aware that she had been drinking green tea at any time, she always thought it her duty to lie awake half through the night afterward – (I have known her to take it in ignorance many a time without such effects) – and consequently green tea was prohibited the house; yet to-day she herself asked for the obnoxious article, under the impression that she was talking about the silk. However, the mistake was soon rectified; and then the silks were unrolled in good truth. By this time the shop was pretty well filled, for it was Cranford market-day, and many of the farmers and country people from the neighbourhood round came in, sleeking down their hair, and glancing shyly about from under their eyelids, as anxious to take back some notion of the unusual gaiety to the mistress or the lasses at home, and yet feeling that they were out of place among the smart shopmen and gay shawls and summer prints. One honest-looking man, however, made his way up to the counter at which we stood, and boldly asked to look at a shawl or two. The other country folk confined themselves to the grocery side; but our neighbour was evidently too full of some kind of intention towards mistress, wife, or daughter, to be shy; and it soon became a question with me, whether he or Miss Matty would keep their shopman the longest time. He thought each shawl more beautiful than the last; and, as for Miss Matty, she smiled and sighed over each fresh bale that was brought out; one colour set off another, and the heap together would, as she said, make even the rainbow look poor.

'I am afraid,' said she, hesitating, 'whichever I choose I shall wish I had taken another. Look at this lovely crimson! it would be so warm in winter. But spring is coming on, you know. I wish I could have a gown for every occasion,' said she, dropping her voice – as we all did in Cranford whenever we talked of anything we wished for but could not afford. 'However,' she continued, in a louder and more cheerful tone, 'it would give me a great deal of trouble to take care of them if I had them; so, I think I'll only take one. But which must it be, my dear?'

LAURENCE STERNE

From A Sentimental Journey

PARIS.

HAIL YE SMALL sweet courtesies of life, for smooth do ye make the road of it! like grace and beauty which beget inclinations to love at first sight; 'tis ye who open this door and let the stranger in.

—Pray, Madame, said I, have the goodness to tell me which way I must turn to go to the Opera comique: — Most willingly, Monsieur, said she, laying aside her work —

I had given a cast with my eye into half a dozen shops as I came along in search of a face not likely to be disordered by such an interruption; till, at last, this hitting my fancy, I had walked in.

She was working a pair of ruffles as she sat in a low chair on the far side of the shop facing the door —

— *Tres volontiers*; most willingly, said she, laying her work down upon a chair next her, and rising up from the low chair she was sitting in, with so chearful a movement and chearful a look, that had I been laying out fifty louis d'ors with her, I should have said — 'This woman is "grateful".'

You must turn, Monsieur, said she, going with me to the door of the shop, and pointing the way down the street I was to take — you must turn first to your left hand — *mais prenez guarde* — there are two turns; and be so good as to take the second — then go down a little way and you'll see a church, and when you are past it, give yourself the trouble to turn directly to the right, and that will lead you to the foot of the *pont neuf*, which you must cross — and there, any one will do himself the pleasure to shew you — . . .

I will not suppose it was the woman's beauty, notwithstanding she was the handsomest grisset, I think, I ever saw, which had much to do with the sense I had of her courtesy; only I remember, when I told her how much I was obliged to her, that I looked very full in her eyes, — and that I repeated my thanks as often as she had done her instructions.

I had not got ten paces from the door, before I found I had forgot every tittle of what she had said — so looking back, and seeing her still standing in the door of the shop as if to look whether I went right or not — I returned back, to ask her whether the first turn was to my right or left — for that I had absolutely forgot — Is it possible! said she, half laughing — 'Tis very possible, replied I, when a man is thinking more of a woman, than of her good advice.

As this was the real truth — she took it, as every woman takes a matter of right, with a slight courtesy.

—*Attendez!* said she, laying her hand upon my arm to detain me, whilst she called a lad out of the back-shop to get ready a parcel of gloves. I am just going to send him, said she, with a packet into that quarter, and if you will have the complaisance to step in, it will be ready in a moment, and he shall attend you to the place.—So I walk'd in with her to the far side of the shop, and taking up the ruffle in my hand which she laid upon the chair, as if I had a mind to sit, she sat down herself in her low chair, and I instantly sat myself down besides her . . .

I had counted twenty pulsations, and was going on fast towards the fortieth, when her husband coming unexpected from a back parlour into the shop, put me a little out in my reckoning.— 'Twas no body but her husband, she said – so I began a fresh score—Monsieur is so good, quoth she, as he pass'd by us, as to give himself the trouble of feeling my pulse—The husband took off his hat, and making me a bow, said, I did him too much honour—and having said that, he put on his hat and walk'd out.

In London a shopkeeper and a shopkeeper's wife seem to be one bone and one flesh: in the several endowments of mind and body, sometimes the one, sometimes the other has it, so as in general to be upon a par, and to tally with each other as nearly as man and wife need to do.

In Paris, there are scarce two orders of beings more different: for the legislative and executive powers of the shop not resting in the husband, he seldom comes there—in some dark and dismal room behind, he sits commerceless in his thrum night-cap, the same rough son of Nature that Nature left him . . .

The beautiful Grisset rose up when I said this, and going behind the counter, reach'd down a parcel and untied it: I advanced to the side over-against her: they were all too large. The beautiful Grisset measured them one by one across my hand—It would not alter the dimensions—She begg'd I would try a single pair, which seemed to be the least—She held it open—my hand slipped into it at once—It will not do, said I, shaking my head a little—No, said she, doing the same thing.

There are certain combined looks of simple subtlety—where whim, and sense, and seriousness, and nonsense, are so blended, that all the languages of Babel set loose together could not express them—they are communicated and caught so instantaneously, that you can scarce say which party is the infecter. I leave it to your men of words to swell pages about it—it is enough in the present to say again, the gloves would not do; so folding our hands within our arms, we both loll'd upon the counter—it was narrow, and there was just room for the parcel to lay between us.

The beautiful Grisset look'd sometimes at the gloves, then side-ways to the window, then at the gloves— and then at me. I was not disposed to break silence—I follow'd her example: so I look'd at the gloves, then to the window, then at the gloves, and then at her—and so on alternately.

I found I lost considerably in every attack—she had a quick black eye, and shot through two such long and silken eye-lashes with such penetration, that she look'd into my very heart and veins—It may seem strange, but I could actually feel she did—

—It is no matter, said I, taking up a couple of the pairs next me, and putting them into my pocket.

I was sensible the beautiful Grisset had not ask'd a single livre above the price—I wish'd she had ask'd a livre more, and was puzzling my brains how to bring the matter about—Do you think, my dear Sir, said she, mistaking my embarrassment, that I could ask a sous too much of a stranger – and of a stranger whose politeness, more than his want of gloves, has done me the honour to lay himself at my mercy?—*M'en croyer capable?*—Faith! not I, said I; and if you were, you are welcome—So counting the money into her hand, and with a lower bow than one generally makes to a shopkeeper's wife, I went out, and her lad with his parcel followed me.

ENID BAGNOLD

From Autobiography

SARAH BERNHARDT WAS coming to London. Frank Harris was to give her a great luncheon at the Savoy. (I found later he was only a guest.) He arranged, he promised, that I should go too. I was wild with excitement. But how should I be dressed? I had what I knew was a smart coat and skirt, black, pin-striped, like a businessman's, and so daringly short that it showed my ankles. White silk stockings and patent shoes with a big buckle. But what about a hat?

On the day of the luncheon, in Bond Street near Cartier's, I saw a white hat in a window, with a big gull's feather. I went in. It cost three or four guineas. I had five shillings on me and a pound in the bank.

I pointed out the urgency, the immediacy, the total necessity – and the steady seventy-five pounds which, though not there at the moment . . . I pointed out my father's name in the telephone book.

'But how am I to know that you're his daughter?' I still wore my school vest. By wriggling and dragging, the sales lady could see the Cash's name-tape sewn at the back of my neck. I went out with the hat.

To see the Parisienne choosing hats is a lesson. An appointment is made. A table with triple mirror is reserved . . . a saleswoman . . . arrives with a satellite who carries a basket of models. One after the other is tried on and borne away. Five, six or seven are chosen. For the Parisienne orders for the season when she has chosen her frocks, and comes in for one or two more when a special occasion arises.

Winifred Boulter, *Night and Day*

PAUL SCOTT
From Staying On

'I HAD NO LUNCH that day, because after I'd put the phone down I remembered he'd said stalls and in those days one dressed for stalls and dress circle, or did if one cared about doing things properly, and I though that if Captain Smalley had misjudged me and turned up in day clothes I could always change back in five minutes but at least he'd know he needn't worry about inviting me out again to a place where it would embarrass him *not* to be dressed.

'So I spent the whole lunch hour in Oxford Street. I almost broke the bank. Not on a dress. I had a long dress, a black chiffon. And I had a stole. Rabbit, dyed as black as sable. It was my only evening rig. I'd brought it up from home in the Spring of that year when I felt myself coming out of my shell and anticipated a need to have it by me in town. And here was the need. What I broke the bank on was a pair of good shoes and a pair of good gloves. Black shoes and black gloves. Oh, I paid the earth. But one had to on things like that.

'And then I bought a bag. How well I remember the bag. An evening bag. Dark green moiré silk, and a chiffon handkerchief to match. Just this one statement of colour, Mr Turner. I have always had to be careful about colour. My eyes never seem to have quite made up their minds about being grey, blue, green or violet. In those days the faint green tinge could be picked up by a green accessory. Later, by wearing deep red. Then the green faded from my eyes forever. But this is woman's talk. It couldn't interest you.

'The black stole, the black chiffon dress, the shoes and gloves, and then the bag. A lovely July evening. I was going to the ball, Mr Turner, and the coach called promptly.

'And he was dressed.'

E. M. DELAFIELD

From The Diary of a Provincial Lady

March 18th:

TRY ON FIVE dresses, but find judgement of their merits very difficult, as hair gets wilder and wilder, and nose more devoid of powder. Am also worried by extraordinary and tactless tendency of saleswoman to emphasize the fact that all the colours I like are very trying by daylight, but will be less so at night. Finally settle on silver tissue with large bow, stipulate for its immediate delivery, am told that this is impossible, reluctantly agree to carry it away with me in cardboard box, and go away wondering if it wouldn't have been better to choose the black chiffon instead.

Hope that Beauty Parlour experiment may enhance self-respect, at present at rather low ebb, but am cheered by going into Fuller's and sending boxes of chocolates to Robin and Vicky respectively. Add peppermint creams for Mademoiselle by an afterthought, as otherwise she may find herself *blessée*. Lunch on oxtail soup, lobster mayonnaise, and cup of coffee, as being menu furthest removed from that obtainable at home.

Beauty Parlour follows. Feel that a good deal could be written on this experience, and even contemplate – in connection with recent observations exchanged between Barbara B. and myself – brightening the pages of our Parish Magazine with result of my reflections, but on second thoughts abandon this, as unlikely to appeal to the Editor (Our Vicar).

Am received by utterly terrifying person with dazzling complexion, indigo-blue hair, and orange nails, presiding over reception room downstairs, but eventually passed on to extremely pretty little creature with auburn bob and charming smile. Am reassured. Am taken to discreet curtained cubicle and put into long chair. Subsequent operations, which take hours and hours, appear to consist of the removal of hundreds of layers of dirt from my face. (These discreetly explained away by charming operator as the result of 'acidity'.) She also plucks away portions of my eyebrows. Very, very painful operation.

Eventually emerge more or less unrecognizable, and greatly improved. Lose my head, and buy Foundation Cream, rouge, powder, lipstick. Foresee grave difficulty in reconciling Robert to the use of these appliances, but decide not to think about this for the present.

GRACE NICHOLS

The Fat Black Woman Goes Shopping

Shopping in London winter
is a real drag for the fat black woman
going from store to store
in search of accommodating clothes
and de weather so cold

Look at the frozen thin mannequins
fixing her with grin
and de pretty face salesgals
exchanging slimming glances
thinking she don't notice

Lord is aggravating

Nothing soft and bright and billowing
to flow like breezy sunlight
when she walking

The fat black woman curses in Swahili/Yoruba
and nation language under her breathing
all this journeying and journeying

The fat black woman could only conclude
that when it come to fashion
the choice is lean

     Nothing much beyond size 14

Inexpensive Small Ladies

'GOING UP' SAID the lift-girl.
  'Cheap frocks, please,' I murmured.
 'Inexpensive Gowns?' said the lift-girl. 'First floor.'
 She was about to slam the gates when a little tired woman in brown appeared
outside, her hands festooned with parcels, and squeezed into the lift.

'Day-dresses,' she panted. 'Not too dear.'

'Inexpensive Gowns?' said the lift-girl. 'First floor.'

Together, but ignoring each other's proximity, I and the little brown woman made our way to the Inexpensive Gowns, and handed ourselves over to the ministrations of two black angels. I call them angels not because they had angelic faces, but because they moved with a slow floating movement through space, wore flowing draperies and were so flat-chested as to be apparently sexless.

With my angel hovering at my side I picked out three frocks from the rail marked 39/11 and a couple more from the one marked 63/-.

'I'd like to try on these ones, please.' The angel's plucked eyebrows arched themselves in surprise and she measured me coolly from her own five-feet-ten.

'You didn't want them for yourself, did you, Modom? I'm afraid these are all far too large. Modom takes an SSW surely?'

'SW,' I corrected her. 'Not *SS*. Will you show me some smaller ones, then?'

'We've nothing less than W in this department,' said the sylph. 'Modom should try the Small Ladies, on the second floor.'

'Oh, I see. I'm so sorry to have troubled you.'

The angel gave a pardoning inclination of the head and wafted the dresses back on to their rails again.

While I was waiting for the lift the little brown woman appeared at my side, looking a shade more tired than before. We glanced tentatively at each other, then rapidly averted our gaze as though afraid that in another moment we might break into conversation.

'Going up?' said the lift-girl. The little brown woman made a dash for the gate. So did I. We collided and smiled apologetically. The ice was cracking.

'Small Ladies, please,' we said with one voice. The smiles changed to rueful grins and the ice trickled away down the lift-shaft unobserved.

Over the Small Ladies' Department hung an air of miniature elegance. Neither the dummy figures nor the attendant angels were taller than five-feet-four. Everything was neat and *petite* and exquisite. Involuntarily I drew myself up; my self-respect returned, my vanity reasserted itself. We were not neglected, after all, we small ones; indeed, all the prettiest things seemed to have been reserved for us – or was it merely that on our fairy-like figures everything looked much nicer?

I picked out a ravishing frock and inquired the price.

'Fourteen-and-a-half guineas,' replied the miniature angel.

I tried not to look as though I had picked up a hot brick, but only as though the frock on closer inspection had ceased to please me. Thereafter I resolved to glance surreptitiously at the tickets before allowing myself to become attracted. But nowhere in the whole case did the figures sink below the forbidding level of

'Seven-seventeen-six.' There was nothing for it but to confess to the angel.

'As a matter of fact I wanted something a good deal cheaper,' I explained apologetically.

'What sort of price did Modom wish to pay?'

'Oh, about four guineas,' I lied. What I wanted to pay, of course, was thirty-nine-and-eleven-pence; but there are some questions that no one even attempts to answer truthfully.

'I'm sorry,' said the angelette, 'but our lowest price here is seven-and-a-half. Modom wanted the Inexpensive Gowns on the first floor.'

'But they're all too *big*,' I protested. 'The department I want is the Inexpensive Small Ladies.'

'I'm sorry,' said the angel again, 'but I'm afraid there's no such thing.' She smiled with gentle finality and turned to another customer.

The little brown woman was already waiting forlornly for the lift.

'Can you explain it?' I asked, dispensing with preliminaries.

She shook her head.

'No. Small women are always rich, that's all. With one exception.'

'Two,' I said bitterly.

After repeating the experiment with the same result at nine other shops, I reached home exhausted.

'Hullo, little woman!' said Jack . . .

Punch (1920s)

MARTIN ARMSTRONG

From Miss Thompson Goes Shopping

In her lone cottage on the downs,
With winds and blizzards and great crowns
Of shining cloud, with wheeling plover
And short grass sweet with the small white clover,
Miss Thompson lived, correct and meek,
A lonely spinster, and every week
On market-day she used to go
Into the little town below,
Tucked in the great downs' hollow bowl,
Like pebbles gathered in a shoal . . .

[SHE VISITS THE BOOTMAKER]
Serenely down the busy stream
Miss Thompson floated in a dream.
Now, hovering bee-like, she would stop
Entranced before some tempting shop,
Getting in people's way and prying
At things she never thought of buying:
Now wafted on without an aim:
Until in course of time she came
To Watson's bootshop. Long she pries
At boots and shoes of every size,
Brown football-boots with bar and stud
For boys that scuffle in the mud,
And dancing-pumps with pointed toes
Glassy as jet, and dull black bows;
Slim ladies' shoes with two-inch heel
And sprinkled beads of gold and steel –
'How anyone can wear such things!'
On either side the doorway springs
(As in a tropic jungle loom
Masses of strange thick-petalled bloom
And fruits misshapen) fold on fold
A growth of sandshoes rubber-soled,
Clambering the doorposts, branching, spawning,
Their barbarous bunches like an awning
Over the windows and the doors.

[IS TEMPTED]
But, framed among the other stores,
Something has caught Miss Thompson's eye
(O worldliness! O vanity!),
A pair of slippers – scarlet plush.
Miss Thompson feels a conscious blush
Suffuse her face, as though her thought
Had ventured further than it ought.
But O that colour's rapturous singing
And the answer in her lone heart ringing!
She turns (O Guardian Angels stop her
From doing anything improper!).
She turns; and see, she stoops and bungles

In through the sandshoes' hanging jungles,
Away from light and common sense,
Into the shop dim-lit and dense
With smells of polish and tanned hide.

[MRS. WATSON]
Soon from a dark recess inside
Fat Mrs Watson comes slip-slop
To mind the business of the shop.
She walks flat-footed with a roll –
A serviceable, homely soul,
With kindly, ugly face like dough,
Hair dull and colourless as tow.
A huge Scotch-pebble fills the space
Between her bosom and her face.
One sees her making beds all day.
Miss Thompson lets her say her say
'So chilly for the time of year.
It's ages since we saw you here.'
Then, heart a-flutter, speech precise,
Describes the shoes and asks the price.
'Them, Miss? Ah, them is six-and-nine.'

[WRESTLES WITH A TEMPTATION]
Miss Thompson shudders down the spine
(Dream of impossible romance).
She eyes them with a wistful glance,
Torn between good and evil. Yes,
For half-a-minute and no less
Miss Thompson strives with seven devils,
Then, soaring over earthly levels,
Turns from the shoes with lingering touch –

[AND IS SAVED]
'Ah, six-and-nine is far too much.
Sorry to trouble you. Goodday!'

[SHE VISITS THE FISHMONGER]
A little further down the way
Stands Miles's fish-shop, whence is shed

So strong a smell of fishes dead
That people of a subtler sense
Hold their breath and hurry thence.
Miss Thompson hovers there and gazes:
Her housewife's knowing eye appraises
Salt and fresh, severely cons
Kippers bright as tarnished bronze . . .
Awhile she paused in timid thought,
Then promptly hurried in and bought
'Two kippers, please. Yes, lovely weather.'
'Two kippers? Sixpence altogether:'
And in her basket laid the pair
Wrapped face to face in newspaper.

[RELAPSES INTO TEMPTATION]
Then on she went, as one half blind,
For things were stirring in her mind:
Then turned about with fixed intent
And, heading for the bootshop, went

[AND FALLS]
Straight in and bought the scarlet slippers,
And popped them in beside the kippers.

ANON

From 'Nothing To Wear, an Episode of City Life'

Miss Flora M'Flimsey, of Madison Square,
Has made three separate journeys to Paris,
And her father assures me, each time she was there,
That she and her friend Mrs Harris
(Not the lady whose name is so famous in history,
But plain Mrs H., without romance or mystery)
Spent six consecutive weeks without stopping,
In one continuous round of shopping;
Shopping alone, and shopping together,
At all hours of the day, and in all sorts of weather;
For all manner of things that a woman can put

On the crown of her head or the sole of her foot,
Or wrap round her shoulders, or fit round her waist,
Or that can be sewed on, or pinned on, or laced,
Or tied on with a string, or stitched on with a bow,
In front or behind, above or below:
For bonnets, mantillas, capes, collars, and shawls;
Dresses for breakfasts, and dinners, and balls;
Dresses to sit in, and stand in, and walk in;
Dresses to dance in, and flirt in, and talk in;
Dresses in which to do nothing at all;
Dresses for winter, spring, summer, and fall;
All of them different in color and pattern,
Silk, muslin, and lace, crape, velvet, and satin,
Brocade, and broadcloth, and other material,
Quite as expensive and much more ethereal;
In short, for all things that could ever be thought of,
Or milliner, modiste, or tradesman be bought of,
From ten-thousand-francs robes to twenty-sous frills;
In all quarters of Paris, and to every store,
While M'Flimsey in vain stormed, scolded, and swore,
They footed the streets, and he footed the bills.

ARNOLD BENNETT
From The Old Wives' Tale

SOPHIA, ON ARRIVING in Paris with the ring on her triumphant finger, had timidly mentioned the subject of frocks. None would have guessed from her tone that she was possessed by the desire for French clothes as by a devil. She had been surprised and delighted by the eagerness of Gerald's response. Gerald, too, was possessed by a devil. He thirsted to see her in French clothes. He knew some of the shops and ateliers in the Rue de la Paix, the Rue de la Chaussée d'Antin, and the Palais Royal. He was much more skilled in the lore of frocks than she, for his previous business in Paris had brought him into relations with the great firms; and Sophia suffered a brief humiliation in the discovery that his private opinion of her dresses was that they were not dresses at all. She had been aware that they were not Parisian, nor even of London; but she had thought them pretty good. It healed her wound, however, to reflect that Gerald had so marvellously kept his own counsel in order to spare her self-love. Gerald had taken her to an establishment in the Chaussée d'Antin. It was not one of what Gerald called *les grandes maisons*, but it was on the very fringe of them, and the real *haute couture* was practised therein; and Gerald was remembered there by name.

Sophia had gone in trembling and ashamed, yet in her heart courageously determined to emerge uncompromisingly French. But the models frightened her. They surpassed even the most fantastic things that she had seen in the streets. She recoiled before them and seemed to hide for refuge in Gerald, as it were appealing to him for moral protection, and answering to him instead of to the saleswoman when the saleswoman offered remarks in stiff English. The prices also frightened her. The simplest trifle here cost sixteen pounds; and her mother's historic 'silk', whose elaborateness had cost twelve pounds, was supposed to have approached the inexpressible! Gerald said that she was not to think about prices. She was, however, forced by some instinct to think about prices – she who at home had scorned the narrowness of life in the Square. In the Square she was understood to be quite without commonsense, hopelessly imprudent; yet here, a spring of sagacity seemed to be welling up in her all the time, a continual anti-dote against the general madness in which she found herself. With extraordinary rapidity she had formed a habit of preaching moderation to Gerald. She hated to 'see money thrown away', and her notion of the boundary line between throw-ing money away and judiciously spending it was still the notion of the Square.

Gerald would laugh. But she would say, piqued and blushing, but self-sure: 'You can laugh!' It was all delicious agreeable.

JENNIFER WAYNE

From The Purple Dress

MY MOTHER TOOK great delight in going to little 'gown shops' in Soho, and bargaining. I came to know Soho quite well, in that pre-Oxford summer. Every gown shop had its full-blown Jewess beaming in the doorway between the small plate-glass windows; but my mother was comically impervious to bland-ishments. She would stump in, make her way down to whatever tatty basement was indicated as the secret source of glamorous snips saved specially for us – and plod through the racks with Anglo-Saxon determination. The Jewesses would coo and cajole; I would stand mute in the background. My mother invariably hooked out 'costumes' which I, left to myself, wouldn't have looked at twice – but which turned out to be both cheap and presentable. I should probably have been persuaded into mauve, pink or totally impracticable white garments at twice the price. Reluctantly I had to admire my mother's implacable good taste, and one had to grin at the way the Jewesses changed their tactics mid-gesture and gave in. They would even compliment her on her rejection of their first offers.

'Ah, I see Modom knows what's *good.*' A nod, and a winning smile. My mother went on looking through the rack.

'Modom has certainly chosen a Quality garment there. Now, that costume is really what I would call Classic. To be honest with you, Modom, not all our customers appreciate Classic Quality. But I could tell, as soon as you came in . . .'

My mother was unmoved, and simply waited to see if the garment fitted me, and whether they would reduce it from £4 to three.

ELIZABETH WETHERELL

From Daisy

'I SUPPOSE THE DRESS is the first thing, Daisy,' he said as we entered the great establishment where everything was to be had; and he inquired for the counter where we should find merinoes. I had no objection ready.

'What colour, Daisy?'

'I want something quiet,' I said.

'Something dark,' said the doctor, seating himself. 'And fine quality. Not green, Daisy, if I might advise. It is too cold.'

'Cold!' said I.

'For this season. It is a very nice colour in summer, Daisy,' he said, smiling.

And he looked on in a kind of amused way, while the clerk of the merinoes and I confronted each other. There was displayed now before me a piece of claret-coloured stuff, dark and bright; a lovely tint and a very beautiful piece of goods. I knew enough of the matter to know that. Fine and thick and lustrous, it just suited my fancy; I knew it was just what my mother would buy; I saw Dr Sandford's eye watch me in its amusement with a glance of expectation. But the stuff was two dollars and a quarter a yard. Yes, it suited me exactly; but what was to become of others if I were covered so luxuriously? And how could I save money if I spent it? It was hard to speak, too, before that shopman, who held the merino in his hand, expecting me to say I would take it; but I had no way to escape that trouble. I turned from the rich folds of claret stuff to the doctor at my side.

'Dr Sandford,' I said, 'I want to get something that will not cost so much.'

'Does it not please you?' he asked.

'Yes; I like it: but I want some stuff that will not cost so much.'

'This is not far above my sister's estimate, Daisy.'

'No –' I said.

'And the difference is a trifle – if you like the piece.'

'I like it,' I said; 'but it is very much above my estimate.'

'You had one of your own!' said the doctor. 'Do you like something else here better? – or what is your estimate, Daisy?'

'I do not want a poor merino,' I said. 'I would rather get some other stuff – if I can. I do not want to give more than a dollar.'

'The young lady may find what will suit her at the plaid counter,' said the shopman, letting fall the rich drapery he had been holding up. 'Just round that corner, sir, to the left.'

Dr Sandford led the way, and I followed. There certainly I found plenty of warm stuffs, in various patterns and colours, and with prices as various; but nothing to match the grave elegance of those claret folds. It was coming down a step, to leave that counter for this. I knew it perfectly well; while I sought out the simplest and prettiest dark small plaid I could find.

'Do you like these things better?' the doctor asked me privately.

'No, sir,' I said.

'Then why come here, Daisy? Pardon me, may I ask?'

'I have other things to get, Dr Sandford,' I said low.

'But, Daisy!' said the doctor, rousing up, 'I have performed my part ill. You are not restricted – your father has not restricted you. I am your banker for whatever sums you may need – for whatever purposes.'

'Yes,' I said, 'I know. Oh no, I know papa has not restricted you; but I think I ought not to spend any more. It is my own affair.'

'And not mine. Pardon me, Daisy; I submit.'

'Please, Dr Sandford, don't speak so!' I said. 'I don't mean that. I mean, it is my own affair and not papa's.'

'Certainly, I have no more to say,' said the doctor, smiling.

'I will tell you all about it,' I said; and then I desired the shopman to cut off the dress I had fixed upon; and we went upstairs to look for cloaks, I feeling hot and confused and half perplexed. I had never worn such a dress as this plaid I had bought in my life. It was nice and good, and pretty too; but it did not match the quality or the elegance of the things my mother always had got for me . . . I followed Dr Sandford up the stairs and into the wilderness of the cloak department, where all manner of elegancies, in silk, and velvet, and cloth, were displayed in orderly confusion. It was a wilderness to me, in the mood of my thoughts. Was I going to repeat here the process just gone through downstairs?

BERTA RUCK
From The Bridge of Kisses

I WAS TO MEET my godmother, Mrs Montague, in town. She met me at the train at Liverpool Street Station. You see, she is one of those people who think that no girl – 'no nice girl' – can possibly be allowed to go about anywhere in town alone until she is one hundred and sixty-three or married!

Aunt Montague looked as if she had been both, ever since the world began! You really could not believe, unless you saw her, that such bygone-agedness could still exist. Not now, in the summer of 1916, with war-time industry going on all round us, and 'quite nice' girls in khaki coats driving Ministry-of-Munitions motor-cars through the thick of the City traffic without turning a hair.

But there was Aunt Montague like a monument to 'Other Days', with a bonnet and a rich satin cape-wrap over her ample form. She said in a deep booming voice: 'Ah! Here you are, Josephine, I am glad to see you. But – surely your skirt is excessively short for a girl of your age?'

My skirt was one of mother's that had been left behind, and which I had put on because it was the only towny-looking garment in the whole house. I also wore mother's second-best high boots. Thank goodness, I can get into them! These, too, I saw, were disapproved of by my godmother.

'I could not bring myself to the extravagance of a taxi in war-time,' said Aunt Montague as we left the station. 'We can go by 'bus and Tube to the shops. I am going to take you to the shops where I bought the material for my trousseau when I was a girl.'

We went by 'bus and Tube. A long, long trail it was, I can tell you! But I was rather buoyed up by the thoughts of the trousseau. I'd been thinking about it all the way up in the train.

Most of my ideas of a trousseau have been taken from my little friend Mollie Molloy. Of course, Mollie has had a lovely bottom-drawer full of trousseau things all ready for ages. Oh, no; not because she has ever been really definitely engaged yet, but so that she might have a few things ready in case she married at a moment's notice.

'Sure, you never know! In war-time and all!' said Mollie once. I thought it a quaint idea, but rather sweet. Her 'things' are sweet, too; you should see the mauve chemise with the little purple embroidered wreath, and the nightie of black silk-voile, patterned with lemon-yellow nasturtiums and tied with an orange satin bow!

I say, I am afraid this is rather a lot about clothes just here, but I can't help it. This is the story of an engagement, after all. Any girl who reads it will want to know about the trousseau all right.

Well, Mollie's theory is that you need have only a few clothes and quite cheap, but they must be pretty and often.

Mother agrees with her. 'What do married men simply pine for? Things to be somehow "different",' said mother once. 'It's the same thing for ever and ever that bores one's man. A girl may not be able to change the style of her face, but she can change the style of her frills. And she ought to, as often as possible, I think.'

Very different from Aunt Montague. My godmother's idea of a trousseau evidently was a stack of things that you got when you married so that you needn't buy anything fresh until you had to be buried. Her one aim and object was that all my trousseau lingerie should last.

'Of course, you wouldn't dream of buying any of those ready-made flimsy French things, so we needn't go and look at them,' she said. 'Things last so much better if one buys really excellent material and then has it made up. Yes. We will now buy twenty dozen yards of longcloth in the thicker quality. I know it well. I had some made up into this embroidered white pettitcoat that I have on at this moment.' Here she lifted up about half an inch of her long, heavy skirt. 'This I wore on my honeymoon. Would you believe it?'

I would. The material still looked so strong and serviceable that you could have made tents out of it. I am afraid my heart sank down, down, down into mother's little suède-topped boots.

Was I to have nothing of an engagement that I liked; not even the trousseau? Oh, dear! Still, I know I oughtn't to make a tragedy of it . . .

'The material I will take to an admirable little needlewoman whom I know, a really deserving woman,' decreed Aunt Montague as we left the department where we'd been purchasing the sailcloth – I mean longcloth. 'She will make them up for you to some really good patterns of my own.'

Aunt Montague's Early Victorian patterns! Couldn't I see them? Prim collars fastened right up to the chin with linen-covered buttons and button-holes. Sleeves down, down to the wrist. I thought of Mollie's shoulder straps; made of four pink ribbons and a rosette!

'And now we will look at some nice thick woollen vests for winter wear,' said Aunt Montague. I longed for mother, whose view on this subject is that wool was meant for the wear of sheep, and sheep alone.

I ventured to suggest our buying stockings first. Stockings I adore; and I've been longing for a pair of those with ivy-leaves embroidered in tiny green beads. Would Aunt Montague think they were extravagant? For a trousseau?

We went on to the hosiery department and Aunt Montague ordered the girl to bring out the kind of stockings that she always got.

You should have seen them. Cashmere . . . I didn't know that they could possibly be got, so thick and serviceable, nowadays? Anyhow, I expect Aunt Montague's £20 helped to buy the last three dozen pairs that have ever been made.

'It's still extravagant to me, but I suppose you had better have just a few pair of silk ones for special occasions,' said my godmother, and I felt a little cheered again. Mother's idea of a pair of silk stockings is for her little feet and ankles to look as if she had dipped them into transparent ink.

But this particular make of silk stockings, that only Aunt Montague seemed to be able to ferret out of all London, might just as well have been cashmere, too, so thick they were, and durable.

I ceased to think of Mollie's or mother's, or my own ideas of a trousseau. I gave it up. My spirit really was broken as I contemplated the bales of good, serviceable, lasting things that nobody could possibly bear.

'There! Now that, I think, allowing for the cost of making, we have laid out our £20 to the very best advantage, Josephine,' said my godmother complacently at last, 'we will go home. Dear me! Is it half-past two already? Perhaps you are quite hungry?'

GEORGE MOORE
From A Drama in Muslin

BUT ABOVE THIS day, and above all other days, was the day that took them spellbound to the foot of a narrow staircase, a humble flight seemingly, but leading to a temple of tightly-stretched floorcloth, tall wardrobes, and groups and lines of lay figures in eternally ladylike attitudes.

'Oh! how do you do, Mrs Barton? We have been expecting you for the last two or three days. I will run upstairs and tell Mrs Symond that you are here; she will be so glad to see you.'

'That is Miss Cooper!' explained Mrs Barton. 'Everyone knows her; she has been with Mrs Symond many years. And, as for dear Mrs Symond, there is no one like her. She knows the truth about everybody. Here she comes,' and Mrs Barton rushed forward and embraced a thin woman with long features.

'And how do you do, dear Mrs Barton, and how well you are looking, and the young ladies? I see Miss Olive has improved since she was in Dublin.' (In an audible whisper.) 'Everyone is talking about her. There is no doubt but that she'll be the belle of the season.' (In a still audible, but lower tone of voice.) 'But tell me, is it true that—'

'Now, now, now!' said Mrs Barton, drowning her words in cascades of silvery laughter, 'I know nothing of what you're saying; ha! ha! ha! no, no – I assure you. I will not—'

Then, as soon as the ladies had recovered their composure, a few questions were asked about her Excellency, the prospects of the Castle season, and the fashions of the year.

'And now tell me,' said Mrs Barton, 'what pretty things have you that would make up nicely for trains?'

'Trains, Mrs Barton? We have some sweet things that would make up beautifully for trains. Miss Cooper, will you kindly fetch over that case of silks that we had over yesterday from Paris?'

'The young ladies must be, of course, in white; for Miss Olive I should like, I think, snowdrops; for you, Mrs Barton, I am uncertain which of two designs I shall recommend. Now, this is a perfectly regal material.'

With words of compliment and solicitation, the black-dressed assistant displayed the armouries of Venus – armouries filled with the deep blue of midnight, with the faint tints of dawn, with strange flowers and birds, with moths, and moons, and stars. Lengths of white silk clear as the notes of violins playing in a minor key; white poplin falling into folds statuesque as the bass of a fugue by Bach; yards of ruby velvet, rich as an air from Verdi played on the piano; tender green velvet, pastoral as hautboys heard beneath trees in a fair Arcadian vale; blue turquoise faille fanciful as the tinkling of a guitar twanged by a Watteau shepherd; gold brocade, sumptuous as organ tones swelling through the jewelled twilight of a nave; scarves and trains of midnight-blue profound as the harmonic snoring of a bassoon; golden daffodils violent as the sound of a cornet; bouquets of pink roses and daisies, charmful and pure as the notes of a flute; white faille, soft draperies of tulle, garlands of white lilac, sprays of white heather, delicate and resonant as the treble voices of children singing carols in dewy English woods; berthas, flounces, plumes, stomachers, lappets, veils, frivolous as the strains of a German waltz played on Liddell's band.

An hour passed, but the difficulty of deciding if Olive's dress should be composed of silk or Irish poplin was very great, for, determined that all should be humiliated, Mrs Barton laid her plans amid designs for night and morning; birds fluttering through leafy trees, birds drowsing on bending boughs, and butterflies folding their wings. At a critical moment, however, an assistant announced that Mrs Scully was waiting. The ladies started; desperate effort was made; rosy clouds and veils of silver tissue were spoken of; but nothing could be settled, and on the staircase the ladies had to squeeze into a corner to allow Violet and Mrs Scully to pass.

'How do you do, Olive? How do you do, Alice? And you, Mrs Barton, how do you do? And what are you going to wear? Have you decided on your dress?'

'Oh! That is a secret that could be told to no one; oh, not for worlds!' said Mrs Barton.

'I'm sure it will be very beautiful,' replied Mrs Scully, with just a reminiscence of the politeness of the Galway grocery business in her voice.

'I hear you have taken a house in Fitzwilliam Square for the season?' said Mrs Barton.

'Yes, we are very comfortable; you must come and see us. You are at the Shelbourne, I believe?'

'Come to tea with us,' cried Violet. 'We are always at home about five.'

'We shall be delighted,' returned Mrs Barton.

Mrs Scully's acquaintance with Mrs Symond was of the slightest; but, knowing that claims to fashion in Dublin are judged by the intimacy you affect with the dressmaker, she shook her warmly by the hand, and addressed her as dear Mrs Symond. To the Christian name of Helen none less than a Countess dare to aspire.

'And how well you are looking, dear Mrs Symond; and when are you going to take your daughters to the Castle?'

'Oh, not for some time yet; my eldest is only sixteen.'

Mrs Symonds had three daughters to bring out, and she hoped when her feet were set on the redoubtable ways of Cork Hill, her fashionable customers would extend to her a cordial helping hand. Mrs Symonds' was one of the myriad little schemes with which Dublin is honeycombed, and although she received Mrs Scully's familiarities somewhat coldly, she kept her eyes fixed upon Violet. The insidious thinness of the girl's figure, and her gay, winsome look interested her, and, as if speaking to herself, she said:

'You will want something very sweet; something quite pure and lovely for Miss Scully?'

Mother and daughter were instantly all attention, and Mrs Symond continued:

'Let me see, I have some Surat silk that would make up sweetly. Miss Cooper, will you have the kindness to fetch those rolls of Surat silk we received yesterday from Paris?'

Then, beautiful as a flower harvesting, the hues and harmonies of earth, ocean, and sky fell before the ravished eyes. The white Surat silk, chaste, beautiful, delicious as that presentiment of shared happiness which fills a young girl's mind when her fancy awakens in the soft spring sunlight; the white faille with tulle and garlands of white lilac, delicate and only as sensuous as the first meetings of sweethearts, when the may is white in the air and the lilac in bloom on the lawn; trains of blue sapphire broché looped with blue ostrich feathers, seductive and artificial as a boudoir plunged in a dream of Ess. bouquet; dove-coloured velvet trains adorned with tulips and tied with bows of brown and pink – temperate as the love that endures when the fiery day of passion has gone down; bodices and trains of daffodil silk, embroidered with shaded maple-leaves, impure as lamp-lit and patchouli-scented couches; trains of white velouture festooned with tulle; trails of snowdrops, icy as lips that have been bought, and cold as a life that lives in a name.

The beautiful silks hissed as they came through the hands of the assistants, cat-like the velvet footfalls of the velvet fell; it was a witches' Sabbath, and out of this terrible caldron each was to draw her share of the world's gifts. Smiling and genial, Mrs Symond stirred the ingredients with a yard measure; the girls came trembling, doubting, hesitating; and the anxious mothers saw what remained of their jeopardized fortunes sliding in a thin golden stream into the flaming furnace that the demon of Cork Hill blew with unintermittent breath.

Secrets, what secrets were held on the subject of the presentation dresses! The obscure Hill was bound with a white frill of anticipation. Olive's fame had gone forth. She was admitted to be the new Venus, and Lord Kilcarney was spoken of as likely to yield to her the coveted coronet. Would he marry her without so much as looking at another girl? was the question on every lip, and in the jealousy thus created the appraisers of Violet's beauty grew bolder. Her thinness was condoned, and her refinement insisted upon. Nor were May Gould and her chances overlooked by the gossips of Merrion Square. Her flirtation with Fred Scully was already a topic of conversation.

FRANCES BRETT YOUNG
From Mr and Mrs Pennington

SUSAN APPROACHED MADAME Allbright's shop with some trepidation. The 'Madame' intimidated her. In Halesby nobody dreamt of buying a frock ready-made: you chose a 'dress-length' and had it made up from a Weldon pattern by Mrs Bagley, the local dressmaker. The black lace evening dress which she coveted had disappeared from the window. It had probably been snapped up by somebody, Susan thought, and her heart fell.

A discreet alarm made a buzzing sound as they entered the shop. It was empty. A dense beige carpet muffled their steps, and the scanty Directoire furniture was quite Parisian. The collection of ravishing clothes with which Susan had expected her eyes to be dazzled was not in evidence. She saw nothing but a few batik scarves thrown negligently on a gilt settee and a number of hats posed coquettishly on tall stands, one of which Muriel, with superb unconcern, began to try on. At that moment a tall and incredibly thin young lady emerged from the curtains at the back. She wore a clinging dress of black satin and was finishing her lunch.

'Yes, Madam? Is there anything I can show you?' she said with a porcelain smile, as she swallowed the last crumb.

Susan nudged Muriel, who, still engrossed with the effect of the hat, replied by way of the mirror into which she was gazing.

'There was an evening frock in the window. Black lace. My friend wants to look at it,' she said.

'A black lace?' the young lady repeated dubiously, her finger to her lips. 'Oh yes, I remember. That little Chanel,' she said. She pronounced this mysterious word as though it rhymed with flannel, which made Susan imagine, by analogy, that it was the name of some new material. Then she turned and dived gracefully into a hanging cupboard from which she extracted the wisp of black lace.

'Yes, isn't it a duck?' she inquired. 'Just over from Paris. Madame gets them by air, you know,' she confided. Then she held it up gracefully and swayed it from side to side with the flimsy skirt trailing, like a toreador exciting the charge of an invisible bull. As she did this Susan was overwhelmed once more with a desire to possess it. 'But it's far too transparent,' she thought: 'you couldn't possibly wear that without a slip underneath.'

'Yes, it isn't so bad,' Muriel said without much enthusiasm. 'How much is it?'

At this blunt question a flicker of shocked surprise veiled the young lady's eyes. As a matter of form she pretended to search for a ticket. 'It's a Chanel, you know,' she said reproachfully. 'I shall have to ask Madame. But you'd like to see it on the model, wouldn't you?'

'I think, if you don't mind, I'd rather....' Susan began. But Muriel interrupted her. 'Yes, that will be much better,' she replied, and took up another hat.

'One moment,' the young lady said, retreating through the curtains with the backward smile of a ballerina who has taken a 'call'. Susan began to wonder what on earth the model might be. She had decided that it was probably a superior version of the full-busted wicker effigy on which Mrs Bagley, her mouth bristling with pins, arranged the queer scraps of material she cut from patterns, when the curtains parted again and the young lady appeared standing transfigured, with one arm statuesquely raised, in the black lace dress. Then, suddenly abandoning this pose, she began to swim forward, with arched back and seductive serpentine movements of the hips familiar to travellers acquainted with the *danse du ventre* but so unfamiliar to Susan as to make her blush. She swam the length of the room, then turned and swam back again; and this manoeuvre, to Susan, was so acutely embarrassing that she could see nothing of the frock which was being displayed: she saw only the spindly legs and knock-knees of the tall young lady, the sallow skin that covered her bony shoulders and chest and, through the black lace, the top of her combinations and grubby mauve shoulder straps.

The whole performance struck Susan as vaguely indecent, but Muriel, apparently, found nothing unusual in it.

'Let me see what it's like,' she said contemptuously. 'The line isn't bad, but the lace isn't any too brilliant,' she went on as she fingered it. 'It might suit me quite well, but it's rather severe for you, Susan.'

'Well, it's Chanel, you know,' said the seductress, as though that excused everything. 'I've a draped charmeuse, a Mollynoo,' she suggested thoughtfully. 'That's a sweet little gown.'

'I might try on the lace,' said Susan, who saw it slipping away from her.

'There's no hurry, darling. Let's look at something else,' said Muriel decidedly.

PAUL GALLICO

From Flowers for Mrs Harris

THEREAFTER, FOR THE next hour and a half, before the enthralled eyes of Mrs Harris, some ten models paraded one hundred and twenty specimens of the highest dressmaker's art to be found in the most degenerately civilized city in the world.

They came in satins, silks, laces, wools, jerseys, cottons, brocades, velvets, twills, broadcloths, tweeds, nets, organzas, and muslins –

They showed frocks, suits, coats, capes, gowns, clothes for cocktails, for the morning, the afternoon, for dinner parties, and formal and stately balls and receptions.

They entered trimmed with fur, bugle beads, sequins, embroidery with gold and silver thread, or stiff with brocades, the colours were wonderfully gay and clashed in daring combinations; the sleeves were long, short, medium, or missing altogether. Necklines ranged from choke to plunge, hemlines wandered at the whim of the designer. Some hips were high, others low, sometimes the breasts were emphasized, sometimes neglected or wholly concealed. The theme of the show was the high waist and hidden hips. There were hints and forecasts of the sack and trapeze to come. Every known fur from Persian lamb, mink, and nutria to Russian baumarten and sable were used in trimming or in the shape of stoles or jackets.

It was not long before Mrs Harris began to become accustomed to this bewildering array of richness and finery and soon came to recognize the various models upon their appearance in rotation.

There was the girl who walked slinky-sly with her stomach protruding a good six inches before her, and the petite one with the come-hither eyes and provocative mouth. There was the model who seemed to be plain until Mrs Harris noted her carriage and quiet air of elegance, and another who was just sufficiently on the plump side to convey the idea to a stout customer. There was the girl with her nose in the air and disdain at her lips, and an opposite type, a red-haired minx who wooed the whole salon as she made her rounds.

And then, of course, there was the one and only Natasha, the star. It was the custom in the salon to applaud when a creation made a particular hit, and Mrs Harris's palms, horny from application to scrubbing brush and mop, led the appreciation each time Natasha appeared looking lovelier than the last. Once, during one of her appearances, the charwoman noticed a tall, blond, pale young man with an odd scar on his face standing outside, staring hungrily as Natasha made an entrance and said to herself: 'Coo, he ain't arf in love with her, he ain't . . .

She was in love herself, was Mrs Harris, with Natasha, with Mme Colbert, but above all with life and the wonderful thing it had become. The back of her card was already covered with pencilled numbers of frocks and dresses and frantic notes, messages and reminders to herself that she would never be able to decipher. How could one choose between them all?

And then Natasha glided into the salon wearing an evening gown, Number 89, called 'Temptation'. Mrs Harris had just a fleeting instant in which to note the enraptured expression on the face of the young man by the door before he turned away quickly as though that was what he had come for, and then it was all up with her. She was lost, dazzled, blinded, overwhelmed by the beauty of the creation. This was IT!!! Thereafter there were yet to come further stunning examples of evening gowns until the traditional appearance of the bridal costume brought the show to a close, but the char saw none of them. Her choice was made. Feverish excitement accelerated her heartbeat. Desire coursed like fire in her veins.

'Temptation' was a black velvet gown, floor length, encrusted half-way from the bottom up with a unique design picked out in beads of jet that gave to the skirt weight and movement. The top was a froth of cream, delicate pink, and white chiffon, tulle and lace from which arose the ivory shoulders and neck and dreamy-eyed dark head of Natasha.

Rarely had a creation been better named. The wearer appeared like Venus arising from the pearly sea, and likewise she presented the seductive figure of a woman emerging from tousled bedclothes. Never had the upper portion of the female form been more alluringly framed.

The salon burst into spontaneous applause at Natasha's appearance and the clacking of Mrs Harris's palms sounded like the beating upon boards with a broomstick.

Cries and murmurs of '*la, la!*' and '*Voyez, c'est formidable!*' arose on all sides from the males present while the fierce old gentleman thumped his cane upon the floor and beamed with ineffable pleasure. The garment covered Natasha most decently and morally and yet was wholly indecent and overwhelmingly alluring.

Mrs Harris was not aware that there was anything extraordinary as to the choice she had made. For she was and eternally would be a woman. She had been young once and in love. She had had a husband to whom her young heart had gone out and to whom she had wished to give and be everything. Life in that sense had not passed her by. He had been shy, embarrassed, tongue-tied, yet she had heard the words love forced haltingly from his lips whispered into her ear. Incongruously, at that moment she thought of the photograph upon her dressing table with herself in the tiered muslin dress that had seemed so grand then, only now she saw herself clad in 'Temptation' in the picture instead.

The bridal model showed herself perfunctorily; the gathering, buzzing as it emerged from the two salons were sucked towards the exit leading to the grand staircase where, lined up like ravens, the *vendeuses*, the black-clad sales women with their little sales books under their arms waited to pounce upon their customers.

Mrs Harris, her small blue eyes glittering like aquamarines, found Mme Colbert. 'Number eighty-nine, Temptytion,' she cried, and then added, 'oh Lor', I 'ope it don't cost more'n what I've got.'

Mme Colbert smiled a thin, sad smile. She might almost have guessed it. 'Temptation' was a poem created in materials by a poet of women, for a young girl in celebration of her freshness and beauty and awakening to the mysterious power of her sex. It was invariably demanded by the faded, the middle-aged, the verging-on-passé women. 'Come,' she said, 'we will go to the back and I will have it brought to you.'

She led her through grey doors into another part of the building, through endless meadows of the soft grey carpeting until at last Mrs Harris came into yet another world that was almost stifling with excitement.

She found herself in a curtained-off cubicle on a corridor that seemed to be a part of an endless maze of similar corridors and cubicles. Each cubicle held a woman like a queen bee in a cell, and through the corridors rushed the worker bees with the honey – armfuls of frilly, frothy garments in colours of plum, raspberry, tamarind, and peach, gentian-flower, cowslip, damask rose, and orchid, to present them where they had been ordered for trial and further inspection.

Here was indeed woman's secret world, where gossip and the latest scandal was exchanged, the battlefield where the struggle against the ravages of age was carried on with the weapons of the dressmaker's art and where fortunes were spent in a single afternoon.

Here, attended by sales women, seamstresses, cutters, fitters, and designers, who hovered about them with tape, scissors, basting needle and thread, and mouths full of pins, rich French women, rich American women, rich German women, super-rich South American women, titled women from England, maharanees from India, and even, it was rumoured, the wife or two of an ambassador or commissar from Russia, spent their afternoons – and their husbands' money.

And here too, in the midst of this thrilling and entrancing hive, surrounded by her own entourage, stood the London charwoman, encased in 'Temptation' – whom it fitted astonishingly, yet logically, since she too was slender, thinned by occupational exercise and too little food.

She issued from the wondrous, frothy foam of seashell pink, sea-cream and pearl white like – Ada 'Arris from Battersea. The creation worked no miracles except in her soul. The scrawny neck and greying head that emerged from the shoulder *décolleté* of the gown, the weathered skin, small button-bright blue eyes, and apple cheeks contrasted with the classic fall of jet-encrusted black velvet panels were grotesque – but still, not wholly so, for the beautiful gown as well as the radiance of the person in it yet managed to lend an odd kind of dignity to this extraordinary figure.

For Mrs Harris had attained her Paradise. She was in a state of dreamed-of and longed-for bliss. All of the hardships, the sacrifices, the economies, and hungers and doings-without she had undergone faded into insignificance. Buying a Paris dress was surely the most wonderful thing that could happen to a woman.

EMILE ZOLA

From The Kill

WHAT MAXIME LOVED was to live among women's skirts, in the midst of their finery, in their rice-powder. He always remained more or less of a girl, with his slim hands, his beardless face, his plump white neck. Renée consulted him seriously about her gowns. He knew the good makers of Paris, summed each of them up in a word, talked about the cunningness of such a one's bonnets and the logic of such another's dresses. At seventeen there was not a milliner whom he had not probed, and not a bootmaker whom he had not studied through and through. This quaint abortion, who during his English lessons read the prospectuses which his perfumer sent him every Friday, could have delivered a brilliant lecture on the fashionable Paris world, customers and purveyors included, at an age when country urchins dare not look their housemaid in the face. Frequently, on his way home from school he would bring back in his tilbury a bonnet, a box of soap, or a piece of jewellery which his stepmother had ordered the preceding day. He had always some strip of musk- scented lace hanging about in his pockets.

But his great treat was to go with Renée to the illustrious Worms, the tailor genius to whom the queens of the Second Empire bowed the knee. The great man's showroom was wide and square, and furnished with huge divans. Maxime entered it with religious emotion. Dresses undoubtedly have a perfume of their own; silk, satin, velvet and lace had mingled their faint aromas with those of hair and of amber-scented shoulders; and the atmosphere of the room retained that sweet-smelling warmth, that fragrance of flesh and of luxury, which transformed the apartment into a chapel consecrated to some secret divinity. It was often necessary for Renée and Maxime to wait for hours; a series of anxious women sat there, waiting their turn, dipping biscuits into glasses of Madeira, helping themselves from the great table in the middle, which was covered with bottles and plates full of cakes. The ladies were at home, they talked without restraint, and when they ensconced themselves around the room, it was as though a flight of white Lesbian doves had alighted on the sofas of a Parisian drawing-room. Maxime, whom they endured and loved for his girlish air, was the only man admitted into the circle. He there tasted delights divine; he glided along the sofas like a supple adder; he was discovered under a skirt, behind a bodice, between two dresses, where he made himself quite small and kept very quiet, inhaling the warm fragrance of his neighbours with the demeanour of a choir-boy partaking of the sacrament.

'That child pokes his nose in everywhere,' said the Baronne de Meinhold, tapping his cheeks.

Then, when the great Worms at last received Renée, Maxime followed her into the consultation room. He had ventured to speak on two or three occasions while the master remained absorbed in the contemplation of his client, as the high-priest of the Beautiful hold that Leonardo da Vinci did in the presence of la Gioconda. The master had deigned to smile upon the correctness of his observations. He made Renée stand up before a glass which rose from the floor to the ceiling, and pondered with knit brows, while Renée, seized with emotion, held her breath, so as not to stir. And after a few minutes the master, as though seized and moved by inspiration, sketched in broad, jerky strokes the work of art which he had just conceived, ejaculating in short phrases:

'A Montespan dress in pale-grey faille ... the skirt describing a rounded basque in front ... large grey satin bows to catch it up on the hips ... and a puffed apron of pearl-grey tulle, the puffs separated by strips of grey satin.'

He pondered once again, seemed to descend to the very depths of his genius, and, with the triumphant facial contortion of a pythoness on her tripod, concluded:

'We will have in the hair, on the top of this bonny head, Psyche's dreamy butterfly, with wings of changeful blue.'

But at other times inspiration was stubborn. The illustrious Worms summoned it in vain, and concentrated his faculties to no purpose. He distorted his eyebrows, turned livid, took his poor head between his hands and shook it in his despair, and beaten, throwing himself into an arm-chair:

'No,' he would mutter, in a pitiful voice, 'no, not today . . . It is not possible . . . You ladies expect too much. The source is exhausted.'

And he showed Renée out, repeating:

'Impossible, impossible, dear lady, you must come back another day . . . I don't grasp you this morning.'

Transl. Serge de Mattos

JEAN RHYS
From Voyage in the Dark

IT WAS FOUR o'clock when I left the flat. I walked along Oxford Street, thinking about my room in Camden Town and that I didn't want to go back to it. There was a black velvet dress in a shop-window, with the skirt slit up so that you could see the light stocking. A girl could look lovely in that, like a doll or a flower. Another dress, with fur round the neck, reminded me of the one that Laurie had worn. Her neck coming out of the fur was a pale-gold colour, very slim and strong-looking.

The clothes of most of the women who passed were like caricatures of the clothes in the shop-windows, but when they stopped to look you saw that their eyes were fixed on the future. 'If I could buy this, then of course I'd be quite different.' Keep hope alive and you can do anything, and that's the way the world goes round, that's the way they keep the world rolling. So much hope for each person. And damned cleverly done too.

MARGARET MITCHELL
From Gone With The Wind

ONE BRIGHT SUMMER morning some weeks later, he reappeared with a brightly trimmed hatbox in his hand and, after finding that Scarlett was alone in the house, he opened it. Wrapped in layers of tissue was a bonnet, a creation that made her cry, 'Oh, the darling thing!' as she reached for it. Starved for the sight, much less the touch, of new clothes, it seemed the loveliest bonnet she had ever seen. It was of dark-green taffeta, lined with watered silk of a pale-jade colour. The ribbons that tied under the chin were as wide as her hand and they, too, were pale green. And curled about the brim of this confection was the perkiest of green ostrich plumes.

'Put it on,' said Rhett, smiling.

She flew across the room to the mirror and popped it on her head, pushing back her hair to show her earrings and tying the ribbon under her chin.

'How do I look?' she cried, pirouetting for his benefit and tossing her head so that the plume danced. But she knew she looked pretty even before she saw confirmation in his eyes. She looked attractively saucy and the green of the lining made her eyes dark emerald and sparkling.

'Oh, Rhett, whose bonnet is it? I'll buy it. I'll give you every cent I've got for it.'

'It's your bonnet,' he said. 'Who else could wear that shade of green? Don't you think I carried the colour of your eyes well in my mind?'

'Did you really have it trimmed just for me?'

'Yes, and there's "Rue de la Paix" on the box, if that means anything to you.'

It meant nothing to her, smiling at her reflection in the mirror. Just at this moment, nothing mattered to her except that she looked utterly charming in the first pretty hat she had put on her head in two years. What she couldn't do with this hat!

Her clothes were incomparable, with just that suggestion of the haphazard which raised them high above the mere *chic* of the mannequin.

Evelyn Waugh, *Vile Bodies*

ROSE MACAULAY
From Personal Pleasures

HOW HANDSOME IT looks, my new dress, fresh from its maker's hands! How elegant, how eximious, how smug, how quaintly fashioned, how all that there is of the most modish! How like other people I shall appear when I wear it! With what respect they will regard me, saying one to another, Look, do you see that woman? She knows how to dress; she is in the mode; indeed, she looks very well. I think I have at other times seen her in dresses three, four, even five years old, altered, as she believes, but not really, to the discerning eye, altered to matter, for they still remain of their epoch, and insufferable to people of good taste and modern outlook, now that there is such gaudy going and such new fashions every day. But to-day she really has a new dress, and a good dress; to-day she really is a Well-Dressed Woman. I like its cut, do not you? And the colour is precisely right.

WILLIAM MAKEPEACE THACKERAY
From Vanity Fair

There are some splendid tailors' shops in the High Street of Southampton, in the fine plate-glass windows of which hang gorgeous waistcoats of all sorts, of silk and velvet, and gold and crimson, and pictures of the last new fashions, in which those wonderful gentlemen with quizzing glasses, and holding on to little boys with exceeding large eyes and curly hair, ogle ladies in riding habits prancing by the statue of Achilles at Apsley House. Jos, although provided with some of the most splendid vests that Calcutta could furnish, thought he could not go to town until he was supplied with one or two of these garments, and selected a crimson satin, embroidered with gold butterflies, and a black and red velvet tartan with white stripes and a rolling collar, with which, and a rich blue satin stock and a gold pin, consisting of a five-barred gate with a horseman in pink enamel jumping over it, he thought he might make his entry into London with some dignity.

7

Weddings

Harriet looked modest for the first time in her Life in a long French lace veil.

The Journals of Elizabeth Fremantle, née Wynne (c. 1800)

The wedding was splendid & I greatly enjoyed it but *oh* the get ups I never saw worse. I'm *sure* English women are dowdier than when I was young. The hats were nearly all as though made by somebody who had once heard about flowers but never seen one – huge muffs of horror.

Nancy Mitford, Letters

Wardrobe account of Trousseau of Princess Phillipa, daughter of Henry IV married to Eric King of Denmark 1406:

5 gowns. 1) cloth of gold worked with white flowers & furred with miniver. 2) red velvert embroidered with pearls furred with ermine. 3) red cloth of gold. 4) ditto. 5) green cloth. Cap of beaver furred with ermine, garnished with silk buttons & tassel, Hood of scarlet cloth; another of black cloth; both furred. Boots 1) of 'shaved' leather (polished) and furred. 2) black leather. 4 pairs of 'puncheons' of white leather. i.e. thin shoes or pumps. 13 pairs of shoes.'

Archeologia Vol. 67

PENELOPE LIVELY
From Treasures of Time

I PUT THE DRESS on; it is lovely; I am lovely. Everything is fuss and excitement, it is all for me. Mother says, 'Stand still, dear, don't fidget, I can't get the veil fixed right. You're not nervous, are you? There, that's better . . .' But I am not nervous: I am not anything. I don't feel anything; this is the happiest day of my life and I don't feel anything. I see the shiny black car in the drive outside, waiting, and father in his wedding clothes. Nellie comes into the room, looking funny in the sort of frock she doesn't like wearing, and a hat. Hugh is in the church now. I think of Hugh, and nothing happens. There is not that delicious, confusing rush of something there was at first, there is nothing much at all. I see Nellie looking at me; she has a funny look – she is . . . she is *sorry* for me.

*

Laura stands at the mirror in the dress. The dress over which we have all been so much exercised, which has been debated and constructed and reconstructed and despaired of and delighted over. She looks beautiful. She looks like a Botticelli angel; her hair shines like water in the sun. Mother is doing something with the veil and Laura stares out of the window and as I come in she turns to see who it is. Her mouth is a little sad cross button like when she was a child: like when she was a child and had got the present she wanted for Christmas or birthday and then it had turned out to be not what she wanted after all. Her eyes are miserable, and a bit scared. She says, 'You look nice, Nellie.' I laugh: because I cannot remember Laura ever saying anything like that before and because I don't think I look nice at all, in my tight, slippery blue silk dress and embarrassing hat. I want to make Laura laugh; I want to cheer her up; it is all wrong for her to be like this today.

JULIAN BARNES
From Talking it Over

I GOT TO MAMAN at 7.00 in the evening the night before my second wedding day. We were both being consciously careful. She settled me down with a cup of coffee and made me put my feet up as if I were already pregnant. Then she picked up my case and went off to unpack it, which made me feel even more as if I'd just come into hospital. I sat there thinking, I hope she doesn't give me any advice, I don't think I could stand it. What's done is done, and what's about to be done can't be changed now. So, let's just be quiet, and watch some rubbish on television, and not talk about anything important.

But – mothers and daughters, mothers and daughters. Approximately ninety seconds later she was back in the room holding up my suit. There was a smile on her face as if I'd suddenly gone senile and needed treating with pitying affection.

'Darling, you packed the wrong clothes.'

I looked up. 'No, Maman.'

'But darling, this *is* the suit I bought you?'

'Yes.' Yes, you know it is. Why do parents go on like prosecuting lawyers, checking the most obvious facts?

'You are proposing to wear *this* tomorrow?'

'Yes, Maman.'

Whereupon the deluge. She started off in French, which is what she does when she's built up a head of steam and needs to let it off. Then she calmed down a little and switched back to English. Her basic line was that I'd clearly taken leave of my senses. Only a seriously disturbed person would dream of getting married twice in the same dress. It offended against good taste, good manners, good dress sense, the Church, everyone present at both ceremonies (though mainly her), fate, luck, world history, and a few other things and people.

'Oliver wanted me to wear it.'

'May I ask why?'

'He said he fell in love with me when I was wearing it.'

Outburst number two. Scandalous, ought to be ashamed, etc. Asking for trouble, etc. Can get married without your mother if that's what you're planning to get married in, etc. It lasted an hour or so, and I ended up handing over the key to my flat. She went off with the suit over her outstretched arm as if it had a dose of radiation.

She returned with a couple of substitutes, which I looked at with indifference.

'You choose, Maman.' I didn't want to fight. Tomorrow wasn't going to be easy, I just hoped one person would be satisfied. But no, it wasn't as simple as that. She wanted me to try on both alternatives. In order to be forgiven my enormous *faux pas*, I was expected to behave like a model. It was ridiculous. I tried them both on.

'Now you choose, Maman.' But that still wasn't good enough. I must choose, I must have opinions. I didn't have an opinion. I didn't have a second choice, I really didn't. It's like saying, Look, Gill, I'm afraid you can't marry Oliver tomorrow, that's out, so who would you like to marry instead? This one or that one?

When I told her this she didn't appreciate the comparison. She thought it in bad taste. Oh well. When I married Stuart I was encouraged only to think of myself. This is *your* day, Gillian, people said. It's your big day. Now I'm marrying Oliver and suddenly it's everyone else's day. Oliver insists on a church wedding which I don't want. Maman insists on a dress which I don't want.

I woke up still being niggled at by dreams. I was writing my name in the sand except it wasn't my name; Oliver started rubbing it out with his foot and Stuart burst into tears. Maman was standing there on the beach, wearing my green wedding suit, looking neither approving nor disapproving. Just waiting. Waiting. If we wait long enough anything and everything will go wrong and you'll be proved right, Maman. But where's the virtue in that?

When we got to the church Oliver was very jumpy. At least we didn't have to process down the aisle: there were only ten of us, and the vicar decided just to gather us at the altar. But the moment we started assembling I could see there was something up.

'I'm sorry,' I said to Oliver. 'She just wouldn't listen to reason.'

He didn't seem to understand. He kept looking over my shoulder towards the church door.

'The dress,' I said, 'I'm sorry about the dress.' It was bright yellow, an optimistic colour as Maman put it, and you would hardly have expected Oliver not to notice the change.

'You look like a jewel,' he said, though his eyes weren't on me.

I wore the wrong colours to both my weddings. I should have been wearing silly optimistic yellow at my first wedding, and cautious pale green at my second.

'And all my worldly goods I with thee share.' That's what I promised.

LOELIA, DUCHESS OF WESTMINSTER
From Grace and Favour

M Y PARENTS WERE married in May 1899 in the Guards Chapel . . .
Press photography was in its infancy, so the society papers had to do the best they could with drawings of the dresses and studio portraits, and *The Gentlewoman* livened up the heads of the bride and bridegroom with a really terrible border of hearts, ribbons and Cupids dressed in bearskins. My mother was robed in crêpe-de-chine, which was considered an original material for a wedding-dress, and her train was held by two little pages in eighteenth century Grenadier costume, which was also considered very original though common enough nowadays. There were twelve bridesmaids in Romney-style dresses who carried staves of lilies and wore hanging from their waists by black velvet ribbons the bridegroom's present, a crystal pendant with blue enamel bands bearing the appropriate motto, '*C'est l'amour qui fait le monde à la ronde.*'

As enthusiastically described by *The Daily Telegraph* and *The Queen*, the clothes of the congregation sound as if they were of unutterable loveliness, though I daresay if one actually saw them one would think them over-trimmed and fussy. My mother, at all events, had the knack of only wearing what suited her, and I have no doubt that when at long last she drove off for her honeymoon she looked absolutely ravishing in her ivory cloth dress with embroidered bodice and pink velvet bows, and her chip straw hat, trimmed with ostrich feathers and wheat. (The hat she preserved and once showed me – it was no bigger than a saucer.)

NANCY MITFORD
From Love in a Cold Climate

FIRST OF ALL we talked about the wedding. Lady Montdore was wonderful when it came to picking over an occasion of that sort; with her gimlet eye nothing escaped her, nor did any charitable inhibitions tone down her comments on what she had observed.

'How extraordinary Lady Kroesig looked, poor woman! I suppose somebody must have told her that the bridegroom's mother should have a bit of everything in her hat – for luck perhaps. Fur, feathers, flowers and a scrap of lace – it was all there and a diamond brooch on top to finish it off nicely. Rose diamonds – I had a good look. It's a funny thing that these people who are supposed to be so rich never seem to have a decent jewel to put on – I've often noticed it. And did you see what mingy little things they gave poor Linda? A cheque – yes, that's all very well but for how much, I wonder? Cultured pearls, at least I imagine so, or they would have been worth quite £10,000, and a hideous little bracelet. No tiara, no necklace, what will the poor child wear at Court?'

STAN BARSTOW
From A Kind of Loving

I'D NEVER BEEN involved in a wedding before and I have to admit it's what you might call an experience.

There's about five hundred people staying overnight before the day, to begin with, and on the morning they're getting ready in lumps all over the place. The house is like a lot of backstage dressing-rooms like you sometimes see in musical pictures and you wouldn't be surprised to see some young lad marching round knocking on all the doors and shouting, 'Five minutes, please,' like they do.

It's even affected the Old Man. I'm just about to go downstairs to get started when he calls me into the bedroom and I find him standing in his undervest and trousers in front of the wardrobe mirror.

'Here, Vic,' he says; 'come an' tell me what you think to these new trousers.'

I sit down on the edge of the bed and look him over. 'Very nice, Dad. They seem to hang all right. Can't really tell, o' course, without your jacket on.'

'I'll just pop it on.'

He does this and then takes another look in the glass. He begins to work his shoulders about as though the tailor's left a few pins in. 'Seems a bit on the slack side to me,' he says.

'Well that's the style now, Dad,' I tell him. 'You'll feel better when you've got your shirt and waistcoat on. And I can't wait while you do that,' I say, as he begins looking round for them.

He's a tall, spare sort of feller, the Old Man is, and really a suit hangs well on him when he lets it. This one's a dark blue, nearly navy, with a faint double stripe in grey. 'I think he's made a right good job of it.' I lean forward and finger the material. 'A nice bit o' cloth an' all.'

'Oh, aye,' the Old Man says in that self-satisfied way he has sometimes; 'you can't diddle me when it comes to pickin' cloth. I know a good length o' cloth when I see one . . .' His voice tails off. He's not at all happy this morning. 'It's t'makin' up 'at worries me,' he says. 'I just don't feel right in it, somehow.'

. . . And then just as I'm turning round to go out I catch sight of these brown shoes under a chair.

'You're not thinkin' o' wearing them today, are you?'

'Eh?' he says. 'What?'

'Your brown shoes.'

'Why not? They're me best.'

'Look,' I say, mustering my patience, 'you don't wear brown shoes with a blue suit. You've heard Stanley Holloway, haven't you?'

'That war a funeral,' he says.

'Well it applies to weddings an' all. You'll have our Chris curling up with shame. Remember there'll be a lot of eyes on you while you're up at the front.'

'They'll never notice me for our Christine.'

'Some of these folk here today make a point of noticing everything,' I tell him. 'Not that three parts of 'em know any better anyway.'

'Oh, damnation,' he says, getting his rag out at last, 'Is'll be glad when it's all over. I don't seem to be able to get owt right some road.'

'You won't be told.'

'Well I can't wear old shoes wi' a new suit,' he says, getting stubborn now.

'An' you can't wear them brown 'uns. I'll ask me mother what she thinks when I go down.'

This is the ace. The Old Man lifts his hand up. 'Ho'd on a minute. There's no need to bring your mother into this: I'm havin' enough trouble as it is.'

Just then I hear the Old Lady shouting from the bottom of the stairs. 'Victor! Are y'there, Victor? The taxi's waiting. Hurry yourself up or you'll have us all late.'

. . . I pull my jacket down and straighten my tie. 'Well I'm ready. Where's our Jim?'

J. T. SMITH

From Nollekens and His Times

THIS LADY'S INTERESTING figure, on her wedding day, was attired in a sacque and petticoat of the most expensive brocaded white silk, resembling net work, enriched with small flowers; which displayed in the variation of the folds a most delicate shade of pink, the uncommon beauty of which was greatly admired. The deep and pointed stomacher was exquisitely gimped and pinked and at the lower part was a large pin, consisting of several diamonds, confining an elegant point lace apron; certainly at that period, rather unfashionable, but on this happy event affectionately worn by the lady in memory of her dear mother, who had presented it to her . . . The sleeves of this dress closely fitted the arm to a little below the elbow from which hung three point lace ruffles of great depth; a handkerchief of the same costly texture partly concealed the beauty of her bosom; wherein, confined by a large bow, was a bouquet of rose-buds, the delicate tints of which were imperceptibly blended with the transparency of her complexion, and not a little increased by the beauty of a triple row of pearls, tied behind with a narrow white satin ribbon. Her beautiful auburn hair, which she never disguised by the use of powder, according to the fashion of the day, was, upon this occasion arranged over a cushion made to fit the head to a considerable height, with large round curls on either side; the whole being surmounted by a small cap of point-lace with plaited flaps to correspond with the apron and ruffled. Her shoes were composed of the same material as her dress, ornamented with silver spangleds and square Bristol buckles, with heels three inches and a half in height; as if she meant to exult in out-topping her husband.

(1821)

The old man started to get himself ready; he'd bought himself a pair of striped trousers and a bobtail coat, all second-hand from the stall in Hoxton market. My sisters just could not keep a straight face. I thought they were going in hysterics when he started to put on a collar and tie; he had never worn one in his life. They eventually got it on for him after a lot of swearing and blinding. The coat was going green with age. He did look a sight, with brown boots, striped trousers, a semi-green bobtail coat and a flat cap.

H. S. Jasper, *A Hoxton Childhood*

Father in his best black coat and grey-striped trousers and Mother resplendent in her pale grey wedding gown with rows and rows of narrow blue velvet ribbon edging its many flounces. The wedding bonnet had long been cast aside, for, as she often said, 'headgear does date so' and on this occasion she wore a tiny blue velvet bonnet, like a little flat mat on her hair, with wide velvet strings tied in a bow under her chin – a new bonnet.

Flora Thompson, *Lark Rise to Candleford*

Bridal Dress

The Gardener stands in his bower door
  Wi' a Primrose in his Hand.
And bye there came a leal Maiden
  As jimp as a Willow wand.

O Ladie! can ye fancie me?
  For to be my bride;
You'll have all the flowers in my garden,
  To be to you a Weed.

The Lily white sall be your smock,
  It becomes your body best;
Your head sall be busk't in Gellyflower
  Wi' the Primrose on your brest.

Your gown sall be the Sweet William,
  Your coat the Camovine;
Your apron of the Sallets neat
  That taste baith sweet and fine.

Your hose sall be the braid Kail-blade
  That is baith braid and lang;
Narrow, narrow, at the cute,
  And braid, braid, at the brawn.

Your gloves sall be the Marigold
  All glittering to your hand;
Weel spread owre wi' blue Blaewart
  That grows in the corn-land.

Old Scotch Ballad

ISABEL COLEGATE
From Statues in a Garden

O F COURSE IT was a perfect wedding. The sun shone, Violet looked sweet, we were all there and in our best.

The reception was in the garden. 'A perfect day,' people said. 'You couldn't have hoped for a better. It all looks so beautiful. A dream wedding.'

There is a photograph of all the bridesmaids walking across the lawn in a long straggling line, out of step. They were wearing heavy white satin dresses, tight about the ankles, so that it is not easy for them to walk. Cicely is holding the skirt up with one hand so that a good deal of bony ankle shows above the black satin buckled shoe. In the other hand she carries, as they all do, an immense bunch of long-stemmed lilies. No, Kitty is not carrying lilies: because she had to hold Violet's train, of course. Kitty wears a shorter dress, but the same lace fichu round her shoulders and bosom, only hers ends in an artificial flower at the waist, theirs in high beaded waistbands. They are all wearing lace caps bound with a black velvet ribbon and bow, and upon the bow, perched like a feather, is a little bunch of orange blossom. Round their necks they wear a thin black velvet ribbon and a gold chain bearing an enamelled locket given to them by the bridegroom. Kitty's hair is about her shoulders: the others of course have theirs pinned up. They all wear long white gloves. Kitty's feet look larger than any of the others' . . .

Cynthia had her own way of dressing. She wore very few trimmings in that year of the beaded fringe, relying rather on line and her own superb carriage. But her hats were enormous.

Here she is in the softest of grey chiffon, the skirt falling in fluted columns from the high waist, a high neck and long full sleeves, her hat a marvellous sweeping brim beneath a curling feather. She had quite a feeling for the dramatic: it was a good hat in which to look desolated by the loss of a daughter. But in this photograph she is not looking desolated (she did cry a little in the church); she is looking untroubled, talking to Lord Tamworth, who is exquisitely dressed himself from top hat to grey spats. He is leaning forward, smiling through his golden beard, telling her probably how beautiful she looks.

HENRY LONGFELLOW

From Hiawatha's Wedding Feast

You shall hear how Pau-Puk-Keewis,
How the handsome Yenadizze
Danced at Hiawatha's wedding; . . .
And the wedding-guests assembled,
Clad in all their richest raiment,
Robes of fur and belts of wampum,
Splendid with their paint and plumage,
Beautiful with beads and tassels . . .

Then the handsome Pau-Puk-Keewis,
He the idle Yenadizze,
He, the merry mischief-maker,
Whom the people call the Storm-Fool,
Rose among the guests assembled . . .

He was dressed in shirt of doe-skin,
White and soft, and fringed with ermine,
All inwrought with beads of wampum;
He was dressed in deer-skin leggings,
Fringed with hedgehog quills and ermine,
And in moccasins of buck-skin
Thick with quills and beads embroidered.
On his head were plumes of swan's down,
On his heels were tails of foxes,
In one hand a fan of feathers,
And a pipe was in the other.

Barred with streaks of red and yellow,
Streaks of blue and bright vermillion,
Shone the face of Pau-Puk-Keewis.
From his forehead fell his tresses,
Smooth and parted like a woman's,
Shining bright with oil, and plaited,
Hung with braids of scented grasses,
As among the guests assembled,
To the sound of flutes and singing,
To the sound of drums and voices,
Rose the handsome Pau-Puk-Keewis,
And began his mystic dances.

8

The Glitter of
the Great and Fashionable

Other women display their jewels, but she lives in the
intimacy of her pearls.

Marcel Proust, *Remembrance of Things Past*

There are no regulations in convents so strict as those imposed upon the great by court etiquette.

Mme de Maintenon (1685)

I love Royalty. They're so clean.

Diana Vreeland

In this garden was the King and five with him apparyelled in garments of purpull satyn, every edge garnished with frysed golde and every garment full of posyes made of letters of fine gold, of bullion as thick as might be. And six Ladyes wore rochettes rouled with crymosyn velvet and set with lettres like Carettes. And after the Kyng and his compaignions had daunsed, he appointed the Ladies, Gentlewomen, and Ambassadours to take the lettres off their garments in token of liberalyte. Which thing the common people perceiving, ranne to them and stripped them. And at this banket a shypman of London caught certayn lettres which he sould to a goldsmith for £3. 14s. 8d.

Edward Hall, *Chronicles of the Pageants and Progress of the English Kings* (1542)

From John Evelyn's Diary

Oct. 18. To Court. It being the first time his Majesty put himself solemnly into the Eastern fashion of vest, changeing doublet, stiff collar, bands and cloake, into a comely vest, after the Persian mode, with girdle or straps, and shoe strings and garters into bouckles, of which some were set with precious stones, resolving never to alter it, and to leave the French mode, which had hitherto obtain'd to our greate expence and reproch. Upon which divers courtiers and gentlemen gave his Majesty gold by way of wager that he would not persist in this resolution. I had sometime before presented an invective against that unconstancy, and our so much affecting the French fashion, to his Majesty, in which I tooke occasion to describe the comliness and usefulnesse of the Persian clothing, in the very same manner his Majesty now clad himselfe. This pamphlet I intitl'd 'Tyrannus, or the Mode', and gave it to his Majesty to reade. I do not impute to this discourse the change which soon happen'd, but it was an identity that I could not but take notice of.

From Fanny Burney's Diaries

M ONDAY, JULY 24, 1786. I rise at six o'clock, dress in a morning gown and cap, and wait my first summons, which is at all times from seven to near eight, but commonly in the exact half hour between them.

Mrs Schwellenberg, since the first weeks, has never come down in the morning at all. The Queen's dress is finished by Mrs Thielky and myself. No maid ever enters the room while the Queen is in it. Mrs Thielky hands the things to me, and I put them on. 'Tis fortunate for me I have not the handing of them. I should never know which to take first, embarrassed as I am, and should run a prodigious risk of giving the gown before the hoop, and the fan before the neck-kerchief.

By eight o'clock, or a little after, for she is extremely expeditious, she is dressed. She then goes out to join the King, and be joined by the Princesses, and they all proceed to the King's chapel in the castle, to prayers, attended by the governesses of the Princesses and the King's equerry.

I then return to my own room for breakfast. I make this meal the most pleasant part of the day; I have a book for my companion, and I allow myself an hour for it. I have my time at my own disposal till a quarter before twelve, except on Wednesdays and Saturdays, when I have it only to a quarter before eleven. These times mentioned call me to the irksome and quick-returning labours of the toilette. The hour advanced on the Wednesdays and Saturdays is for curling and craping the hair, which it now requires twice a week.

A quarter before one is the usual time for the Queen to start dressing for the day. Mrs Schwellenberg then constantly attends; so do I; Mrs Thielky of course, at all times. We help her off with her gown, and on with her powdering things, and then the hairdresser is admitted. She generally reads the newspapers during that operation. She never forgets to send me away while she is powdering, with a consideration not to spoil my clothes that one would not expect belonged to her high station.

When I return I find her removed to her state dressing-room, if any room in this private mansion can have the epithet of state. There, in a very short time, her dress is finished. She then says she won't detain me, and I hear and see no more of her till bed-time.

From The Letters of Lady Mary Wortley Montagu

I AM NOW IN my Turkish Habit . . . tis admirably becoming. The first peice of my dresse is a pair of drawers, very full, that reach to my shoes and conceal the legs more modestly than your Petticoats. They are of a thin rose colour damask brocaded with silver flowers, my shoes of white kid Leather embrodier'd with Gold. Over this hangs my Smock of a fine white silk Gause edg'd with Embrodiery. This smock has wide sleeves hanging halfe way down the Arm and is clos'd at the Neck with a diamond button, but the shape and colour of the bosom very well to be distinguish'd through it. The Antery is a wastcoat made close to the shape, of white and Gold Damask, with very long sleeves falling back and fring'd with deep Gold fringe, and should have Diamond or pearl Buttons. My Caftan of the same stuff with my Drawers is a robe exactly fited to my shape and reaching to my feet, with very long straight falling sleeves. Over this is the Girdle of about 4 fingers broad, which all that can afford have entirely of Diamonds or other precious stones. Those that will not be at that expence have it of exquisite Embrodiery on Satin, but it must be fasten'd before with a clasp of Di'monds. The Curdee is a loose Robe they throw off or put on according to the Weather, being of a rich Brocade (mine is green and Gold) either lin'd with Ermine or Sables; the sleeves reach very little below the Shoulders. The Headress is compos'd of a Cap call'd Talpock, which is in winter of fine velvet embrodier'd with pearls or Di'monds and in summer of a light shineing silver stuff. This is fix'd on one side of the Head, hanging a little way down with a Gold Tassel and bound on either with a circle of Di'monds (as I have seen several) or a rich embrodier'd Handkerchief. On the other side of the Head the Hair is laid flat, and here the Ladys are at Liberty to shew their fancys, some putting Flowers, other a plume of Heron's feather, and, in short, what they please, but the most general fashion is a large Bouquet of Jewels made like natural flowers, that is, the buds of Pearl, the roses of different colour'd Rubys, the Jess'mines of Di'monds, Jonquils of Topazes, etc., so well set and enammell'd tis hard to imagine any thing of that kind so beautifull. The Hair hangs at its full length behind, divided into tresses briaded with pearl or riband, which is allways in great Quantity.

OCTAVE UZANNE

From Fashion in Paris

On Marie Antoinette's toilette

SHAWLS. JEWELS. STUFFS, gew-gaws of every kind, were perpetually brought her and everything she bought, never asking the price, and, for the most part, straightway forgetting what she had purchased . . . From the very outset she gave her lady-in-waiting and her lady of the bedchamber to understand that they were to have nothing to say to her wardrobe. Everything connected with that was arranged between herself and the waiting-women, of whom she had seven or eight. Her toilette consumed a great deal of time. Certain operations directed to the maintenance of her personal beauty, and in which cosmetics played a part, she kept entirely to herself. When these were over she had her hair dressed. During this ceremony she wore a long and very elegant wrapper, trimmed with lace. Her chemises and petticoats were all embroidered and lace-trimmed. She changed her inner garment, and all her linen, three times each day, and never wore a pair of stockings twice. If the *dames du palais* came to the door while her hair was being dressed, they were allowed to enter. When her hair was arranged, great baskets were brought her, containing a selection of gowns, bonnets, and shawls. In summer, these gowns were of muslin or cambric, much embroidered and elaborately adorned. In winter there were coats of silken or woollen material, or velvet. The Empress chose her garments for the day. In the morning she always wore a hat or bonnet, trimmed with flowers or feathers, and high long-sleeved dresses. She had between three and four hundred shawls.

MME DE LA TOUR DU PIN

From Memoirs

MME D'HÉNIN TOLD us that the Queen wished me to be presented the following Sunday. I had been married on Monday, and it was on Tuesday that my aunt told my grandmother of the Queen's wish . . .

The next day, I accordingly left for Paris with my aunt, Mme d'Hénin, and spent the next two mornings with M. Huart, my dancing master. It is impossible to conceive of anything more ridiculous than those rehearsals of the presentation. M. Huart, a large man, his hair very well dressed and white with powder, wore a billowing underskirt and stood at the far end of the room to represent the Queen. He told me what I had to do, sometimes taking the part of the lady who was to present me and sometimes that of the Queen. Standing at the far end of the room, he showed me just when to remove my glove and bow to kiss the hem of the Queen's gown. He showed me the gesture she would make to prevent me. Nothing was forgotten or overlooked in these rehearsals, which went on for three or four hours. I wore a train and the wide paniers of Court dress, but above and below was my ordinary morning dress, and my hair was only very simply pinned up. It was all very funny.

I was presented on Sunday morning, after Mass. I was 'en grand corps'; that is to say, wearing a special bodice without shoulders, laced at the back, but narrow enough for the lacings, four inches wide at the bottom, to show a chemise of the finest lawn through which it could easily be seen if the wearer's skin were not white. This chemise had sleeves, but they were only three inches deep and the shoulders were uncovered. From the top of the arm to the elbow fell three or four flounces of blonde lace. The throat was bare. Mine was partly covered by the seven or eight rows of large diamonds which the Queen had kindly lent me. The front of the bodice was as if laced with rows of diamonds and on my head were more diamonds, some in clusters and some in aigrets.

The gown itself was very lovely. On account of my half-mourning, it was all in white and the entire skirt was embroidered with pearls and silver.

Thanks to M. Huart's good coaching, I made my three curtseys very well. I removed my glove and put it on again not too awkwardly. Then I went to receive the accolade from the King . . .

(1778)

In the 2d yeere of Queene Elizabeth, her silk-woman, Mistress Montagu, presented her Majestie, for a new yeare's gift, a pair of black silk knit stockings, the which, after a few day's wearing, pleased her highness so well, that she sent for Mistress Montagu, and asked her where she had them, and if she could help her to any more; who answering, said, 'I *made* them very carefully of purpose only for your Majestie, and seeing them please you so well, I will presently set more in hand.' 'Do (quoth the queene), for indeed I like silk stockings so well, because they are pleasant, fine, and delicate, that henceforth I will wear no more cloth stockings.'

John Stow, *Chronicles of England* (1580)

The king's coronation day was being celebrated . . . The ladies' hoops did not differ at all, for the London ones are just as large as those in Paris; the train, however, which at Versailles trails as a mark of respect, is here held up for the same reason, and only the queen allows hers to hang loose. It was a delightful moment for me, when I offered my hand to the countess for her to step into her hoop, to which the skirt was already fixed; it was made of silver floss, with twining roses, the petals all of foil, like a rose-hedge in which a beauteous nymph, garlanded with flowers, wanted to hide, asking me to lend a hand. The sack with sleeves was of the same silver floss, trimmed with rich blonde lace, flowers and pearls. Nothing is gained by fastening up the train, for a great length is required so as to form a number of deep folds as it loops. I accompanied her to St James' Palace, saw many fine ladies and gentlemen, the former wearing a quantity of diamonds, which, however, the countess did not do, it being forbidden at the Danish court, and the noble lady remains loyal to her native traditions.

The Diary of Sophie V. La Roche (1786)

From The Selected Letters of Somerville and Ross

To Edith Somerville, on the coronation of George V

June 23rd, 1911

Dear Edith,

Here while awaiting the procession I begin a letter – and the comfort is great of a seat here. I am up in the next room, remote from all disturbances – and I know that my seat is there, in front of the western-most drawing window – with an awning over it, and I have but to step into it, at ten o'clock or so. Yesterday morning I was away out of the house at 7 – and into the little electric railway from Battersea Park to Victoria, armed with my ticket for St James' Palace, and the cherry brandy – and sandwiches – and opera glasses and a white striped coat and skirt, with the black collar that you don't like. At Victoria I picked up Nora who is close beside there – and I was thankful to have her – as although the crowd was not great the motors and carriages were *streaming* to the Abbey – it was great and lasting fun to see the Peers and Peeresses therein – but too like the stage, only so much better than any stage. They looked so competent for their parts – sat, and held their heads rightly with their coronets in their laps as well as I could see . . . My ticket with the Chamberlain's name opened all routes . . . once at St James' Palace you could circulate anywhere, as a space around it was kept clear. Here I went and viewed the Second Day Procession – of which more anon. I got in round the corner by the Ambassador's court, and winding stair took me to the roof of the chapel – a lovely place all clean and white, and just beside the clock tower a stand was set forth to hold about thirty people . . . It was very cold and blustery up there, and a heavy shower descended at 8.30 – most depressing and also perishing – and the umbrellas dripped on the seats, and I felt very low for the sake of the poor royalties – all the time a cease-less cataract of carriages passed down St James' Street for the Abbey – with scarlet and ermine laps and fronts showing very gloriously – and the coronets in laps – one could see the glint of them – (N.B. I had opera glasses) and perishing bare necks and chilly long white gloves – nothing can set forth the splendour of some of the Peers or semi-royalties carriages. Hammer-cloths of every hue, heavy with gold, and coats of arms – footmen with long beatle backs, same as hammer-cloth – each coachman a ball of glory, in the hollow centre of his hammer-cloth. Three-cornered hats, powder – one knew it was the genuine article – the carriages dug out and done up, the liveries 'just so' – and such lovely colours – misty yellow, strawberry red – soft blue. It was like Fairyland. The horses were A1 – and their harnesses wonderful – all crusted with gold or silver and these old high carriages with tremendous coats of arms . . . I could not see the King within the gold sway-ing coach; he was the far side from me and I was high up, but the Queen looked very noble, *very* white, but holding her head beautifully with its crown upon it – It was undoubtedly moving in some strange way. They certainly, in their help-less greatness, appeal to chivalry – I stood up and cheered and yelled and waved, and there was a fine roll of it went with them. Then the four children, poor little Princess Mary bowing with a good anxious and pale face, and her hair down her back under her coronet . . .

Yours ever
Martin

MRS STONE

From Chronicles of Fashion

DETAILS OF ROYAL WARDROBES
A HUNDRED YEARS AGO
(FOUND AMONGST LADY SUFFOLK'S PAPERS.)

———

WINTER CLOTHES.
What was delivered yearly for each Princess.
Two rich coats, embroider'd, trim'd, or rich stuff.
One velvet, or rich silk.
Three coats, brocaded or damask.
A damask nightgown.
Two silk under petticoats, trim'd with gold or silver.

———

SUMMER CLOTHES.

Three flower'd coats, one of them with silver.

Three plain or striped lustrings.

One nightgown; four silk hoops.

Their Royal Highnesses, Princess Mary, and Princess Louisa's
Linnen, delivered every two years for each Princess.

QUANTITIES.	PRICE.
Eighteen day shifts,.....................	10s. per ell.
Eighteen nightshifts, trimmed,	8s. per ell: the lace 10s. per yard.
Eighteen fine petticats, five dimity, or Indian quilting, computed at half-yard wide	} 7s. per yard: making 2s. each.
Twelve pairs of thread stockens,	7s. 6d. per pair.
Twelve nightcaps, laced,...............	10s. per yard.
Twelve hoods, cambrick Holand,..	14s. per yard; making 1s. 6d. a suit.
Six petticoats, over-hoops, Indian quilting, about..............	} 3l. 3s. per petticoat: making 12s.
Two dozen pocket handkerchiefs, cambrick,................................	} 4l. 4s. per piece; making 1s. 6d.
Whilst their Royal Highnesses were in bibs and aprons, they had six suits of broad lace for aprons, but the caps and ruffles were much narrower; they came to about...................	} 20l. the suit; making 10s.
It must be remembered they had for birthdays very fine entire lace suits, which came to,..........	} 50l. or 60l. per suit.

(1870)

Marianne is busy learning to make shoes . . . What think you of Princess
Charlotte learning the trade? It rather discomposes me as it is not an amusement for a Queen of England.

The Letter-Bag of Lady Elizabeth Spencer-Stanhope (1806–73)

LADY SYDNEY MORGAN
From France

A T LAST, AFTER full two hours' efforts, and more suffering from heat and apprehension than I ever endured, we passed the last barrier, and arrived at the palladium of the royal toilette. A long suite of beautiful rooms were thrown open, whose lofty walls were thickly covered with robes of every hue, tint, web, and texture, from the imperial drapery of coronation splendour, to the simple *robe-de-chambre* of British lace and British muslin; from the diamond coronet to the *bonnet-de-nuit*; while platforms, or counters, surrounding each room, were guarded off from the unhallowed touch of plebeian curiosity by silken cords, and placed under the surveillance of the priests and priestesses of the toilette, in grand pontificals. These formed the sanctuary of all the minor attributes of the royal wardrobe. Every article of female dress, from the most necessary to the most superfluous, was here arranged, not by dozens, but by hundreds. Here the Queen of Sheba might have died of envy; here the treasures of the 'forty thieves', or the 'cave of Baba Abdalla', were rivalled or surpassed, not only in splendour but extent. The life of the old Countess of Dumont would have been too short, though spent in dressing, to exhaust such a wardrobe as here presented itself; and if such were the sumptuous provision to be made for the future daughters of France, it may be truly said that 'Solomon, in all his glory, was not arrayed like one of these.'

(1817)

MARY, LADY MONKSWELL
From Journals

W E SAW THE Chinese Ambassador pass by covered with jewels & in splendid robes, the two women in little baby caps, one mass of jewels, & faces *painted* white, an extraordinary sight. When I passed through and made my curtseys I retained just enough presence of mind to observe that the old Queen was sitting & the Princess of Wales was standing by her side. I was a little put off my stroke because the rosettes inside the corners of my train on the gold lining caught such a firm hold on the carpet that my train was nearly pulled off my back. It did not show but it felt very heavy.

DAISY ASHFORD

From The Young Visiters

OH YES WHAT fun said Mr Salteena have you any notion what a levie is my man.

Procurio gave a superier smile. It is a party given by the Queen to very superier peaple but this one is given by the Prince of Wales as the Queen is not quite her usual self today. It will be at Buckingham palace so you will drive with his lordship.

Mr Salteena was fearfully excited. What shall I weare he gasped.

Well of course you ought to have black satin knickerbockers and a hat with white feathers also garters and a star or two.

You supprise me said Mr Salteena I have none of those articles.

Well said Procurio kindly his lordship will lend you his second best cocked hat as you are obliged to wear one and I think with a little thourght I might rig you up so as to pass muster.

Then they rumaged among Mr Salteenas things and Procurio got very intelligent and advised Mr Salteena to were his black evening suit and role up his trousers. He also lent him a pair of white silk stockings which he fastened tightly round his knees with red rosettes. Then he quickly cut out a star in silver paper and pinned it to his chest and also added a strip of red ribbon across his shirt front. Then Mr Salteena survayed himself in the glass. Is it a fancy dress party he asked.

No they always were that kind of thing but wait till you see his Lordship – if you are ready sir I will conduct you in.

Mr Salteena followed Procurio up countless stairs till they came to the Earls compartments and tapped on the bedroom door.

Come in cried a merry voice and in they strode.

I have done my best with Mr Salteena my lord I trust he will do the hat of course will make a deal of difference.

Mr Salteena bowed nervously wishing he had got correct knickerbockers as his trousers did not feel too firm in spite of the garters.

Not half bad cried the earl try on the hat Salteena it is on my bed. Mr Salteena placed it on his head and the feathers and gold braid became him very well but he felt very jellous of the earl who looked a sight for the gods. He had proper satin knickerbockers with diamond clasps and buckled shoes and black silk stockings which showed up his long fine legs. He had a floppy shirt of softist muslin with real lace collar and cuffs. A sword hung at his side and a crimson sash was round his waist and a splendid cocked hat on his head. His blue eyes twinkled as he pulled on a pair of white kid gloves.

Well come on Salteena he cried and dont be nervus I will get you a pair of knickers tomorrow. Will you get a hansome Procurio.

Presently the earl and Mr Salteena were clattering away to Buckingham palace.

You wont mind if I introduce you as Lord Hyssops do you said the earl as he lit his pipe. You see you are sort of mixed up with the family so it wont matter and will look better.

So it would said Mr Salteena what do we do at the levie.

Oh we strole round and eat ices and champaigne and that kind of thing and sometimes there is a little music.

Is there any dancing asked Mr Salteena.

Well not always said the Earl.

I am glad of that said Mr Salteena I am not so nimble as I was and my garters are a trifle tight.

Sometimes we talk about the laws and politics said the earl if Her Majesty is in that kind of mood.

The earl twiddled his mustache and slapped his leg with his white glove as calmly as could be. Mr Salteena purspired rarther hard and gave a hitch to his garters to make sure.

Then the portles divided and their names were shouted in chorus by countless domesticks. The sumshious room was packed with men of a noble nature dressed like the earl in satin knickerboccers etc and with ladies of every hue with long trains and jewels by the dozen. You could hardly moove in the gay throng. Dukes were as nought as there were a good lot of princes and Arch Dukes as it was a very superier levie indeed. The earl and Mr Salteena struggled through the crowd till they came to a platform draped with white velvet. Here on a golden chair was seated the prince of Wales in a lovely ermine cloak and a small but costly crown. He was chatting quite genially with some of the crowd.

Just then the splendid edifice appeared in view and Mr Salteena licked his dry lips at sight of the vast crowd. All round were carrages full of costly peaple and outside the railings stood tall Life Guards keeping off the mere peaple who had gathered to watch the nobility clatter up. Lord Clincham began to bow right and left raising his cocked hat to his friends. There was a lot of laughter and friendly words as the cab finally drew up at the front door. Two tall life guards whisked open the doors and one of them kindly tipped the cabman. Mr Salteena followed his lordship up the grand steps trying to feel as homely as he could. Then a splendid looking fellow in a red tunick and a sort of black velvet tam a shanter stepped forward from the throng shouting what name please.

The Earl of Clincham and Lord Hyssops calmly replied the earl gently nudging Mr Salteena to act up. Mr Salteena nodded and blinked at the menial as much as to say all is well and then he and the earl hung up their cocked hats on two pegs.

This way cried a deep voice and another menial apeared wearing stiff white britches top boots and a green velvit coat with a leather belt also a very shiny top hat. They followed this fellow down countless corridoors and finally came to big folding doors.

Up clambered the earl followed at top speed by Mr Salteena.

Hullo Clincham cried the Prince quite homely and not at all grand so glad you turned up – quite a squash eh.

A bit over powering your Highness said the earl who was quite used to all this may I introduce my friend Lord Hyssops he is staying with me so I thought I would bring him along if you dont mind Prince.

Not at all cried the genial prince looking rarther supprised. Mr Salteena bowed so low he nearly fell off the platform and as the prince put out a hand Mr Salteena thought he had better kiss it. The Prince smiled kindly I am pleased to see you Lord Hyssops he said in a regal voice.

Then the Earl chipped in and how is the dear Queen he said reveruntly.

Not up to much said his Highness she feels the heat poor soul and he waved to a placard which said in large letters The Queen is indisposed.

Presently his Highness rose I think I will have a quiet glass of champaigne he said you come too Clincham and bring your friend the Diplomats are arriving and I am not much in the mood for deep talk I have already signed a dozen documents so I have done my duty.

They all went out by a private door and found themselves in a smaller but gorgous room. The Prince tapped on the table and instantly two menials in red tunics appeared. Bring three glasses of champaigne commanded the prince and some ices he added majestikally. The goods appeared as if by majic and the prince drew out a cigar case and passed it round.

One grows weary of Court Life he remarked.

LADY DOROTHY NEVILL
From Reminiscences

A S LATE AS the fifties quite a number of peers wore blue coats and brass buttons. Lord Redesdale, for instance, wore a swallow-tailed blue coat with brass buttons, a white necktie and shoes tied with a bow of black ribbon. Nobody ever saw him in any other suit except at a levée. On the whole there has been comparatively little change in gentlemen's dress during the last half-century, though, of course, minor variations have been frequent. Not so very many years ago quite a number of men wore white duck trousers with a frock-coat in summer. The ducks seem now to have totally disappeared whilst I fear the frock-coat is in a fair way to follow them. The hideous, though convenient, cloth cap is a quite modern invention, as was the dinner jacket, which appears after a hard fight to have been conquered by the old swallow-tailed evening coat, which was probably never so firmly established in public favour as it is to-day. The top-hat, though threatened, still holds its own. A great change has taken place in the shape of this headgear since the sixties, when it was far higher than it is now, and thoroughly deserved the appellation of 'stove-pipe', which the Americans, I believe, still call it. During the sixties there was a craze amongst men for large and loud checks and plaids. Some people carried this to a great extreme. The modern tendency would appear to be to suppress all eccentricity of colour or cut in man's dress. In fact, the whole object of a well-dressed gentleman is now to escape notice by the unobtrusive nature of his well-cut clothes. This was not always the case in the past, when West End tailors permitted themselves various extravagancies.

In the fifties the sleeves of men's coats began to be made very full indeed. At last they became almost gigot sleeves, which caused it to be said that the 'peg-tops' (as the full trousers then fashionable were called) were leaving the gentlemen's legs, and taking shelter under their arms.

In my early childhood there were still men living, who had not abandoned the eighteenth-century fashion of wearing a wig. This custom, indeed, did not entirely die out with the coming of the nineteenth century, some old-fashioned people continuing to wear these head-coverings as late as the early thirties. The last man to wear a pigtail is said to have been one of the Cambridge dons, who retained it as late as the year 1835. The higher clergy did not abandon their wigs till a somewhat later date.

(1906)

CAPT. GRONOW
From Reminiscences

IN 1816, WHEN I was residing in Paris, I used to have all my clothes made by Straub, in the Rue Richelieu . . . As I went out a great deal into the world, and was every night at some ball or party, I found that knee-breeches were only worn by a few old fogies; trousers and shoes being the usual costume of all the young men of the day . . .

I mention the following somewhat trivial circumstance to give some notion of the absurd severity in matters of dress and etiquette of Brummell's worthy pupil, the Prince Regent. A few days after my arrival, I received an invitation to a party at Manchester House, from Lady Hertford, 'to have the honour of meeting the Prince'. I went there dressed 'à la Française', and quite correctly, as I imagined, with white neckcloth and waistcoat, and black trousers, shoes, and silk stockings.

The Prince had dined there, and I found him in the octagon-room, surrounded by all the great ladies of the Court. After making my bow, and retiring to the further part of the room, I sat down by the beautiful Lady Heathcote, and had engaged in conversation with her for some time, when Horace Seymour tapped me on the shoulder, and said, 'the "great man"', meaning the Prince, 'is very much surprised that you should have ventured to appear in his presence without knee-breeches. He considers it as a want of proper respect for him.' This very disagreeable hint drove me away from Manchester House in a moment, in no very pleasant mood . . . In the morning, being on guard, I mentioned what occurred, with some chagrin, to my colonel, Lord Frederick Bentinck, who good-naturedly told me not to take the matter to heart, as it was really of no consequence; and he added – 'Depend upon it, Gronow, the Prince, who is a lover of novelty, will wear trousers himself before the year is out, and then you may laugh at him.' Lord Frederick proved a true prophet, for in less than a month I had the satisfaction of seeing 'the finest gentleman in Europe' at a ball at Lady Cholmondeley's, dressed exactly as I had been at Lady Hertford's, and Lord Fife, who was in attendance upon the Prince, congratulated me upon the fact that his royal master had deigned to take example from the young Welshman.

(1816)

I try and take him to pieces, and find silk stockings, paddings, stays, a coat with frogs and a fur collar, a star and blue ribbon, a pocket-handkerchief prodigiously scented, one of Truefitt's best nutty-brown wigs reeking with oil, a set of teeth and a huge black stock, underwaistcoats, more underwaistcoats, and then nothing.

William Makepeace Thackeray, *The Four Georges*

Cleanliness is not an aristocratic invention.

James Laver, *letter to a girl on the future of clothes*

BEAU NASH
Rules to be observed at Bath

1. That a visit of ceremony at first coming, and another at going away, are all that is expected or desired by ladies of quality and fashion – except impertinents.

2. That ladies coming to the ball appoint a time for their footmen coming to wait on them home, to prevent disturbances and inconveniences to themselves and others.

3. That gentlemen of fashion never appearing in a morning before the ladies in gowns and caps, show breeding and respect.

4. That no person take it ill that any one goes to another's play or breakfast, and not theirs; except captious by nature.

5. That no gentleman give his ticket for the balls to any gentlewomen. – N.B. Unless he has none of his acquaintance.

6. That gentlemen crowding before the ladies at the ball, show ill-manners; and that none do so in future, – except such as respect nobody but themselves.

7. That no gentleman or lady take it ill that another dances before them; – except such as have no pretence to dance at all.

8. That the elder ladies and children be content with a second bench at the ball, as being past or not come to perfection.

9. That the younger ladies take notice how many eyes observe them. – N.B. This does not extend to the Have-at-alls.

10. That all whisperers of lies and scandal be taken for their authors.

11. That all repeaters of such lies and scandal be shunned by all company, – except such as have been guilty of the same crime. – N.B. Several men of no character, old women and young ones of questioned reputation, are great authors of lies in these places, being of the sect of levellers.

Would you see our law-giver, Mr. Nash, whose white hat commands more respect and non-resistance than the Crowns of some Kings, though now worn on a head that is in the eightieth year of its age? To promote society, good manners, and a coalition of parties and ranks; to suppress scandal and late hours, are his views; and he succeeds rather better than his brother-monarchs generally do; hasten then your steps; for he may be soon carried off the stage of life, as the greatest must fall to the worm's repast . . .

Letter from Henrietta, Lady Luxborough, to William Shenstone, 1752

LORD BYRON

From Beppo: A Venetian Story

'Tis known, at least it should be, that throughout
　　All countries of the Catholic persuasion,
Some weeks before Shrove Tuesday comes about,
　　The people take their fill of recreation,
And buy repentance, ere they grow devout,
　　However high their rank, or low their station,
With fiddling, feating, dancing, drinking, masking,
And other things which may be had for asking.

The moment night with dusky mantle covers
　　The skies (and the more duskily the better),
The time less liked by husbands than by lovers
　　Begins, and prudery flings aside her fetter;
And gaiety on restless tiptoe hovers,
　　Giggling with all the gallants who beset her;
And there are songs and quavers, roaring, humming,
Guitars, and every other sort of strumming.

And there are dresses splendid, but fantastical,
　　Masks of all times and nations, Turks and Jews,
And harlequins and clowns, with feats gymnastical,
　　Greeks, Romans, Yankee-doodles, and Hindoos;
All kinds of dress, except the ecclesiastical,
　　All people, as their fancies hit, may choose,
But no one in these parts may quiz the clergy -
Therefore take heed, ye Freethinkers! I charge ye.

You'd better walk about begirt with briars,
　　Instead of coat and smallclothes, than put on
A single stitch reflecting upon friars,
　　Although you swore it only was in fun;
They'd haul you o'er the coals, and stir the fires
　　Of Phlegethon with every mother's son,
Nor say one mass to cool the cauldron's bubble
That boiled your bones, unless you paid them double.

But saving this, you may put on whate'er
   You like by way of doublet, cape, or cloak,
Such as in Monmouth Street, or in Rag Fair,
   Would rig you out in seriousness or joke;
And even in Italy such places are,
   With prettier name in softer accents spoke,
For, bating Covent Garden, I can hit on
No place that's called 'Piazza' in Great Britain.

This feast is named the Carnival, which being
   Interpreted, implies 'farewell to flesh':
So called, because the name and thing agreeing,
   Through Lent they live on fish both salt and fresh.
But why they usher Lent with so much glee in,
   Is more than I can tell, although I guess
'Tis as we take a glass with friends at parting,
In the stage-coach or packet, just at starting.

J. B. S. MORRITT
From Letters and Journals

IF AN ENGLISHMAN wore his shoes on his head I believe he would have imitators here, as we are in high vogue and received with great cordiality. We presented Mrs Philips's letters to Madame Ferrari and the Bishop of Nancy, and met with much civility, and offers of more if we stayed. I was so extremely tired of being quizzy in a dress coat that I followed the example at last of every single Englishman I have met, and made up once more my uniform. As it is a custom in most corps here for a man to be allowed to wear any uniform he has once had, though he is no longer in the corps, there is nothing improper in it. However, don't tell Stanley, as he makes a fuss about these things. Elliot and everybody advised me to do it, and I found that all foreigners, English and others, make a practice of it with less right than I have. Stockdale has sported a grave black dress coat, and looks *Doctor Stockdale* at least. I only wish you could see either of us full dressed, as our figures are excellent.

(1794–6)

WILLIAM OLDYS
From Life of Raleigh

IT WAS COMMON with him [the Duke of Buckingham] at an ordinary dancing, to have his clothes trimmed with great diamond buttons, and to have diamond hatbands, cockades, and ear-rings, to be yoked with great and manifold ropes and knots of pearl, in short, to be manacled, fettered, and imprisoned in jewels; insomuch that, on going to Paris in 1625, he had twenty-five suits of clothes made, the richest that embroidery, lace, velvet, gold, and gems could contribute; one of which was a white uncut velvet, set all over, both suit and cloak, with diamonds, valued at 80,000*l.*, besides a great feather, stuck all over with diamonds, as were also his girdle, sword, hatband, and spurs.

(1736)

LADY CHAWORTH
From Belvoir Castle Calendar

MR BERNARD HOWARD made one of the greatest and most absolute French feasts that ever I saw last Tuesday, att Somerset House, and but eleven of us att it; and the clothes last night at the Queenes birth-night ball was infinite rich, especially Mis Phraser, who put downe all for a gowne, black velvet, imbroydered with all sorts of slips inbost worke of gold and silver, and peticote one broad ermine and gold lace all over; yet I doe not aprove the fancy of either, though they say cost £800.

(1676)

GIUSEPPE DI LAMPEDUSA
From The Leopard

THE PRINCESS MARIA Stella climbed into the carriage, sat down on the blue satin cushions and gathered around her as many rustling folds of her dress as she could. Meanwhile Concetta and Carolina were also getting in; they sat down in front of her, their identical pink dresses exhaling a faint scent of violets. Then a heavy foot on the running board made the barouche heel over on its high springs; Don Fabrizio was getting in too. The carriage was crammed, waves of silk, hoops of three crinolines, billowed, clashed, mingled almost to the height of their heads; beneath was a tight press of foot-gear, the girls' silken slippers, the Princess's russet ones, the Prince's patent leather pumps: each suffered from the other's feet and could find nowhere to put his own.

CHARLES DICKENS
From Bleak House

IT IS BUT a glimpse of the world of fashion that we want on this same miry afternoon. It is not so unlike the Court of Chancery, but that we may pass from the one scene to the other, as the crow flies. Both the world of fashion and the Court of Chancery are things of precedent and usage: oversleeping Rip Van Winkles, who have played at strange games through a deal of thundery weather; sleeping beauties, whom the Knight will wake one day, when all the stopped spits in the kitchen shall begin to turn prodigiously!

It is not a large world. Relatively even to this world of ours, which has its limits too (as your Highness shall find when you have made the tour of it, and are come to the brink of the void beyond), it is a very little speck. There is much good in it; there are many good and true people in it; it has its appointed place. But the evil of it is, that it is a world wrapped up in too much jeweller's cotton and fine wool, and cannot hear the rushing of the larger worlds, and cannot see them as they circle round the sun. It is a deadened world, and its growth is sometimes unhealthy for want of air.

My Lady Dedlock has returned to her house in town for a few days previous to her departure for Paris, where her ladyship intends to stay some weeks; after which her movements are uncertain. The fashionable intelligence says so, for the comfort of the Parisians, and it knows all fashionable things. To know things otherwise, were to be unfashionable. . .

My Lady Dedlock, having conquered *her* world, fell, not into the melting, but rather into the freezing mood. An exhausted composure, a worn-out placidity, an equanimity of fatigue not to be ruffled by interest or satisfaction, are the trophies of her victory. She is perfectly well bred. If she could be translated to Heaven tomorrow, she might be expected to ascend without any rapture.

She has beauty still, and, if it be not in its heyday, it is not yet in its autumn. She has a fine face – originally of a character that would be rather called very pretty than handsome, but improved into classicality by the acquired expression of her fashionable state. Her figure is elegant, and has the effect of being tall. Not that she is so, but that 'the most is made,' as the Honourable Bob Stables has frequently asserted upon oath, 'of all her points.' The same authority observes, that she is perfectly got up; and remarks, in commendation of her hair especially, that she is the best-groomed woman in the whole stud.

EUGENIE FOA

From Livres des cent et un

To be a woman of fashion, and that is not so easy, I assure you, you must be a little more than twenty years of age, a little less than thirty; fat or lean is of no consequence, fair, dark, or chestnut colour is of no matter, except that the dark woman will last some few hours longer than the fair.

The woman of fashion is always dressed with simplicity and elegance; no jewels . . . The farseeing creature will keep them to make herself remarked when her reign is over.

The woman of fashion will purchase her hats at *Simon*'s, her bonnets at *Herbeault*'s, her shoes at *Michael*'s, her boots at *Gilot*'s, her gloves at *Boivin*'s; she will only wear the flowers of *Batton* and the feathers of *Cartier*.

The woman of fashion has no appointed tailor; it is she who invents a cut or makes it of value; only once, observe this well, once only she will have a dress made at *Palmyre's*, never twice; Palmyre repeats herself, and it is desolating to find at a ball three dresses of which the physiognomy agrees with your own . . . it is enough to give you the vapours.

The woman of fashion arrives at the ball; in alighting from her carriage, she is engaged to dance; on the staircase she is engaged, on the landing she is engaged; she was engaged the previous evening, the evening before that, at the last ball; she has more invitations on entering the room than she will dance quadrilles the whole night long.

The woman of fashion is surrounded so that she cannot breathe, engaged so that she knows not to whom to answer, suffocated with compliments, if compliments suffocate, and intoxicated with incense (incense intoxicates), it is charming.

She remains a short time at the ball, as a flash of lightning, the time to dazzle, and then away; the same effect is repeated at two other balls; she departs, returns home in good time, long before fatigue and dancing have deadened the brightness of her eyes, uncurled her hair, taken the shine off her dress. She must have it said of her: 'She only came for an instant, she has so many invitations, so many duties of society to fulfil! One caught a sight of her with difficulty; but never, never did she look so pretty!'

The woman of fashion gets up late, passes her mornings at home, looks after her household affairs, if she has neither mother nor mother-in-law to do it for her; or she takes care of her children, if she has any, or she paints, plays, for, in the nineteenth century, women do all this and avow it . . . Towards four o'clock she gets into a carriage which conducts her to the Bois, at the gate of which attends or does not attend her a horse already bridled for her, which her gallooned servant holds in leash, himself mounted on a fine horse. Then at her side some cavaliers caracole, seven or eight sparks, her partners of last night.

Is it bad weather? Madame goes to pay visits, to make purchases. Then the dinner, then the Bouffes or the Opera, from there to the ball, and so on and so on till spring, an epoch at which the woman who respects herself, the woman who has the slightest regard for her reputation, quits Paris, goes into the country, and returns more beautiful, more fresh than ever at the commencement of winter.

(1886)

The Duchess of Devonshire's Ball

IT WAS A wonderful season for fancy dress balls, Mrs Arthur Paget leading the way before Easter with her very successful *poudré* dance, and Mrs Oppenheim following suit with her flower-ball. The glory of these was overshadowed, however, by the brilliant historic and fancy ball given by the Duchess of Devonshire, and attended by many members of the Royal family. Even in anticipation this ball created a sensation only second to that caused by the Jubilee itself, and it is said that there were ladies who prepared their costumes for the great occasion, but never received an invitation. Great ladies are sometimes capricious, and the fact of being on their visiting list and having been invited to previous entertainments does not at all ensure a continuance of favours.

On July 2nd the great event came off, and the fact that *The Times* devoted four columns to a description of the ball is indicative of the stir it made.

In tissue of silver and cloth of gold, and richly jewelled from head to foot, stood the stately Zenobia, Duchess of Devonshire, at the head of her marble stairway, to receive her guests of all the ages – queens who had stepped out of history to grace the scene, queens from the idyllic stories of long ago, queens from ancient Persia and Abyssinia, and queens from Fairyland. Was not Titania there herself, with glittering wings and lily wand? And the beautiful fair-haired queen, before whom all other queens bent and performed obeisance as she passed, fair Marguerite de Valois, in gleaming snowy satin and high lace collar, with silver-lined train of cloth of gold, was she not our own Princess, the queen of hearts? Her jewels were magnificent indeed, the diamond crown reflected in multitudinous bands and rivers of quivering light from the diamonds and pearls upon her neck. The Princesses in her suite were her own daughters and her daughter-in-law – Princess Victoria in palest citron, the Duchess of Fife in white, Princess Charles of Denmark in pale pink, and the Duchess of York in blue. The Prince of Wales, as Grand Master of the Knights Hospitallers of Malta, in black velvet and white satin, led the Princess to the dais prepared for her, and the glittering processions began to file past, according to their historic period and date. Among the Royal spectators were the Duke of Connaught as an Elizabethan general, looking extremely well in his steel cuirass, inlaid with gold, and dark grey velvet doublet, and trunks slashed with gold-embroidered grey satin; the Duke of York, in the character of the Earl of Cumberland of Elizabeth's reign, also in grey velvet cape and doublet, the trunks crimson velvet slashed with grey, the high grey suède boots rolled outwards at the top, and in the front of his grey felt hat a jewelled cordelière glove, representing that given by good Queen Bess to her faithful Cumberland. Prince Christian, as Earl of Lincoln, wore white satin and velvet, his black velvet cape being lined with ermine. Princess Christian, in eighteenth-century costume of pink and gold, had her hair looped with pearls. Prince Charles of Denmark was very handsome in purple and mauve as a Danish gentleman of the last century, and the Duke of Fife, in royal blue, was a courtier of Marguerite de Valois, as in duty bound. The Marchioness of Lorne was at her best and brightest in red wig and Gretchen white. The Duchess of Connaught was Anne of Austria, in amber velvet brocade, her hair arranged in short ringlets under a jewelled cap: the high Vandyck collar was thickly sewn with pearls and gold. The Duchess of Teck, as Electress of Hanover, looked every inch a queen in her lovely Frédéric gown of orange velvet, the full skirt sewn on with rows of large pearls. Fine old point and royal ermine made the bodice a thing of beauty, and ermine also trimmed the skirt; a very picturesque arrangement of lace falling from one side and caught up in the hair, with a splendid necklace of pearls and diamonds, completed an exact reproduction from a miniature at Hampton Court.

Among the various courts were those of King Arthur, the Doge of Venice, Queen Marie Thérèse, Queen Elizabeth, and Catherine II of Russia. Enid was personated by Lady Ashburton in white cut velvet. Mrs Willy Walker was a pretty Vivian in lurid and sinuous draperies. Her husband, Major Walker, was Merlin, and the knights, in chain armour, white tabards richly broidered, crested helmets, and velvet mantles, were Lord Ashburton, Earl Rodney, Earl Bathurst, Sir Lister Kaye, and the Hon. G. Hood.

Lady Tweedmouth was gorgeously arrayed as Queen Elizabeth, and was surrounded by a numerous Court, including Lord Tweedmouth, Lord Battersea, the Earl of Sandwich, and Lord Frederic Hamilton, to say nothing of six stalwart halberdiers, one of whom was the Duke of Roxburghe, whose Duchess was bravely attired as an Elizabethan lady of high degree. Lady Raincliffe, as Catherine of Russia, was a marvel of millinery in yellow and gold, ermine and rubies. Her lords and ladies emulated her splendour, and among the most successful were the Duchess of Newcastle, Lady Yarborough, Lady Henry Bentinck,

Lord Raincliffe, and Mr Cresswell.

The Countess of Warwick, as Queen Marie Antoinette, in white and blue, with golden fleur-de-lys upon her velvet train, was the centre of a picturesque group, among whom were the Earl of Essex dressed as his ancestor of that period, and the Earl of Mar and Kellie as Sir Walter Raleigh.

Lady Edmonstone was a perfect picture as Mary, Queen of Scots. The Duchess of Sutherland looked prettier than ever as Charlotte Corday in revolutionary red. The Duchess of Hamilton went as Mary Hamilton in Elizabethan days, all in white satin and gold embroidery.

There were three Queens of Sheba, and Paris himself could scarcely have decided to which the apple of beauty should have been awarded. Lovely Lady Cynthia Graham was one, in white satin embroidered in gold and silver and bright rose. Princess Henry of Pless was another, and her dress was absolutely magnificent in its barbaric splendour of turquoise, emerald, amethyst, and ruby, caught in a web of finest gold, and spread thickly upon the dress and train of diaphanous gauze in purple and gold, its shifting light seeming to mingle with that of the jewels. Black attendants bore her train along, and among her girl attendants was her pretty sister, Miss Cornwallis West, in an Ethiopian dress of snowy crêpe, girdled with jewels under a flowing robe of gold tissue. A drapery of gold and pink shot tissue was held round the hips by jewelled wings, and the pleated Liberty silk underdress was hemmed with pink roses, repeating the flowers in the hair.

Lady Archibald Campbell wore a beautiful dress as 'Artemis', goddess of the chase. It was in palest green crêpe de chine, embroidered by hand with glittering silver thread and crystals, which resembled dewdrops. The tunic opened at the side to show an underdress of pale, steely-blue crêpe. Floating scarves of pale blue and green chiffon suggested moonlight. The green chiffon sleeves were held together by crystals. The headdress consisted of a star of crystal on the forehead, and a crescent moon in mother-o'-pearl, lit by electric light.

The Duchess of Leeds wore a lovely dress as Lalla Rookh. Tommy Moore would have beheld his ideal realised. But where was Feramorz? Lady Meysey Thompson, as Elizabeth, Queen of Bohemia, was in orange velvet, yellow satin, and old lace collar; the orange velvet cape sewn with silver, had a garland of lilies slung at the back.

Countess Clary, Countess Kinsky, and Countess Isabel Deym went as the three sisters of Napoleon I in dresses which were perfect copies of an engraving by Isabey. All three being tall, handsome, and graceful, the effect was excellent. Lady Angela Forbes also was Queen of Naples. Miss Muriel Wilson made a splendid Vashti, in white crêpe and silver, with bands of diamonds in her hair, a lotus flower at one side, and a pomegranate at the other.

The Princess of Wales, as Marguerite of Valois, looked quite lovely, but H.R.H. refused to wear the quaint coif of the period, and consequently had a rather modern air. The Duchess of Devonshire was not very well suited as Zenobia, though dressed with the utmost Oriental magnificence. The truth is that many were overweighted and overshadowed by their clothes, the wearers sinking into insignificance in comparison with the splendours of their array. Another circumstance that rather marred the occasion was the disproportionate size of the rooms to the enormous company assembled, and the consequent impossibility of gaining an adequate idea of the scene. A very large hall would be needed in order to display to proper advantage the various quadrilles in which the characters belonging to the different courts joined. This idea was borrowed from the fancy ball given at Marlborough House several years ago.

Many of the dark-haired ladies chose to wear light wigs, while numbers of fair-haired beauties donned dark hair for the occasion. The Duchess of Portland was ill-advised to abandon her own beautiful auburn hair, which is one of the most charming points of her appearance. She spoiled herself with her fair curls. The Duchess of Sutherland, on the contrary, never looked prettier than in the dark locks of Charlotte Corday. Mrs Ronalds, as the Goddess of Music, made a sensation with her electrically lighted head-dress, but had constantly to retire to be lighted up. Princess Charles of Denmark was very much admired. The Countess of Dudley wore a marvellous dress as Queen Esther, a mass of embroidery under a floating robe of peach-tinted gauze, with pale poppies and superb jewels almost covering her head. Every woman there seemed to have emptied her jewel casket over herself, and many of the men were wonderfully jewelled. Lord Rosebery had five hundred pounds' worth of diamond buttons on his Horace Walpole costume. The manner in which serious-minded statesmen and others, who might be supposed to be, like the Laird o' Cockpen, 'ta'en up wi' the things o' the State', dressed up for the ball, spending very high sums on their costumes, was nothing short of surprising. The average price of their costumes was £200 apiece, and in some cases the hire of the jewellery amounted to considerably more. Lord Kenyon and Mr Montagu Guest were the finest men in the rooms. The Hungarian National Anthem was played as the Marchioness of Londonderry's procession passed the Royal dais. The beautiful Marchioness represented the Empress Marie Thérèse, surrounded by a brilliant court. The Duke of Devonshire was Charles V of Germany, and among other well-known men were Earl Spencer as a Florentine noble, Mr Chaplin as General Lefebvre, Mr Joseph Chamberlain (in rose-coloured silk) as a Louis Quinze seigneur, the Hon. Gathorne Hardy in Louis XV dress, Mr Asquith a Roundhead, Lord James of Hereford as Sir Thomas More, Lord Halsbury as George III, and Viscount Peel as a Doge of Venice.

Of the beauties, the most conspicuous were Lady de Grey, a magnificent Cleopatra, Lady de Trafford, a too-lovely Semiramis, Mrs Jack Menzies as Titania, the Countess of Westmorland as Hebe, and the Duchess of Leeds as Lalla Rookh.

The Countess of Suffolk's dress was copied from the painting of a Countess of Suffolk – Maria Constantia – date 1766, skirt of black moiré, with hanging sleeves and draped bodice of chiffon sparkling with embroidery. The Duke of Somerset went as the Protector Somerset, in jetted black velvet; Lord Ellesmere as James I, in grey satin trunks embroidered in large pearls, jewelled grey velvet mantle, etc.; Lord Hyde as Romeo; Lord Winchester as an officer of the Coldstream Guard, 1700; Lord Stavordale as Petrarch when young, in violet crêpe robe, doublet slashed with damask rose velvet and gold laurel wreath. Lady Muriel Fox Strangways, as Lady Sarah Lennox, one of Queen Charlotte's brides-maids, wore the identical bodice, white satin and silver. The Hon. Bridget Harbord, as 'Bride of Abydos,' had a lovely clinging robe, all silver and white, and a little cap embroidered in pearls. Lady Belper, as Ann Page, was in pale blue broché, the slashed sleeves filled in with large puffs of lisse, and a white front to the gown. The Hon. Mrs George Beckett, as Marie Leczinski, wore a very hand-some brocade with chiné roses, worked over with sprays of leaves in gold, emeralds, and diamonds, set in with gold embroidery; the white brocade train-mantle was lined with pink. Mrs Rupert Beckett's white velvet train of the same period was lined with pink. Her gown was silver and white brocade trimmed with lace and crystal embroidery.

Lord Burton, as Cardinal Dubois, was one of the successes of the evening. The different courts had to advance in fours to pass before the Royalties, but the master of the ceremonies thought Lord Burton and Lord Lathom, as the Doge of Venice, so imposing in themselves that they came past alone, or with only their train-bearers.

Sir Henry Irving looked in late, as Cardinal Wolsey. The Royalties did not leave until three, or past. The Duke and Duchess of York were the first to go. The Duchess of Teck walked round with Lord Lathom. The Duke was dressed as an Austrian officer. Prince Francis wore the red coat and uniform of an offi-cer of the Dragoon Guards, and looked very handsome, as did Prince Alexander in the blue coat of a Gentleman of the Guard. Lord Basil Blackwood was in the blue and red uniform of a German officer, date 1818. The Duchess of Marlborough looked very pretty in her pale green Watteau dress wreathed with roses, her hair slightly powdered, with black feathers and roses. Lady Westmorland, as Hebe, was greatly admired, but the enormous eagle on her shoulder was considered by some to be too heavy. The Orientals salaamed. The Hon. Mrs Talbot, as Brunhilde, was much cumbered with her shield and spear.

Lady Gwendolen Cecil looked very well as Portia, in a red robe. The Hon. Mrs George Curzon was a perfect picture in white and blue, with a blue velvet hat at the back of her head. Many of the guests were unable to sit down, so unwieldy were their dresses. A Joan of Arc slipped on the stairs, not being able to manage the marble steps in her iron or steel shoes. Mrs Asquith, either intentionally or accidentally, prostrated herself at the feet of the Royal party.

Several ladies got very much out of temper with the heavy properties they had chosen to carry, and the wearers of velvet and fur-trimmed dresses felt the tropical heat of the night very much, even in the gardens, which were beautifully illuminated. One or two great ladies were observed to be in a frightful passion. Perhaps this was in some degree owing to the heat imparted by white wigs.

In taking leave of the Duchess, the Prince remarked that it was the prettiest ball he had seen for five-and-twenty years. Earlier in the evening, while the Prince was talking to Lady Randolph Churchill – who was so exquisitely dressed as Théodora that someone said that her portrait should be sent to Sardou – a tall and handsome man came up and held out his hand. The Prince took it, and asked, in a puzzled tone, 'Who are you?'

Lady Randolph laughed. 'It is your son-in-law,' she said, 'Prince Charles of Denmark.'

Dawn was just beginning to break, when the Princess of Wales went out on the terrace in the garden and sat down, admiring the lovely light in the sky. A gentleman bent low before her. 'Your collar is crooked, sir,' she said, and with her own pretty fingers Her Royal Highness straightened it for him. He was Mr Arthur Balfour.

At half-past four the Royalties left, and soon the rooms were empty, after having been filled with a crowd that suggested a scene out of 'The Arabian Nights'.

From *The Woman at Home* (1897)

OSBERT SITWELL
From The Scarlet Tree

THE THIN WOMAN, like the ugly woman, hardly aspired to be a *femme fatale* until Léon Bakst had introduced her as paragon into Western Europe. The waist, alone, had to be slim, the body must jut out in front and behind. The staymaker, rather than the costume-designer, appeared to be fashion dictator of that time, and, though the waist had not to be as minute as formerly, a good deal of constrictive torture, comparable to that caused in the contemporary Chinese Empire by fashionable binding of feet, still existed. As for the rest, every adjunct must be conventional and costly; the dresses must be cut very low, while on the contrary the white kid gloves without which at dinner the women would have deemed themselves naked, and which could only be worn once, must reach as high as possible above the elbow. The mode was not yet fully modish, but all these women except the governesses, when present, and the members of the fun brigade, bore about them, nevertheless, the air of the latest mode of the minute; an atmosphere that had been banished from the English *femme du monde* for over seventy years; a period during which it had been confined to women of a different sort, on the smartness of whose appearance had depended their livelihood. Not since the florid days of King George IV had fashion been similarly triumphant.

It seemed as though this world, new born, would last for ever.

EMILE ZOLA

From Nana

A S EXCITED AS if the Grand Prix was going to decide her fortune, Nana wished to take up her position against a barrier beside the winning-post. She had come there very early and was one of the first arrivals in her silver-fitted landau, to which were harnessed four magnificent white horses in Duke d'Aumont style, a present from Count Muffat. When she had appeared at the entrance to the enclosure, with two postilions on the left-side trotting horses and two footmen sitting motionless at the back of the carriage, there was a scuffle among the crowd as though a queen were passing. She wore the colours of the Vandeuvres stable, blue and white, in a very wonderful costume: the little bodice and blue silk tunic fitted tightly to her body, turning up at the back in an enormous bustle which showed off her hips most audaciously in that period when full skirts were worn. The frock was of black satin with white satin sleeves, a sash of white satin crosswise over the shoulder, the whole set off with a silvery wrap which sparkled in the sunshine. To go with it, and to look more like a jockey, she wore on her head a blue toque with a white plume on her chignon, from which the golden tresses fell down her back like an enormous sandy-coloured pigtail.

It struck twelve. They would have to wait three hours for the Grand Prix to be run. When the landau drew up alongside the barrier, Nana settled herself at her ease, as if at home. Out of mere caprice she had taken Bijou and Louiset with her. The dog lay in her skirts shivering with cold in spite of the heat; and the poor little waxen-faced child, dressed up in ribbons and lace, looked dumb and pale in the open air. Nevertheless, without worrying about her neighbours, the young woman chatted in a very loud voice with Georges and Philippe Hugon.

They were sitting facing her on the opposite seat among such a pile of bouquets, white roses and blue myosotis, that they disappeared up to the shoulders . . .

In the meantime the enclosure was filling up. Carriages were continually arriving by the Porte de la Cascade in an endless compact file. There were big omnibuses like the 'Pauline', which started from the Boulevard des Italiens loaded with its fifty passengers, and was making its way to line up on the right of the stands. And then there were dog-carts, victorias and landaus in superb good taste mixed with lamentable cabs jolted along by old nags; and four-in-hands with drivers urging on their four horses, and mail-coaches with their masters high up on the outside seats, leaving the servants inside to take care of the baskets of champagne; and spider-buggies with the enormous wheels reflecting a dazzle of steel, and light tandems as delicate as pieces of clockwork, spinning along to a jingle of bells. Occasionally a horseman rode past; or a surge of pedestrians scattered in fright among the medley of vehicles. To those on the grass, the distant rumble coming from the avenues in the Bois suddenly ended in a dull rustling. Nothing could be heard but the hubbub of the growing crowd, shouts, calls, crackings of a whip fading into the air. And after the gusts of wind, when the sun reappeared on the edge of a cloud, a golden beam lit up the harness and the varnished panels, making the ladies' dresses glow, and in that transparent haze the coachmen high up on their seats flashed their great whips . . .

She had stood up to choose a bookmaker with the right sort of face, but in the meantime, on catching sight of a whole crowd of her acquaintances, forgot what she wanted. Besides the Mignons, Gaga, Clarisse, and Blanche, there were, right and left, behind and in the middle of the mass of carriages which now penned in her landau, Tatan Néné in the company of Maria Blond in a victoria, Caroline Héquet with her mother and two gentlemen in a light four-wheeled carriage with a folding hood, and Louise Violaine was herself driving a little wicker pony-carriage beribboned with the orange-and-green colours of the Méchain stable, while Léa de Horn was on the high seat of a mail-coach where a party of young people were kicking up a shindy. Further away, in an eight-springed carriage fitted out in aristocratic fashion, Lucy Stewart in a very simple black silk dress was giving herself an air of distinction beside a tall youth in the uniform of a midshipman. But what took Nana's breath away was to see Simone arrive in a tandem driven by Steiner, who had a footman sitting behind as stiff as a poker with his arms crossed. Simone was dazzling, all in white satin striped with yellow and covered with diamonds from her waist to her hat; while the banker, holding out an enormous whip, was galloping his two horses in tandem, the leader a little chestnut with a short mouse-like trot, the second a big brown bay, a fine stepper which trotted beautifully.

Transl. Charles Duff

MRS E. M. WARD
From Memories of Ninety Years

W E WERE UP at 6 a.m., and took a memorable walk through the streets. We saw about as motley a gathering as it would be possible to conceive, packed in dense masses. Farmers, wearing broad-brimmed beaver hats, long tailcoats which were donned only on special occasions, bright-coloured waistcoats, and tight breeches, were accompanied by their families. Their wives and daughters, with cheeks like roses, were decked out in stiffly starched print frocks, adorned with flowers and ribbons, and large bonnets. Foreigners of every country mingled with the crowd. Beautifully dressed gentlepeople, the crinoline in evidence, well-to-do tradesmen, clergymen, country doctors, and pickpockets formed such a jumble of humanity as I never saw before. Families had spent the night on doorways, the police treating such vagrants with indifference, and they were having an early meal as we squeezed through the crowd. Cold sausages and bacon were being dealt out by heads of families, children were regaled with milk from enormous bottles, and I saw an old Irishwoman smoking a pipe contentedly. We passed through Hay Hill into Berkeley Square, and the scenes changed. Numbers of people of good social standing had driven up to town overnight, and had slept in their carriages, the horses having been taken out. They were determined to see the Great Exhibition, and were ready to greet the Queen and Royal Family at the precise moment of their arrival. Powdered footmen were preparing breakfast on the pavement, kettles were singing, and the smell of bacon and eggs frying greeted us, whilst fine ladies, in lovely attire, declared they were fainting for a cup of tea. Footmen, distracted by these appeals and the novel manner of serving breakfast, were tumbling over each other. This was about 6.30 a.m.

MARCEL PROUST
From Remembrance of Things Past

S WANN HAD A wonderful scarf of oriental silk, blue and pink, which he had bought because it was exactly that worn by Our Lady in the *Magnificat*. But Mme Swann refused to wear it. Once only she allowed her husband to order her a dress covered all over with daisies, cornflowers, forget-me-nots and campanulas, like that of the Primavera. And sometimes in the evening, when she was tired, he would quietly draw my attention to the way in which she was giving, quite unconsciously, to her pensive hands the uncontrolled, almost distraught movement of the Virgin who dips her pen into the inkpot that the angel holds out to her, before writing upon the sacred page on which is already traced the word '*Magnificat*'. But he added, 'Whatever you do, don't say anything about it to her; if she knew she was doing it, she would change her pose at once.'

Save at these moments of involuntary relaxation, in which Swann essayed to recapture the melancholy cadence of Botticelli, Odette seemed now to be cut out in a single figure, wholly confined within a line which, following the contours of the woman, had abandoned the winding paths, the capricious re-entrants and salients, the radial points, the elaborate dispersions of the fashions of former days, but also, where it was her anatomy that went wrong by making unnecessary digressions within or without the ideal circumference traced for it, was able to rectify, by a bold stroke, the errors of nature, to make up, along a whole section of its course, for the failure as well of the human as of the textile element. The pads, the preposterous 'bustle' had disappeared, as well as those tailed corsets which, projecting under the skirt and stiffened by rods of whalebone, had so long amplified Odette with an artificial stomach and had given her the appearance of being composed of several incongruous pieces which there was no individuality to bind together. The vertical fall of fringes, the curve of trimmings had made way for the inflexion of a body which made silk palpitate as a siren stirs the waves, gave to cambric a human expression now that it had been liberated, like a creature that had taken shape and drawn breath, from the long chaos and nebulous envelopment of fashions at length dethroned. But Mme Swann had chosen, had contrived to preserve some vestiges of certain of these, in the very thick of the more recent fashions that had supplanted them. When in the evening, finding myself unable to work and feeling certain that Gilberte had gone to the theatre with friends, I paid a surprise visit to her parents, I used often to find Mme Swann in an elegant dishabille the skirt of which, of one of those rich dark colours, blood-red or orange, which seemed always as though they meant something very special, because they were no longer the fashion, was crossed diagonally, though not concealed, by a broad band of black lace which recalled the flounces of an earlier day. When on a still chilly afternoon in Spring she had taken me (before my rupture with her daughter) to the Jardin d'Acclimatation, under her coat, which she opened or buttoned up according as the exercise made her feel warm, the dog-toothed border of her blouse suggested a glimpse of the lapel of some non-existent waistcoat such as she had been accustomed to wear, some years earlier, when she had liked their edges to have the same slight indentations; and her scarf – of that same 'Scotch tartan' to which she had remained faithful, but whose tones she had so far softened, red becoming pink and blue lilac, that one might almost have taken it for one of those pigeon's-breast taffetas which were the latest novelty – was knotted in such a way under her chin, without one's being able to make out where it was fastened, that one could not help being reminded of those bonnet-strings which were now no longer worn. She need only 'hold out' like this for a little longer and young men attempting to understand her theory of dress would say: 'Mme Swann is quite a period in herself, isn't she?' As in a fine literary style which overlays with its different forms and so strengthens a tradition which lies concealed among them, so in Mme Swann's attire those half-hinted memories of waistcoats or of ringlets, sometimes a tendency, at once repressed, towards the 'all aboard', or even a distant and vague allusion to the 'chase me' kept alive beneath the concrete form the unfinished likeness of other, older forms which you would not have succeeded, now, in making a tailor or a dressmaker reproduce, but about which your thoughts incessantly hovered, and enwrapped Mme Swann in a cloak of nobility – perhaps because the sheer use-lessness of these fripperies made them seem meant to serve some more than utilitarian purpose, perhaps because of the traces they preserved of vanished years, or else because there was a sort of personality permeating this lady's wardrobe, which gave to the most dissimilar of her costumes a distinct family likeness. One felt that she did not dress simply for the comfort or the adornment of her body; she was surrounded by her garments as by the delicate and spiritu-alised machinery of a whole form of civilisation.

When Gilberte, who, as a rule, gave her tea-parties on the days when her moth-er was 'at home', had for some reason to go out, and I was therefore free to attend Mme Swann's 'kettledrum', I would find her dressed in one of her lovely gowns, some of which were of taffeta, others of grosgrain, or of velvet, or of *crêpe-de-Chine*, or satin or silk, gowns which, not being loose like those that she general-ly wore in the house but buttoned up tight as though she were just going out in them, gave to her stay-at-home laziness on those afternoons something alert and energetic. And no doubt the daring simplicity of their cut was singularly appro-priate to her figure and to her movements, which her sleeves appeared to be symbolising in colours that varied from day to day: one would have said that there was a sudden determination in the blue velvet, an easy-going good humour in the white taffeta, and that a sort of supreme discretion full of dignity in her way of holding out her arm had, in order to become visible, put on the appear-ance, dazzling with the smile of one who had made great sacrifices, of the black *crêpe-de-Chine*. But at the same time these animated gowns took from the com-plication of their trimmings, none of which had any practical value or served any conceivable purpose, something detached, pensive, secret, in harmony with the melancholy which Mme Swann never failed to shew, at least in the shadows under her eyes and the drooping arches of her hands. Beneath the profusion of sap-phire charms, enamelled four-leaf clovers, silver medals, gold medallions, turquoise amulets, ruby chains and topaz chestnuts there would be, on the dress itself, some design carried out in colour which pursued across the surface of an inserted panel a preconceived existence of its own, some row of little satin buttons, which buttoned nothing and could not be unbuttoned, a strip of braid that sought to please the eye with the minuteness, the discretion of a delicate reminder; and these, as well as the trinkets, had the effect – for otherwise there would have been no possible justification of their presence – of disclosing a secret intention, being a pledge of affection, keeping a secret, ministering to a superstition, commemorating a recovery from sickness, a granted wish, a love affair or a 'philippine'. And now and then in the blue velvet of the bodice a hint of 'slashes', in the Henri II style, in the gown of black satin a slight swelling which, if it was in the sleeves, just below the shoulders, made one think of the 'leg of mutton' sleeves of 1830, or if, on the other hand, it was beneath the skirt, with its Louis XV paniers, gave the dress a just perceptible air of being 'fancy dress' and at all events, by insinuating beneath the life of the present day a vague reminiscence of the past, blended with the person of Mme Swann the charm of certain heroines of history or romance. And if I were to draw her attention to this: 'I don't play golf,' she would answer, 'like so many of my friends. So I should have no excuse for going about, as they do, in sweaters.'

Transl. F. Scott Moncrieff

GUSTAVE FLAUBERT
From Madame Bovary

WHEN THE OPENING quadrille was over, the floor was left free for the groups of men standing about and the liveried servants, who carried huge trays. Along the line of seated women, painted fans moved to and fro, bouquets half hid the smiles of the faces, and gold-topped scent-bottles twirled in loosely closed hands, the white gloves of which showed the shape of the nails and compressed the flesh at the wrist. Lace trimmings, diamond brooches, medallion bracelets, trembled on the bodices, glittered on the bosoms, tinkled on the bare arms. The hair of the ladies, pressed well down over the brow and coiled on the neck, was crowned by clusters or branches of forget-me-not, jasmine, pomegranate-flowers, wheat or corn-flowers. Peacefully reposing in their places, sour-faced mothers wore red turbans.

Emma's heart beat a little when, her partner holding her finger-tips, she advanced to place herself in line and awaited the stroke of the violin bow, before commencing the dance. But soon her agitation disappeared; and balancing herself to the rhythm of the orchestra, she glided forward with light swaying movements of her neck. A smile rose to her lips at certain tender tones of the violin, which played alone sometimes, when the other instruments were silent; you could hear the light chink of the golden louis as they were placed on the tables in the next room; then all would begin again at once, the cornet-à-piston launched forth a sonorous crash, feet moved again in time, skirts floated out and touched each other lightly in passing, hands were given and released; the same eyes, after being lowered before you, returned to fix themselves on yours.

A few men (about fifteen), ranging in age from twenty-five to forty, scattered among the dancers or talking near the doorways, were distinguishable among the crowd by an air of breeding, whatever the differences between them in point of age, dress, or appearance.

Their clothes, better cut, seemed of a softer cloth; and their hair, combed down in ringlets towards the temples, seemed made glossy by finer pomades. They had the complexion of wealth, that white skin which is enhanced by the paleness of porcelain, the moire of satin, the polish of handsome furniture, and which is maintained in health by a carefully chosen diet of delicate food. Their necks moved within low cravats; their long whiskers fell over turned-down collars; they wiped their lips on handkerchiefs embroidered with a large monogram, from which there was diffused a pleasant perfume. Those who were beginning to grow old had an air of youth, while some suggestion of maturity was visible in the countenance of the younger men. In their indifferent glances floated the tranquility of passion daily satisfied; and, through their suave manners, there pierced that particular brutality which is communicated by the domination of half-yielding things, in which force is exercised and vanity amused, by the management of thoroughbred horses and the society of degraded women.

Transl. Henry James

There were many visitors to the house, amongst whom were the beautiful Mrs Langtry and Mrs Wheeler, both friends of my still beautiful mother. I well remember their curious concertina-shaped bustles and little pork-pie hats decorated with silk pom-poms, and their tippets, either of fur or eiderdown, which barely covered their shoulders. My mother once showed me a hat which had been sent her as a present by the late Duke of Fife; it was made of a ptarmigan, the head of which stuck out in front so that when she put it on her head it gave the impression of the bird sitting on a nest.

George Cornwallis-West, *Edwardian Hey-Days* (1930)

ANGUS WILSON

From For Whom the Cloche Tolls

How that funny old photograph recalls it all! We still hadn't got quite away from the idea that Woman was a sort of lampstand to be hung with decorations. Those great hats and cloaks and veilings! We thought them very pretty, I'm afraid. Of course, we weren't all as excessive as poor Maisie. No matter how much she spent on her clothes, she never looked quite right. Her figure didn't really help; it had neither the proportion to be called 'fine' nor the carriage to be called graceful. Later when the more 'petite' figure became fashionable, she tried every ridiculous fad in order to reduce, and, of course, always looked haggard and drawn as a result. But, apart from her figure, she just did not know how to *wear* her clothes. No matter what Paquin or Molyneux did for her, she always added some little colour or ornament which completely destroyed the effect. Even when she was in mourning, she insisted on adding a great gold buckle and tassel! I remember so well the very day this photograph was taken, I was wearing a plain black gabardine coat-frock with appliqué jet and a simple black satin toque with an egret – the whole thing costing about one quarter of Maisie's clothes – and yet I flatter myself . . . But then simplicity is the hallmark of good taste, as we began to see a few years later. The little snap that my nephew Tata took of me pasting scraps into this very album will show what I mean. Just a plain rust silk stockinette frock with jade green jazz design, and a jade green and rust *apache* scarf. It was really the prettiest period imaginable, with its charming neat shingled heads. My hair had a lovely auburn tinge then – Bridget has just the same – and I always wore something green, if only a scarf or handkerchief – to set it off. But I seem to be writing all about myself – Harold would say no woman could resist the temptation to do so! – and I had meant this to be a little tribute to Maisie and the children!

Doesn't dear Bridget look sweet, despite the ugly waist-line? I don't think it's just fancy to see already not only the fascinating debutante of Cecil Beaton's famous photograph, but also the splendid wife and mother she is now.

I think the reason my generation bobbed and shingled their hair, flattened their bosoms and lowered their waists, was not that we wanted to be masculine but that we did not want to be emotional. War widows, many of them still wearing crepe and widow's weeds in the Victorian tradition, had full bosoms, full skirts and fluffed out hair . . . it was anti-sentiment . . . not . . . anti-feminine.

Barbara Cartland, *We Danced All Night*

I think her avarice, her dirt, and her vivacity are all increased. Her dress, like her languages, is a *galimatias* of several countries; the ground-work rags, and the embroidery nastiness. She needs no cap, no handkerchief, no gown, no petticoat, no shoes. An old black-lace hood represents the first; the fur of a horseman's coat, which replaces the third, serves for the second; a dimity petticoat is deputy, and officiates for the fourth; and slippers act the part of the last.

Horace Walpole on Lady Mary Wortley Montague

LORD BERNERS
From First Childhood

IN APPEARANCE LADY Bourchier was not unlike Holbein's portrait of Bloody Mary with just a touch of Charley's Aunt. In fact her coiffure might have been modelled upon that of the latter, and she wore a lace cap with two large, melancholy black bows on it, which always made me think of a couple of crows perching on the roof of a Methodist chapel. There was indeed something very peculiar about all her clothes. Though she usually wore a simple costume of black silk resembling in style the dresses worn by Queen Victoria in her later years, the garment was not as simple as it looked. It appeared to possess the faculty of increasing or diminishing in volume like the sails of a ship. It was rumoured that, concealed beneath her skirts, there was an elaborate system of strings and pulleys for raising her petticoats off the ground whenever she walked in the garden. Whether this was the case or not I imagine nobody had ever ventured to probe. It is certain that, whenever she went out of doors, her clothes used to assume a curious bunched-up appearance behind, which made her look like an emu.

CELIA FIENNES
From Through England on a Side Saddle in the Time of William and Mary

THE LADYES GOES into the bath with Garments made of a fine yellow canvas, which is stiff and made large with great sleeves like a parsons gown; the water fills it up so that its borne off that your shape is not seen, it does not cling close as other linning, which Lookes sadly in the poorer sort that go in their own linning. The Gentlemen have drawers and wastcoates of the same sort of canvas, this is the best linning, for the bath water will Change any other yellow. When you go out of the bath you go within a doore that leads to Steps which you ascend by degrees that are in the water, . . . you still ascend severall more steps and let your Canvass drop of by degrees into the water, which your women guides take off, and the meane tyme your maides flings a garment of flannell made like a Nightgown with great sleeves over your head, and ye guides take ye taile and so pulls it on you Just as you rise ye steps, and yr other garment drops off so you are wrapped up in ye flannell and your nightgown on ye top, and your slippers and so you are set in Chaire, . . . then a Couple of men with staves takes and Carryes you to your lodging and sets you at yr bedside where you go to bed and lye and sweate some time as you please.

I may mention for your consolation that Mr Byng (a tall gentlemanly blasé-looking man) was dressed from head to foot in unbleached linen; while Babbie may take a slight satisfaction to her curiosity de femme from knowing how a Paget attires herself of a morning to sit under a beech tree – a white-flowered muslin pelisse, over pale blue satin; a black lace scarf fastened against her heart with a little gold horse-shoe; her white neck tolerably revealed, and set off with a brooch of diamonds; immense gold bracelets, an immense gold chain; a little white silk bonnet with a profusion of blond and flowers; thus she had prepared herself for being rural! But with all this finery, she looked a good-hearted rattling, clever haveral sort of woman. Her account of Lord Londonderry's sentimental dedication to his wife was perfect – 'from a goose to a goose' – and she defended herself with her pocket handkerchief against the wasps, with an energy.

Jane Welsh Carlyle, *Correspondence*

ANGELA CARTER
From Wise Children

'WHAT SHALL WE wear tonight?' said Nora . . .
    'Tell you what,' I said to Nora. 'You put on some Shalimar, tonight; I'll use Mitsouko.' . . .
    'Quite like old times,' she said with a glint.
    'Don't let's exaggerate.' . . .
    As we opened up the wardrobe, we saw ourselves swimming in the mirrored door as if in a pool of dust and, for a split second, in soft focus, we truly looked

like girls, again. And going through those cast-offs was a trip down Memory Lane and a half, I can tell you. First, there was the lingerie – silk, satin, lace, eau de nil, blush rose, flesh, black and red ribbons, straight up and down things from the twenties, slithering things from the thirties, curvy things from the forties, waspies, merry widows, uplift bras. At the very bottom of the pile, I seized on something navy blue – the bloomers from our dancing class! From Miss Worthington's dancing class! To think that Grandma had kept our old bloomers!

Then there were the frocks. Some things we'd put away in plastic bags: bias-cut silk jersey, beaded sheaths that weighed a ton. Others we'd covered up with sheets, the big net skirts, the taffeta crinolines, halter necks, strapless, backless, etc. etc. etc., all heaped high on Grandma's bed.

'Half a century of evening wear,' said Nora. 'A history of the world in party frocks.'

LORD BERNERS
From First Childhood

MRS LAFONTAINE AND her companion were the apotheosis of a certain type of Englishwoman still happily to be met with on the Continent. Both of them had the slightly prominent teeth of the traditional 'fille d'Albion'. Their high fringes in the Queen Alexandra style were crowned with hats perched at a slanting angle which made them look as though they were just about to loop the loop. The gestures of the two ladies were brisk and decided, their voices rather loud and authoritative. One could visualise them moving through foreign crowds, oblivious of mockery, wholly concentrated on the enjoyment of 'being abroad'.

CAPT. MARRYAT
From Mr Midshipman Easy

MISS JULIA HICKS, as we before observed, set the fashions at Tetuan, and her style of dress was not unbecoming. The Moorish women wore large veils, or they may be called what you will, for their head-dresses descend to their heels at times and cover the whole body, leaving an eye to peep with, and hiding everything else. Now Miss found this much more convenient than the bonnet, as she might walk out in the heat of the sun without burning her fair skin, and stare at everybody and everything without being stared at in return. She therefore never went out without one of these overalls, composed of several yards of fine muslin. Her dress in the house was usually of coloured sarcenet, for a small vessel came into the port one day during her father's lifetime, unloaded a great quantity of bales of goods with English marks, and, as the vessel had gone out in ballast, there was a surmise on his part by what means they came into the captain's possession. He therefore cited the captain up to the governor, but the affair was amicably arranged by the vice-consul receiving about one quarter of the cargo in bales of silks and muslins. Miss Hicks had therefore all her dresses of blue, green, and yellow sarcenet, which, with the white muslin overall, made her as conspicuous as the only Frankish lady in the town had a right to be, and there was not a dog which barked in Tetuan which did not know the sister of the vice-consul, although few had seen her face.

COLETTE
From Julie de Carneilham

S HE UNDRESSED SLOWLY, and created a breath of air between the studio and the kitchen before going straight to a little mother-of-pearl fitted box, without a lock, which was hidden in the hanging-cupboard. She undid a bundle of letters, picked out a sheet of paper bearing a sixty-centime stamp, and re-read it. '*I hereby testify that I have received, in the nature of a loan, from Madame Julius Becker* . . .' She folded it up at once, and put back everything in good order.

She scattered her remaining hundred and forty francs and the platinum chain over her bedside table. Then she put on her damp bath-robe and sat down to make out a list. 'Two tailor-made suits. Four blouses. Two v. pretty pullovers. A long overcoat. An afternoon dress. Stockings, gloves, shoes, hats (two only). Underclothes. A very smart mackintosh.' She took the chain solemnly into the kitchen to weigh it on the scales; but she could not find the weights. She lay listening to the wind sweeping across the sheet-zinc of the roof, and then turned the lamp on again and picked up the list. Opposite 'underclothes' she wrote 'For whose benefit?' and then crossed it out and went back to bed.

*

The days following were measured out to Julie in equal doses of disappointment and intoxication. She went to a Dressmaking House where she unearthed an elderly and rebellious saleswoman, who wore a bang of carrot-coloured tow on her forehead, told horrifying tales about the days of vitriol- throwing, and smoked in the w.c. But she made the clumsy mistake of saying to Julie, 'Ah, in our day, Countess . . .', and Julie squandered eight out of her ten thousand francs at another dressmaker's.

'But what are you doing?' Lucie Albert complained into the telephone. 'Nobody seems to see you any more.'

'I'm working,' Julie answered importantly. 'Come round if you like and I'll teach you how to knit washable sports-gloves.'

Her experimental bent and her skill with her hands had returned to her. She gilded a pair of mules, and tried painting a solution of *vernis-Martin* over an old biscuit box, which turned out like an enormous caramel. Finally, she knitted some gloves and a scarf out of very thick pink string, over which Lucie Albert was lost in admiration. The huge, nocturnal eyes of the little pianist-cashier blinked sleepily as she tried to follow the needles, for she could only manage to relax when sitting at a table in a bar or outside a café.

'I've seen some lovely washable gloves in the Rue Fontaine,' she said. 'They've even got some sky-blue ones.'

'Knitted by machinery,' said Lucie.

'Yes. And what if they are? They're just as good.'

Brand-new, dashing, self-centred, dressed up in grey and black, smartly gloved and wearing a pink scarf, Julie went out one morning at eleven o'clock. There was a yellow, end-of-August sun, and she stopped in front of the glass between two shop windows. 'A woman like that,' she thought, 'can still look a knockout if she's properly dressed. That little felt hat with the wood-pigeon's feather is a pure marvel. All the outfit needs is a dark grey man. But that's an expensive accessory.'

Transl. Patrick Leigh Fermor

ISABEL COLGATE

From Statues in a Garden

AND HERE SHE is in her black velvet and all her diamonds, pausing at the top of the stairs which lead, so conveniently for dramatic effect, down into the crowded reception-room. And the faces turn, obediently. And she pauses, pretending to look for her hostess, turning her head with its elaborate gleaming pile of hair first to one side then to the other, on the famous long white neck. And how gloriously white the shoulders and the bosom, how fine the moulding of the arms, how wide the great dark gaze of the eyes. But the pause is not a moment too long. She begins to move, and Aylmer, happy in his role, follows a step or two behind, and she glides down the stairs with the velvet spreading out behind her, and her smile begins slowly and widens for her hostess, and she stretched out both jewelled hands, as it were, impulsively, and what a benefit she bestows!

And later an ambassador says, 'I must tell you that I think you make the most beautiful entrances,' and is quite ravished by the serene happiness of the smile with which she answers, '*Don't* I?'

ANTHONY TROLLOPE
From Barchester Towers

SHE HAD BEEN a beauty, and even now, at fifty-five, she was a handsome woman. Her dress was always perfect: she never dressed but once in the day, and never appeared till between three and four; but when she did appear, she appeared at her best. Whether the toil rested partly with her, or wholly with her handmaid, it is not for such a one as the author even to imagine. The structure of her attire was always elaborate, and yet never overlaboured. She was rich in apparel, but not bedizened with finery; her ornaments were costly, rare, and such as could not fail to attract notice, but they did not look as though worn with that purpose. She well knew the great architectural secret of decorating her constructions, and never descended to construct a decoration. But when we have said that Mrs Stanhope knew how to dress, and used her knowledge daily, we have said all. Other purpose in life she had none.

Dressed in black silk, with a ruby cross as well as her customary string of pearls round her neck, she presided.

Aldous Huxley, *Crome Yellow*

ARNOLD BENNETT
From The Old Wives' Tale

SHE LOOKED CURIOUSLY at Madame Foucault, who was carefully made up and arranged for the street, in a dress of yellow tussore with blue ornaments, bright lemon-coloured gloves, a little blue bonnet, and a little white parasol not wider when opened than her shoulders. Cheeks, lips, and eyes were heavily charged with rouge, powder, or black. And that too abundant waist had been most cunningly confined in a belt that descended beneath, instead of rising above, the lower masses of the vast torso. The general effect was worthy of the effort that must have gone to it. Madame Foucault was not rejuvenated by her toilette, but it almost procured her pardon for the crime of being over forty, fat, creased, and worn out. It was one of those defeats that are a triumph.

'You are very chic,' said Sophia, uttering her admiration.

'Ah!' said Madame Foucault, shrugging the shoulders of disillusion. 'Chic! What does that do?'

But she was pleased.

ALPHONSE DAUDET

From Sappho

'GET UP QUICKLY, we're going to have lunch in the country.'
'In the country?'

'Yes, at Enghien, at Rosa's. She's invited us both.' At first he said no, but she insisted: Rosa would never forgive a refusal. 'You might come for my sake. I do enough, I should think.'

The place was by the lake at Enghien and looked out on a vast lawn sweeping down to a little boat-house where some rowing-boats and punts were moored, swaying lightly on the water. The house itself was a large chalet, marvellously decorated and furnished, with mirrors let into the ceilings and walls to reflect the sparkle of the water and the superb young hornbeams growing in the park, already a-quiver with the first hurried touches of green, and the flowering lilac. There were servants in immaculate livery; there were walks where not a twig lay on the ground; it was a credit to Rosario's and old Pilar's joint vigilance.

The rest of the party was at table when they arrived, for they had been misdirected and had wasted time going all round the lake, along little paths between high garden walls. Jean was completely put out of countenance by the chilly welcome given them by the mistress of the house, who was furious at having been kept waiting, and by the extraordinary appearance of the hags, looking like the Fatal Sisters themselves, to whom Rosa introduced him, her voice hoarse as a drayman's. They were three *élégantes*, as the most expensive cocottes referred to themselves: three ancient whores who had been among the most brilliant figures of the Second Empire, with names as famous as any great poet's or any victorious general's – Wilkie Cob, Sombreuse, and Clara Desfous.

The *élégantes* were smart enough even now, certainly, got up to the nines in the latest fashion, in pale summery colours, all exquisite lace and ribbons from their little collars down to their little boots. Only how withered, how raddled and frizzed! There Sombreuse sat with blank, lashless eyes, her lower lip hanging, and fumbled about with plate, fork, or glass. La Desfous was a vast blotchy-looking woman with a hot-water bottle at her feet and her poor gnarled rheumatic fingers spread out on the tablecloth to show off her glittering rings, which were as difficult to get on and off as the rings of a Chinese puzzle. Cob was very slim, but her youthful figure only made her lean fleshless face seem more horrible than ever; with her mop of yellow tow-like hair she looked like a sick clown. Ruined and desperate, she had gone to try a last fling at Monte Carlo and had come back without a penny, frantic with love for a handsome croupier who had not wanted to have anything to do with her. Rosa had taken her in and fed her and was making a great boast of it.

All these women knew Fanny, whom they greeted with a patronizingly friendly: 'Well, how are things, dear?' The fact was that in her dress made of stuff costing three francs a yard and with no jewel but Kuyper's red brooch, she looked like a raw recruit among these ghastly old women who had long ago won their stripes on the field of amorous adventure and who looked more spectral than ever framed in this luxurious setting, the light reflected from lake and sky, and the air coming in through the dining-room windows, gusty with scents of spring.

There was also old Mother Pilar, 'the monkey', as she called herself, talking her broken French interlarded with Spanish. Indeed she looked a thorough macacus, with her loose, rough skin and an expression of ferocious spite on her face, always grimacing, her hair cut short like a man's and grey over her ears. Her old black satin dress was topped with a big blue collar like a master mariner's.

Transl. Eithne Wilkins

SIR WALTER SCOTT
From The Antiquary

THE ELDERLY LADY rustled in silks and satins, and bore upon her head a structure resembling the fashion in the ladies' memorandum-book for the year 1770 – a superb piece of architecture, not much less than a modern Gothic castle, of which the curls might represent the turrets, the black pins the *chevaux de frise*, and the lappets the banners.

The face, which, like that of the ancient statues of Vesta, was thus crowned with towers, was large and long, and peaked at nose and chin, and bore, in other respects, such a ludicrous resemblance to the physiognomy of Mr Jonathan Oldbuck, that Lovel, had they not appeared at once, like Sebastian and Viola in the last scene of the 'Twelfth Night', might have supposed that the figure before him was his old friend masquerading in female attire. An antique flowered silk gown graced the extraordinary person to whom belonged this unparalleled tête, which her brother was wont to say was fitter for a turban for Mahound or

Termagant, than a headgear for a reasonable creature, or Christian gentlewoman. Two long and bony arms were terminated at the elbows by triple blond ruffles, and being folded saltire-ways in front of her person, and decorated with long gloves of a bright vermillion colour, presented no bad resemblance to a pair of gigantic lobsters. High-heeled shoes, and a short silk cloak, thrown in easy negligence over her shoulders, completed the exterior of Miss Griselda Oldbuck.

ADA LEVERSON
From Love's Shadow

Lady cannon had never been seen after half-past seven except in evening dress, generally a velvet dress of some dark crimson or bottle-green, so tightly-fitting as to give her an appearance of being rather upholstered than clothed. Her cloaks were always like well-hung curtains, her trains like heavy carpets; one might fancy that she got her gowns from Gillows. Her pearl dog- collar, her diamond ear-rings, her dark red fringe and the other details of her toilette were put on with the same precision when she dined alone with Sir Charles as if she were going to a ceremonious reception. She was a very tall, fine-looking woman. In Paris, where she sometimes went to see Ella at school, she attracted much public attention as *une femme superbe*. Frenchmen were heard to remark to one another that her husband *ne devrait pas s'embêter* (which, as a matter of fact, was precisely what he did – to extinction); and even in the streets when she walked out the gamins used to exclaim, '*Voilà l'Arc de Triomphe qui se promène!*' – to her intense fury and gratification. She was still handsome, with hard, wide-open blue eyes, and straight features. She always held her head as if she were being photographed in a tiara *en profil perdu*. It was in this attitude that she had often been photographed and was now most usually seen; and it seemed so characteristic that even her husband, if he accidentally caught a glimpse of her full-face, hastily altered his position to one whence he could behold her at right angles.

As she grew older, the profile in the photographs had become more and more *perdu*; the last one showed chiefly the back of her head, besides a basket of flowers, and a double staircase, leading (one hoped) at least to one of the upper rooms in Buckingham Palace.

VITA SACKVILLE WEST
From The Edwardians

YES, SHE WAS indeed a beautiful woman, she decided, catching sight of herself in a long mirror as she came out of the cloak-room at Buckingham Palace. She was alone in the passage, but for the beef-eaters, and they affected her no more than so many pieces of furniture. She could take stock of herself in the mirror without any consciousness of men watching her; beef-eaters were not men, they were effigies stuck down at intervals; no more men than sentries, or dummies in suits of armour. So she loitered, having come out of the cloak-room only to face an unexpected mirror that returned to her, full-length, the image of the complete woman she might have postulated from the head-and-shoulders revealed to her in the mirror propped on the cloak-room table. There, she had scrutinised a lovely head, something after the manner of Lely, she thought – having been told so innumerable times – and the bare shoulders, oyster satin, and pearls of Lely, all of which she affected on state occasions because she knew they accorded with her type of beauty. Here, in the long mirror, she saw herself not only as a kit-cat, but full-length: oyster satin flowing out at her feet, pearls vanishing into the valley between her breasts, pearls looped round her wrists, a rosy scarf tossed round her shoulders. She wore no tiara. The fact that Lady Roehampton wore no tiara at Court balls made other women say, with a half-deprecatory, half-envious laugh, that Lady Roehampton was an unconventional woman. Such daring was almost insolent. It was almost rude. But the Order of St John of Jerusalem caught and held her rosy scarf.

From Samuel Pepys's Diary

29 November. Lords Day. This morning I put on my best black cloth suit trimmed with scarlett ribbon, very neat, with my cloak lined with velvett and a new beaver, which altogether is very noble, with my black silk knit canons I bought a month ago. I to church alone, my wife not going; and there I find my Lady Batten in a velvet gowne, which vexed me that she should be in it before my wife, or that I am able to put her into one; but what cannot be, cannot be. However, when I came home I told my wife of it; and to see my weakness, I could on the sudden have found my heart to have offered her one, but second thoughts put it by: and indeed, it would undo me to think of doing as Sir W. Batten and his Lady do, who hath a good estate besides his office.

JOHN BUCHAN

From The Dancing Floor

I HAD A SHARP impression of the change which five years had brought. This was not, like a pre-war ball, part of the ceremonial of an assured and orderly world. These people were dancing as savages danced – to get rid of or to engender excitement. Apollo had been ousted by Dionysos. The nigger in the band who came forward now and then and sang some gibberish was the true master of ceremonies. I said as much to Vernon, and he nodded. He was watching with a curious intensity the faces that passed us.

'Everybody is leaner,' I said, 'and lighter on their feet. That's why they want to dance. But the women have lost their looks.'

'The women!' he murmured. 'Look at that, I beseech you!'

It was a tall girl, who was dancing with a handsome young Jew, and dancing as I thought, with a notable grace. She was very slim and clearly very young, and I dare say would have been pretty, if she had let herself alone. I caught a glimpse of fine eyes, and her head was set on her neck like a flower on its stalk. But some imp had inspired her to desecrate the gifts of the Almighty. Her hair was bobbed, she had too much paint and powder on her face, she had some kind of barbaric jewels in her ears which put her head out of drawing, and she wore a preposterous white dress. Don't ask me to describe it, for I am not an expert in millinery; but it seemed to me wrong by every canon of decency and art. It had been made, no doubt, with the intention of being provocative, and its audacious lines certainly revealed a great deal of its wearer's body. But the impression was rather of an outrage perpetrated on something beautiful, a foolish ill-bred joke.

IAN FLEMING

From Casino Royale

B OND FELT HER presence strongly. While he and Mathis talked, he turned from time to time towards her, politely including her in the conversation, but adding up the impressions recorded by each glance.

Her hair was very black and she wore it cut square and low on the nape of the neck, framing her face to below the clear and beautiful line of her jaw. Although it was heavy and moved with the movements of her head, she did not constantly pat it back into place, but let it alone. Her eyes were wide apart and deep blue and they gazed candidly back at Bond with a touch of ironical disinterest which, to his annoyance, he found he would like to shatter, roughly. Her skin was lightly sun-tanned and bore no trace of make-up except on her mouth which was wide and sensual. Her bare arms and hands had a quality of repose and the general impression of restraint in her appearance and movements was carried even to her finger-nails which were unpainted and cut short. Round her neck she wore a plain gold chain of wide flat links and on the fourth finger of the right hand a broad topaz ring. Her medium-length dress was of grey soie sauvage with a square-cut bodice, lasciviously tight across her fine breasts. The skirt was close-ly pleated and flowered down from a narrow, but not a thin, waist. She wore a three-inch, handstitched black belt. A handstitched black sabretache rested on the chair beside her, together with a wide cart-wheel hat of gold straw, its crown encircled by a thin black velvet ribbon which tied at the back in a short bow. Her shoes were square-toed of plain black leather.

Bond was excited by her beauty and intrigued by her composure. The prospect of working with her stimulated him. At the same time he felt a vague disquiet. On an impulse he touched wood.

TOM WOLFE
From The Bonfire of the Vanities

HE SURVEYED THE crowd and immediately sensed a pattern . . . *presque vu!* *presque vu!* almost seen! . . . and yet he couldn't have put it into words. That would have been beyond him. All the men and women in this hall were arranged in clusters, conversational bouquets, so to speak. There were no solitary figures, no strays. All faces were white. (Black faces might show up, occasionally, at fash-ionable charity dinners but not in fashionable private homes.) There were no men under thirty-five and precious few under forty. The women came in two varieties. First, there were women in their late thirties and in their forties and older (women 'of a certain age'), all of them skin and bones (starved to near per-fection). To compensate for the concupiscence missing from their juiceless ribs and atrophied backsides, they turned to the dress designers. This season no puffs, flounces, pleats, ruffles, bibs, bows, battings, scallops, laces, darts, or shirs on the bias were too extreme. They were the social X rays, to use the phrase that had bubbled up into Sherman's own brain. Second, there were the so-called Lemon Tarts. These were women in their twenties or early thirties, mostly blondes (the Lemon in the Tarts), who were the second, third, and fourth wives or live-in girlfriends of men over forty or fifty or sixty (or seventy), the sort of women men refer to, quite without thinking, as *girls*. This season the Tart was able to flaunt the natural advantages of youth by showing her legs from well above the knee and emphasizing her round bottom (something no X ray had). What was entirely missing from *chez* Bavardage was that manner of woman who is neither very young nor very old, who has laid in a lining of subcutaneous fat, who glows with plumpness and a rosy face that speaks, without a word, of home and hearth and hot food ready at six and stories read aloud at night and conversations while seated on the edge of the bed, just before the Sandman comes. In short, no one ever invited . . . Mother.

S. J. PERELMAN
From Long Time No Sheepskin

IMMERSED IN THE last canto of *Don Juan* over a quiet sundowner, I had paid no special attention to the two young matrons at the table next to mine. One of them, I was vaguely aware, was a lush blonde with honey-coloured hair, clad in a wool dress of forest green edged in rickrack, gunmetal stockings, black suède pumps, and a nutria jacket. The other, a rather smouldering brunette, wore a pin-checked tweed suit with poodle scatter pins on the lapel, brown oxfords, a cocoa-coloured riding hat, three-quarter-length tan gloves, and an American-broadtail stole. The light in the bar was too dim to determine whether their lingerie had come from Bendel's or Bonwit's, but everything proclaimed them to be women not visibly harassed by the spectre of want.

Bite on the Bullet or, Under the Spreading Atrophy

ANGELA CARTER
From Wise Children

WHAT A JOY IT is to dance and sing!
We're stuck in the period at which we peaked, of course. All women do. We'd feel mutilated if you made us wipe off our Joan Crawford mouths and we always do our hair up in great big Victory rolls when we go out. We've still got lots of it, thank God, iron grey though it may be and tucked away in scarves, turban-style, this very moment, to hide the curlers. We always make an effort. We paint an inch thick. We put on our faces before we come down to breakfast, the Max Factor Pan-Stik, the false eyelashes with the three coats of mascara, everything. We used to polish our eyelids with Vaseline, when we were girls, but we

gave up on that during the war and now use just a simple mushroom shadow for day plus a hint of tobacco brown, to deepen the tone, and a charcoal eyeliner. Our fingernails match our toenails match our lipstick match our rouge. Revlon, Fire and Ice. The habit of applying warpaint outlasts the battle; haven't had a man for yonks but still we slap it on. Nobody could say the Chance girls were going gently into that good night.

We'd got our best kimonos on, because it was our birthday. Real silk, mine mauve with a plum-blossom design on the back, Nora's crimson with a chrysanthemum. Our beloved Uncle Perry, that is, the late, and by his nieces grievously lamented, Peregrine Hazard, sent us back our kimonos from Nagasaki, years ago, before Pearl Harbor, when he was on one of his trips. Underneath, camiknickers with a French lace trim, lilac satin for me, crushed rose crepe for her. Tasty, eh? Course, we were wearing camiknickers before they *came back*.

WENDY COPE

Advertisement

The lady takes *The Times* and *Vogue*,
Wears Dior dresses, Gucci shoes,
Puts fresh-cut flowers round her room
And lots of carrots in her stews.

A moss-green Volvo, morning walks,
And holidays in Guadeloupe;
Long winter evenings by the fire
With Proust and cream of carrot soup

Raw carrots on a summer lawn,
Champagne, a Gioconda smile;
Glazed carrots in a silver dish
For Sunday lunch. They call it style.

Making Cocoa for Kingsley Amis

By and large they are at their best dressed for a brisk walk in the rain but they can look awe-inspiring at Hunt Balls and above all at weddings.

Douglas Sutherland on English Ladies in *The English Gentleman's Wife*

9

Getting it Wrong

Vulgarity is a very important ingredient in life. I'm a
great believer in vulgarity – if it's got vitality. A little
bad taste is like a nice splash of paprika. We all need a
splash of bad taste – it's hearty, it's physical . . . No
taste is what I'm against.

Diana Vreeland

She wears her clothes, as if they were thrown on her with a pitchfork.

Jonathan Swift, *A Complete Collection of Polite and Ingenious Conversation*

'Look, Adam, look!'

'Look at what, dear?'

Thus it was that the first husband failed to notice the first hat of the first wife.

Marcel Vertes, *Art and Fashion*

OGDEN NASH

The Drop of a Hat

Darling, what is that?
That, angel, is a hat.
Are you positive? Are you certain?
Are you sure it's not a curtain?
Shall you really place your head in it?
How's for keeping cake or bread in it?
Do not wear it on your head;
Find some other use instead.
Say a cloth for drying dishes,
Or a net for catching fishes,
Or a veil by night to veto
The bill of the mosquito?
Darling, what is that?
Are you sure it is a hat?
And if so, what was the matter

With the hatter?
Was he troubled? Was he ill?
Was he laughing fit to kill?
Oh, what was on his mind
As he designed?
Had he gone without his supper?
Was he dressing in an upper?
Did he plot a wily plan
To annoy his fellow man?
Is its aspect, rear and frontal,
Intended to disgruntle,
Or was it accidental
And is he now repental?
Are memoirs of the brim
Now agony to him?
Do visions of the crown
Drag his spirits down?
Oh, may the Furies batter
That eleven-fingered hatter!
May doom and gloom enswaddle
The creator of this model!
I hope he made a lot of them,
That dozens he has got of them;
I hope he has a harem,
And all his spouses warem.

The English women are nothing by halves; they are the perfection of beauty, or they are the extreme of ugliness, and they then cease to be women: they are fossilised beings, unknown to creation, the infinitely varied species of which defy classification. One looks like an old horse, another an old bird. Several remind one of the dromedary, others the bison.

Mme de Girardin, *Letters* (1838)

Imagine a sugar loaf covered with gold embroidery and you'll have a fairly accurate idea of her figure.

Comtesse de Boigne on Queen Charlotte in old age.

She looked like a fat asparagus whose head had been dipped in dressing and then put in a warm place to dry. She dried in patches. A caravan of pearls crawled upwards from her bosom to her throat, and she said to Mr Trehawke Tush, the novelist: 'The only decent cocktails you can get in Paris are at the Ritz Bar, but the people are so odd. My Archie wants to stand for Parliament. What do you think?'

Michael Arlen, *The Green Hat*

She was got up in the fashion. A mauve silk dress with eighteen flounces, and about eighteen hundred steel buttons that glittered your sight away; a 'zouave' jacket, worked with gold; a black straw hat with no visible brim perched on the top of her skull, garnished in front with what court milliners are pleased to call a '*plume de coq*', but which by its size and height, might have been taken for a '*coq*' himself, while a white ostrich feather was carried round and did duty behind, and a spangled hair-net hung down to her waist. Gloriously grand was Afy that day; and if I had only a photographing machine at hand – or whatever may be the scientific name for the thing – you should certainly have been regaled with the sight of her.

Mrs Henry Wood, *East Lynne*

I must not here omit an Adventure which happened to us in a Country Church upon the Frontiers of Cornwall. As we were in the midst of the Service, a Lady who is the chief Woman of the Place and had passed the Winter at London with her Husband, entered the Congregation in a little Head-dress and a Hoop'd-Petticoat. The People, who were wonderfully startled at such a sight, all of them rose up. Some stared at the Prodigious Bottom, and some at the little Top of this strange Dress. In the mean time the Lady of the Manor filled the Area of the Church, and walked up to her Pew with an unspeakable Satisfaction, amidst the Whispers, Conjectures and Astonishments of the whole Congregation.

The Spectator (1711)

MME DE SÉVIGNÉ
From Letters

THEY WORE FINE clothes and their collars and presented an excellent appearance. On Saturday it was the turn of all the others, including two Marshals of France who had not attended on the previous occasion. Maréchal de Bellefonds looked utterly ridiculous, because, through modesty and indifference to his appearance, he had omitted to put any ribbons at the knees of his Court breeches, and so looked quite naked. The company as a whole was splendid, and M. de La Trousse among the best; he had some difficulty with his wig: one of the side pieces worked round to the back of his head and stayed there, so that his cheek was quite uncovered; he kept on pulling at it, but the part that was causing the trouble would not move – it was rather annoying. Then M. de Montchevreuil and M. de Villars, who were in the same line, became so frantically hooked up with each other, their swords, ribbons, lace, and all their trimmings all got so mixed up, jumbled together, and entangled, all the little hooked parts were so perfectly intertwined, that no man's hand could separate them; the more they tried to do so, the more entangled they became, like the links of Roger's armour. In the end, as the whole ceremony and all the bowing and movements were held up, they had to be torn apart by force, and the stronger man won. But what completely upset the dignity of the ceremony was the negligence of good old D'Hocquincourt, who was dressed so much in the manner of a Provençal or a Breton that, as his Court breeches were not so accommodating as the ones he usually wears, his shirt would not remain tucked into them, however much he pleaded with it. For, realizing the state he was in, he tried continually to put himself in order, but always without avail, so that Madame la Dauphine could no longer restrain herself from bursting into a peal of laughter. It was a great pity: it very nearly shook the King's majesty, and never, in the records of the Order, has such a mishap been seen.

HIPPOLYTE TAINE
From Notes sur l'Angleterre

From five to seven, review of toilettes; beauty and finery abound. Colours are outrageously crude, and the figures ungraceful. Crinolines too hooped, and badly hooped, in lumps, or in geometrical cones; green flounces, dressed with gold embroidery, flowered dresses, a profusion of light gauze, masses of hair, curled and hanging loose, crowned with small hats covered with flowers; the hat is over-trimmed, the hair too shiny and sticks severely on the temples. The mantle or the cloak falls shapelessly over the hips, the skirt is absurdly puffed out, and the whole effect is bad – badly chosen, badly made, badly arranged, badly put on and the loud colouring simply shrieks out.

(1872)

Honest Fuller relates, that 'Sir Philip Calthorpe, who lived in the reign of King Henry the Seventh, having sent as much cloth of fine French Tawny as would make him a gown, to a tailor in Norwich, it happened that one John Drakes, a shoemaker, coming into the shop, liked it so well, that he went and bought of the same as much for himself, enjoining the tailor to make it of the same fashion. The knight being informed thereof, commanded the tailor to cut his gown as full of holes, as his shears could make; which so purged John Drakes of his proud humour, that he would never be of that gentleman's fashion again.'

Percy Anecdotes (1823)

DOROTHY CANFIELD
From The Bent Twig

THE QUESTION OF clothes, usually such a sorely insoluble problem for academic people of small means, was solved by the Marshalls in an eccentric, easy-going manner which was considered by the other faculty families as nothing less than treasonable to their caste. Professor Marshall, it is true, having to make a public appearance on the campus every day, was generally, like every other professor, undistinguishable from a commercial traveler. But Mrs Marshall, who often let a good many days pass without a trip to town, had adopted early in her married life a sort of home uniform, which year after year she wore in one form or another. It varied according to the season, and according to the occasion on which she wore it, but it had certain unchanging characteristics. It was always very plain as to line, and simple as to cut, having a skirt neither full nor scant, a waist crossed in front with a white fichu, and sleeves reaching just below the elbow with white turn-back cuffs. As Mrs Marshall, though not at all pretty, was a tall, upright, powerfully built woman, with a dark, shapely head gallantly poised on her shoulders, this garb, whether short-skirted, of blue serge in the morning, or trailing, of ruby-colored cashmere in the evening, was very becoming to her. But there is no denying that it was always startlingly and outrageously unfashionable. At a time when every woman and female child in the United States had more cloth in her sleeves than in all the rest of her dress, the rounded muscles of Mrs Marshall's arm, showing through the fabric of her sleeves, smote shockingly upon the eye of the ordinary observer, trained to the American habit of sheep-like uniformity of appearance. And at the time when the front of every woman's waist fell far below her belt in a copiously blousing sag, Mrs Marshall's trim tautness had in it something horrifying. It must be said for her that she did not go out of her way to inflict these concussions upon the brains of spectators, since she always had in her closet one evening dress and one street dress, sufficiently approximating the prevailing style to pass unnoticed. These costumes lasted long, and they took in the long run but little from the Marshall exchequer: for she wore them seldom, only assuming what her husband called, with a laugh, her 'disguise' when going into town.

E. F. BENSON
From Miss Mapp

DIVA WAS SITTING at the open drawing-room window of her house in the High Street, cutting with a pair of sharp nail scissors into the old chintz curtains which her maid had told her no longer 'paid for the mending'. So, since they refused to pay for their mending any more, she was preparing to make them pay, pretty smartly, too, in other ways. The pattern was of little bunches of pink roses peeping out through trellis work, and it was these which she had just began to cut out. Though Tilling was noted for the ingenuity with which its more fashionable ladies devised novel and quaint effects in their dress in an economical manner, Diva felt sure, ransack her memory though she might, that nobody had thought of *this* before.

The hot weather had continued late into September and showed no signs of breaking yet, and it would be agreeable to her and acutely painful to others that just at the end of the summer she should appear in a perfectly new costume, before the days of jumpers and heavy skirts and large woollen scarves came in. She was preparing, therefore, to take the light white jacket which she wore over her blouse, and cover the broad collar and cuffs of it with these pretty roses. The belt of the skirt would be similarly decorated, and so would the edge of it, if there were enough clean ones. The jacket and skirt had already gone to the dyer's, and would be back in a day or two, white no longer, but of a rich purple hue, and by that time she would have hundreds of these little pink roses ready to be tacked on. Perhaps a piece of the chintz, trellis and all, could be sewn over the belt, but she was determined to have single little bunches of roses peppered all over the collar and cuffs of the jacket and, if possible, round the edge of the skirt. She had already tried the effect, and was of the opinion that nobody could possibly guess what the origin of these roses was. When carefully sewn on they looked as if they were a design in the stuff.

She let the circumcised roses fall on to the window seat, and from time to time, when they grew numerous, swept them into a cardboard box. Though she worked with zealous diligence, she had an eye to the movements in the street outside, for it was shopping hour, and there were many observations to be made. She had not anything like Miss Mapp's genius for conjecture, but her memory was appallingly good, and this was the third morning running on which Elizabeth had gone into the grocer's. It was odd to go to your grocer's every day like that: groceries twice a week was sufficient for most people. From here, on the floor above the street, she could easily look into Elizabeth's basket, and she certainly was carrying nothing away with her from the grocer's, for the only thing there was a small bottle done up in white paper with sealing wax, which, Diva had no need to be told, certainly came from the chemist's, and was no doubt connected with too many plums.

Miss Mapp crossed the street to the pavement below Diva's house, and precisely as she reached it, Diva's maid opened the door into the drawing room, bringing in the second post, or rather not bringing in the second post, but the announcement that there wasn't any second post. This opening of the door caused a draught, and the bunches of roses which littered the window seat rose brightly in the air. Diva managed to beat most of them down again, but two fluttered out of the window. Precisely then, and at no other time, Miss Mapp looked up, and one settled on her face, the other fell into her basket. Her trained faculties were all on the alert, and she thrust them both inside her glove for future consideration, without stopping to examine them just then. She only knew that they were little pink roses, and that they had fluttered out of Diva's window . . .

She paused on the pavement, and remembered that Diva had not yet expressed regret about the worsted, and that she still 'popped' as much as ever. Then Diva deserved a punishment of some sort, and happily, at that very moment, she thought of a subject on which she might be able to make her uncomfortable. The street was full, and it would be pretty to call up to her, instead of ringing her bell, in order to save trouble to poor overworked Janet. (Diva only kept two servants, though of course poverty was no crime.)

'Diva darling!' she cooed.

Diva's head looked out like a cuckoo in a clock preparing to chime the hour. 'Hullo!' she said. 'Want me?'

'May I pop up for a moment, dear?' said Miss Mapp. 'That's to say if you're not very busy.'

From Joyce Grenfell Requests the Pleasure

MANY OF [MY grandmother's] dresses were made by Madame Marthe, one of the dressmakers of whom it was said: 'She cuts so beautifully.' Maybe she did, but not when she made my white velvet wedding dress. I argued about having to have it made by her, but the chorus of my mother, Granny and Aunt Margaret said that Marthe cuts *so* beautifully, and I was defeated. The mistake may have been my determination to design the dress myself. I had strong ideas, often wrong, but after all it was my wedding and I knew what I wanted: a plain, square-necked dress with long sleeves and a full skirt ending in a long train. What I got was roughly this but complicated by much cross-cutting and clever draping, sleeves too tight under the arms even after I complained, and a square neck that didn't sit flat. Madame Marthe made a meal of the dress and I stood patiently for fittings, full of hope that she must know what she was doing. She pulled and pruned, made little French noises and said it was *ravissante*, but then she didn't have to wear it. It must be admitted that I probably wasn't the right shape for cross-cutting, but it was up to Madame Marthe to spot this and contrive. In the photograph, taken in a gale as we left St Margaret's Westminster, on 12 December 1929, the general effect wasn't too bad, but when I came to try and have it converted into a dress to wear for dinner-parties, the velvet was found to be the kind that marked if you breathed near it and it wouldn't take dye. I kept it in a big cardboard box where it slowly turned yellow and then I hardened my heart and threw it out.

LADY CLODAGH ANSON
From Victorian Days

THE MOST TIRESOME part of going to live abroad undoubtedly is having to listen to the expert advice given by your friends and relations as to what clothes you will require, but in whatever direction of the world you may be going, one thing is quite certain – everybody will say to you: 'My dear, what you really will want is a good pair of strong boots.' None of my friends had ever been to Texas, but every single soul I met made the same remark. I bought high boots, and medium-sized boots, boots that laced up all the way, boots that laced up a little bit in the middle; in fact, every known kind of boot, but now I look back on my life in Texas – I do not ever remember wearing any boots at all. It was usually much too hot, and though there were families of rattlesnakes living under the house, I got so accustomed to the idea of them that I just took a chance;

anyhow, they hardly ever came out till late evening when it began to get dark.

Nobody seemed to think that I should need any other kind of clothing; in fact, one friend of mine, who happened to see some trousseau under-garments being packed for the journey, said: 'Surely you won't want those in Texas?' in rather a shocked voice.

JULIA KEAY

From With Passport and Parasol: the adventures of seven Victorian ladies

THE POLICE CHIEF was furious. These were no ordinary travellers; they carried a letter of introduction from none other than Her Majesty the Empress Marie Fedorovna herself, together with instructions to whomever it may concern that they were to be given every assistance. The people of Zlatoust should be ashamed of showing so little respect.

Had he but known it, the stouter of the two dignitaries at his side had every sympathy with the crowd, and did not blame them in the least for grinning. She knew she looked ridiculous; she hated looking ridiculous, and there was not a single thing she could do about it. It was not surprising that they stared for I was broadened and lengthened by so many inches I had failed to recognise myself in the looking glass.

I had on a whole outfit of warm undergarments, then a loose kind of body lined with flannel, a very thickly wadded eiderdown ulster with sleeves long enough to cover the hands entirely, the fur collar reaching high enough to cover the head and face. Then a sheepskin reaching to the feet and furnished with a collar to come over the fur one. Then over the sheepskin I had to wear a dacha, which is a fur coat made of reindeer skin.

And even now I have not come to the end of the list. I wore a long pair of stockings made of long hair, over them a pair of gentleman's thickest hunting stockings, over them a pair of Russian boots made of felt coming high up over the knees and over a pair of brown felt vaalenkies. All this immense load of wool and fur and skins to cover a bit of frail and feeble humanity – yet there was not an ounce too much, as after-experience showed.

The 'bit of frail and feeble humanity' inside this shapeless bundle was Miss Kate Marsden; her companion, similarly accoutred, was Miss Ada Field, a shadowy figure reminiscent of Amelia Edward's nameless friend 'L', and they were on their way to Siberia.

L. M. MONTGOMERY
From Anne of Green Gables

'WELL, HOW DO you like them?' said Marilla.

Anne was standing in the gable-room, looking solemnly at three new dresses spread out on the bed. One was of snuffy-coloured gingham which Marilla had been tempted to buy from a pedlar the preceding summer because it looked so serviceable; one was of black-and-white checked sateen which she had picked up at a bargain counter in the winter; and one was a stiff print of an ugly blue shade which she had purchased that week at a Carmody store.

She had made them up herself, and they were all made alike – plain skirts pulled tightly to plain waists, with sleeves as plain as waist and skirt and tight as sleeves could be.

'I'll imagine that I like them,' said Anne soberly.

'I don't want you to imagine it,' said Marilla, offended. 'Oh, I can see you don't like the dresses! What is the matter with them? Aren't they neat and clean and new?'

'Yes.'

'Then why don't you like them?'

'They're – they're not – pretty,' said Anne, reluctantly.

'Pretty!' Marilla sniffed. 'I didn't trouble my head about getting pretty dresses for you. I don't believe in pampering vanity, Anne, I'll tell you that right off. Those dresses are good, sensible, serviceable dresses, without any frills or furbelows about them, and they're all you'll get this summer. The brown gingham and the blue print will do you for school when you begin to go. The sateen is for Church and Sunday school. I'll expect you to keep them neat and clean and not to tear them. I should think you'd be grateful to get most anything after those skimpy wincey things you've been wearing.

'Oh, I *am* grateful,' protested Anne. 'But I'd be ever so much gratefuller if – if you'd made just one of them with puffed sleeves. Puffed sleeves are so fashionable now. It would give me such a thrill, Marilla, just to wear a dress with puffed sleeves.'

'Well, you'll have to do without your thrill. I hadn't any material to waste on puffed sleeves. I think they are ridiculous-looking things anyhow. I prefer the plain, sensible ones.'

'But I'd rather look ridiculous when everybody else does than plain and sensible all by myself,' persisted Anne mournfully.

'Trust you for that! Well, hang those dresses carefully up in your closet, and then sit down and learn the Sunday school lesson. I got a quarterly from Mr Bell for you, and you'll go to Sunday school tomorrow,' said Marilla, disappearing downstairs in high dudgeon.

Anne clasped her hands and looked at the three dresses.

'I did hope there would be a white one with puffed sleeves,' she whispered disconsolately. 'I prayed for one, but I didn't much expect it on that account. I didn't suppose God would have time to bother about a little orphan girl's dress. I knew I'd just have to depend on Marilla for it. Well, fortunately, I can imagine that one of them is of snow-white muslin with lovely lace frills and two puffed sleeves.'

CARSON McCULLERS
From The Member of the Wedding

'SHUT YOUR EYES!' she called. 'Don't watch me coming down the stairs. Don't open your eyes until I tell you.'

It was as though the four walls of the kitchen watched her, and the skillet hanging on the wall was a watching round black eye. The piano-tuning was for a minute silent. Berenice sat with her head bowed, as though she was in church. And John Henry had his head bowed also, but he was peeking. F. Jasmine stood at the foot of the stairs and placed her left hand on her hip.

'Oh, how pretty!' John Henry said.

Berenice raised her head, and when she saw F. Jasmine her face was a study. The dark eye looked from the silver hair ribbon to the soles of the silver slippers. She said nothing.

'Now tell me your honest opinion,' F. Jasmine said.

But Berenice looked at the orange satin evening dress and shook her head and did not comment. At first she shook her head with little short turns, but the longer she stared, the longer these shakes became, until at the last shake F. Jasmine heard her neck crack.

'What's the matter?' F. Jasmine asked.

'I thought you was going to get a pink dress.'

'But when I got in the store I changed my mind. What is wrong with this dress? Don't you like it, Berenice?'

'No,' said Berenice, 'It don't do.'

'What do you mean? It don't do.'

'Exactly that. It just don't do.'

F. Jasmine turned to look in the mirror, and she still thought the dress was beautiful. But Berenice had a sour and stubborn look on her face, an expression like that of a long-eared mule, and F. Jasmine could not understand.

'But I don't see what you mean,' she complained. 'What is wrong?'

Berenice folded her arms over her chest and said: 'Well, if you don't see it I can't explain it to you. Look there at your head, to begin with.'

F. Jasmine looked at her head in the mirror.

'You had all your hair shaved off like a convict, and now you tie a silver ribbon around this head without any hair. It just looks peculiar.'

'Oh, but I'm washing my hair tonight and going to try to curl it,' F. Jasmine said.

'And look at them elbows,' Berenice continued. 'Here you got on this grown woman's evening dress. Orange satin. And that brown crust on your elbows. The two things just don't mix.'

F. Jasmine hunched her shoulders and covered her rusty elbows with her hands.

Berenice gave her head another wide shake, then bunched her lips in judgement. 'Take it back down to the store.'

'But I can't!' said F. Jasmine. 'It's bargain basement. They don't take back.'

Berenice always had two mottoes. One was the known saying that you can't make a silk purse out of a sow's ear. And the other was the motto that you have to cut your suit according to the cloth, and make the best of what you have. So F. Jasmine was not certain if it was the last of these mottoes that made Berenice change her mind, or if she really began to improve her feelings about the dress. Anyway, Berenice stared for several seconds with her head to one side, and finally said:

'Come here. We'll make it fit better at the waist and see what we can do.'

'I think you're just not accustomed to seeing anybody dressed up,' F. Jasmine said.

'I'm not accustomed to human Christmas trees in August.'

So Berenice took off the sash and patted and pulled the dress in various places. F. Jasmine stood stiff like a hatrack and let her work with the dress. John Henry had got up from his chair and was watching, with the napkin still tied around his neck.

'Frankie's dress looks like a Christmas tree,' he said.

'Two-faced Judas!' F. Jasmine said. 'You just now said it was pretty. Old double-faced Judas!'. . .

'Step back a little now,' said Berenice.

She had pinned the waist higher and done one thing and another to the dress. F. Jasmine looked in the mirror over the sink. She could only see herself from the chest up, so after admiring this top part of herself, she stood on a chair and looked at the middle section. Then she began to clear away a corner of the table so she could climb up and see in the mirror the silver shoes, but Berenice prevented her.

'Don't you honestly think it is pretty?' F. Jasmine said. 'I think so. Seriously, Berenice. Give me your candy opinion.'

But Berenice rose up and spoke in an accusing voice: 'I never knew somebody so unreasonable! You ask me my candy opinion, and I give it to you. Then you ask me again, and I give it to you. But what you want is not my honest opinion, but my good opinion on something I know is wrong. Now what kind of way is that to act?'

'All right,' F. Jasmmine said. 'I only want to look good.'

'Well, you look very well,' said Berenice, 'Pretty is as pretty does.'

GIUSEPPE DI LAMPEDUSA
From The Leopard

NOW, WITH HIS sensibility to presages and symbols, he saw revolution in that white tie and two black tails moving at this moment up the stairs of his own home. Not only was he, the Prince, no longer the major land-owner in Donnafugata, but he now found himself forced to receive, when in afternoon dress himself, a guest appearing in evening clothes. His distress was great; it still lasted as he moved mechanically towards the door to receive his guest. When he saw him, however, his agonies were somewhat eased.

Though perfectly adequate as a political demonstration it was obvious that as tailoring, Don Calogero's tail-coat was a disastrous failure. The stuff was excellent, the style modern, but the cut appalling. The Word from London had been most inadequately made flesh in a tailor from Girgenti to whom Don Calogero had gone with his tenacious avarice. The wings of his cravat pointed straight to heaven in mute supplication, his huge collar was shapeless, and, what is more, it is our painful but necessary duty to add that the Mayor's feet were shod in buttoned boots.

*

The girls, incomprehensible beings for whom a ball is fun and not a tedious worldly duty, were chatting away gaily in low voices; the Princess Maria Stella felt her bag to assure herself she'd brought her little bottle of sal volatile; Don Fabrizio was enjoying in anticipation the effect of Angelica's beauty on all those who did not know her and of Tancredi's luck on all those who knew him too well. But a shadow lay across his contentment; what about Don Calogero's tail-coat? Certainly not like the one worn at Donnafugata; he had been put into the hands of Tancredi, who had dragged him off to the best tailor and even been present at fittings. Officially the result had seemed to satisfy him the other day; but in confidence he had said, 'The coat is the best we can do; Angelica's father lacks chic.' That was undeniable; but Tancredi had guaranteed a perfect shave and decently polished shoes. That was something.

ANTHONY POWELL
From Books Do Furnish a Room

ALTHOUGH THE SPRING weather was still decidedly chilly, he was dressed in a pale ochre-coloured tropical suit, almost transparent in texture, on top of which he wore an overcoat, black and belted like Quiggin's Partisan number, but of cloth, for some reason familiarly official in cut. This heavy garment, rather too short for Trapnel's height of well over six feet, was at the same time too full, in view of his spare, almost emaciated body. Its weight emphasized the flimsiness of the tussore trousers below. The greatcoat turned out, much later, to have belonged to Bagshaw during his RAF service, disposed of on terms unspecified, possibly donated, to Trapnel, who had caused it to be dyed black. The pride Trapnel obviously took in the coat was certainly not untainted by an implied, though unjustified, aspiration to ex-officer status.

The walking stick struck a completely different note. Its wood unremarkable, but the knob, ivory, more likely bone, crudely carved in the shape of a skull, was rather like old Skerrett's head at Erridge's funeral. This stick clearly bulked large in Trapnel equipment. It set the tone far more than the RAF greatcoat or tropical suit. For the rest, he was hatless, wore a dark blue sports shirt frayed at the collar, an emerald green tie patterned with naked women, was shod in grey suede brothel-creepers. These last, then relatively new, were destined to survive a long time, indeed until their rubber soles, worn to the thinness of paper, had become all but detached from fibreless uppers, sounding a kind of dismal applause as they flapped rhythmically against the weary pavement trodden beneath.

The general effect, chiefly caused by the stick, was the Eighteen-Nineties, the *décadence*; putting things at their least eclectic, a contemptuous rejection of currently popular male modes in grey flannel demob suits with pork-pie hats, bowler-crowned British Warms, hooded duffles, or even those varied outfits like Quiggin's, to be seen here and there, that suggested recent service in the *maquis*. All such were rejected. One could not help speculating whether an eye-glass would not be produced – Trapnel was reported to have sported one for a brief period, until broken in a pub brawl – insomuch that the figure he recalled, familiar from some advertisement advocating a brand of chocolates or cigarettes, similarly equipped with beard and cane, wore an eye-glass on a broad ribbon, though additionally rigged out in full evening dress, an order round his neck, opera cloak over his shoulder. In Trapnel's case, the final effect had that touch of surrealism which redeems from complete absurdity, though such redemption was a near thing, only narrowly achieved.

It came back of course to the question of money . . . A less vulgarly, a less obviously purchasing or parading person she couldn't have imagined; but it prevailed even as the truth of truths that the girl couldn't get away from her wealth . . . It was in the fine folds of the helplessly expensive little black frock . . . it was in the curious and splendid coils of hair, 'done' with no eye whatever to the *mode du jour*, that peeped from under the corresponding indifference of her hat, the merely personal tradition that suggested a sort of noble inelegance.

Henry James, *The Wings of a Dove*

And then Mrs Fitz-Adam reappeared in Cranford ('as bold as a lion,' Miss Pole said), a well-to-do widow, dressed in rustling black silk, so soon after her husband's death, that poor Miss Jenkyns was justified in the remark she made, that 'bombazine would have shown a deeper sense of her loss'.

Mrs Gaskell, *Cranford*

But reason and brooches and bracelets do not go in company: the girl who has not the sense to perceive that her person is disfigured, and not beautified, by parcels of brass and tin (for they are generally little better) and other hardware, stuck about her body; the girl that is so foolish as not to perceive, that when silks and cottons and cambrics, in their neatest form, have done their best, nothing more is to be done; – the girl that cannot perceive this, is too great a fool to be trusted with the purse of any man.

William Cobbett, *Advice to Young Men* (1829)

Hector Protector was dressed all in green;
Hector Protector was sent to the Queen,
The Queen did not like him,
Nor more did the King:
So Hector Protector was sent back again.

Nursery Rhyme, Anon

'Pray how many suits does she wear out in a year?' – 'Oh, dear Sir! A fine lady's clothes are not old by being worn but by being seen.'

Richard Steele, *The Tender Husband* (1705)

From The Morning Chronicle:
Fashion Reports: 'A young lady by attending to the literal meaning of one of the Monthly Reports was shocked to find that her sleeves and her tunic were actually three days old; and another fainted away on being told that her border was of a colour which had been seen the week before, and that her antique shirt was not new.'

(1808)

JEROME K. JEROME
From Three Men in a Boat

I URGED UPON GEORGE, however, how much pleasanter it would be to have Harris clean and fresh about the boat, even if we did have to take a few more hundredweight of provisions; and he got to see it in my light, and withdrew his opposition to Harris's bath. Agreed, finally, that we should take *three* bath towels, so as not to keep each other waiting.

For clothes, George said two suits of flannel would be sufficient as we could wash them ourselves, in the river, when they got dirty. We asked him if he had ever tried washing flannels in the river, and he replied: 'No, not exactly himself like, but he knew some fellows who had, and it was easy enough'; and Harris and I were weak enough to fancy he knew what he was talking about, and that three respectable young men, without position or influence, and with no experience in washing, could really clean their own shirts and trousers in the River Thames with a bit of soap.

We were to learn in the days to come, when it was too late, that George was a miserable impostor, who could evidently have known nothing whatever about the matter. If you had seen these clothes after – but, as the shilling shockers say, we anticipate.

GEORGE AND WEEDON GROSSMITH
From The Diary of a Nobody

B Y-THE-BY, I will never choose another cloth pattern at night. I ordered a new suit of dittos for the garden at Edwards', and chose the pattern by gaslight, and they seemed to be a quiet pepper-and-salt mixture with white stripes down. They came home this morning, and to my horror, I found it was quite a flash-looking suit. There was a lot of green with bright yellow-coloured stripes.

I tried on the coat, and was annoyed to find Carrie giggling. She said: 'What mixture did you say you asked for?'

I said: 'A quiet pepper-and-salt.'

Carrie said: 'Well, it looks more like mustard, if you want to know the truth.'

BRIGID BROPHY
From In Transit

L EAN FORWARD: CLEAR throat: Pardon (international pron.), would you please tell me what sex I am? . . .

Going, in a matter that was, after all, elemental, straight to the point, I looked down my sitting body to the point where my legs met.

I was wearing trousers.

They were of black corduroy (the thick, broad-ribbed kind). They opened down the front by a zip, a few of whose metallic railway sleepers I could see at the top of the track but the rest of which was concealed by fly.

At the region round and below the base of the fly I peered closely down . . .

To my surprise, deduction was not easy. What baffled me seemed to be that mine were not close-fitting trousers. A second scrutiny shewed that up as inexact. It was rather that they closely followed their, not my, configuration.

So far from presenting a significant lack of bulges, the region made a whole rolling landscape of bulges. The difficulty was to know which, if any, were significant.

Corduroy seemed a material contradictorily both soft and stiff. It draped softly, but it created airpockets of its own to be draped over. It was virtually erectile tissue in its own right. Indeed, I was now doubly glad of my adult knowledge of anatomical possibility. If I'd had to go on the evidence of my trousers alone, I would have been obliged to believe that an exceptionally long penis took its rise half-way down the inside of my left thigh and presently curled like coral over the front of my leg towards my knee.

Obviously, corduroy would not disclose to sight alone when it was rolling over flesh and blood and when it was rolling over a ridge of air.

I opened my right hand and placed it, palm down, on top of the junction of my legs.

Gently, I pressed.

My palm reported a perceptible thickening. I pressed harder and realized that all I had discovered was the double thickness where that unyielding material had been formed into the fly.

I edged my fingertips (which I now realized would be more sensitive than my palm) towards the seam and, pressing harder, let my fingers begin to curl into a grasping position.

Suddenly conscious of the non-concealment afforded by that narrow triangle of table, I flicked a look up at my companion.

He was staring directly at my hand.

From the Diary of Francis Kilvert

12 June 1874

A T SHANKLIN ONE had to adopt the detestable custom of bathing in drawers. If ladies don't like to see men naked why don't they keep away from the sight? To-day I had a pair of drawers given me which I could not keep on. The rough waves stripped them off and tore them down round my ankles. While thus fettered I was seized and flung down by a heavy sea which retreating suddenly left me lying naked on the sharp shingle from which I rose streaming with blood. After this I took the wretched and dangerous rag off and of course there were some ladies looking on as I came up out of the water.

1761. When Mr Bubb Dodington 'paid his court at St James' to the present queen upon her nuptials he approached to kiss her hand decked in an embroidered suit of silk with lilac waistcoat and breeches, the latter of which in the act of kneeling forgot their duty and broke loose from their moorings in a very indecorous and uncourtly manner.

Memoirs of Richard Cumberland

From Augustus Carp Esq., by himself, Being the Autobiography of a Really Good Man

U PON THE MANTELPIECE stood an oval mirror, indecently surrounded by likenesses of Cupid, and beside it a nude female, fashioned in bronze, was extracting a thorn from her left calf. Flushing involuntarily, I turned away from these only to observe upon a French-looking writing-table a large photograph of an elderly man, pathetically signed 'Your aff. Chrysostom.' Beneath this, in a confusion that was probably characteristic, lay a half-finished letter to somebody called Loo-Loo and several others addressed to 'Dearest Nina' that I did not hesitate to peruse. Most of these, as I discovered, were but little more than the vapid productions of obvious worldlings. But two were invitations to card parties and one, to my horror, contained the word 'blasted'.

This was the one, indeed, upon which I was engaged when the door of the room was abruptly thrown open with a lack of refinement that I ought perhaps to have expected, but that for a moment completely unnerved me. In fact, it did more. For in the effort to recover myself the rug upon which I was standing slid across the floor, leaving behind it not only the upper and middle but the lower middle portions of my frame. Poised in mid-air, my feet having accompanied the rug, I was entirely unable to support these, and was obliged in consequence to assume with the extremest suddenness a sedentary position upon the parquet. Nor was that all. For when, at the third attempt, I succeeded in once more standing upright, the left of my two posterior trouser-buttons fell with a sharp metallic sound upon the floor. Here it paused for a moment, and then standing upon its circumference followed the rug in the direction of Mrs Lorton.

'Dear me,' she said, 'I'm afraid I interrupted you. Is this your button?'

She stooped and picked it up.

With a supreme effort, and despite the most poignant anguish, I regained command of myself and requested her to return it. Hardly had she done so, however, when there came a second metallic sound, and the comrade of the first button also rolled to her feet.

'Oh, dear,' she said, 'isn't that the other one? What do you suppose will happen now?'

Only those who have experienced the extreme discomfort of the simultaneous loss of both posterior trouser-buttons, and the consequent approach to the back of the neck of the bifurcation-point of the braces, will be able to appreciate the enormous handicap under which Providence had now seen fit to place me. In the manual effort, too, which became instantly necessary to prevent the downward corrugation of my trousers, the first button slipped from my grasp and again bounced upon the parquet.

'Oh, I say,' said Mrs Lorton, 'is this a new kind of game, or are you trying to put me at my ease?'

With a silent but powerful petition, I drew myself as erect as the circumstances permitted.

'It is neither a game,' I said, holding up my trousers, 'nor am I entering into personal relations with you. In fact, it is my duty to make it quite clear to you that you are no sort of temptation to me.'

Clad in some close-fitting fabric that exuded a most licentious scent, I could see at once that these well-chosen words had had a profound and immediate effect upon her. Turning her back on me, she emitted a hoarse gasp, and then collapsing upon the sofa, she lay there choking and convulsed in what appeared to be an attack of acute hysteria. Startled but unmoved, and still sustaining my trousers, I gravely awaited her recovery.

'Oh dear,' she said, wiping her eyes, and then after looking at me again, she collapsed once more. Then she sat up, fanning herself with her handkerchief.

'You must really forgive me,' she said, 'but you looked so stern.'

BARRY PAIN

From Eliza Getting On

M Y GREY FLANNEL trousers had been put away for the winter with some of Pigley's Patent Preservative. This is sold in penny packets; and so little is needed that one packet might very well last a man a life-time. Quite a small pinch of it will not only keep moth away, but will destroy any moth that already happens to be there. Eliza, who is quite enthusiastic about it, says that it would suffocate an elephant. The only real trouble about it is that the smell does undoubtedly cling. My system, with clothes that have been put away with the preservative, is to hang them on a line in the garden for twenty-four hours. This removes the worst of the smell, and the rest passes off slowly in use. In about a week or ten days it becomes hardly noticeable. It is a case where tact helps, as it does in so many things in life. For instance, Miss Sakers surprised us once by a call when the suit I was wearing still carried a considerable reminder of the patent preservative. I simply turned to Eliza and said carelessly: 'My dear, I am afraid the plumber has not made quite a success of that gas-leak.' Of course, Eliza had to mess the whole thing up by saying that we had not got any gas-leak, and she didn't know what I was talking about. But otherwise it would have passed off very nicely.

However, it was about those grey flannel trousers that I wished to speak. They had been made to my order by a fair-price tailor two years before, and were still distinctly good. They had been worn only on my annual holidays, and occasionally on a fine Saturday afternoon. Light flannel trousers on a Sunday are things I have always set my face against, whatever the opinion of the majority may be. This spring I had given them twenty-four hours on a clothes-line in the garden – naturally in a secluded spot where they could not possibly be overlooked – and, Saturday afternoon being fine and sunny, I took them up to my room to put on. And a very sharp disappointment I got.

I joined Eliza in the garden. 'Hullo,' she said, 'I thought you were going to put on those grey flannel trousers?'

'That had been my intention,' I said. 'However, I find that my express orders have been disregarded. Those trousers have been washed. Washed, mark you. And, as was inevitable, they have shrunk. It is impossible to make them meet at the waist without causing me great physical discomfort. There's twelve-and-six thrown on the dust-heap, sacrificed to your obstinacy. Why couldn't they have been dry-cleaned at home by our own simple process, as I directed?'

'They were,' said Eliza.

'Not washed?'

'No.'

'But could a chemical preservative in the form of a dry powder cause material to shrink?'

'No,' said Eliza, 'but a man getting fatter might cause his clothes to get too tight for him.'

I must admit that the idea had already crossed my mind once or twice, but I had shut my eyes to it. I was now very seriously disturbed. I went to the station and weighed myself on one of those penny-in-the-slot machines. I have been told that these are often inaccurate, and I could only hope that this was the case now.

I talked it over with Eliza on my return from the station, and she said that, of course, the only thing for it was more exercise. So I mowed the lawn twice and rolled the paths. And what was the result? At dinner I had an appetite that it was hopeless to fight against. The thing is what is called, I believe, a vicious circle.

GEORGE AND WEEDON GROSSMITH
From The Diary of a Nobody

August 1

Ordered a new pair of trousers at Edwards's, and told them not to cut them so loose over the boot; the last pair being so loose and also tight at the knee, looked like a sailor's, and I heard Pitt, that objectionable youth at the office, call out 'Hornpipe' as I passed his desk. Carrie has ordered of Miss Jibbons a pink Garibaldi and blue-serge skirt, which I always think looks so pretty at the seaside. In the evening she trimmed herself a little sailor-hat, while I read to her the *Exchange and Mart*. We had a good laugh over my trying on the hat when she had finished it; Carrie saying it looked so funny with my beard, and how the people would have roared if I went on the stage like it.

August 2

Mrs Beck wrote to say we could have our usual rooms at Broadstairs. That's off our mind. Bought a coloured shirt and a pair of tan-coloured boots, which I see many of the swell clerks wearing in the City, and hear are all the 'go'.

August 3

A beautiful day. Looking forward to to-morrow. Carrie bought a parasol about five feet long. I told her it was ridiculous. She said: 'Mrs James, of Sutton, has one twice as long', so the matter dropped. I bought a capital hat for hot weather at the seaside. I don't know what it is called, but it is the shape of the helmet worn in India, only made of straw. Got three new ties, two coloured handkerchiefs, and a pair of navy-blue socks at Pope Brothers. Spent the evening packing . . .

August 16

Lupin positively refused to walk down the Parade with me because I was wearing my new straw helmet with my frock-coat. I don't know what the boy is coming to.

The Short Body'd Gown

Ye lads and ye lasses of country and city,
I pray you give ear to my humorous ditty,
Concerning the fashion just come from town,
A whimsical dress call'd the short body'd gown.

This humorous dress that's now call'd the mode,
Surpasses all fashions that e'er was in vogue,
There's not a young miss in the country all round,
But must be stuff'd up in a short body'd gown.

Last Midsummer-day Sally went to the fair,
For to sell her yarn. Oh, how she did stare!
Both wives, maids, and widows, in every shop round,
They all were dress'd up in a short body'd gown!

So home in the evening Miss Sally she hies,
And told it her mother with greatest surprize,
Saying, 'Two hanks a-day I will spin the week round,
Until I can purchase a short body'd gown.'

The mother surpriz'd, only thought it a jest,
Saying, 'Sally, your old fashion'd gown fits you best,
So leave this new fashion to folks in the town,
And don't waste your cloth in a short body'd gown.'

* * *

Both maids, wives, and widows, you'd think were all wild,
And all look as if they were got with child;
Neither baloons, nor turbans, or all fashions round,
Will fit them, unless they've a new body'd gown.'

(Anon, 1801)

VIRGINIA WOOLF

From The New Dress

MABEL HAD HER first serious suspicion that something was wrong as she took her cloak off and Mrs Barnet, while handing her the mirror and touching the brushes and thus drawing her attention, perhaps rather markedly, to all the appliances for tidying and improving hair, complexion, clothes, which existed on the dressing table, confirmed the suspicion – that it was not right, not quite right, which growing stronger as she went upstairs and springing at her, with conviction as she greeted Clarissa Dalloway, she went straight to the far end of the room, to a shaded corner where a looking-glass hung and looked. No! It was not *right*. And at once the misery which she always tried to hide, the profound disssatisfaction – the sense she had had, ever since she was a child, of being inferior to other people – set upon her, relentlessly, remorselessly, with an intensity which she could not beat off, as she would when she woke at night at home, by reading Borrow or Scott; for oh these men, oh these women, all were thinking – 'What's Mabel wearing? What a fright she looks! What a hideous new dress!' – their eyelids flickering as they came up and then their lids shutting rather tight. It was her own appalling inadequacy; her cowardice: her mean, water- sprinkled blood that depressed her. And at once the whole of the room where, for ever so many hours, she had planned with the little dressmaker how it was to go, seemed sordid, repulsive: and her own drawing-room so shabby, and herself, going out, puffed up with vanity as she touched the letters on the hall table and said: 'How dull!' to show off – all this now seemed unutterably silly, paltry, and provincial. All this had been absolutely destroyed, shown up, exploded, the moment she came into Mrs Dalloway's drawing-room.

What she had thought that evening when, sitting over the teacups, Mrs Dalloway's invitation came, was that, of course, she could not be fashionable. It was absurd to pretend it even – fashion meant cut, meant style, meant thirty guineas at least – but why not be original? Why not be herself, anyhow? And, getting up, she had taken that old fashion book of her mother's, a Paris fashion book of the time of the Empire, and had thought how much prettier, more dignified, and more womanly they were then, and so set herself – oh, it was foolish – trying to be like them, pluming heself in fact, upon being modest and old-fashioned, and very charming, giving herself up, no doubt about it, to an orgy of self-love, which deserved to be chastised, and so rigged herself out like this.

But she dared not look in the glass. She could not face the whole horror – the pale yellow, idiotically old-fashioned silk dress with its long skirt and its high sleeves and its waist and all the things that looked so charming in the fashion book, but not on her, not among all these ordinary people. She felt like a dressmaker's dummy standing there, for young people to stick pins into.

'But, my dear, it's perfectly charming!' Rose Shaw said, looking her up and down with that little satirical pucker of the lips which she expected – Rose herself being dressed in the height of fashion, precisely like everybody else always . . .

Miss Milan said that the skirt could not well be longer; if anything the skirt, said Miss Milan, puckering her forehead, considering with all her wits about her, must be shorter; and she felt, suddenly, honestly, full of love for Miss Milan, much, much fonder of Miss Milan than of any one in the whole world, and could have cried for pity that she should be crawling on the floor with her mouth full of pins, and her face red and her eyes bulging – that one human being should be doing this for another, and she saw them all as human beings merely, and herself going off to her party, and Miss Milan pulling the cover over the canary's cage, or letting him pick a hemp-seed from between her lips, and the thought of it, of this side of human nature and its patience and its endurance and its being content with such miserable, scanty, sordid, little pleasures filled her eyes with tears.

And now the whole thing had vanished. The dress, the room, the love, the pity, the scrolloping looking-glass, and the canary's cage – all had vanished, and here she was in a corner of Mrs Dalloway's drawing-room, suffering tortures, woken wide awake to reality.

But it was all so paltry, weak-blooded, and petty-minded to care so much at her age with two children, to be still so utterly dependent on people's opinions and not have principles or convictions, not to be able to say as other people did, 'There's Shakespeare! There's death! We're all weevils in a captain's biscuit' – or whatever it was that people did say.

She faced herself straight in the glass; she pecked at her left shoulder; she issued out into the room, as if spears were thrown at her yellow dress from all sides. But instead of looking fierce or tragic, as Rose Shaw would have done – Rose would have looked like Boadicea – she looked foolish and self-conscious, and simpered like a schoolgirl and slouched across the room, positively slinking, as if she were a beaten mongrel, and looked at a picture, an engraving. As if one went to a party to look at a picture! Everybody knew why she did it – it was from shame, from humiliation.

DAPHNE DU MAURIER
From Rebecca

I BEGAN TO GET in a panic about my costume. It seemed so feeble not to be able to think of anything, and I kept remembering all the people who would come, from Kerrith and round about, the bishop's wife who had enjoyed herself so much, the last time, Beatrice and Giles, that tiresome Lady Crowan, and many more people I did not know and who had never seen me, they would every one of them have some criticism to offer, some curiosity to know what sort of effort I should make . . .

In the evening, when I was changing for dinner, there was a knock at my bedroom door. I called 'Come in,' thinking it was Clarice. The door opened and it was not Clarice. It was Mrs Danvers . . .

'So you have not decided yet what you will wear?' she said. There was a hint of derision in her voice, a trace of odd satisfaction . . .

'I wonder you don't copy one of the pictures in the gallery,' she said.

I pretended to file my nails. They were too short and too brittle, but the action gave me something to do and I did not have to look at her . . .

'All the pictures in the gallery would make good costumes,' said Mrs Danvers, 'especially that one of the young lady in white, with her hat in her hand . . .'

*

I found Clarice waiting for me in my bedroom, her round face scarlet with excitement. We giggled at one another like schoolgirls, and I bade her lock my door. There was much sound of tissue paper, rustling and mysterious. We spoke to one another softly like conspirators, we walked on tiptoe. I felt like a child again on the eve of Christmas. This padding to and fro in my room with bare feet, the little furtive bursts of laughter, the stifled exclamations, reminded me of hanging up my stocking long ago. Maxim was safe in his dressing-room, and the way through was barred against him. Clarice alone was my ally and favoured friend. The dress fitted perfectly. I stood still, hardly able to restrain my impatience while Clarice hooked me up with fumbling fingers.

'It's handsome, Madam,' she kept saying, leaning back on her heels to look at me. 'It's a dress fit for the Queen of England.'

'What about under the left shoulder there,' I said, anxiously. 'That strap of mine, is it going to show?'

'No, Madam, nothing shows.'

'How is it? How do I look?' I did not wait for her answer, I twisted and turned in front of the mirror, I frowned, I smiled. I felt different already, no longer hampered by my appearance. My own dull personality was submerged at last. 'Give me the wig, ' I said excitedly, 'careful, don't crush it, the curls mustn't be flat. They are supposed to stand out from the face.' Clarice stood behind my shoulder, I saw her round face beyond mine in the reflection of the looking-glass, her eyes shining, her mouth a little open. I brushed my own hair sleek behind my ears. I took hold of the soft gleaming curls with trembling fingers, laughing under my breath, looking up at Clarice.

'Oh, Clarice,' I said, 'what will Mr de Winter say?'. . .

*

They all stared at me like dumb things. Beatrice uttered a little cry and put her hand to her mouth. I went on smiling, I put one hand on the banister.

'How do you do, Mr de Winter,' I said.

Maxim had not moved. He stared up at me, his glass in his hand. There was no colour in his face. It was ashen white. I saw Frank go to him as though he would speak, but Maxim shook him off. I hesitated, one foot already on the stairs. Something was wrong, they had not understood. Why was Maxim looking like that? Why did they all stand like dummies, like people in a trance?

Then Maxim moved forward to the stairs, his eyes never leaving my face.

'What the hell do you think you are doing?' he asked. His eyes blazed in anger. His face was still ashen white.

I could not move, I went on standing there, my hand on the banister.

'It's the picture,' I said, terrified at his eyes, at his voice. 'It's the picture, the one in the gallery.'

There was a long silence. We went on staring at each other. Nobody moved in the hall. I swallowed, my hand moved to my throat. 'What is it?' I said. 'What have I done?'

If only they would not stare at me like that with dull blank faces. If only somebody would say something. When Maxim spoke again I did not recognize his voice. It was still and quiet, icy cold, not a voice I knew.

'Go and change,' he said, 'it does not matter what you put on. Find an ordinary evening frock, anything will do. Go now, before anybody comes.'

I could not speak, I went on staring at him. His eyes were the only living things in the white mask of his face.

'What are you standing there for?' he said, his voice harsh and queer. 'Didn't you hear what I said?'

I turned and ran blindly through the archway to the corridors beyond. I caught a glimpse of the astonished face of the drummer who had announced me. I brushed past him, stumbling, not looking where I went. Tears blinded my eyes.

LOUISA M. ALCOTT
From Good Wives

A FEW DAYS BEFORE she had done a dreadful thing, and it weighed upon her conscience. Sallie had been buying silks, and Meg longed for a new one – just a handsome light one for parties, her black silk was so common, and thin things for evening wear were only proper for girls. Aunt March usually gave the sisters a present of twenty-five dollars apiece at New Year, that was only a month to wait, and here was a lovely violet silk going at a bargain, and she had the money, if she only dared to take it. John always said what was his was hers; but would he think it right to spend not only the prospective five-and-twenty, but another five-and-twenty out of the household fund? That was the question. Sallie had urged her to do it, had offered to loan the money, and with the best intentions in life, had tempted Meg beyond her strength. In an evil moment the shopman held up the lovely, shimmering folds, and said, 'A bargain, I assure you, ma'am.' She answered, 'I'll take it'; and it was cut off and paid for, and Sallie had exulted, and she had laughed as if it were a thing of no consequence, and driven away, feeling as if she had stolen something, and the police were after her.

When she got home, she tried to assuage the pangs of remorse by spreading forth the lovely silk; but it looked less silvery now, didn't become her, after all, and the words 'fifty dollars' seemed stamped like a pattern down each breadth. She put it away; but it haunted her, not delightfully, as a new dress should, but dreadfully, like the ghost of a folly that was not easily laid. When John got out his books that night, Meg's heart sank, and for the first time in her married life, she was afraid of her husband.

ANITA LOOS
From Gentlemen Prefer Blondes

So Lady Shelton was really delighted to have we Americans come to her house. I mean she took Dorothy and I into the back parlor and tried to sell us some bead headbands she seems to make by sewing quite a few beads on a piece of ribbon to tie around your head in the evening. So I asked her how much they were and she said 5 pounds. So I asked her how much it was in money and it seems it is 25 dollars. I mean I am going to have quite a hard time with Dorothy in London because she should not say what she said about an English lady. I mean she should not say that she really thought that Lady Shelton's head-bands were quite useful because any girl who would pay 25 dollars for one of them would need to have her head bandaged.

We had a great deal of company, eleven damsels . . . they had amongst them, on their heads, an acre and a half of shrubbery, besides slopes, grass-plats, tulip-beds, clumps of peonies, kitchen-gardens and green-houses.

								Hannah More (1773)

LYNNE REID BANKS
From The L-shaped Room

She came at last, swathed in mink, ushered in by the perspiring PRO. The photographers reluctantly put their glasses down and picked up their cameras as the PRO, his hands daintily plucking at the collar of the mink, prepared to unveil the famous figure. When every camera was in place, he whisked the coat away.

It really was the most extraordinary outfit I've ever seen. The red hair flowed over bare white shoulders. The celebrated bust, looking like two dunces' caps applied to her chest, was encased in a puce halter-necked sweater which left all but essentials bare. Her sizable bottom and not-too-marvellous legs were thinly coated with bright yellow silk jeans ending just below the knee; her bare feet were thrust into pink mules with diamond spike-heels. She also wore a diamond brooch at her waist, the size of a buckler.

For a second there was an unbelieving silence – then a chorus of whistles and concerted pops and tinkles as every flashbulb in the room went off.

'Eeh, booger me,' murmered the little comic, who was standing near me. 'Have I got to 'ave me picture taken alongside of that? I'll feel like a seaside postcard.'

While all the posed pictures were being taken I was edging round among the columnists saying, 'Please, give us a break, don't put in that it happened at Drummonds. This is supposed to be a respectable hotel.'

This was what I knew James would have done; the boys laughed wryly.

'Don't blame you. Don't worry. Thanks for the drinks, Janie.'

It was nearly over. I had a small breather in which to feel pleased that there was this part of me that could take over, like an automatic pilot, and carry on as usual. I knew that not one person had guessed there was anything wrong.

At this moment, Madam, who knew me, shrieked to me over the heads of the crowd: 'You – there – please! I'm simply dying of thirst. Could you do you think possibly find me a small drink?' The waiters were all busy at that moment so I picked up a full glass from the table and fought my way to where she was holding court in the middle of the mass – standing up, of course. She couldn't sit down; the yellow pants were too tight. I handed her the drink, and she smiled at me with all her splendid teeth and said, 'Thank you. The men are all being so unkind, they're making fun of my relaxing clothes. Don't you think they're divinely chic?'

At this moment, at this precise moment, a feeling came over me that I hadn't had for nearly a month. My face went deathly cold and saliva rushed into my mouth. There'd been no warning. I clutched my throat and gasped. Madam's smile froze on her lips. 'What's the matter?' asked someone. 'I'm going to be sick,' I replied hollowly. A passage was cleared through the crowd like magic, and although they were all kindly men, a great shout of irrepressible laughter went up as I fled. As I left the room I heard the little comic bellow, 'That's what she thinks o' thy relaxing clothes, ducks, and I must say I see what she means!'

A black silk balloon towing a black-and-white striped parachute proved to be old Mrs Budge . . . the spikes of her black-and-white sunshade menaced the eyes of Priscilla Wimbush, who towered over her – a massive figure dressed in purple and topped with a queenly toque on which the nodding black plumes recalled the splendours of a first-class Parisian funeral.

Aldous Huxley, *Crome Yellow*

1671. March 18th. Madame the Duchess de Nevers came in with her hair dressed in the most ludicrous fashion, though you know that as a rule I like uncommon styles. La Martin had had the fancy to create a new coiffure and

had cropped her! Her hair had been cut and rolled on paper curlers which
had made her suffer death and agony a whole night long. Her head was like a
little round cabbage – nothing at the sides. My dear, it is the most ridiculous
sight you can imagine.

Mme de Sévigné, *Letters*

MRS FRANCES TROLLOPE
From The Domestic Manners of the Americans

THOUGH THE EXPENSE of the ladies' dress greatly exceeds, in proportion to
their general style of living, that of the ladies of Europe, it is very far (excepting in Philadelphia) from being in good taste. They do not consult the seasons
in the colours or in the style of their costume; I have often shivered at seeing a
young beauty picking her way through the snow with a pale rose-coloured bonnet, set on the very top of her head: I knew one young lady whose pretty little
ear was actually frost-bitten from being thus exposed. They never wear muffs or
boots, and appear extremely shocked at the sight of comfortable walking shoes
and cotton stockings, even when they have to step to their sleighs over ice and
snow. They walk in the middle of winter with their poor little toes pinched into
a miniature slipper, incapable of excluding as much moisture as might bedew a
primrose. I must say in their excuse, however, that they have, almost universally,
extremely pretty feet.

(1832)

Boots and shoes are the greatest trouble of my life. Everything else one can
turn and turn about, and make old look like new; but there's no coaxing boots
and shoes to look better than they are.

George Eliot, *Letters*

EDNA O'BRIEN
From The Girl with Green Eyes

DO YOU LIKE them, Will?' I said, as he made a face at my new white shoes.
The toes were so long that I had to walk sideways going upstairs. I put them
on because Baba and I were going to a wine-tasting reception that night. We read

about it in the papers and Baba said that we'd crash it. We had crashed two other functions – a fashion show and a private showing of a travel film of Ireland. (All lies, about dark-haired girls roaming around Connemara in red petticoats. No wonder they had to show it in private.)

At half five, customers began to flock in on their way from work, and around six Mrs Burns came out, to let me go off.

'Very stuffy here,' she said to Willie. A hint to mean that we shouldn't have the oil heater on. Stuffy! There were draughts everywhere and a great division between the floor and the wainscoting.

I made my face up in the hall and put on rouge, eye-shadow, and lashings of ashes-of-roses perfume. The very name ashes-of-roses made me feel alluring. Willie sneaked me in a good sugar bag, so that I could bring my shoes in the bag, and wear my wellingtons. The gutters were overflowing outside, and rain beat against the skylight in the upstairs hall.

'Don't do anything I wouldn't do,' he said, as he let me out by the hall door and whistled as I ran to the bus shelter a few yards down the road. It was raining madly.

The bus was empty, as there were very few people going down to the centre of the city at that hour of evening. It was too early for the pictures. There were toffee papers and cigarette packets on the floor and the bus had a sweaty smell. It was a poor neighbourhood.

I read a paper which I found on the seat beside me. There was a long article by a priest, telling how he'd been tortured in China. I knew a lot about that sort of thing, because in the convent where I went to school the nun used to read those stories to us on Saturday nights. As a treat she used to read a paper called *The Standard*. It was full of stories about priests' toe-nails being pulled off and nuns shut up in dark rooms with rats.

I almost missed my stop, because I had been engrossed in this long article by the Irish priest.

Baba was waiting for me outside the hotel. She looked like something off a Christmas tree. She had a new fur muff and her hair-set was held in place with lacquer.

'Mother o' God where are you off to in your wellingtons?' she asked.

I looked down at my feet and realized with desolation that I'd left my shoes on the bus.

There was nothing for it but to cross the road and wait for the bus on its return journey. It was an unsheltered bus-stop and Baba's hair style got flattened. Then, to make everything worse, my shoes were not on the bus and there was a different conductor. He said that the other conductor must have handed them in to the lost property office on the way to his tea.

STAN BARSTOW

From The Human Element

'**L**ook, there's Lottie Sharpe.'

I turn round and look over into the next yard, where a girl's walking by: a slim little bit, all dressed up in nylons and high heels and even a fancy little hat.

'I wish I looked like that,' Thelma says, sort of quiet and wistful like, and I can tell she's talking to herself, not to me. I take a good look at her, standing nearly as big as me, with that sort of suet-pudding face of hers, and I see what she means, but I say nothing.

'Lottie's gettin' married next month.'

There it is: they're all alike. Getting married and spending some poor feller's brass is all they think about. I say nothing.

Thelma watches right till Lottie turns the corner into the entry, then she gives a big sigh, right down inside herself.

'I'll tell 'em to be gettin' ready, then.'

She goes back across the yard. Her overall's tight and stretched across her fat behind and I can see the red backs of her knees.

I reckon I've had it for today and I begin to pick my gear up.

We go along the street to the bus stop. Ma Baynes is walking in front, wearing white holiday shoes and carrying the sandwiches in a tartan shopping bag. Old Man Baynes, in a new cap and cricket shirt, strolls along beside her sucking at his pipe and saying nothing.

I'm walking behind with Thelma, carrying the portable radio. Thelma's changed into a thin cotton frock that's as short and tight as the overall she had on earlier. I wonder if she has any clothes she doesn't look as though she's grown out of. Now and then I take a look down at my new shoes. They're a light tan, with long toes. I've had my eye on them for weeks, along with a pair with inch-thick crêpe soles, and I've had a lot of trouble making up my mind between them. But these are definitely dressier: a smashing pair of shoes. They'll be fine when a bit of the newness has worn off. Just now they've developed a bit of a squeak and once Thelma looks down and giggles. I give her a look and move away from her and try to look as if I'm not with them at all, and hoping like mad we won't run into any of the bods from the Works.

We sit downstairs on the bus. Just out of manners I have a bit of a difference with Old Man Baynes about who's going to get the fares. But I soon give in when I see one or two of the other passengers looking round. It's the Bayneses' treat anyway and I don't want to attract attention and have everybody taking me for Thelma's young man.

JOHN GALSWORTHY
From The Man of Property

PHILIP BOSINNEY WAS known to be a young man without fortune, but Forsyte girls had become engaged to such before, and had actually married them. It was not altogether for this reason, therefore, that the minds of the Forsytes misgave them. They could not have explained the origin of a misgiving obscured by the mist of family gossip. A story was undoubtedly told that he had paid his duty call to Aunts Ann, Juley, and Hester, in a soft grey hat – a soft grey hat, not even a new one – a dusty thing with a shapeless crown. 'So extraordinary, my dear – so odd!' Aunt Hester, passing through the little, dark hall (she was rather short-sighted), had tried to 'shoo' it off a chair, taking it for a strange, disreputable cat – Tommy had such disgraceful friends! She was disturbed when it did not move.

Like an artist for ever seeking to discover the significant trifle which embodies the whole character of a scene, or place, or person, so those unconscious artists – the Forsytes – had fastened by intuition on this hat; it was their significant trifle, the detail in which was embedded the meaning of the whole matter; for each had asked himself: 'Come, now, should I have paid that visit in that hat?' and each had answered 'No!' and some, with more imagination than others, had added: 'It would never have come into my head!'

George, on hearing the story, grinned. The hat had obviously been worn as a practical joke! He himself was a connoisseur of such.

'Very haughty!' he said, "the wild Buccaneer!'

And this *mot*, 'The Buccaneer', was bandied from mouth to mouth, till it became the favourite mode of alluding to Bosinney.

Her aunts reproached June afterwards about the hat.

'We don't think you ought to let him, dear!' they had said.

June had answered in her imperious brisk way, like the little embodiment of will she was:

'Oh! what does it matter? Phil never knows what he's got on!'

No one had credited an answer so outrageous. A man not know what he had on? No, no!

EVELYN WAUGH
From Vile Bodies

ADAM ALSO ATTEMPTED in an unobtrusive way to exercise some influence over the clothes of his readers. *'I noticed at the Café de la Paix yesterday evening'*, he wrote, *'that two of the smartest men in the room were wearing black suède shoes with their evening clothes – one of them, who shall be nameless, was a Very Important Person indeed. I hear that this fashion, which comes, like so many others, from New York, is likely to become popular over here this season.'* A few days later he mentioned Captain Stuart-Kerr's appearance at the Embassy *'wearing, of course, the ultra-fashionable black suède shoes'*. In a week he was gratified to notice that Johnny Hoop and Archie Schwert had both followed Captain Stuart-Kerr's lead, while in a fortnight the big emporiums of ready-made clothes in Regent Street had transposed their tickets in the windows and arranged rows of black suède shoes on a silver step labelled 'For evening wear'.

His attempt to introduce a bottle-green bowler hat, however, was not successful; in fact, a 'well-known St James's Street hatter', when interviewed by an evening paper on the subject, said that he had never seen or heard of such a thing, and though he would not refuse to construct one if requested to by an old customer, he was of the opinion that no old customer of his would require a hat of that kind (though there was a sad case of an impoverished old beau who attempted to stain a grey hat with green ink, as once in years gone by he had been used to dye the carnation for his buttonhole).

DAISY ASHFORD
From The Young Visiters

ONE MORNING MR Salteena came down to brekfast and found Ethel had come down first which was strange. Is the tea made Ethel he said rubbing his hands. Yes said Ethel and such a quear shaped parcel has come for you. Yes indeed it was a quear shape parcel it was a hat box tied down very tight and a letter stuffed between the string. Well well said Mr Salteena parcels do turn quear I will read the letter first and so saying he tore open the letter and this is what it said.

MY DEAR ALFRED.
I want you to come for a stop with me so I have sent you a top hat wraped up in tishu paper inside the box. Will you wear it staying with me because it is very

uncommon. Please bring one of your young ladies whichever is the prettiest in the face.

> I remain Yours truely
> BERNARD CLARK.

Well said Mr Salteena I shall take you to stay Ethel and fancy him sending me a top hat. Then Mr S opened the box and there lay the most splendid top hat of a lovly rich tone rarther like grapes with a ribbon round compleat.

Well said Mr Salteena peevishly I dont know if I shall like it the bow of the ribbon is too flighty for my age.

NANCY MITFORD
From Love in a Cold Climate

MY MOTHER HAD given me an evening dress from Mainbocher which seemed specially designed for such an occasion; it had a white pleated chiffon skirt, and black silk jersey top with a high neck and long sleeves, which was tucked into a wide, black, patent-leather belt. Wearing this with my only jewel, a diamond clip sent by my father, I thought I was not only nicely, but also suitably, dressed. My father, incidentally, had turned a deaf ear to Lady Montdore's suggestion that he should buy me a place, and had declared himself to be too utterly ruined even to increase my allowance on my marriage. He did, however, send a cheque and this pretty jewel . . .

I saw at once that my dress would not do. Norma told me afterwards, when pointing out the many fearful gaffes which I was supposed to have made during the course of the evening, that as a bride I would have been expected to wear my wedding dress at our first dinner party. But, even apart from that blunder, a jersey top, however Parisian, was obviously unacceptable for evening wear in high Oxford society. The other women present were either in lace or marocain, décolleté to the waist behind, and with bare arms. Their dresses were in shades of biscuit, and so were they.

WINIFRED FOLEY
From A Child in the Forest

BECAUSE I COULD only shuffle along in my sandals, I started for chapel well before time. We had to wait in the little vestry; then make a grand entrance

..

into chapel. When I arrived, a few girls were there already, among them Eunice. . . .

There she sat today, clad from top to toe in white, except for the pink rose-buds and blue forget-me-nots round her straw hat. She had long brown curls as well, and a pretty face. There couldn't have been much left for her to ask God for. It didn't seem fair!

Gladys, my best friend, was there, and she too was nearly all in white, but I didn't mind about her. Gladys could have been dressed in fairy gossamer, and I wouldn't have grudged her it. She was kind and nice to everybody, especially me. She patted the place on the wooden form next to her for me to sit down.

All the glory I had felt in my sandals, white socks, and straw hat (which I'd thought quite passable with the frayed ends at the back) vanished. Compared with the others, I was going to look a proper gypsy. I just managed to hold back the tears and make a concentrated study of my white socks. Presently Nell Wills shuffled in. It wasn't her shoes that handicapped *her*. It was her dress!

Nell had eleven brothers and sisters. A couple of the girls were in service, and a couple of the boys worked down the pit when there was any work. All the same, it was a miracle where Nell's mum had found the money to buy the white material and lace edging for Nell's dress. Considering Mrs Wills was mother of twelve children, she hadn't much notion of relating the shape of the dress to the body's needs. It was just a straight tube with two smaller straight tubes sewn in for sleeves, and a hole left in the top for Nell's head to go through.

The lace edging had gone round the neck and sleeves, but only two-thirds round the narrow skirt bottom. This had been made even narrower by a one-sided tuck, so that the lace might fit. The whole gave an interesting lop-sided effect, and it also made it nearly impossible for Nell to walk. Still, it did have the glory of being all white. I would gladly have swapped my dark flounces for it . . .

Any pleasure I'd anticipated from reciting my poem had evaporated before I took my seat, conscious that my outlandish appearance spoilt the show . . .

I started off well enough, and everyone suffered me with quiet politeness. Too quiet; I could hear a faint crackling noise coming from my hat. It was difficult to concentrate on my pious poem, wondering what was happening up there on my head; and it became even more difficult when I saw the big ribbon boss on Mrs Dee's hat begin to shake. She was shaking too, with suppressed laughter . . .

Like the rippling of a breeze in a cornfield, her laughter spread to everyone in the audience. I knew now what they were laughing at – my hat. The inadequate stitching must have come undone, and I could picture the braid standing up in a spiral above it.

The poor choirmaster, who'd spent patient weeks coaching us for this day, was sticking his chin in and out in nervous bewilderment at this collapse of events. I felt terribly guilty, but the whole thing seemed so comical. So I had a fit of giggles and laughed till the tears came, then sat down. The closing hymn was 'Jesus Loves Me'. Even if I hadn't been so choked up, I wouldn't have had the nerve to sing it.

MARGARET KENNEDY
From The Constant Nymph

FLORENCE HAD TOLD Teresa to put on her new white frock. It was a maidenly garment of embroidered muslin with sleeves to cover her sharp elbows and a high yoke which hid the hollows in her young neck. A white ribbon spanned the broad middle of the dress in that region where it was to be hoped she might some day have a waist, and other white bows tied up her tail of fair hair. Also she had new patent leather shoes, with steel buckles, and thick, black silk stockings. All this gear was designed for school parties and concerts, and became her almost as little as it would have become that Delphic Sibyl whom she so closely resembled. Its infantile scantiness emphasised everything that was out of scale in her person: the lanky awkwardness of her rapid growth, and the shy, abrupt grandeur of some of her gestures. She peered at the glass rather dismally and could not help feeling that she looked foolish.

'God in His wisdom gave you that face,' she informed her reflection, 'and Florence in her wisdom gave you that dress. But they don't understand the value of team work. And neither of them consulted your feelings very much. It's not your beauty, my girl, that will get you into trouble in this world.'

REBECCA WEST
From Sunflower

SHE HURRIED ON with her head down until she bumped into a woman who was coming out of the shop. Looking up to apologise she found that the little body's eyes were set derisively on her coat, which was a very lovely fantasy in checks by Molyneux. She was not hurt by that, for often before she had noticed that good clothes, like any other form of fine art, were always greeted with ridicule when they were brought out into the open among ordinary people; and she knew that there is nothing base about this ridicule, since it springs, like the giggling of children who are taken to see a tragedy, not from a lack of sensibility but from its excess. Children are as far as possible from all knowledge of tragedy, ordinary people have few chances of encountering the rarer sorts of decoration, so these contacts are to them news of an unfamiliar variation in life. They are dismayed that it should exist at all, for it intimates that life covers a range far wider than the octave of their daily routine and that the demands which it may make upon them are endless and incalculable. They are dismayed, too, at its quality: for the beauty of tragedy, and the beauty of good clothes, which is one and the same beauty, asks from those who use it a sympathetic nobility and an unembittered but firm discontent with the emotion that is not right, with the colour, the line that is not right. It sends them off on that search for harmony which is as delicious as love for a woman who is perfect and loving, as agonising as love for a woman about whom one knows nothing, not even that she has been born. This is a hard thing to lay on children, on simple people. They will not have it, they pretend that what they have seen is of no significance, and merely a ludicrous accident of folly which calls for nothing from the sane but laughter. Essington had made her see all that when she had told him how the people in Cricklewood Broadway had giggled at her when her car had broken down on the way to the Fairshams' at Harrow, and she had had to step out into the street in a Nicole Groult picture gown and cloak.

GEORGE ELIOT
From The Mill on the Floss

THE DODSONS WERE certainly a handsome family, and Mrs Glegg was not the least handsome of the sisters. As she sat in Mrs Tulliver's arm-chair, no impartial observer could have denied that for a woman of fifty she had a very comely face and figure, though Tom and Maggie considered their aunt Glegg as the type of ugliness. It is true she despised the advantages of costume, for though, as she often observed, no woman had better clothes, it was not her way to wear her new things out before her old ones. Other women, if they liked, might have their best thread-lace in every wash, but when Mrs Glegg died, it would be found that she had better lace laid by in the right-hand drawer of her wardrobe, in the Spotted Chamber, than ever Mrs Wooll of St Ogg's had bought in her life, although Mrs Wooll wore her lace before it was paid for. So of her curled fronts: Mrs Glegg had doubtless the glossiest and crispest brown curls in her drawers, as well as curls in various degrees of fuzzy laxness; but to look out on the weekday world from under a crisp and glossy front, would be to introduce a most dreamlike and unpleasant confusion between the sacred and the secular. Occasionally, indeed, Mrs Glegg wore one of her third-best fronts on a weekday visit, but not at a sister's house; especially not at Mrs Tulliver's, who, since her marriage, had hurt her sister's feelings greatly by wearing her own hair, though, as Mrs Glegg observed to Mrs Deane, a mother of a family, like Bessy, with a husband always going to law, might have been expected to know better. But Bessy was always weak!

So if Mrs Glegg's front to-day was more fuzzy and lax than usual, she had a design under it: she intended the most pointed and cutting allusion to Mrs Tulliver's bunches of blond curls, separated from each other by a due wave of smoothness on each side of the parting. Mrs Tulliver had shed tears several times at sister Glegg's unkindness on the subject of these unmatronly curls, but the consciousness of looking the handsomer for them, naturally administered support. Mrs Glegg chose to wear her bonnet in the house to-day – untied and tilted slightly, of course – a frequent practice of hers when she was on a visit, and happened to be in a severe humour: she didn't know what draughts there might be in strange houses. For the same reason she wore a small sable tippet, which reached just to her shoulders, and was very far from meeting across her well-formed chest, while her long neck was protected by a *chevaux-de-frise* of miscellaneous frilling. One would need to be learned in the fashions of those times to know how far in the rear of them Mrs Glegg's slate-coloured silk gown must have been; but from certain constellations of small yellow spots upon it, and a mouldy odour about it suggestive of a damp clothes-chest, it was probable that it belonged to a stratum of garments just old enough to have come recently into wear.

ANGUS WILSON
From Anglo-Saxon Attitudes

R OSE LORIMER, STRUGGLING with weighed-down shopping baskets, made her immense way among the marble and mosaic of the Corner House, caught a passing view of herself in a mirror and was pleased. She had always affirmed that women scholars were primarily women and should not disregard the demands of feminine fashions. To advertise learning by disregard of dress was to be odd, and Dr Lorimer disliked oddity more than anything. The vast intellectual excitement of her researches since the war had not left her a lot of time for thinking about clothes, but her mother had always said that with a good fur coat, however old, one could not go wrong; and for her own part, she had added a bold dash of colour to cheer our drab English winter – woman's contribution to banish gloom. Twenty years ago, of course, she reflected, straw hats with flowers would have been out of place in December, but the dictates of fashion were so much less strict nowadays, it seemed. And then Dr Lorimer had always loved artificial flowers, especially roses.

Clarissa Crane, searching the vast marble tea-room with a certain distaste, suddenly recognized her learned hostess and felt deeply embarrassed. In all this drab collection of matinée-goers and pantomime parties, that only could be her. She had expected somebody dowdy, indeed had worn her old green tweed suit in deference to the academic occasion, but she had not been prepared for someone quite so outrageously odd, so completely a 'fright'. Dr Lorimer was mountainous, not only up and down, but round and round as well, and then her clothes were so strange – that old, old fur coat, making almost no pretence of the large safety-pins that held it together, and, above the huge, aimlessly smiling grey face, a small toque composed entirely of artificial pink roses and set askew on a bundle of tumbling black coils and escaping hairpins. Clarissa, with a sensitive novelist's eye, dreaded to think into what strange realm the poor creature's mind had strayed; with a woman of the world's tact, however, she cried, 'Dr Lorimer, this is so awfully kind of you!'

'*PIERRE!*' I heard Randy screaming outside the door. I turned the lock and pulled the light cord. Then I backed into my mother's sable coat (smelling of old Joy and stale Diorissimo) and sat beneath it cross-legged among the boots. Above me were two more racks of coats going up high into the ceiling. Old fur coats, English children's coats with leather leggings, ski parkas, rain capes, trench coats, autographed slickers from our camp days, school blazers with name tapes in the necks and forgotten skate keys in the pockets, velvet evening coats, brocade coats, polo coats, mink coats . . . thirty-five years of changing fashions and four grown daughters . . . thirty-five years of buying and spending and raising kids and screaming . . . and what did my mother have to show for it? Her sable, her mink, and her resentment?

Erica Jong, *Fear of Flying*

'I like the air of this Ruffle mightily. The French are certainly the most agreeable people. Do they wear 'em so low?'

'Exactly . . . The bottom of the Lace must agree with the tip of your Ladyship's little finger. To wear it higher wou'd show too much of your Ladyship's arm.'

'Which I would not do by any means; it looks like a washer-woman to bare above the Ring.'

William Burnaby, *The Reform'd Wife* (1700)

Ladies at the theatre

The goddess of fashion suffers from a quotidian fever which, it has often been noticed, at a certain degree of heat runs to madness; as the get-up of four ladies attested, who entered a box during the third play, with such wonderfully fantastic caps and hats perched on their head, that they were received by the entire audience with loud derision. Their neckerchiefs were puffed up so high that their noses were scarcely visible, and their nosegays were like huge shrubs, large enough to conceal a person. In less than a quarter of an hour, when the scene had changed to a market-square in any case, four women walked on to the stage dressed equally foolishly, and hailed the four ladies in the box as their friends.

The Diary of Sophie V. La Roche

And in these times the Devil appeared in the shape of a monster. No wonder; for the frivolity of the English, always taking up the folly of foreigners in the variety of their clothes and not foreseeing future evils coming through this, they began to wear hoods so small that they barely covered the shoulder (much less the head).

Chronicle of John Reading (1365)

Give Chloe a bushel of horse-hair and wool,
Of paste and pomatum a pound,
Ten yards of gay ribbon to deck her sweet skull,
And gauze to encompass it round.
Let her flaps fly behind for a yard at the least,
Let her curls meet just under her chin;
Let these curls be supported to keep up the jest
With a hundred instead of one pin.
Let her gown be tucked up to the hip on each side,
Shoes too high for to walk or to jump,
And to deck the sweet creature complete for a bride
Let the cork-cutter make her a rump.

Universal Magazine (1776)

WILLIAM MAKEPEACE THACKERAY
From The Book of Snobs

POMPEY HICKS IS giving elaborate directions to his servant, and asking loudly, 'Davis, where's the dwessing-case?' and 'Davis, you'd best take the pistol-case into the cabin.' Little Pompey travels with a dressing-case, and without a beard: whom he is going to shoot with his pistols, who on earth can tell? and what he is to do with his servant but wait upon him, I am at a loss to conjecture.

Look at honest Nathan Houndsditch and his lady, and their little son. What a noble air of blazing contentment illuminates the features of those Snobs of Eastern race! What a toilette Houndsditch's is! What rings and chains, what gold-headed canes and diamonds, what a tuft the rogue has got to his chin (the rogue! he will never spare himself any cheap enjoyment). Little Houndsditch has a little cane with a gilt head and little mosaic ornaments – altogether an extra air. As for the lady, she is all the colours of the rainbow! – she has a pink parasol with a white lining, and a yellow bonnet, and an emerald green shawl, and a shot-silk pelisse; and drab boots and rhubarb-coloured gloves; and parti-coloured glass buttons, expanding from the size of a fourpenny-piece to a crown, glitter and twiddle all down the front of her gorgeous costume. I have said before, I like to look at 'the Peoples' on their gala days, they are so picturesquely and outrageously splendid and happy.

> The gawdy gossip, when she's set agog,
> In jewels dressed, and at each ear a bob,
> Goes flaunting out, and, in her trim of pride,
> Think all she says or does, is justified.
>
> John Dryden, *The Book-Learned Wife*

P. G. WODEHOUSE
From The Amazing Hat Mystery

'WELL, BE THAT as it may,' he went on, his cheeks suffused to a certain extent, 'I love that girl, Nelson, and she's coming with me to the first day of Ascot, and I'm relying on this new hat of mine to do just that extra bit that's needed in the way of making her reciprocate my passion. Having only met her so far at country houses, I've never yet flashed upon her in a topper.'. . .

'These new hats are pretty well bound to do the trick, I should say, wouldn't you?'

'Infallibly. Where girls are concerned, there is nothing that brings home the gravy like a well-fitting topper.'. . .

The lid was OK absolutely: and on the following morning Percy, having spent the interval polishing it with stout, assembled the boots, the spats, the trousers, the coat, the flowered waistcoat, the collar, the shirt, the quiet grey tie, and the good old gardenia, and set off in a taxi for the house where Elizabeth was staying. And presently he was ringing the bell and being told she would be down in a minute, and eventually down she came, looking perfectly marvellous.

'What ho, what ho!' said Percy.

'Hullo, Percy,' said Elizabeth.

Now, naturally, up to this moment Percy had been standing with bared head. At this point, he put the hat on. He wanted her to get the full effect suddenly in a good light. And very strategic, too. I mean to say, it would have been the act of a juggins to have waited till they were in the taxi, because in a taxi all toppers look much alike.

So Percy popped the hat on his head with a meaning glance and stood waiting for the uncontrollable round of applause.

And instead of clapping her little hands in girlish ecstasy and doing Spring dances round him, this young Bottsworth gave a soft gurgling scream not unlike a coloratura soprano choking on a fish-bone.

Then she blinked and became calmer.

'It's all right,' she said, 'The momentary weakness has passed. Tell me, Percy, when do you open?'

'Open?' said Percy, not having the remotest.

'On the Halls. Aren't you going to sing comic songs on the Music Halls?'

Percy's perplexity deepened.

'Me? No. How? Why? What do you mean?'

'I thought that hat must be part of the make-up and that you were trying it on the dog. I couldn't think of any other reason why you should wear one six sizes too small.'

Percy gasped.

'You aren't suggesting this hat doesn't fit me?'

'It doesn't fit you by a mile.'

'But it's a Bodmin.'

'Call it that if you like. I call it a public outrage.'

Percy was appalled. I mean, naturally. A nice thing for a chap to give his heart to a girl and then find her talking in this hideous, flippant way of sacred subjects . . .

'Possibly,' he said, coldly, 'you would prefer to go to this bally race-meeting alone?'

'You bet I'm going alone. You don't suppose I mean to be seen in broad daylight in the paddock at Ascot with a hat like that.'

Percy stepped back and bowed formally.

'Drive on, driver,' he said to the driver, and the driver drove on.

R. P. WESTON AND BERT LEE
Brahn Boots

Our Aunt Hannah's passed away,
We'd her funeral today,
And it was a posh affair –
Had to have two p'licemen there!

The 'earse was luv'ly all plate glass,
And wot a corfin! oak and brass!
We'd fah-sands weepin', flahers gaore,
But Jim, our cousin – what d'yer fink 'e wore?

Why Brahn boots! I ask yer – brahn boots!
Fancy comin' to a funeral in brahn boots!
I will admit 'e 'ad a nice black tie,
Black finger nails and a nice black eye:

But yer can't see people orf when they die in brahn boots!
And Aunt 'ad been so very good to 'im.
Done all that any muvver could fer 'im.
And Jim, her son, to show his clars

Rolls up to make it all a farce
In brahn boots – I ask yer – brahn boots!
While all the rest
Wore decent black and mourning suits.

I'll own he didn't seem so gay,
In fact he cried best part the way,
But straight, he reg'lar spoilt our day
Wiv 'is brahn boots.

In the graveyard we left Jim,
None of us said much to him.
Yus, we all give 'im the bird.
Then by accident we 'eard

'E'd given 'is black boots to Jim Small.
A bloke wot 'ad no boots at all.
So p'raps Aunt Hannah doesn't mind
She did like people who was good and kind.

But brahn boots! I ask yer – brahn boots!
Fancy coming to a funeral in brahn boots!
And we could 'ear the neighbours all remark
'Wot,'im chief mourner? Wot a bloomin' lark!

'Why 'e looks more like a Bookmaker's clerk – in brahn boots!'
That's why we 'ad to be so rude to 'im,
That's why we never said 'Ow do!' to 'im,
We didn't know – he didn't say,

He'd give 'is other boots away.
But brahn boots! I ask yer – brahn boots!
While all the rest
Wore decent black and mourning suits!

But some day up at Heaven's gate
Poor Jim, all nerves, will stand and wait
Till an angel whispers 'Come in, Mate.
Where's yer brahn boots?'

(1910)

He stood up. Hello. Were those two buttons of my waistcoat open all the time? Women enjoy it. Never tell you. But we. Excuse, miss, there's a (whh!) just a (whh!) fluff. Or their skirt behind, placket unhooked. Glimpses of the moon. Annoyed if you don't. Why didn't you tell me before. Still like you better untidy. Good job it wasn't farther south.

James Joyce, *Ulysses*

You buy yourself a new suit of clothes;
The care you give it, God only knows;
The material, of course, is the very best yet;
You get it pressed and pressed and pressed yet;
You keep it free from specks so tiny –
What thanks do you get? The pants get shiny.

Samuel Hoffenstein, *Poems in Praise of Practically Nothing*

WILLIAM MAKEPEACE THACKERAY
From The Book of Snobs

EXAMPLE IS THE best of precepts; so let us begin with a true and authentic story, showing how young aristocratic Snobs are reared, and how early their snobbishness may be made to bloom. A beautiful and fashionable lady (pardon, gracious madam, that your story should be made public; but it is so moral that it ought to be known to the universal world) told me that in her early youth she had a little acquaintance, who is now indeed a beautiful and fashionable lady too. In mentioning Miss Snobky, daughter of Sir Snobby Snobky, whose presentation at Court caused such a sensation, need I say more?

When Miss Snobky was so very young as to be in the nursery regions, and to walk of early mornings in St James's park, protected by a French governess and followed by a huge hirsute flunkey in the canary-coloured livery of the Snobkys, she used occasionally in these promenades to meet with young Lord Claude Lollipop, the Marquis of Sillabub's younger son. In the very height of the season, from some unexplained cause, the Snobkys suddenly determined upon leaving town. Miss Snobky spoke to her female friend and confidante. 'What will poor Claude Lollipop say when he hears of my absence?' asked the tender-hearted child.

'Oh, perhaps he won't hear of it,' answers the confidante.

'*My dear, he will read it in the papers,*' replied the dear little fashionable rogue of seven years old. She knew already her importance, and how all the world of England, how all the would-be-genteel people, how all the silver-fork worshippers, how all the tattle-mongers, how all the grocers' ladies, the tailors' ladies, the attorneys' and merchants' ladies, and the people living in Clapham and Brunswick Square – who have no more chance of consorting with a Snobky than my beloved reader has of dining with the Emperor of China – yet watched the movements of the Snobkys with interest, and were glad to know when they came to London and left it.

Here is the account of Miss Snobky's dress, and that of her mother, Lady Snobky, from the papers:–

'MISS SNOBKY.

'Habit de Cour, composed of a yellow nankeen illusion dress over a slip of rich pea-green corduroy, trimmed en tablier, with bouquets of Brussels sprouts: the body and sleeves handsomely trimmed with calimanco, and festooned with a pink train and white radishes. Head-dress, carrots and lappets.

'LADY SNOBKY

'Costume de Cour, composed of a train of the most superb Pekin bandannas, elegantly trimmed with spangles, tinfoil, and red-tape. Bodice and under-dress of sky-blue velveteen, trimmed with bouffants and nœuds of bell-pulls. Stomacher, a muffin. Head-dress, a bird's nest, with a bird of paradise, over a rich brass knocker en ferronnière. This splendid costume, by Madame Crinoline, of Regent Street, was the object of universal admiration.'

This is what you read. Oh, Mrs Ellis! Oh, mothers, daughters, aunts, grand-mothers of England, this is the sort of writing which is put in the newspapers for you! How can you help being the mothers, daughters, etc., of Snobs, so long as this balderdash is set before you?

You stuff the little rosy foot of a Chinese young lady of fashion into a slipper that is about the size of a salt-cruet, and keep the poor little toes there impris-oned and twisted up so long that the dwarfishness becomes irremediable. Later, the foot would not expand to the natural size were you to give her a washing-tub for a shoe; and for all her life she has little feet, and is a cripple. Oh, my dear Miss Wiggins, thank your stars that those beautiful feet of yours – though, I declare, when you walk, they are so small as to be almost invisible – thank your stars that society never so practised upon them; but look around and see how many friends of ours in the highest circles have had their *brains* so prematurely and hopeless-ly pinched and distorted.

How can you expect that those poor creatures are to move naturally when the world and their parents have mutilated them so cruelly? As long as a *Court Circular* exists, how the deuce are people whose names are chronicled in it ever to believe themselves the equals of the cringing race which daily reads that abominable trash? I believe that ours is the only country in the world now where the *Court Circular* remains in full flourish – where you read, 'This day his Royal Highness Prince Pattypan was taken an airing in his go-cart.' 'The Princess Pimminy was taken a drive, attended by her ladies of honour, and accompanied by her doll,' etc. We laugh at the solemnity with which Saint Simon announces that *Sa Majesté se médicamente aujourd'-hui*. Under our very noses the same folly is daily going on.

'I have just had my hair dressed. You cant think how oddly my head feels, full of powder and black pins and a great cushion on the top of it. When I shall be able to make use of a comb for myself I cannot tell, for my hair is so much entangled, *frizled* they call it, that I fear it will be very difficult.'

Fanny Burney, Evelina

How long had her hair been dressed? Three weeks. 'Dont that lay you under the necessity of dressing your hair every evening?' 'Oh Lord, Sir, a head properly made up, with pins paste & pomatum, will keep a month very well.'

Arthur Murphy, The Old Maid (1756)

I went the other morning to make a visit to an elderly aunt of mine, when I found her tendering her head to the ingenious Mr Gilchrist, who has lately obliged the public with a most excellent essay upon hair. He asked her how long it was since her head had been opened or repaired. She answered, not above nine weeks. To which he replied, that was as long as a head could well go in the summer, and that therefore it was proper to deliver it now; for he confessed that it begun to be a little *hazarde*.

When Mr Gilchrist opened my aunt's head, as he called it, I must confess its effluvias affected my sense of smelling disagreeably, which stench, however, did not surprize me when I observed the great variety of materials employed in raising the dirty fabrick. False locks to supply the great deficiency of native hair, pomatum with profusion, greasy wool to bolster up the adopted locks, and gray powder to conceal at once age and dirt, and all these caulked together by pins of an indecent length and corresponding color. When the comb was applied to the natural hair, I observed swarms of animalculas running about in the utmost consternation and in different directions, upon which I put my chair a little further from the table and asked the operator whether that numerous swarm did not from time to time send out colonies to other parts of the body? He assured me that they could not; for that the quantity of powder and pomatum formed a glutinous matter, which like lime twiggs to birds, caught and clogged the little natives and prevented their migration. Here I observed my aunt to be in a good deal of confusion, and she told me that she would not detain me any longer from better company; for that the operations of the toilette were not a very agreeable spectacle to bystanders, but that they were an unavoidable evil; for, after all, if one did not dress a little like other people, one should be pointed at as one went along.

The London Magazine (Anon, 1768)

'Their woolly white hair, and fiery faces, make them look more like skinned sheep than human beings.'

Lady Mary Wortley Montague, on French hair fashions in the 1730s

10

The Thrills of Undressing

Brevity is the soul of lingerie.

Dorothy Parker

Women are most alarmingly plastic. Their very physique seems to change from age to age.

James Laver, *A Letter to a Girl on the Future of Clothes*

Fashion has such wonderful power over the French mind that it can actually transform the body so as to suit the exigency of the moment.

Captain Gronow, *Reminiscences* (1816)

You would be surprised if you saw Mary and me now, for we have got some new French stays and are become such wonderful shapes that every time I see myself in the glass I open the eyes of astonishment and lift up the voice of admiration.

Cecilia, The Life and Letters of Cecilia Ridley, 1819–45

While I am conniving at low stays and short petticoats I will permit no lady whatsoever to make both ends meet.

Edward Moore, *The World* (1753)

There has been a young gentlewoman overturned and terribly bruised by her *Vulcanian stays*. They now wear a steel busk down their middle and a rail of the same metal across their breasts. If a hero attempts to storm such strong lines and comes to a close engagement he must lie as ill at ease as St Lawrence on his gridirion.

Horace Walpole, *Miscellaneous Letters*

ROBERT HERRICK
Delight in Disorder

A sweet disorder in the dress
Kindles in clothes a wantonness:
A lawn about the shoulders thrown
Into a fine distraction:
An erring lace, which here and there
Enthrals the crimson stomacher:
A cuff neglectful, and thereby
Ribbands to flow confusedly:
A winning wave, deserving note,
In the tempestuous petticoat:
A care show-string, in whose tie
I see a wild civility:
Do more bewitch me than when art
Is too precise in every part.

In Defence of Sh★★ld★rs

'NOW THAT,' I observed, 'is what I call a really pretty girl.'
'Oh, where?' said Nicola with the rather studied enthusiasm of the wife who is determined to be generous at all costs.

'Over there by the door. Don't you think so?'

'She is rather,' Nicola admitted.

'Well-dressed too,' I continued.

'Oh, Oliver, how *can* you. . . ?'

'Why, what's wrong?' I asked innocently.

'My dear,' said Nicola in a shocked tone, 'can't you see? *She's showing her shoulders.*'

'Well, what about it?'

'Well, it simply isn't done, that's all. Look round you and see.'

I looked. And at that moment I perceived for the first time what you, no doubt, have known for weeks, that shoulders this year are 'off'. I had noticed, of course, that Nicola's own evening frock had little puffy sleeves of the kind that small girls used to wear at parties when I was a small boy; but I had put that down to a personal and rather engaging whim of her own, not realising that she was wearing them in obedience to the latest taboo.

I do not know what remote Olympian authority is responsible for this sudden decision that shoulders are indecent; but at any rate his word seems to be law, for about two-thirds of the women in the room had respected it in one way or another. Some, like Nicola, wore tiny puff-sleeves; others little lace capes; others, again, mere wisps of drapery that rather daringly, as the wearer moved, gave glimpses of the forbidden area. The remaining third, it is true, flouted the decree, but it seemed to me that they did so self-consciously, with the defiant air of those who are making a last stand for freedom. I began to feel quite intrigued about shoulders, and on glancing again at the girl by the door I was forced to admit that she did look surprisingly undressed.

It is all very bewildering and rather sad. Shoulders are pretty things – at least most of them are. I wouldn't mind betting that there are more pretty shoulders than pretty faces (even after dividing the number in half to make up for the fact that a woman has two shoulders and only one face); there are certainly more pretty shoulders than pretty ears, elbows, hands and other bits of themselves which women do not feel in the least shy of showing. Why, then, should we be deprived of the sight of these charming features?

I admit that, so far as I know, no poet has yet written a 'Sonnet to His Mistress's Shoulder' (why not? 'Bolder,' 'colder,' 'older . . .' what possibilities!), but I distinctly remember reading once that there is a girl's Christian name which means 'maiden with the white shoulders' – Guinevere or Gwenllian or Wufflefride or one of those: you know the kind.

Anyway, shoulders have always been respectable mentionable objects up to now, and I protest vehemently against their being arbitrarily relegated to the ranks of the Things One Doesn't talk About. Unless something is done quickly even the word itself will soon become taboo, and we shall be reduced, in our conversation, to euphemism, as, she 'gave him the cold upper-arm'; and on paper to asterisks, as 'I let them have it straight from the sh**ld*r.'

Will the day even come when, in modesty's name, we shall be forced to write on our menus, '*Ép**le de mouton*'?

Punch (1920s)

It is the fashion for a lady to undress herself to go abroad and to dress only when she stays at home.

Edward Moore, *The World* (1753)

Among the causes which are cited to account for the decreasing rate of increase of the French population, it is thought that the spread of the Crinoline contagion is proving most injurious in its effects upon the census. The mode now prevailing is one of such extravagance that it is continually demanding fresh sacrifice, and ladies have to choose between a fine dress and a family, for no income but a Rothschild's can provide for both. This results, for the most part, as we learn by the 'Examiner', that – 'where you would see with English habits half a dozen healthy boys and girls walking with their parents, you see instead, in the Bois de Boulogne, a fine lady in a handsome open carriage.'

Punch (1857)

For what Reason I will not pretend to say, but the Ladies have found some Inconvenience surely in the circular 'Hoop', that they have chang'd it to that extensive oblong Form they now wear; If that was complain'd of as an Incumbrance, I am certain this must be much more troublesome in the Management both within Doors and without; I have been in a moderate large Room, where there have been but two Ladies, who had not Space enough to move without lifting up their Petticoats higher than their Grandmothers would have thought decent; I believe every one has observed to what Pains a Lady is put, to reduce that wide extended Petticoat to the narrow Limits of a Chair or a Chariot; But let her manage her getting in or out ever so skilfully or modestly, yet, she makes but a very grotesque Figure with her Petticoats standing up half way the Glasses, and her Head just peeping out above them. However, as by Women of Quality some greater Liberties will be taken than is any Way consistent for private Persons to attempt, I would desire my fair Country women, who have no Chairs or Chariots, to reduce the exhorbitant Extent of their Petticoat when they walk in publick Places: But it were to be wish'd, that the Sex in general would introduce a more reasonable Fashion for Coats, and confine them within the Bounds of Decency and Moderation. I know no other Argument should sooner prevail with them, than to acquaint them it is a Mode very disagreeable to the Men in general, as it is in particular to Your Humble Servant . . .

London Magazine (1768)

Rose is wearing expensive underwear of black lace. There is a subtle, erotic sheen to it. I can think of half a dozen girls straight away who would look alluring in it. Not Rose. She belongs to the age of white underwear – slips and stockings; the kind of things you see in old films from the fifties and early sixties. After all, this was her time.

Christopher Burns, Angelo's Pasion

Away with silks, away with Lawn,
Ile have no sceans,[1] or Curtains drawn;
Give me my Mistress, as she is,
Drest in her nak't simplicities:
For as my Heart ene so mine Eye
Is wone with flesh, not *Drapery*.

Robert Herrick

[1] hangings

JANE WELSH CARLYLE
From New Letters & Memorials

To Mrs Russell
Oct. 21 1862

BUT THE ROSE coloured petticoat, Oh my Dear! I must tell you about the first appearance of *that*! I put it on the second day, and the black silk tunic trimmed with half-a-yard-wide lace (imitation), with long falling sleeves lined with rose-colour; and a great bunch of rose-coloured ribbon on my breast, and smaller boughs at the wrists of my white under-sleeves. It was really, as Miss Baring said, 'quite a costume!' And in spite of its prettiness, I couldn't help feeling nervous about appearing, for the first time, in a guise which would make me remarked by all the *women*, at least! So I dressed in good time, that I mightn't have to walk into the drawing room when many people were down. There had been some uncertainty about the dinner hour that day, as people were coming from London by a late train. At all events, I should hear the gong sound for dressing, I thought, half an hour before dinner; and in the mean time I sat down, all ready, to read a novel. How long I had sat without hearing either bell or gong I can't say; but I was startled from my reading by a sharp knock at my bedroom door, and the voice of one of the man-servants informing me 'everybody was gone in to dinner!' Upon my honour, I can believe some hardened wretches have gone out to be hanged with less emotion than I had in hurrying along the corridor and down the great staircase, to have the two leaves of the dining room door flung wide open before me by two footmen! and then to walk up the great room to my seat at the dinner-table, everybody's head turned to see *who* was so late! To put the finishing stroke to my agony, the rose-coloured petticoat was a trifle too long in front for the stooping way in which I walked, and was like to trip me at every step! – But bad moments and good moments, and all moments pass over! I got into my seat, Lord knows how, and any one who had heard me complaining aloud to Lady A. up the table, that the gong had never been sounded, would have fancied me endowed with all the self-possession I could have wished.

Another ordeal was in store for me and my 'costume' later. Being Sunday night, the Bishop was to read a Chapter and say Prayers in that same dining room before all the servants, and such of the visitors as would attend. Eight-and-thirty servants were seated along two sides of the room; the men all in a line, and the women all in a line; and with these thirty-eight pairs of eyes on me (six pairs of them belonging to Ladies' maids!!) I had to sail up, in all that rose-colour, to the top of the room, on the opposite side, *first*! the other Ladies being members of the family pushed me into that horrid dignity. And the same in going out; I had to walk the length of the room, like to trip myself at every step, with the petticoat and the embarrassment! before one of that frightful line of servants budged. It took all the compliments paid me on the costume to give me courage to put it on a second time! As an old Aunt of Mr C's said, when she had become somehow possessed of a one-pound note and didn't know where on earth to hide it for safety, 'They're troubled that hae' the worl', and troubled that want it.'

E. NESBIT

From The Railway Children

T HEY GOT DOWN the steep stairs. Bobbie was pale and shivering. Peter's face looked thinner than usual. Phyllis was red-faced and damp with anxiety.

'Oh, how hot I am!' she said; 'and I thought it was going to be cold; I wish we hadn't put on our – ' she stopped short, and then ended in quite a different tone – 'our flannel petticoats.'

Bobbie turned at the bottom of the stairs.

'Oh, yes,' she cried, '*they're* red! Let's take them off.'

They did, and with the petticoats rolled up under their arms, ran along the railway, skirting the newly fallen mound of stones and rocks and earth, and bent, crushed, twisted trees. They ran at their best pace. Peter led, but the girls were not far behind. They reached the corner that hid the mound from the straight line of railway that ran half a mile without a curve or corner.

'Now,' said Peter, taking hold of the largest flannel petticoat.

'You're not' – Phyllis faltered – 'you're not going to *tear* them?'

'Shut up,' said Peter, with brief sternness.

'Oh, yes,' said Bobbie, 'tear them into little bits if you like. Don't you see, Phil, if we can't stop the train, there'll be a real live accident, with people *killed*. Oh, horrible! Here, Peter, you'll never tear it through the band!'

She took the red flannel petticoat from him and tore it off an inch from the band. Then she tore the other in the same way.

'There!' said Peter, tearing in his turn. He divided each petticoat into three pieces. 'Now, we've got six flags.' He looked at the watch again. 'And we've got seven minutes. We must have flagstaffs.'

The knives given to the boys are, for some odd reason, seldom of the kind of steel that keeps sharp. The young saplings had to be broken off. Two came up by the roots. The leaves were stripped from them.

'We must cut holes in the flags, and run the sticks through the holes,' said Peter. And the holes were cut. The knife was sharp enough to cut flannel with. Two of the flags were set up in heaps of loose stones beneath the sleepers of the down line. Then Phyllis and Roberta took each a flag, and stood ready to wave it as soon as the train came in sight.

'I shall have the other two myself,' said Peter, 'because it was my idea to wave something red.'

'They're our petticoats, though,' Phyllis was beginning, but Bobbie interrupted –

'Oh, what does it matter who waves what, if we can only save the train?'. . .

It seemed to her that they had been standing there for hours and hours, holding those silly little red flannel flags that no one would ever notice. The train wouldn't care. It would go rushing by them and tear round the corner and go crashing into that awful mound. And everyone would be killed. Her hands grew very cold and trembled so that she could hardly hold the flag. And then came the distant rumble and hum of the metals, and a puff of white steam showed far away along the stretch of line.

'Stand firm,' said Peter, 'and wave like mad! When it gets to that big furze bush step back, but go on waving! Don't stand *on* the line, Bobbie!'

The train came rattling along very, very fast.

'They don't see us! They won't see us! It's all no good!' cried Bobbie.

The two little flags on the line swayed as the roaring train shook and loosened the heaps of loose stones that held them up. One of them slowly leaned over and fell on the line. Bobbie jumped forward and caught it up, and waved it; her hands did not tremble now.

It seemed that the train came on as fast as ever. It was very near now.

'Keep off the line, you silly cuckoo!' said Peter, fiercely.

'It's no good,' Bobbie said again.

'Stand back!' cried Peter, suddenly, and he dragged Phyllis back by the arm.

But Bobbie cried, 'Not yet, not yet!' and waved her two flags right over the line. The front of the engine looked black and enormous. Its voice was loud and harsh.

'Oh, stop, stop, stop!' cried Bobbie. No one heard her. At least Peter and Phyllis didn't, for the oncoming rush of the train covered the sound of her voice with a mountain of sound. But afterwards they used to wonder whether the engine itself had not heard her. It seemed almost as though it had – for it slackened swiftly, slackened and stopped, not twenty yards from the place where Bobbie's two flags waved over the line. She saw the great black engine stop dead, but somehow she could not stop waving the flags. And when the driver and the fireman had got off the engine and Peter and Phyllis had gone to meet them and pour out their excited tale of the awful mound just round the corner, Bobbie still waved the flags but more and more feebly and jerkily.

When the others turned towards her she was lying across the line with her hands flung forward and still gripping the sticks of the little red flannel flags.

The engine-driver picked her up, carried her to the train, and laid her on the cushions of a first-class carriage.

'Gone right off in a faint,' he said, 'poor little woman. And no wonder. I'll just 'ave a look at this 'ere mound of yours, and then we'll run you back to the station and get her seen to.'

CHARLES CAVERS

From Hades! The Ladies!

THEY ARE GONE – I had a young lady this week who was married at St Paul's, Westminster, without one. It is incredible. It is the end of an epoch. The petticoats I have seen and sold, they flutter and flaunt and furbelow in my memory, and now they are no more.

There were the decent flannel ones – the common sort in red or with feather cross-stitch to relieve their plainness. There were the cream flannel ones with scalloping and even Swiss embroidery. There were the lawn ones with Valenciennes lace – rows and rows of it. There were the seemly nainsook ones which virginal brides bought.

There were, too, for those and such as those, the princess petticoat with no waistband, but with bodice all in a piece. There were the moirette ones and those of real silk moiré. There were those, too, of many uses – one body, but a detachable frill for morning, noon, and evening wear which Lee in Sloane Street invented. There were those net ones with flounces as well as tucks. There were the rich, handsome petticoats in satin: we had a department in Whiteley's where we sold nothing else, and all men selling them, too. There were those of glacé silk with a delicious soft frou-frou as the wearer walked – and now they are all gone, every one.

The petticoat is as dead and done with as chain armour or sedan chairs, and I – and the world which understood these things – am left lamenting.

What would Robert Herrick write to-day – where would he find an inspiration to write –

> A winning wave, deserving note
> In the tempestuous petticoat.

Sir John Suckling would be devastated. He would have to look in his lady's eyes – a less interesting spectacle than in the days when he remarked that –

> Her feet beneath her petticoat
> Like little mice stole in and out.

The lament which I pen is a post-epilogue. The bride's aunt, the aunt of her who went to St Paul's, Westminster, with serene assurance but no petticoat, said it in my hearing. 'No petticoat, nothing at all, my dear Olive; well, I do declare!'

I declare, too. Women will learn again that to declare no petticoats is to declare no trumps in the game of life.

Washing gowns of all kinds are the ton. Dark dutch chintzes are very much worn and now I think of it I must tell you I never had a gown so admired as my Irish lawn. It has been wash'd three times and appears now if any thing better than when new, so tell Mr Porter if you think of it. It is always taken for a dutch chintz but I take care to publish its country. As a Dress gown I have brought down a Robe a la Turque – violet colour – the petticoat and vest white – Tiffany gauze and pale yellow Ribbons – with that a sash and buckle under the Robe. Gauze gowns and clear muslin gowns are much worn in full dress.

The undress Hats are straw, chip or Cellbridge or Cane, of the dimensions pretty nearly of your round tea table, two rows of narrow ribbon or one of broad round the crown.

Betsey Sheridan's *Journal* (1784–1790)

The justice in a cotton nightcap with a little perky tassel, sat on a chair tying his drawers at the knee, preparatory to inducting his legs into his pantaloons – if any single damsel in years, who may read this, will forgive this slight revelation as to the mysteries of a gentleman's toilette. The pantaloons assumed and the braces fastened, the justice threw his nightcap on to the bed.

Mrs Henry Wood, *East Lynne* (1861)

JEAN GENET
From Querelle of Brest

STANDING THERE ON the carpet, her bare feet flat on the floor, her figure no longer had the impressive extra height afforded her by her high–heeled shoes. The plump curves of her thighs had no meaning now that they no longer were swathed in and swayed beneath the heavy folds of a silky dress. Her bosom was less provocative. All of this she felt instinctively, and also that anger could be expressed in the real tragic manner only when properly supported on the theatrical buskin, and could increase only with the body tightly swathed, allowing no pendulous part of it to appear. Madame Lysiane regretted the time when women were set on a pedestal. She regretted the days of buss-bodices, stays, whale-bones that stiffened the body and gave it authority enough to rule over conduct, and sufficient ferocity. She would have liked to be able to squeeze together the edges of a stiff and flexible pair of pink stays, at the bottom of which would be dangling four suspenders, flapping against her legs. But she was stark naked, her feet planted firmly on the floor. Something just as monstrous in its inconsistency as this inner monologue began to undermine and upset her poise. 'Shall I be shamed into thinking myself a clumping Big Bertha in carpet slippers? But I am . . .' Thereupon her spirit failed her and she was overcome with terrible confusion as the vision of two febrile muscular bodies came forcibly yet inescapably before her eyes, and, facing them, the softly crumbling mass of her own too fat body. She stepped into her shoes and regained something of her former stature.

BERYL BAINBRIDGE
From The Dressmaker

THE AUNTS PUT on their flannel nightgowns over their clothes and then undressed, poking up the fire to make a blaze before removing their corsets. The girl sat withdrawn on the sofa, stroking the spine of the cat, while the two women grunted and twisted on the hearth rug, struggling to undo the numerous hooks that confined them, until, panting and triumphant, they tore free the great pink garments and dropped them to the floor, where they lay like cricket pads, still holding the shape of their owners, and the little dangling suspenders sparkling in the firelight. Dull then after such exertions, mesmerised by the heat of the fire, the aunts stood rubbing the flannel nightgowns to and fro across their stomachs, breathing slow and deep. After a while they sat down on either side of the fender and removed their stockings. Out on the woollen rug, lastly, came their strange yellow feet, the toes curled inwards against the warmth.

A lady's leg is a dangerous sight, in whatever colour it appears; but, when it is enclosed in white, it makes an irresistible attack upon us.

The Universal Spectator (1737)

. . . next to no clothing, there is nothing more ravishing than an easy dishabille.

The Connoisseur (1754)

'Madame du V. a French lady, appeared in public in a dress entirely a la guillotine. That is to say, in a scarlet stuff, with pantaloons descending to the sole of the feet, and covered with a slight transparent gauze; the breasts entirely bare, as well as the arms up as high as the shoulders, the hair from behind drawn back very tight and fastened emblematically on the top of the head.'

Gentleman's Magazine (1801)

The crowd itself was gay and pretty and those who had real beauty are wonderfully distinguished by the present dress . . . and the transparent dresses that leave you certain there is no chemise beneath! the fault of the reigning fashion when carried to its extreme, even for the youngest and handsomest, is, to say the truth, *indecency*. Not that it shows so much more than people have done at many other times, but that it both shows and covers, in a certain way, very much answering certain descriptions our precious neighbours the French used to give in their instructive novels. The figures one meets walking in the street with footmen behind them are exactly what Crébillon would have painted lying on a sopha to receive a lover. And in a high wind! . . . Don't imagine me an old maid growling at the young people for some of the most remarkable statues in wet drapery are very fully my contemporaries at least.

> Lady Louisa Stuart, *Gleanings from an Old Portfolio* (1778)

'Miladi' very handsome woman, but she and all the women were decolletées in a beastly fashion – damn the aristocratic standard of fashion; nothing will ever make me think it right or decent that I should see a lady's armpit flesh-folds when I am speaking to her.

> George du Maurier, letter to his mother after dining
> with the Earl and Countess Somers (1862)

The upstart impudence and innovation of naked breasts, and cutting or hallowing downe the neck of womens garments below their shoulders, an exorbitant and shamefull enormity and habit, much worn by our semi-Adamits, is another meere peice of refined Barbarisme . . .

Another foolish affection there is in young Virgins, though grown big enough to be wiser, but that they are led blind-fold by custome to a fashion pernitious beyond imagination; who thinking a Slender-Waste a great beauty, strive all that they possibly can by streight-lacing themselves, to attain unto a wand-like smalnesse of Waste, never thinking themselves fine enough untill they can span their Waste.

> John Bulwer, *Artificial Changeling* (1653)

> The woman looked immortal. How they told,
> Those alabaster shoulders and bare breasts,
> On which the pearls, drowned out of sight in milk,
> Were lost, excepting the ruby-clasp!
> They split the amaranth velvet-bodice down
> To the waist or nearly, with the audacious press

Of full-breathed beauty. If the heart within
Were half as white! – but, if it were, perhaps,
The breast were closer covered, and the sight
less aspectable, by half, too.

Elizabeth Barrett Browning, *Aurora Leigh*

The crowd presses round her. Is she naked? I am in doubt. Come still
nearer; this deserves my pencil. I see her light pantaloons, comparable to the
famous skin breeches of Mgr. le Comte d'Artois, whom four great lackeys
raised in air to let fall into his vestment, so that there should be no crease.
Clothed in this all day, it became necessary to unbreech him in the evening by
raising him in the same manner and with still greater efforts. The feminine
pantaloons, I say, exceedingly tight although of silk, surpass perhaps the
famous breeches by their complete closeness; they are trimmed with a sort of
bracelets. The jacket is cut sloping in the most skilful fashion, and under a
gauze, artistically painted, palpitate the reservoirs of maternity. A chemise of
fine lawn allows the legs and thighs to be seen, which are embraced by circles
of gold and diamonds. A crowd of young people environ her with the
language of dissolute joy. Another daring feat of *Marveilleuse*, and we might
see among us the antique dances of the daughters of Laconia; there remains
so little to let fall that I know not if true modesty would not be a gainer by the
removal of that transparent veil. The flesh-coloured pantaloons, applied
straitly to the skin, excite the imagination and allow to be seen only at the
best and most hidden forms and allurements; . . . and these are the fine days
which follow those of Robespierre!

Louis Mercier, quoted in Octave Uzanne, *Frenchwoman of the Century*

The wise woman with a limited dress allowance will invest a great deal of it in
underwear.

Mrs Eric Pritchard, *The Cult of Chiffon* (1902)

BARONESS STAFFA
From The Lady's Dressing-Room

UNDERGARMENTS MAY BE simple, but they should be as irreproachable as, or more so, than the dress, which even one spot disgraces. They should be as gracefully cut as possible, and if they can be cut out of very good material so much the better.

Happily, the taste for underclothing made of coloured surah silk or cambric has lost ground for some time back. Many women of refined tastes, indeed, never gave up white linen or cambric, or even simple calico, which can be so easily washed.

Chemises made of printed cambric, or pink, blue, and mauve surah, have this drawback – they cannot be thoroughly washed. Moreoever, they are in somewhat doubtful taste.

A virtuous woman has a repugnance to excessive luxury in her underclothing. She does not like too much lace or embroidery or ribbons and bows. She has them trimmed, of course, but with a certain sobriety which speaks in her favour; she likes them to be elegant, assuredly, so far as she can afford it, but she denies herself the abuse of and over-richness of trimming. She prefers comparatively simple underlinen, which there is no fear of washing, and which can be changed daily.

Coloured stockings begin to be less worn in summer, and only with shoes. With boots, we are coming back to white thread or cotton stockings.

All women who wear long stockings have for some time been in the habit of gartering them above the knee, and it is only in out-of-the-way country parts that to do this cords, tapes, and bits of string are sometimes used. The most humble servant-maid who is a little civilized buys elastic garters with buckles.

Garters should always be clean and fresh, never ragged or shabby. In America the garters do not match; a pair is composed of one yellow and the other black, or one yellow and the other blue, etc., but one of the two is always yellow: it is said that this brings good luck.

Everyone cannot bear a garter as tight as it should be. Their legs swell under pressure, and varicose veins form. In this case the stockings should be fastened to the stays by ribbons (suspenders). But accidents might happen; for if the ribbon, which must be well stretched to hold up the stocking, were to break, down comes the stocking over the heel! My advice is to wear at the same time a garter not at all tight, but sufficiently so to hold up the stocking, in case of accidents, until the damage can be repaired.

To wear the garter below the knee is against all rules of taste. If the chemise, the drawers, the little under-petticoat, and the slip-bodice could all be made to match, it would be in charmingly good taste. They should in that case be of fine nainsouk or fine cambric, with embroideries or valenciennes. The prettiest chemise is cut out either round or heart-shape. A ribbon run in tightens it a little round the shoulders. It is also buttoned on the shoulder. The neck and shoulders are edged with valenciennes or a light embroidery. The chemise must be neither too wide nor too long. It should not fill up needlessly either the stays or the drawers.

The night chemise should reach down to the feet and have long sleeves. It is trimmed with frills, embroideries, or lace, and is finished off with a large collar, falling to the shoulders in pleats. Ribbons are sometimes put in at the collar and cuffs. It is, of course, made of washing material.

(1892)

Dearest Mamma – Yesterday was the best day we have had yet; the nice men had not to field at all, and the stupid cricket was over at four o'clock, and so we went into the gardens and lay in hammocks, and Miss La Touche had such nice shoes on, but her ankles are thick.

The Rooses told me it wasn't 'quite nice' for girls to loll in hammocks (and they sat on chairs) – that you could only do it when you are married; but I believe it is because they don't have pretty enough petticoats. Anyway, Lady Doraine and that horrid Smith creature made a place for me in the empty hammock between them, and, as I knew my 'frillies' were all right, I hammocked too, and it was *lovely*.

Elinor Glyn, *The Visits of Elizabeth*

JOHN GAY
From The Petticoat

> Yet found too late,
> The Petticoat too wide, the door too strait;
> Entrance by force she oft attempts to gain,
> Betty's assistance, too, she calls in vain,
> The stubborn whalebone bears her back again.
> Vex'd at the balk, on foot she trips her way,
> For woman's will admits of no delay;
> On either side a faithful slave attends,
> And safe from harm the Petticoat defends.

'Bosom Secrets.' – When a lady of Mr Punch's acquaintance was in Paris not very long ago, she ordered a dress at a famous Modiste's but found, when she tried it on that she could hardly breathe. On her complaining to the Modiste that the dress was too tight over the chest, 'Que voulez-vous, Madame?' exclaimed the faithful follower – if not framer – of the fashion. 'On ne porte plus de gorge.' (Bosoms are not worn now.) 'Qu'est-ce qu'on fait donc?' asked her innocent English customer. 'Mais, Madame, on ôte la ouate.' (Oh, they take out the wadding) was the equally innocent answer. Punch had never fully appreciated the bearings of this perfectly true story till the other day when he came upon the following paragraph in one of the leading ladies' journals: 'Buy a pair of Maintenon corsets, fitting your waist measure. The other parts of the corset will be proportioned as you ought to be. Put the corset on, and fill the vacant spaces with fine jewellers' wool, then tack on a piece of soft silk or cambric over the bust thus formed to keep the wool in place, renewing it as often as required. This is the most natural and effectual mode of improving the figure which I have heard of.' Now Punch sees how exactly the Parisian Modiste's plan came home to her own business and her customers' bosoms.

Punch (1877)

As Jack, above a draper's shop
Saw written 'Bombazeen',
Here, Bet, says he, I pray you stop
And tell what that may mean.
It means fair lady's dress, she cried,
Who now go naked nearly,
For 'tis so thin, and drawn aside,
'tis bum-be-seen most clearly.

The Spirit of The Public Journals (Anon 1806)

Ladies, old and young, at this period, wore preposterous pads behind; and, as if this fashion wanted a counterbalance, enormous false bosoms were contrived of puffed gauze, so that they might be compared to pouter pigeons.

Henry Angelo, *Reminiscences* (c.1785)

> If skirts get any shorter
> Said the flapper with a sob
> There'll be two more cheeks to powder
> And one more place to 'bob'.

James Laver

It is difficult to see why lace should be so expensive; it is mostly holes.

Mary Wilson Little

SHENA MACKAY
From Dunedin

'I TAKE MY TEXT this morning from the Book of Job, Chapter XLI, verse I. "Canst thou draw out Leviathan with an hook?" ' He had read with a heavy heart of the seas round the Australian and New Zealand coast running red with the blood of whales and seals from May to October as the whaling fleets pursued them to their breeding and mating grounds until they were hunted almost to extinction, of the Sodom and Gomorrah that man had made of the beautiful Bay of Islands, the site of the notorious whaling station. Darwin had called the white population there 'the very refuse of society' and had been pleased to leave behind the debauched riffraff who plundered the seas and reduced their living creatures to blubber. The stench of boiling oil hung over the passengers and crew grouped on the deck as he accused: 'And you ladies in the congregation might pause to think, as you lace your corsets in your vanity, of the cost of that whalebone, of the protracted agony of a noble beast, of mothers heavy with young, of calves and fathers of families slain indiscriminately, of that cache of oil in the head of the sperm whale, shed for you, which in the sight of God is as precious as the ointment in the jar of alabaster with which a sinful woman anointed the feet of Jesus Christ . . .'

There were murmurings, uneasy shiftings and blushes, as if Darwin and whalebone corsets in a sermon constituted profanity. Those familiar with the word sperm were outraged; Louisa felt her dress billow like a bulky sail at the references to mothers heavy with child, and stared scarlet-faced at the sea. And yet, his vulgarity had been redeemed, even blessed by divine approval, when at the words, 'Oh ye whales, and all that move in the waters, bless ye the Lord: praise him and magnify him for ever', a school of porpoises had risen, leaping and curvetting over the green waves, joining in with the congregation.

OSCAR WILDE
From Art and Decoration

FROM THE SIXTEENTH century to our own day there is hardly any form of torture that has not been inflicted on girls, and endured by women, in obedience to the dictates of an unreasonable and monstrous Fashion. 'In order to obtain a real Spanish figure,' says Montaigne, 'what a Gehenna of suffering will not women endure, drawn in and compressed by great *coches* entering the flesh; nay, sometimes they even die thereof!' 'A few days after my arrival at school,' Mrs Somerville tells us in her memoirs, 'although perfectly straight and well made, I was enclosed in stiff stays, with a steel busk in front; while above my frock, bands drew my shoulders back till the shoulder-blades met. Then a steel rod with a semi-circle, which went under my chin, was clasped to the steel busk in my stays. In this constrained state I and most of the younger girls had to prepare our lessons'; and in the life of Miss Edgeworth we read that, being sent to a certain fashionable establishment, 'she underwent all the usual tortures of back-boards, iron collars and dumbs, and also (because she was a very tiny person) the unusual one of being hung by the neck to draw out the muscles and increase the growth', a signal failure in her case. Indeed, instances of absolute mutilation and misery are so common in the past that it is unnecessary to multiply them; but it is really sad to think that in our own day a civilized woman can hang on to a cross-bar while her maid laces her waist into a fifteen-inch circle. To begin with, the waist is not a circle at all, but an oval; nor can there be any greater error than to imagine that an unnaturally small waist gives an air of grace, or even of slightness, to the whole figure. Its effect, as a rule, is simply to exaggerate the width of the shoulders and the hips; and those whose figures possess that stateliness which is called stoutness by the vulgar, convert what is a quality into a defect by yielding to the silly edicts of Fashion on the subject of tight-lacing.

> Do lace me tighter, sister dear,
>   I never had supposed
> It would give me so much pleasure.
>   'My dear, the corset's closed.'
> Then I must get a smaller pair
>   To clasp my slender waist;
> Full well you know I cannot bear,
>   To feel I'm not tight-laced.
> Oh, the pleasure of tight-lacing,

I that have tried, can tell;
Besides that, as to the figure,
I feel I'm quite a belle.
This is the teaching of my lay,
Lace tightly while you can;
Be sure you'll soon forget the pain
You feel when you began.

Englishwoman's Domestic Magazine (Anon, 1800s)

FRANCIS DAVISON
Madrigal

My Love in her attire doth show her wit,
It doth so well become her;
For every season she hath dressings fit,
For Winter, Spring, and Summer.
No beauty she doth miss
When all her robes are on:
But Beauty's self she is
When all her robes are gone.

From *Poetical Rhapsody* (1602)

THOMAS PYNCHON
From The Crying of Lot 49

OEDIPA SKIPPED INTO the bathroom, which happened also to have a walk-in closet, quickly undressed and began putting on as much as she could of the clothing she'd brought with her: six pairs of panties in assorted colours, girdle, three pairs of nylons, three brassieres, two pairs stretch slacks, four half-slips, one black sheath, two summer dresses, half dozen A-line skirts, three sweaters, two blouses, quilted wrapper, baby blue peignoir and old Orlon muu-muu. Bracelets then, scatterpins, earrings, a pendant. It all seemed to take hours to put on and she could hardly walk when she was finished. She made the mistake of looking at herself in a full-length mirror, saw a beach ball with feet, and laughed so violently she fell over, taking a can of hair spray on the sink with her. The can hit the floor, something broke, and with a great outsurge of pressure the stuff commenced atomizing, propelling the can swiftly about the bathroom. Metzger rushed in to find Oedipa rolling around, trying to get back on her feet, amid a great sticky miasma of fragrant lacquer. 'Oh, for Pete's sake,' he said in his Baby Igor voice. The can, hissing malignantly, bounced off the toilet and whizzed by Metzger's right ear, missing by maybe a quarter of an inch. Metzger hit the deck and cowered with Oedipa as the can continued its high-speed caroming; from the other room came a slow, deep crescendo of naval bombardment, machine-gun, howitzer and small-arms fire, screams and chopped-off prayers of dying infantry. She looked up past his eyelids, into the staring ceiling light, her field of vision cut across by wild, flashing over-flights of the can, whose pressure seemed inexhaustible. She was scared but nowhere near sober. The can knew where it was going, she sensed, or something fast enough, God or a digital machine, might have computed in advance the complex web of its travel; but she wasn't fast enough, and knew only that it might hit them at any moment, at whichever clip it was doing, a hundred miles an hour. 'Metzger,' she moaned, and sank her teeth into his upper arm, through the sharkskin.

ANAÏS NIN

From Delta of Venus

THEY LEFT TOGETHER and got into the back seat of Leila's black limousine. Leila leaned over Elena and covered her mouth with her own full lips in one interminable kiss in which Elena nearly lost consciousness. Their hats fell off as they threw their heads back against the seats. Leila engulfed her. Elena's mouth fell on Leila's throat, in the slit of her black dress, which was open between the breasts. She only had to push the silk away with her mouth to feel the beginning of the breasts.

'Are you going to elude me again?' asked Leila.

Elena pressed her fingers against the silk-covered hips, feeling the richness of the hips, the fullness of the thighs, caressing her. The tantalizing smoothness of the skin and the silk of the dress melted into one another. She felt the little prominence of the garter. She wanted to push open Leila's knees, right there. Leila gave an order to the chauffeur Elena did not hear. The car changed direction. 'This is an abduction,' said Leila, laughing deeply.

MILAN KUNDERA
From The Unbearable Lightness of Being

S ABINA WAS NOW by herself. She went back to the mirror, still in her underwear. She put the bowler hat back on her head and had a long look at herself. She was amazed at the number of years she had spent pursuing one lost moment.

Once, during a visit to her studio many years before, the bowler hat had caught Tomas's fancy. He had set it on his head and looked at himself in the large mirror which, as in the Geneva studio, leaned against the wall. He wanted to see what he would have looked like as a nineteenth-century mayor. When Sabina started undressing, he put the hat on her head. There they stood in front of the mirror (they always stood in front of the mirror while she undressed), watching themselves. She stripped to her underwear, but still had the hat on her head. And all at once she realized they were both excited by what they saw in the mirror.

What could have excited them so? A moment before, the hat on her head had seemed nothing but a joke. Was excitement really a mere step away from laughter?

Yes. When they looked at each other in the mirror that time, all she saw for the first few seconds was a comic situation. But suddenly the comic became veiled by excitement: the bowler hat no longer signified a joke; it signified violence; violence against Sabina, against her dignity as a woman. She saw her bare legs and thin panties with her pubic triangle showing through. The lingerie enhanced the charm of her femininity, while the hard masculine hat denied it, violated and ridiculed it. The fact that Tomas stood beside her fully dressed meant that the essence of what they both saw was far from good clean fun (if it had been fun he was after, he, too, would have had to strip and don a bowler hat); it was humiliation. But instead of spurning it, she proudly, provocatively played it for all it was worth, as if submitting of her own will to public rape; and suddenly, unable to wait any longer, she pulled Tomas down to the floor. The bowler hat rolled under the table, and they began thrashing about on the rug at the foot of the mirror.

COLETTE
From Claudine Married

R ÉZI SLEEPS IN a long, dark bedroom and dresses in a gallery. But I like this inconvenient, perpetually overheated dressing-room. And Rézi dresses and undresses in it by a kind of magical process. Sitting very demurely in a low armchair, I watch her admiringly.

While still in her chemise, she does her hair. That marvellous hair, tinted pink by the blinding electric light, green by the low streak of blue daylight, shimmers when she tosses her head to shake it out. At all hours of the day, this false double light from the inadequate window and the over-bright bulbs illuminates Rézi with a theatrical glare.

She brushes her dancing cloud of hair . . . A wave of her wand and, in a flash, thanks to a magic comb, all that gold is gathered up into a shining, twisted knot on the nape of her neck, with every ripple subdued. How on earth does it stay put? Wide-eyed, I am on the verge of imploring: 'Do it again!' Rézi does not wait for my request. Another wave of the wand and the pretty woman in the chemise rises up, sheathed in a dark cloth dress and wearing a hat, ready to go out. The straitlaced corsets, the impertinent knickers, the soft and silent petticoat, have flung themselves on her like eager birds. Then Rézi gives me a triumphant look and laughs.

Her undressing is just as magical. The garments drop all at once, as if they were stuck together, and this charming creature retains nothing but her chemise . . . and her hat. How that irritates me and amazes me! She pins it on her head before she puts on her corsets, she leaves it on till she has taken off her stockings. She wears a hat in her bath, she tells me.

'But why this worship of headgear?'

'I don't know. Something to do with modesty, perhaps. If I had to escape in the middle of the night because the house was on fire, I wouldn't mind running out in the street completely naked, but not without a hat.'

'Honestly? The firemen would have a treat!'

Transl. Antonia White

From Walter: My Secret Life

THE OMNIBUS, WHEN stopped, got crammed full, and went slowly and noisily jolting on its way over a quite newly macadamized road. The mist changed as we got further out to a fog which filled the omnibus, and all was dark. 'How cramped my legs are,' said the lady. 'I like yours against mine, they are so nice, and it's so nice and warm,' I replied. To my astonishment she gave me a gentle punch in my ribs with her left hand. 'Oh, for shame.' 'Stretch them out,' said I, encouraged. 'I can't.' 'Shall I stretch them apart for you?' Another pinch. 'What's the best way of stretching legs?' 'I don't know.' 'Why, put something between them,' I said. Another pinch. All was said in a low tone. No one could have heard but us two, no one could have known what was going on. A fat old man who stunk of brandy and water was on the lady's right, and he was snoring so loudly that people laughed. Vic could not hear me, tho opposite to the lady, thro the noise in passing over the rough road.

She's randy, thought I – who is she? A kept woman perhaps, – and I wished Victoria out of the way. I ungloved my hands, and put my right hand on her thigh. She made no resistance. 'They are close together, they are cramped really, open them wider.' 'I can't, this old snoring man's legs are against mine.' 'Lift one over the other.' She did. I kept my hand there and began gently pinching her thigh. 'That's your garter,' I whispered, feeling a little lump. 'Are you sure?' 'I'll make sure.' Stooping a little, I dropped my right hand down, and pulled up her clothes. There was such a weight of them that my hand could only get up gradually. I felt her calf, and that it was in silk. She let me. 'Oh your heavy clothes,' I whispered. She put the leg down and far from the other, half moved her bum as if to ease her position, and the next instant her clothes being looser, I had one hand on to her thigh above her garter, and pushed it slowly higher up till my little finger was buried in the thatch of her motte, and my other fingers lay a little down grasping her left thigh, but I could not get them far enough to feel her notch, and the weight and pressure of her clothes against my wrist was almost painful. She put her hand down, but only to pull her clothes forwards fearing perhaps that passing a gas-light might disclose our position. All that increased the drag on my wrist and arm, for I was using my right hand, that being next to her, and my knuckles were outwards till I reached her knee and now was only sideways on her thigh – a difficult position, with heavy clothes against it.

FRANK NORRIS

From McTeague

THEY WERE ALL very tired, and went to bed early. After great discussion it was decided that Marcus would sleep upon the lounge in the front parlour. Trina would sleep with August, giving up her room to McTeague. Selina went to her home, a block or so above the Sieppes's. At nine o'clock Mr Sieppe showed McTeague to his room and left him to himself with a newly lighted candle.

For a long time after Mr Sieppe had gone McTeague stood motionless in the middle of the room, his elbows pressed close to his sides, looking obliquely from the corners of his eyes. He hardly dared to move. He was in Trina's room . . .

McTeague was in his lady's bower, it seemed to him a little nest, intimate, discreet. He felt hideously out of place. He was an intruder: he, with his enormous feet, his colossal bones, his crude, brutal gestures. The mere weight of his limbs, he was sure, would crush the little bedstead like an egg-shell.

Then, as this first sensation wore off, he began to feel the charm of the little chamber. It was as though Trina were close by, but invisible. McTeague felt all the delight of her presence without the embarrassment that usually accompanied it. He was near to her, nearer than he had ever been before. He saw into her daily life, her little ways and manners, her habits, her very thoughts. And was there not in the air of that room a certain faint perfume that he knew, that recalled her to his mind with marvellous vividness?

As he put the candle down upon the bureau he saw her hairbrush lying there. Instantly he picked it up, and, without knowing why, held it to his face. With what a delicious odour was it redolent! That heavy, enervating odour of her hair – her wonderful royal hair! The smell of that little hairbrush was talismanic. He had but to close his eyes to see her as distinctly as in a mirror. He saw her tiny, round figure, dressed all in black for, curiously enough, it was his very first impression of Trina that came back to him now – not the Trina of the later occasions, not the Trina of the blue cloth skirt and white sailor. He saw her as he had seen her the day that Marcus had introduced them: saw her pale, round face; her narrow, half-open eyes, blue like the eyes of a baby; her tiny, pale ears, suggestive of anaemia; the freckles across the bridge of her nose; her pale lips; the tiara of royal black hair; and, above all, the delicious poise of the head, tipped back as though by the weight of all that hair – the poise that thrust out her chin a little, with her movement that was so confiding, so innocent, so nearly infantile.

McTeague went softly about the room from one object to another, beholding Trina in everything he touched or looked at. He came at last to the closet door. It was ajar. He opened it wide, and paused upon the threshold.

Trina's clothes were hanging there – skirts and waists, jackets, and stiff white petticoats. What a vision! For an instant McTeague caught his breath, spellbound. If he had suddenly discovered Trina herself there, smiling at him, holding out her hands, he could hardly have been more overcome. Instantly he recognized the black dress she had worn on that famous first day. There it was, the little jacket she had carried over her arm the day he had terrified her with his blundering declaration, and still others, and others, a whole group of Trinas faced him there. He went farther into the closet, touching the clothes gingerly, stroking them softly with his huge leathern palms. As he stirred them a delicate perfume disengaged itself from the folds. Ah, that exquisite feminine odour! It was not only her hair now, it was Trina herself – her mouth, her hands, her neck; the indescribably sweet, fleshly aroma that was a part of her, pure and clean, and redolent of youth and freshness. All at once, seized with an unreasonable impulse, McTeague opened his huge arms and gathered the little garments close to him, plunging his face deep amongst them, savouring their delicious odour with long breaths of luxury and supreme content.

..

Rose has just seen in the concierge's lodge the night-clothes – or morning-clothes if you prefer – that our neighbour La Deslions sends by her maid to the house of the man to whom she is giving a night. It seems that she has a different outfit for each of her lovers in the colour that he prefers. This one consists of a white satin dressing-gown, quilted and pinked, with gold-embroidered slippers in the same colour – a dressing-gown costing between twelve and fifteen hundred francs – a nightdress in batiste trimmed with Valenciennes lace, with embroidered insertions costing three hundred francs, and a petticoat trimmed with three lace flounces at three or four hundred francs each, a total of some three thousand francs taken to any house whose master can afford her.

Goncourt Brothers, *Diaries*

VLADIMIR NABOKOV
From Lolita

WHAT NEXT? I PROCEEDED to the business center of Parkington and devoted the whole afternoon (the weather had cleared, the wet town was like silver-and-glass) to buying beautiful things for Lo. Goodness, what crazy purchases were prompted by the poignant predilection Humbert had in those days for check weaves, bright cottons, frills, puffed-out short sleeves, soft pleats, snug-fitting bodices and generously full skirts! Oh Lolita, you are my girl, as Vee was Poe's and Bea Dante's, and what little girl would not like to whirl in a circular skirt and scanties? Did I have something special in mind? coaxing voices asked me. Swimming suits? We have them in all shades. Dream pink, frosted aqua, glans mauve, tulip red, oolala black. What about playsuits? Slips? No slips. Lo and I loathed slips.

One of my guides in these matters was an anthropometric entry made by her mother on Lo's twelfth birthday (the reader remembers that Know-Your-Child book). I had the feeling that Charlotte, moved by obscure motives of envy and dislike, had added an inch here, a pound there; but since the nymphet had no doubt grown somewhat in the last seven months, I thought I could safely accept most of those January measurements: hip girth, twenty-nine inches; thigh and neck circumference, eleven; chest circumference, twenty-seven; upper arm girth, eight; waist, twenty-three; stature, fifty-seven inches; weight, seventy-eight pounds; figure, linear; intelligence quotient, 121; vermiform appendix present, thank God.

Apart from measurements, I could of course visualize Lolita with hallucinational lucidity; and nursing as I did a tingle on my breastbone at the exact spot her silky top had come level once or twice with my heart; and feeling as I did her warm weight in my lap (so that, in a sense, I was always 'with Lolita' as a woman is 'with child'), I was not surprised to discover later that my computation had been more or less correct. Having moreover studied a midsummer sale book, it was with a very knowing air that I examined various pretty articles, sport shoes, sneakers, pumps of crushed kid for crushed kids. The painted girl in black who attended to all these poignant needs of mine turned parental scholarship and precise description into commercial euphemisms, such as '*petite*'. Another, much older woman, in a white dress, with a pancake make-up, seemed to be oddly impressed by my knowledge of junior fashions; perhaps I had a midget for mistress; so, when shown a skirt with two 'cute' pockets in front, I intentionally put a naïve male question and was rewarded by a smiling demonstration of the way the zipper worked in the back of the skirt. I had next great fun with all kinds of shorts and briefs – phantom little Lolitas dancing, falling, daisying all over the counter. We rounded up the deal with some prim cotton pajamas in popular butcher-boy style. Humbert, the popular butcher.

There is a touch of the mythological and the enchanted in those large stores where according to ads a career girl can get a complete desk-to-date wardrobe, and where little sister can dream of the day when her wool jersey will make the boys in the back row of the classroom drool. Lifesize plastic figures of snubbed-nosed children with dun-colored, greenish, brown-dotted, faunish faces floated around me. I realized I was the only shopper in that rather eerie place where I moved about fish-like, in a glaucous aquarium. I sensed strange thoughts form in the minds of the languid ladies that escorted me from counter to counter, from rock ledge to seaweed, and the belts and the bracelets I chose seemed to fall from siren hands into transparent water. I bought an elegant valise, had my purchases put into it, and repaired to the nearest hotel, well pleased with my day.

ARMISTEAD MAUPIN

From Tales of the City

'CROWDED, HUH?' THE man at the bar was wearing Levi's, a rugby shirt and red-white-and-blue tigers. He had a pleasant, square-jawed face that reminded Michael of people he had once known in the Campus Crusade for Christ.

'What is it?' Michael asked. 'A full moon or something?'

'Got me. I don't keep up with that crap.'

Point One in his favour. Despite Mona's proselytizing, Michael was not big on astrology freaks. He grinned.

Go ahead, Michael told himself. Ply him with cheap jokes. Have no shame.

'Don't tell anybody, but the moon's in Uranus.'

The man stared dumbly, then got it. 'The moon's in your anus. That's a riot!' The man obviously liked him. 'What are you drinking?'

'Calistoga water.'

'I figured that.'

'Why?'

'I don't know. You're . . . healthy-looking.'

'Thanks.'

The man extended his hand. 'I'm Chuck.'

'Michael.'

'Hi, Mike.'

'Michael.'

'Oh . . . You know what, man? I gotta tell you the truth. I scoped you out when you walked in here . . . and I said, "That's the one, Chuck!" I swear to God!'

What *was* it with this butch number? 'Keep it up,' Michael grinned. 'I can use the strokes.'

'You know what it was, man?'

'No.'

The man smiled self-assuredly, then pointed to Michael's shoes. 'Them.'

'My shoes.'

He nodded. 'Weejuns.'

'Yeah?'

'And white socks.'

'I see.'

'They new?'

'The Weejuns?'

'No. I just had them half-soled.'

The man shook his head reverentially, still staring at the loafers. 'Half-soled. Far fucking out!'

'Excuse me, are you . . . ?'

'How many pairs you got?'

'Just these.'

'I have six pairs. Black, brown, scotch grain . . .'

'You like 'em, huh?'

'You seen my ad in *The Advocate*?'

'No.'

'It says . . .' He held his hand up to make it graphic for Michael. ' "Bass

Weejuns." Big capital letters, like.'

'Catchy wording.'

'I get a lotta calls. Collegiate types. Lotta guys get sick of the glitter fairies in this town.'

'I can imagine.'

The man moved closer, lowering his voice. 'You ever . . . done it in 'em?'

'Not to my recollection. Look . . . if you've got six pairs, how come you're not wearing any tonight?'

The man was aghast at his *faux pas*. 'I always wear my Tigers with my rugby shirt!'

'Right.'

He held his foot up for examination. 'They're just like Billy Sive's. In *The Front Runner*.'

EMILE ZOLA
From Nana

'HE'LL NEVER GET dry; he's going to catch cold,' said Nana, seeing Georges shivering.

And not a pair of trousers in the house! She was on the point of recalling the gardener when she had an idea. Zoé, who was unpacking the trunks in a dressing-room, was fetching madame's linen for her to change clothes; a chemise, petticoats, and a lady's dressing-gown.

'But that's just perfect!' exclaimed the young woman. 'Zizi can put the whole lot on. How's that! You're not disgusted with me . . . When your clothes are dry you'll put them on again, and be off quickly so as not to be scolded by your mamma . . . Hurry up, I'm also going to change clothes in the little room.'

Ten minutes later when she reappeared in a dressing-gown she clasped her hands in rapture.

'Oh, the pet! How sweet he is as a little woman!'

He had simply slipped on a long nightdress trimmed with a lace insertion, a pair of embroidered drawers; and the lady's dressing-gown, a long cambric garment also trimmed with lace. With his bare arms slightly tanned, his light brown hair, still wet, falling on his neck, he looked like a girl in these garments.

'Why, he's as slender as me!' said Nana, taking him by the waist. 'Zoé, come and see how it suits him . . . Just fancy! It's made for him, except the bodice part, which is too loose . . . He hasn't as much there as I have, poor Zizi.'

'Yes, of course, I lack a bit there,' said Georges, smiling.

They all three became cheerful. Nana had begun to button the lady's dressing-gown from top to bottom so that it should be decent. She turned him round like a doll, giving him little pats, making the skirt stand out behind. And she questioned him, asking him if he felt well, if he was warm. Yes, hang it all, of course he was well. Nothing was warmer than a woman's chemise: if he could, he'd always have worn one. He wriggled round inside it, delighted by the fine texture of the material of that loose garment which felt so comfortable, and in which he thought he could feel something of Nana's warm life.

Transl. Charles Duff

ANAÏS NIN
Artists and Models

'HE SAID, "DON'T go. I won't touch you. I just love to see women in lovely underwear. I won't move from here. And if you want me to pay you more, all you have to do is wear my favorite piece of underwear and pose for fifteen minutes. I will give you five dollars more. You can reach for it yourself. It is right above your head on the shelf there."

'Well, I did reach for the package. It was the loveliest piece of underwear you ever saw – the finest black lace, like a spider web really, and the panties were slit back and front, slit and edged with fine lace. The brassière was cut in such a way as to expose the nipples through triangles. I hesitated because I was wondering if this would not excite the man too much, if he would attack me.

'He said, "Don't worry. I don't really like women. I never touch them. I like only underwear." I just like to see women in lovely underwear.'

11

The Practical Approach

What with one thing and another, ladies were
completely dependent on their maids – and a
friend of my mother's went to bed in her tiara
because she could not get it off herself.

Loelia, Duchess of Westminster, *Grace and Favour*

A Lord's Toilet

'SEE THAT YOUR lord has a clean shirt and hose, a tunic a doublet and a long coat if he wear such, his hose well-brushed, his socks at hand, his shoes or slippers as brown as a water leech . . .

When he rises make ready the foot sheet . . . over the cushion and chair spread this sheet . . . and see that you have a kerchief and a comb to comb your lord's head before he is fully dressed . . . First hold out to him his tunic, then his doublet while he puts in his arms, and have his stomacher well aired to keep off harm, as also his stockings and socks, and so shall he go warm all day. Then draw on his socks and his hose on well and truss them up to the height that suits him, lace his doublet in every hole, and put around his neck and on his shoulders a kerchief; and then gently comb his head with an ivory comb, and give him water wherewith to wash his hands and face . . .

Then get him such as he asks for, and hold it out for him to put on, and put on his girdle, if he wear one, tight or loose, arrange his robe in the proper fashion give him a hood or hat for his head, a cloak or cape for the house, according as it be fair or foul.

From *The Babees Book* (Anon, 1447)

thick wadded calico rapper, a musk-coloured velvet mantle lined with squirrel skins, eight night-shifts, four pair of silk stockings curiously darned, six pair of laced shoes, new and old, with the heels of half two inches higher than their fellows; a quilted petticoat of the largest size, and one of canvas with whalebone hoops; three pair of stays, bolstered below the left shoulder, two pair of hips of the newest fashion, six roundabout aprons with pockets, and four striped muslin night-rails very little frayed.

The Tatler (c. 1720)

Cottage girls whose parents can scarcely get bread to eat, and certainly cannot get butter to their bread, must nevertheless have their frilled habit-shirts and their long-sleeved gowns . . . It becomes the duty of landholders and proprietors of estates to check as much as possible this ruinous propensity in the country people.

Akermann's Repository (1809)

JASPER MAYNE
The Merchant's Wedding

I am never drest
Without a sermon; but am forc'd to prove
The lawfulness of curling irons before
She'll crisp me in a morning; I must shew
Texts for the fashions of my gowns; she'll ask
Where jewels are commanded, or what lady
I'th' primitive times wore ropes of pearls and rubies.
My toilet's her aversion; her whole service
Is a mere confutation of my cloathes.

(1710)

He has the assurance to appear at the sideboard in a pair of filthy Nankeen breeches made to fit so extremely tight that a less curious observer might have mistaken them for no breeches at all . . . the fellow seems to have thrown off every appearance of decency.

Edward Moore, *On The Appearance of a Manservant* (1755)

OUIDA

From Under Two Flags

'I DON'T SAY BUT what he's difficult to please with his Tops,' said Mr Rake, factotum to the Hon. Bertie Cecil, of the 1st Life Guards, with that article of hunting toggery suspended in his right hand as he paused, before going upstairs, to deliver his opinions with characteristic weight and vivacity to the stud-groom, 'he is uncommon particular about 'em; and if his leathers ain't as white as snow he'll never touch 'em, tho' as soon as the pack come nigh him at Royallieu, the leathers might just as well never have been cleaned, them hounds jump about him so; old Champion's at his saddle before you can say Davy Jones. Tops are trials, I ain't denying that, specially when you've jacks, and moccasins, and moor boots, and Russia-leather crickets, and turf hacks, and Hythe boots, and waterproofs, and all manner of varnish things for dress, that none of the boys will do right unless you look after 'em yourself. But is it likely that he should know what a worry a Top's complexion is, and how hard it is to come right with all the Fast Brown polishing in the world? how should *he* guess what a piece of work it is to get 'em all of a color, and how like they are to come mottled, and how a'most sure they'll ten to one go off dark just as they're growing yellow, and put you to shame, let you do what you will to make 'em cut a shine over the country? How should *he* know? *I* don't complain of that; bless you he never thinks. It's "do this, Rake," "do that," and *he* never remember 't isn't done by magic. But he's a true gentleman, Mr Cecil; never grudge a guinea, or a fiver to you; never out of temper neither, always have a kind word for you if you want, thoro'bred every inch of him; see him bring down a rocketter, or lift his horse over the Broad Water! He's a gentleman – not like your snobs that have nothing sound about 'em but their cash, and swept out their shops before they bought their fine feathers! – and I'll be d—d if I care what I do for him.'

With which peroration to his born-enemy the stud-groom, with whom he waged a perpetual and most lively feud, Rake flourished the tops that had been under discussion, and triumphant, as he invariably was, ran up the back stairs of his master's lodgings in Piccadilly, opposite the Green Park, and with a rap on the panels entered his master's bed-room.

A Guardsman at home is always, if anything, rather more luxuriously accommodated than a young Duchess, and Bertie Cecil was never behind his fellows in anything; besides, he was one of the cracks of the Household, and women sent him pretty things enough to fill the Palais Royal. The dressing-table was littered with Bohemian glass and gold-stoppered bottles, and all the perfumes of Araby represented by Breidenbach and Rimmel. The dressing-case was of silver, with the name studded on the lid in turquoises; the brushes, boot-jacks, boot-trees, whip-stands, were of ivory and tortoiseshell; a couple of tiger-skins were on the hearth with a retriever and blue greyhound in possession; above the mantlepiece were crossed swords in all the varieties of gilt, gold, silver, ivory, aluminium, chiselled and embossed hilts; and on the walls were a few perfect French pictures, with the portraits of a greyhound drawn by Landseer, of a steeplechaser by Harry Hall, one or two of Herring's hunters, and two or three fair women in crayons. The hangings of the room were silken and rose-coloured, and a delicious confusion prevailed through it pell-mell, box-spurs, hunting-stirrups, cartridge-cases, curb-chains, muzzle-loaders, hunting-flasks, and white gauntlets, being mixed up with Paris novels, pink notes, point-lace ties, bracelets, and bouquets to be dispatched to various destinations, and velvet and silk bags for bank-notes, cigars, or vesuvians, embroidered by feminine fingers and as useless as those pretty fingers themselves. On the softest of sofas, half-dressed, and having half an hour before plashed like a water-dog out of the bath, as big as a small pond, in the dressing-chamber beyond, was the Hon. Bertie himself, second son of Viscount Royallieu, known generally on the Brigades as 'Beauty'. The appellative, gained at Eton, was in no way undeserved; when the smoke cleared away that was circling round him out of a great meerschaum-bowl, it showed a face of as much delicacy and brilliancy as a woman's, handsome, thoro'bred, languid, nonchalant, with a certain latent recklessness under the impassive calm of habit, and a singular softness given to the large, dark hazel eyes by the unusual length of the lashes over them. His features were exceedingly fair, fair as the fairest girl's; his hair was of the softest, silkiest, brightest chestnut; his mouth very beautifully shaped; on the whole, with a certain gentle, mournful love-me look that his eyes had with them, it was no wonder that great ladies and gay lionnes alike gave him the palm as the handsomest man in all the Household Regiments – not even excepting that splendid golden-haired Colossus, his oldest friend and closest comrade, known as 'the Seraph'.

He looked at the new tops that Rake swung in his hand, and shook his head.

'Better, Rake; but not right yet. *Can't* you get that tawny color in the tiger's skin there? You go so much to brown.'

Rake shook his head in turn, as he set down the incorrigible tops beside six pairs of their fellows, and six times six of every other sort of boots that the covert side, the heather, the flat, or the 'sweet shady side of Pall Mall' ever knew.

'Do my best, sir; but Polish don't come nigh Nature, Mr Cecil.'

VITA SACKVILLE WEST
From The Edwardians

Button vanished into the dressing-room, and for a while there was silence, broken only by irritable exclamations from within. These inner mysteries of his mother's toilet were unknown to Sebastian, but Viola knew well enough what was going on: her mother was seated, poking at her hair meanwhile with fretful but experienced fingers, while Button knelt before her, carefully drawing the silk stockings on to her feet and smoothing them nicely up the leg. Then her mother would rise, and, standing in her chemise, would allow the maid to fit the long stays of pink coutil, heavily boned, round her hips and slender figure, fastening the busk down the front, after many adjustments; then the suspenders would be clipped to the stockings; then the lacing would follow, beginning at the waist and travelling gradually up and down, until the necessary proportions had been achieved. The silk laces and their tags would fly out, under the maid's deft fingers, with the flick of a skilled worker mending a net. Then the pads of pink satin would be brought, and fastened into place on the hips and under the arms, still further to accentuate the smallness of the waist. Then the drawers; and then the petticoat would be spread into a ring on the floor, and Lucy would step into it on her high-heeled shoes, allowing Button to draw it up and tie the tapes. Then Button would throw the dressing-gown round her shoulders again – Viola had followed the process well, for here the door opened, and the duchess emerged.

MRS HENRY WOOD
From Verner's Pride

In the commodious dressing-room at Verner's Pride, appropriated to its new mistress, Mrs Verner, stood the housekeeper, Tynn, lifting her hands and her eyes. You once saw the chamber of John Massingbird, in this same house, in a tolerable litter; but that was as nothing compared with the litter in this dressing-room, piles and piles of it, one heap by the side of another. Mary Tynn stood screwed against the wainscoting of the wall; she had got in, but to get out was another matter: there was not a free place where she could put her foot. Strictly speaking, perhaps, it could not be called litter, and Mrs Verner and her French maid would have been alike indignant at hearing it so classed. Robes of rich and rare texture; silks standing on end with magnificence; dinner attire, than which nothing could be more exquisite; ball dresses in all sorts of gossamer fabrics; under-skirts, glistening with their soft lustre; morning costumes, pure and costly; shawls of

Cashmere and other *recherché* stuffs, enough to stock a shop; mantles of every known make; bonnets that would send an English milliner crazy; veils charming to look upon; laces that might rival Lady Verner's embroideries, their price fabulous; handkerchiefs that surely never were made for use; dozens of delicately-tinted gloves, cased in ornamental boxes, costing as much as they did; every description of expensive *chaussure*; and trinkets, the drawn cheques for which must have caused Lionel Verner's sober bankers to stare. Tynn might well heave her hands and eyes in dismay. On the chairs, on the tables, on the drawers, on the floor, on every conceivable place and space they lay; a goodly mass of vanity, just unpacked from their cases.

Flitting about amidst them was a damsel of coquettish appearance, with a fair skin, light hair, and her nose a turn-up. Her gray gown was flounced to the waist, her small cap of lace, its pink strings flying, was lodged on the back of her head. It was Mademoiselle Benoite, Mrs Verner's French maid, one she had picked up in Paris. Whatever other qualities the damsel might lack, she had enough of confidence. Not many hours yet in the house, and she was assuming more authority in it than her mistress did.

Mr and Mrs Verner had returned the night before, Mademoiselle Benoite and her packages making part of their train. A whole *fourgon* could not have been sufficient to convey these packages from the French capital to the frontier. Phœby, the simple country maid whom Sibylla had taken to Paris with her, found her place a sinecure since the engagement of Mademoiselle Benoite. She stood now on the opposite side of the room to Tynn, humbly waiting Mademoiselle Benoite's imperious commands.

'Where on earth will you stow 'em away?' cried Tynn, in her wonder. 'You'll want a length of rooms to do it in.'

'Where I stow 'em away!' retorted Mademoiselle Benoite, in her fluent speech, but broken English. 'I stow 'em where I please. Note you that, Madame Teen. Par example! The château is grand enough.'

'What has its grandeur got to do with it?' was Mary Tynn's answer. She knew but little of French phrases.

'Now, then, what for you stand there, with your eyes staring and your hands idle?' demanded Mademoiselle Benoite sharply, turning her attack on Phœby.

'If you'll tell me what to do, I'll do it,' replied the girl. 'I could help to put the things up, if you'd show me where to begin.'

'I like to see you dare to put a finger on one of these things!' returned Mademoiselle Benoite. 'You can confine your services to sewing, and to waiting upon me; but not you dare to interfere with my lady's toilette. Tiens, I am capable, I hope! I'd give up the best service to-morrow where I had not sole power! Go you down to the of-fice, and order me a cup of chocolate, and wait you and bring it up to me. That maudite drogue, that coffee, this morning, has made me as thirsty as a panthère.'

'What a sight of money those things must have cost!' cried she.

'What that matter?' returned the lady's maid. 'The purse of a milor Anglais can stand anything.'

'What did she buy them for?' went on Tynn. 'For what purpose?'

'*Bon!*' ejaculated Mademoiselle. 'She buy them to wear. What else you suppose she buy them for?'

'Why! she would never wear out the half of them in all her whole life!' uttered Tynn, speaking the true sentiments of her heart. 'She could not.'

'Much you know of things, Madame Teen!' was the answer, delivered in undisguised contempt for Tynn's primitive ignorance. 'They'll not last her six months.'

'Six months!' shrieked Tynn. 'She couldn't come to an end of them dresses in six months, if she wore three a day, and never put on a dress a second time!'

'She want to wear more than three different a day sometimes. And it not the mode now to put on a robe more than once,' returned Mademoiselle Benoite carelessly.

Tynn could only open her mouth. 'If they are to but put on but once, what becomes of 'em afterwards?' questioned she, when she could find breath to speak.

Phœby, glancing across at Mrs Tynn, turned somewhat hesitatingly to pick her way out of the room. The housekeeper, though not half understanding, contrived to make out that the morning coffee was not approved of. The French mademoiselle had breakfasted with her, and, in Mrs Tynn's opinion, the coffee had been perfect, fit for the table of her betters.

'Is it the coffee that you are abusing?' asked she. 'What was the matter with it?'

'*Ciel!* You ask what the matter with it!' returned Mademoiselle Benoite, in her rapid tongue. 'It was everything the matter with it. It was all bad. It was drogue, I say; médicine. There!'

'Well, I'm sure!' resentfully returned the housekeeper. 'Now, I happened to make that coffee myself this morning – Tynn, he's particular in his coffee, he is – and I put in –'

'I not care if you put in the whole canastre,' vehemently interrupted Mademoiselle Benoite. 'You English know not to make coffee. All the two years I lived in London with Madame la Duchesse, I never got one cup of coffee that was not enough to choke me. And they used pounds of it in the house, where they might have used ounces. Bah! You can make tea, I not say no; but you cannot make coffee. Now, then! I want a great number sheets of silk-paper.'

'Silk-paper?' repeated Tynn, whom the item puzzled. 'What's that?'

'You know not what silk-paper is!' angrily returned Mademoiselle Benoite. '*Quelle ignorance!*' she apostrophised, not caring whether she was understood or not. '*Elle ne connait pas ce que c'est, papier-de-soie!* I must have it, and a great deal of it, do you hear? It is as common as anything – silk-paper.'

'Things common in France mayn't be common with us,' retorted Mrs Tynn. 'What is it for?'

'It is for some of these articles. If I put them by without the paper-silk round them in the cartons, they'll not keep their colour.'

'Perhaps you mean silver-paper,' said Mary Tynn. 'Tissue-paper, I have heard my Lady Verner call it. There's none in the house, Madmisel Bennot.'

'Madmisel Bennot' stamped her foot. 'A house without silk-paper in it! When you knew my lady was coming home!'

'I didn't know she'd bring – a host of things with her that she has brought,' was the answering shaft lanced by Mrs Tynn.

'Don't you see that I am waiting? Will you send out for some?'

'It's not to be had in Deerham,' said Mrs Tynn. 'If it must be had, one of the men must go to Heartburg. Why won't the paper do that was over 'em before?'

'There not enough of that. And I choose to have fresh, I do.'

'Well, you had better give your own orders about it,' said Mary Tynn. 'And then, if there's any mistake, it'll be nobody's fault, you know.'

Mademoiselle Benoite did not on the instant reply. She had her hands full just then. In reaching over for a particular bonnet, she managed to turn a dozen or two on to the floor. Tynn watched the picking up process, and listened to the various ejaculations that accompanied it, in much grimness.

'Oh, they good for jupons – petticoats, you call it. Some may be worn a second time; they can be changed by other trimmings to look like new. And the rest will be good for me: Madame la Duchesse gave me a great deal. "*Tenez, ma fille,*" she would say, "*regardez dans ma garde-robe, et prenez autani que vous voudrez.*" She always spoke to me in French.'

Tynn wished there had been no French invented, so far as her comprehension was concerned. While she stood, undecided what reply to make, wishing very much to express her decided opinion upon the extravagance she saw around her, yet deterred from it by remembering that Mrs Verner was now her mistress, Phœby entered with the chocolate. The girl put it down on the mantelpiece – there was no other place – and then made a sign to Mrs Tynn that she wished to speak with her. They both left the room.

'Am I to be at the beck and call of that French madmizel?' she resentfully asked. 'I was not engaged for that, Mrs Tynn.'

'It seems we are all to be at her beck and call, to hear her go on,' was Mrs Tynn's wrathful rejoinder. 'Of course it can't be tolerated. We shall see in a day or two. Phœby, girl, what could possess Mrs Verner to buy all them cart-loads of finery? She must have spent the money like water.'

'So she did,' acquiesced Phœby. 'She did nothing all day long but drive about from one place to another and choose pretty things. You should see the china that's coming over!'

DOROTHY WORDSWORTH
From Grasmere Journal

TUESDAY, DECEMBER 22, 1801. As we came up the White Moss, we met an old man, who I saw was a beggar by his two bags hanging over his shoulders; but I let him pass. He said nothing, and my heart smote me. I turned back and said:

'You are begging?'

'Ay,' says he.

I gave him something. William, judging from his appearance, joined in:

'I suppose you were a sailor?'

'Ay,' he replied, 'I have been fifty-seven years at sea, twelve of them on board a man-of-war under Sir Hugh Palmer.'

'Why have you not a pension?'

'I have no pension, but I could have got into Greenwich Hospital, but all my officers are dead.'

He was seventy-five years of age, had a freshish colour in his cheeks, grey hair, a decent hat with a binding round the edge, the hat worn brown and glossy, his shoes were small thin shoes, pretty good. They had belonged to a gentleman. His coat was frock shaped, coming over his thighs. It had been joined up at the seams behind with paler blue, to let it out, and there were three bell-shaped patches of darker blue behind, where the buttons had been. His breeches were either of fustian or grey cloth, with strings hanging down, whole and tight. He had a checked shirt on, and a small coloured handkerchief tied round his neck. His bags were hung over each shoulder, and lay on each side of him, below his breast. One was brownish, and of coarse stuff, the other was white with meal on the outside, and his blue waistcoat was whitened with meal.

The apparel of the inmates [of the farms] was in all cases comfortable, though seldom gaudy. Almost everything was made at home, except the gudeman's black bonnet, and the gudewife's velvet hood. Their clothing was all made from their own fleeces, or from their own home-made lint; spun by their own maids, and woven, wauked [fulled], and dyed by their own customary webster [weaver], wauker, and litster [dyer], from the nighest town; whilst the tailor from the same village (commonly the Kirkton, one with the parish church) made up the clothes, on the top of the kitchen table, under the gudewife's own eye, or careful superintendence, so that not a shaping or shred of it could escape: – even the shoes were made of their own bought-in leather, by the country sutor.

George Robertson, *Rural Recollections* (1829)

R. S. SURTEES
From Mr Sponge's Sporting Tour

NOTHING BESPEAKS THE character of a dealer's trade more than the servants and hangers-on of the establishment. The civiler in manner, and the better they are 'put on', the higher the standing of the master, and the better the stamp of the horses.

Those about Mr Buckram's were of a very shady order. Dirty-shirted, sloggering, baggy-breeched, slangey-gaitered fellows, with the word 'gin' indelibly imprinted on their faces. Peter Leather, the head man, was one of the fallen angels of servitude. He had once driven a duke – the Duke of Dazzleton – having nothing whatever to do but dress himself and climb into his well-indented richly fringed throne, with a helper at each horse's head to 'let go' at a nod from his broad laced three-cornered hat. Then having got in his cargo (or rubbish, as he used to call them), he would start off at a pace that was truly terrific, cutting out this vehicle, shooting past that, all but grazing a third, anathematizing the 'buses, and abusing the draymen. We don't know how he might be with the queen, but he certainly drove as though he thought nobody had any business in the street while the Duchess of Dazzleton wanted it. The duchess liked going fast, and Peter accommodated her. The duke jobbed his horses and didn't care about pace, and so things might have gone on very comfortably, if Peter one afternoon hadn't run his pole into the panel of a very plain but very neat yellow barouche, passing the end of New Bond Street, which having nothing but a simple crest – a stag's head on the panel – made him think it belonged to some bulky cit, taking the air with his rib, but who, unfortunately, turned out to be no less a person than Sir Giles Nabem, Knight, the great police magistrate, upon one of whose myrmidons in plain clothes, who came to the rescue, Peter committed a most violent assault, for which unlucky casualty his worship furnished him with rotatory occupation for his fat calves in the 'H. of C.', as the clerk shortly designated the House of Correction. Thither Peter went, and in lieu of his lace-bedaubed coat, gold-gartered plushes, stockings, and buckled shoes, he was dressed up in a suit of tight-fitting yellow and black-striped worsteds, that gave him the appearance of a wasp without wings. Peter Leather then tumbled regularly down the staircase of servitude, the greatness of his fall being occasionally broken by landing in some inferior place. From the Duke of Dazzleton's, or rather from the tread-mill, he went to the Marquis of Mammon, whom he very soon left because he wouldn't wear a second-hand wig. From the marquis he got hired to the great Irish Earl of Coarsegab, who expected him to wash the carriage, wait at table, and do other incidentals never contemplated by a London coachman. Peter threw this place up with indignation on being told to take the letters to the post. He then lived on his 'means' for a while, a thing that is much finer in theory than in practice, and having about exhausted his substance and placed the bulk of his apparel in safe keeping, he condescended to take a place as job coachman in a livery-stable – a 'horses let by the hour, day, or month' one, in which he enacted as many characters, at least made as many different appearances, as the late Mr Mathews used to do in his celebrated 'At Homes'. One day Peter would be seen ducking under the mews' entrance in one of those greasy, painfully well-brushed hats, the certain precursors of soiled linen and seedy, most seedy-covered buttoned coats, that would puzzle a conjuror to say whether they were black, or grey, or olive, or invisible green turned visible brown. Then another day he might be seen in old Mrs Gadabout's sky-blue livery, with a tarnished, gold-laced hat, nodding over his nose; and on a third he would shine forth in Mrs Major-General Flareup's cockaded one, with a worsted shoulder-knot, and a much over-daubed light drab livery coat, with crimson inexpressibles, so tight as to astonish a beholder how he ever got into them. Humiliation, however, has its limits as well as other things; and Peter having been invited to descend from his box – alas! a regular country patent leather one, and invest himself in a Quaker-collared blue coat, with a red vest, and a pair of blue trousers with a broad red stripe down the sides, to drive the Honourable old Miss Wrinkleton, of Harley Street, to Court in a 'one oss pianoforte-case,' as he called a Clarence, he could stand it no longer, and, chucking the nether garments into the fire, he rushed frantically up the area-steps, mounted his box, and quilted the old crocodile of a horse all the way home, accompanying each cut with an imprecation such as '*me* make a guy of myself!' (whip) '*me* put on sich things!' (whip, whip) '*me* drive down Sin Jimses-street!' (whip, whip, whip), '*I'd* see her – fust!' (whip, whip, whip), cutting at the old horse just as if he was laying it into Miss Wrinkleton, so that by the time he got home he had established a considerable lather on the old nag, which his master resenting a row ensued, the sequel of which may readily be imagined. After assisting Mrs Clearstarch, the Kilburn laundress, in getting in and taking out her washing, for a few weeks, chance at last landed him at Mr Benjamin Buckram's, from whence he is now about to be removed to become our hero Mr Sponge's Sancho Panza, in his fox-hunting, fortune-hunting career, and disseminate in remote parts his doctrines of the real honour and dignity of servitude. Now to the inspection.

Peter Leather, having a peep-hole as well as his master, on seeing Mr Sponge arrive, had given himself an extra rub over, and covered his dirty shirt with a clean, well-tied, white kerchief, and a whole coloured scarlet waistcoat, late the property of one of his noble employers, in hopes that Sponge's visit might lead to something. Peter was about sick of the suburbs, and thought, of course, that he couldn't be worse off than where he was.

Just as I had finished my toilet, Jersey came into my room in great agitation. He was expected to wear what he called the 'funny trousers' – not knee breeches, but trousers fastened just below the calf of the leg and showing the socks. Unfortunately his black silk socks were marked in white, and he said I must pick out the markings – which was impossible all in a minute, and the rooms somewhat dimly lit. However, my maid suggested inking over the marks, to my immense relief, and all was well.

Lady Jersey, *Fifty-one Years of Victorian Life*

He wore a deerstalker hat, so sodden and shredded it looked like a helping of breakfast food, and round the waist of his mackintosh, which was belted with string, hung a collection of pots and spoons.

Rattling like a dustbin, he sat down beside me and began pulling off his boots.

Laurie Lee, *As I Walked Out One Midsummer Morning*

One of the facts of war that had most impressed me had been Mamma's ability suddenly to do without Miss Draper, and to go off to Etaples with only a small suitcase as her luggage. Now, I recalled the daily services that Miss Draper had always done for Mamma: drawing her bath and scenting it with rose-geranium bath salts; setting out her underclothes under their lace cover; kneeling on the floor to put on Mamma's stockings, lacing Mamma into her stays (as though she were reining in a runaway horse); doing her hair; pinning her veil on to her hat; buttoning up her gloves; putting her powder and cigarettes and money into her bag. And, behind the scenes, washing, ironing, mending. It had quite worried me to think of Mamma bereft of all this help.

Sonia Keppel, Edwardian Daughter

BERTA RUCK

From The Courtship of Rosamond Fayre

CATCHING TOGETHER HER blue crêpe kimona, she stepped across to the window again. With a little jingle of brass rings she drew the cream-coloured casement curtains, catching, as she did so, the sound of a crunching step on the gravel outside, the whiff of a cigarette.

'Alone. I wonder what he's thinking about. Waiting for Eleanor to come down, of course,' said Rosamond Fayre as she stepped back.

Behind those drawn curtains she snapped on the lights. They shone on that waiting parcel, a square white carton box with a dressmaker's name ('Madame Cora') splashed in scarlet letters across it, containing a new evening frock for Miss Fayre, who spent what Eleanor privately considered an utterly disproportionate amount of her salary upon clothes.

'I wonder what Eleanor is going to put on "for Him"?' mused Rosamond as she sat down on the bed and cut the scarlet strings of the box. 'Surely she'll stop having a soul above dressing to please a man now? Lots of girls could take Eleanor's looks and make them rather Spanish and piquante. But will she?'

Layer after layer of tissue paper rustled at her feet with the sound of drifted autumn leaves.

Rosamond took out the frock.

It was of three-tiered pink, fading from the deep blush of the lowest flounce to the creamy heart of the corsage, and but for the shot-weighed hems it would have seemed light as a silken scarf across her arm.

'Now there's something really mysterious about a woman's pretty frock that's not been put on yet,' thought Rosamond. Her eyes drank in the dainty colour. 'She doesn't yet know what will happen to her while she's wearing it. How can Eleanor call clothes '*so inessential*'? A frock? Why, it's a fateful thing! Now, this –'

She stepped into the pink sheath.

'Will it be an unlucky frock? A hoodoo? Some are!' She drew it up about her pliant column of a body. 'Or will it be a "frock of fascination" that brings a good time whenever or wherever it's worn? Perhaps!' She slipped sculptured arms into those short transparent sleeves. 'Oh! Feels like crisp butterfly's wings against one! Yes! Surely Eleanor will learn to enjoy clothes for his sake? Surely he'll teach her that? Though I don't think much of him, even if he does romp up and down the Andes with castings on his back. (Obstinate-looking back.) Now, which is the – ah, here –'

She joined the silken waist-belt, humming her old song:

> '*My father's a hedger and ditcher –*
> *My mother must card and spin –*

Fancy when they spun all their own frocks!'

With busy enjoyment she fastened silver snaps down the front, still humming –

> '*But I'm a poor little critcher*

That's it –'

She coaxed a tiny hook into a silken loop,

> '*And money comes slowly in!*

Now!'

.She turned to the long glass of her wardrobe a glance of triumphant enquiry.

Yes!

It was a success.

Ah, blessed fashions of Nineteen Fourteen, that revived all the frilly, feminine vanity and charm, with none of the rigidity of the Crinoline Period! That corolla of petal shapes spreading below the hips as the girl that lent it movement turned slowly, lifted an arm, took a step aside and back again! Why, this garment was just a flower made into a frock! She smiled with frankest pleasure at her own white-framed reflection. And the last cunning touch was to overlay it with that film of misty-blue chiffon which softened all that warmer colour with just the quality of pink rose-leaves!

'My frock; distinctly mine!' murmured the girl. 'I've never looked so nice in anything. I'll write and tell Mrs Cora that. Clever little woman! Worth double what she charges. It is nice! M–m!'

She pursed her mouth into the shape of a kiss wafted to that preening, radiant image of gold-and-white-and-rose.

'Rather a darling! The frock, I mean, of course. Oh, I shall be happy in this, I know. Is it too idiotically silly and frivolous, after all, to think it matters so much? It's not looked upon as frivolous to enjoy a good picture? No! That's artistic interest. Then why isn't it "artistic" to enjoy actually being the delightful colouring and the graceful "line", and all that? It gives such pleasure, and not only to oneself,' mused Rosamond. 'Now, shall I, or not, wear just a bud fastened into the lace here?'

She had chosen that bud from the bowl of roses set on her corner writing-table; she was pinning it in when a sudden thought checked her.

'Why –'

The smile faded from her face. A little unreasonable chill seemed to pass over her.

Why, she had forgotten. This brand-new frock was not for wearing at dinner to-night! This was for 'special' occasions; parties. She'd only been trying it on to see if it needed to be sent back for any alteration. It wasn't as if *her* sweetheart had just come home. *She'd* nobody – nothing to dress for, to make herself into charming pictures for, to-night. Yet here she was prinking, tittivating and taking thought of her appearance, just as if she were, say, in Eleanor's place!

The lace at her breast stirred over a little sigh. 'Rather a pity, Rosamond, that you haven't got – somebody nice of your own to admire you just now, she thought. 'This frock simply calls for it! . . . Well, some day, perhaps, before it's quite worn out – ! But I had better make haste and get out of it, now –'

Rather slowly she began to unfasten those snaps, – 'since it does fit all right.' She coaxed that tiny hook out of that silken noose.

Then, with a jerk, she stepped out of the frock, and gave a little laugh. Her face cleared into gaiety again.

Briskly she began putting the new vanity away, humming as she did so, the end of her old song:

'Last night the dogs did bark.
(I hope dinner won't be long. I'm quite hungry.)
And I went out to see –
(Better stuff this tissue-paper back into the sleeves.)
And every lass had a spark,
But there's nobody comes for me!'

She turned back to the wardrobe.

'The old black ninon rag, I suppose –'

That old black ninon rag flattered her neck and shoulders as even the rose-pink lisse had not done. – 'And perhaps my one and only remaining piece of modest jewellery –'

This was a tiny antique paste slide and clasp on a velvet ribbon. Another girl might wear black, to show up the contrast with her throat, but Rosamond's neckband was of velvet insolently white, inviting comparison with the skin against which it could scarcely be seen.

She was fastening the clasp as the purr of the gong through the house rose into a growl and died down again to a mutter.

'Good . . . There is dinner. I wonder if Mr Ted Urquhart thinks that the secretary ought to be having it in the housekeeper's room, with a frock right up to her chin, and a neat little white turnover collar?' meditated the secretary as she came downstairs. 'Of course I shall have to show him, now, that I do know "my place", and that I realise I'm merely a menial in this house. No part of my duty to dress for the young master of the house, even if I did have to write love letters to him! His house. What a pity I don't wear an apron,' she concluded with an inward chuckle as she walked demurely into the oak-panelled dining-room of which the long table below the chandelier was unused except for a large party.

ROBERT ROBERTS
From The Classic Slum

AGAIN, BECAUSE OF the heat and slippery floors, women worked barefoot, dressed in little more than calico shifts . . . clogs and shawls were, of course, standard wear for all . . . the girl who first defied this tradition in one of Lancashire's largest mills, remembered the 'stares, skits and sneers' of fellow workers 60 years after. Her parents had put her to weaving. They lived, however, in one of the newer suburbs with its parloured houses and small back gardens. To be seen in such a district returning from the mill in clogs and shawl would have meant instant social demotion for the whole family. She was sent to the weaving shed wearing coat and shoes and thereby shocked a whole establishment . . . was a 'forward little bitch' 'setting above herself'. So clearly in fact did headwear denote class that in Glasgow separate clubs existed for 'hat' girls and 'shawls' girls.

THOMAS HARDY
From The Dorset Farm Labourer, Past and Present

THE HIRING FAIR OF recent years presents an appearance unlike that of former times. A glance up the high street of the town on a Candlemass-fair day twenty or thirty years ago revealed a crowd whose general colour was whity-brown flecked with white. Black was almost absent, the few farmers who wore that shade, being hardly discernible. Now the crowd is as dark as a London crowd. The change is owing to the rage for cloth clothes which possesses the labourers of today. Formerly they came in smock frocks and gaiters, the shepherds with their crooks, the carters with a zone of whipcord round their hats, thatchers with a straw tucked into the brim, and so on. Now, with the exception of the crook in the hands of an occasional old shepherd, there is no mark of speciality in the groups, who might be tailors or undertakers for what they exhibit externally. Out of a group of eight, for example, who talk together in the middle of the road, one only wears corduroy trousers. Two wear cloth pilot coats and black trousers, two patterned tweed suits with black canvas overalls, the remaining four suits being of faded broadcloth. To a great extent these are their Sunday suits but the genuine white smock frock of Russian duck and whity-brown one of drabber, are rarely seen now afield, except on the shoulders of old men. Where smocks are worn by the young and middle-aged, they are of a blue material. The mechanic's 'slop' has also been adopted, but a mangy old coat is preferred, so that often a group of these honest fellows on the arable has the aspect of a body of tramps up to some mischief in the field, rather than its natural tillers at work...

The peculiarity of the English urban poor (which M. Taine ridicules and unfavourably contrasts with the taste of the Continental working-people) – their preferences for the cast-off clothes of a richer class to a special attire of their own – has, in fact, reached the Dorset farm folk. Like the men, the women are, pictorially, less interesting than they used to be. Instead of the wing bonnet like the tilt of a wagon, cotton gown, bright hued neckerchief, and strong flat boots and shoes, they (the younger ones at least) wear shabby millinery bonnets and hats with beads and feathers, 'material' dresses, and boot-heels almost as foolishly shaped as those of ladies of highest education.

ALAN JOBSON

From An Hourglass on the Run

GRANDMOTHER MADE GRANDFATHER'S shirts, each of which took four yards of calico that cost threepence a yard. This was folded over like a sheet of paper to the length of the garment, not exactly in half, allowing the back to be longer than the front; and the calico was doubled, back to front, down to the bottom of the armpits. It was then sewn up the side, with gussets by the flaps, and gussets again at the neck. That is, the material was stitched to fit with the tucks rather than any should be cut away. The arms were put in square, and when the shirt was worn the shoulders fell away over the upper arm. This sounds a bit uncomfortable, but it gave ample room for movement. Sometimes she used tin buttons, quite flat, bought for a penny a dozen of Mary Mullinger at the door; but sometimes they were three-fold linen ones.

Grandfather's shirts were his most important undergarments, since he never wore vests and pants. As his trousers were always lined he seldom felt the cold and it was always said they would stand up of their own accord, without legs in them; but they used to say that also of grandmother's worsted stockings that started life by being black, and then changed to green as the years rolled by! He usually wore a neckcloth that varied from turkey twill, striped material to plain white linen.

His trousers were fastened below the knees by a wisp of hay or a bootlace, the latter bearing the name of 'ligers, which was a corruption, presumably, of Elijahs.

This gave greater freedom to the knees and was kinder to the trousers during work in the field; besides, it helped to keep the bottoms out of the wet. Black bone buttons were used, fastened on with wax thread, bought by the ounce, as in his opinion reel-thread was of no use. Later he complained that the new buttons, presumably meaning those made by machine, wore the thread to bits. In summer the heavy trousers were discarded and those of drabbet substituted, while the buttons, starting white, soon turned to a lovely ivory shade. This drabbet was strong stuff, and was used also for the smocks. An odd piece would be turned into a Long Melford purse, which was shaped like a modern tobacco pouch. All his trousers were fitted with a fob pocket to hold his turnip watch, which for safety's sake was also tied to his braces.

Besides making his shirts grandmother knitted his braces of white thread, with a cross-over at the back, and on the front straps were two or three button-holes to allow for adjustment. As there was no metal there were no iron marks to contend with. She knitted his garters as well.

Needless to say, grandfather had several shirts, but there was one in particular of which he was very proud. It was a splendid, ample creation of calico, made by his mother for his seventeenth birthday, and begun soon after his birth. Made like the others in cut it differed from them in having a series of pleats down the front. It served him for special occasions all his long life.

The old people were always careful about changing their clothes, especially the casting off of any garment, taking due note of the month, however hot the sun, calling to mind those who had been caught unawares:

> Beneath this little mound of clay
> Lies Captain Ephraim Daniels,
> Who chose the dangerous month of May
> To change his winter flannels . . .

Grandfather would never work with his shirtsleeves rolled up. His bare arms might get blistered and blood poisoning ensue. Neither would farmers hereabouts allow the womenfolk to work in the field with their gowns on. They had to take them off and work in their shifts. That sort of condition was readily complied with by Harriet, who had only one gown, and was never likely to have another. So she took it off, folded it up, patches and all. All the same, it was a happy time for everybody, especially the children . . .

Most of grandfather's co-labourers wore smocks. They were decorated with those exquisite specimens of stitchcraft denoting the wearer's calling as a husbandman. He could remember when these were woven by the womenfolk in the cottage homesteads, of flax that had been grown in garden or field, retted by these same housewives, and spun into a web by their own firesides. Indeed, in his young days it had been the custom in farmhouses for the servants to be so occupied at certain periods. Needless to say, grandmother could always tell a piece of linen from a piece of cotton, because if she wetted the tip of her finger with spittle and put it on the cloth, if it was linen it would 'spot' right through!

GEORGE EWART EVANS
From The Horse in the Furrow

FOR WALKING OUT and for Sundays he had a cord jacket and cord trousers. But the trousers were no ordinary trousers: they were *whole-falls*, that is, trousers with a flap that let down in front like a sailor's. They were also bell-bottomed, with a sixteen inch knee and a twenty-two inch bottom. The outside of the trouser-leg was trimmed with steel-faced horse-shoe buttons. Some of the more dress-conscious horsemen ordered a special kind of trimming on the leg – an inlet or gusset of black velvet, running from the bottom of the trousers, on the outside, and tapering to a point somewhere near the knee. Four or five horse-shoe buttons were sewn to this gusset as an extra decoration.

The jacket had flap-pockets; and fancy stitching on the jacket was usual. 'They'd have what we called a *vandyck* back and sleeves – a fancy stitch something like waves – on the shoulders and the cuffs. Some of them wanted pint-pots worked in fancy stitch on the back, or maybe a horse's head or even a fox-head. The owd horseman knew what he wanted; and it weren't no use a-tryin' to tell him what to have. Those owd country-bo's had wunnerful good clothes: do you know that? They went in for warmth. They'd have their breeches and leggin's lined with flannelette – lined with *swansdown*, they used to say – or fluffy calico. The cloth for their suits was *cord* (corduroy), as I've told you; but sometimes they went in for a suit of heavy tweed – *staple tweed* it was called; and at that time they made it as hard as a board. It were wunnerful stuff. It never wore up. It lasted them fourteen or fifteen years. The cost? Well, about fifty year ago a suit of staple tweed cost £3 10s. Now today . . . but aside from the cost I couldn't make a suit like that today: I couldn't get the material. Breeches and leggings cost 17s. 6d.

'They dressed warm and comfortable, a style of their own. A big silver chain across the front of the weskit, and a big owd tarnip watch at the end of it. On the head they wore a hard hat with a high crown, or a billy cock with a pheasant's or woodcock's feather tucked into the band at the side. We sometimes made an over-coat for one of those owd country-bo's – a head horseman, for instance. This was always a *melton* overcoat. Melton is a thick, very tightly woven woollen cloth.

The weave is so tight, wet will never get through it. Here's a piece of real owd melton, the owd stuff. I keep it specially to remind me what it was like. Feel it. And feel this. Here's a piece of what they make and call melton today. They still *call* it melton; but look at the difference: the heart has gone right out of the cloth. The owd stuff wouldn't wear up. You could hand the overcoat over to your son when you'd finished with it; and he could hand it over to his son . . .

'Not so long ago a very old man came into my shop and told me what he'd bought from my father at one of the sales nearly fifty years ago. He had a cap, muffler – a square of brightly coloured artificial silk – a shirt, vest, pants, a suit and a pair of boots and he still had some change out of his gold sovereign. And he reckoned he was well clothed. Today, a farm-worker will go on to a field with a tractor; and he'll be wearing, like as not, flannel trousers and a pair of dancing pumps. But in those days they were dressed for the job. They kept warm. Now I remember calling on a farm-worker: I was fitting him for something, I believe. This is what he was wearing: a thick vest, long pants, cords, shirt and muffler, two ordinary waist-coats, a sleeved waistcoat, a cardigan and a jacket. That old boy worked hard enough in the field, if it was only in carrying all that stuff around with him!

'But the ordinary worker's dress for Sunday was a square-cut, long, black vel-vet jacket with short revers and about six buttons down the front; a very good cord trousers, medium drab in colour; and a bowler hat with a *set* (or straight) brim – the curly brimmed bowler was the wear for the *toffs*, the gentry. The mak-ers of these bowlers always put a peacock's feather on the side of the hat. Every man liked a feather in his hat. Often a new bowler hat had a clay-pipe stuck in the band as well; or even a cigar. You could get a *sure-shot* cigar for tuppence in those days.

'The bowler was made of stiff felt. They also wore a billycock, a tallish hat made of semi-stiff felt with a black band round it just above the brim. The band was made of silk, worked in an oak-leaf pattern. The farmers and sometimes the head horsemen wore a *square-crown* or *half-high* hat made of stiff felt . . .

There were only two or three kinds of shirt on the market then – white and black-and-white, that is a white shirt with a thin black stripe. The working man never bought a shirt with a collar – there wasn't one made in fact. They wore leather collars with their shirts – no tie. These leather collars were about an inch-and-a-half deep, and had a patent leather surface on the outside. This patent leather was decorated with vertical, coloured stripes – usually black and white. The big advantage of these collars was that they were easily washed. The wear-er had only to wipe the surface with a wet flannel to have a clean collar – at least on the outside.'

FLORA THOMPSON
From Lark Rise to Candleford

DELIGHTED AS THE women were with the letters from their daughters, it was the occasional parcels of clothing they sent that caused the greatest excitement. As soon as a parcel was taken indoors, neighbours who had seen Old Postie arrive with it would drop in, as though by accident, and stay to admire, or sometimes to criticise, the contents.

All except the aged women, who wore what they had been accustomed to wearing and were satisfied, were very particular about their clothes. Anything did for everyday wear, as long as it was clean and whole and could be covered with a decent white apron; it was the 'Sunday best' that had to be just so. 'Better be out of the world than out of the fashion' was one of their sayings. To be appreciated, the hat or coat contained in the parcel had to be in the fashion, and the hamlet had a fashion of its own, a year or two behind outside standards, and strictly limited as to style and colour.

The daughter's or other kinswoman's clothes were sure to be appreciated, for they had usually already been seen and admired when the girl was at home for her holiday, and had indeed helped to set the standard of what was worn. The garments bestowed by the mistresses were unfamiliar and often somewhat in advance of the hamlet vogue, and so were often rejected for personal wear as 'a bit queer' and cut down for the children; though the mothers often wished a year or two later when that particular fashion arrived that they had kept them for themselves. Then they had colour prejudices. A red frock! Only a fast hussy would wear red. Or green – sure to bring any wearer bad luck! There was a positive taboo on green in the hamlet; nobody would wear it until it had been home-dyed navy or brown. Yellow ranked with red as immodest; but there was not much yellow worn anywhere in the 'eighties. On the whole, they preferred dark or neutral colours; but there was one exception; blue had nothing against it. Marine and sky blue were the favourite shades, both very bright and crude.

Much prettier were the colours of the servant girls' print morning dresses – lilac, or pink, or buff, sprigged with white – which were cut down for the little girls to wear on May Day and for churchgoing throughout the summer.

To the mothers the cut was even more important than the colour. If sleeves were worn wide they liked them to be very wide; if narrow, skin tight. Skirts in those days did not vary in length; they were made to touch the ground. But they were sometimes trimmed with frills or flounces or bunched up at the back, and the women would spend days altering this trimming to make it just right, or turning gathers into pleats or pleats into gathers.

The hamlet's fashion lag was the salvation of its wardrobes, for a style became 'all the go' there just as the outer world was discarding it, and good, little-worn specimens came that way by means of the parcels. *The* Sunday garment at the beginning of the decade was the tippet, a little shoulder cape of black silk or satin with a long, dangling fringe. All the women and some of the girls had these, and they were worn proudly to church or Sunday school with a posy of roses or geraniums pinned in front.

Hats were of the chimney-pot variety, a tall cylinder of straw, with a very narrow brim and a spray of artificial flowers trained up the front. Later in the decade, the shape changed to wide brims and squashed crowns. The chimney-pot hat had had its day, and the women declared they would not be seen going to the privy in one.

Then there were the bustles, at first looked upon with horror, and no wonder! but after a year or two the most popular fashion ever known in the hamlet and the one which lasted longest. They cost nothing, as they could be made at home from any piece of old cloth rolled up into a cushion and worn under any frock. Soon all the women, excepting the aged, and all the girls, excepting the tiniest, were peacocking in their bustles, and they wore them so long that Edmund was old enough in the day of their decline to say that he had seen the last bustle on earth going round the Rise on a woman with a bucket of pig-wash.

This devotion to fashion gave a spice to life and helped to make bearable the underlying poverty. But the poverty was there; one might have a velvet tippet and no shoes worth mentioning; or a smart frock, but no coat; and the same applied to the children's clothes and the sheets and towels and cups and saucepans. There was never enough of anything, except food.

It is of little use for me to tell you that Hetty's cheek was like a rose-petal, that dimples played about her pouting lips, that her large dark eyes hid a soft roguishness under their long lashes, and that her curly hair, though all pushed back under her round cap while she was at work, stole back in dark delicate rings on her forehead, and about her white shell-like ears; it is of little use for me to say how lovely was the contour of her pink-and-white neckerchief, tucked into her low plum-coloured stuff bodice, or how the linen buttermaking apron, with its bib, seemed a thing to be imitated in silk by duchesses, since it fell in such charming lines, or how her brown stockings and thick-soled buckled shoes lost all that clumsiness which they must certainly have had when empty of her feet and ankle; – of little use, unless you have seen a woman who affected you as Hetty affected her beholders, for otherwise, though you might conjure up the image of a lovely woman, she would not in the least resemble that distracting kitten-like maiden.

George Eliot, *Adam Bede*

Since he lived six times as many working-days as Sundays, Oak's appearance in his old clothes was most peculiarly his own – the mental picture formed by his neighbours in imagining him being always dressed in that way. He wore a low-crowned felt hat, spread out at the base by tight jamming upon the head for security in high winds, and a coat like Dr Johnson's; his lower extremities being encased in ordinary leather leggings and boots emphatically large, affording to each foot a roomy apartment so constructed that any wearer might stand in a river all day long and know nothing about it – their maker being a conscientious man who always endeavoured to compensate for any weakness in his cut by unstinted dimension and solidity.

Thomas Hardy, *Far From the Madding Crowd*

Old Nance got up to go and begin her duties at once. Then the farmer, looking at her clothes, said he would give her something more to protect her from the weather on such a bleak day. He got her an old felt hat, a big old, frieze overcoat, and a pair of old leather leggings. When she had put on these somewhat cumbrous things, and had tied her hat firmly on with a strip of cloth, and fastened the coat at the waist with a cord, she was told to go to the head-shepherd and ask him to direct her to the field where the rooks were troublesome. Then when she was setting out the farmer called her back and gave her an ancient, rusty gun to scare the birds. 'It isn't loaded,' he said, with a grim smile. 'I don't allow powder and shot, but if you'll point it at them they'll fly fast enough.'

Thus arrayed and armed she set forth, and Caleb seeing her approach at a distance was amazed at her grotesque appearance, and even more amazed still when she explained who and what she was and asked him to direct her to the field of swedes.

W. H. Hudson, *A Shepherd's Life*

DYLAN THOMAS
From Holiday Memory

AUGUST BANK HOLIDAY. A tune on an ice-cream cornet. A slap of sea and a tickle of sand. A fanfare of sunshades opening. A wince and whinny of bathers dancing into deceptive water. A tuck of dresses. A rolling of trousers. A compromise of paddlers . . .

There was no need, that holiday morning, for the sluggardly boys to be shouted down to breakfast; out of their jumbled beds they tumbled, scrambled into their rumpled clothes; quickly at the bath-room basin they catlicked their hands and faces, but never forgot to run the water loud and long as though they washed like colliers; in front of the cracked looking-glass bordered with cigarette-cards, in their treasure-trove bedrooms, they whisked a gap-tooth comb through their surly hair; and with shining cheeks and noses and tidemarked necks, they took the stairs three at a time.

But for all their scramble and scamper, clamour on the landing, catlick and toothbrush flick, hair-whisk and stair-jump, their sisters were always there before them. Up with the lady lark, they had prinked and frizzed and hot-ironed; and smug in their blossoming dresses, ribboned for the sun, in gym-shoes white as the blanco'd snow, neat and silly with doilies and tomatoes they helped in the higgledy kitchen. They were calm; they were virtuous; they had washed their necks; they did not romp, or fidget; and only the smallest sister put out her tongue at the noisy boys . . .

Pale young men with larded hair and Valentino-black side-whiskers, fags stuck to their lower lips, squinted along their swivel-sighted rifles and aimed at ping-pong balls dancing on fountains.

In knife-creased, silver-grey, skirt-like Oxford bags, and a sleeveless, scarlet, zip-fastened shirt with yellow horizontal stripes, a collier at the strength-machine spat on his hands, raised the hammer, and brought it Thoring down. The bell rang for Blaina . . .

Draggled and stout-wanting mothers, with haphazard hats, hostile hatpins, buns awry . . .

A daring dash of schoolboys, safely, shoulder to shoulder, with their father's trilbies cocked at a desperate angle over one eye, winked at and whistled after the procession past the swings of two girls arm-in-arm: always one pert and pretty, and always one with glasses.

From *Quite Early One Morning*

'My chief dexterity was in robbing the ladies – there is a peculiar delicacy required in whipping one's hand up a lady's petticoats and carrying off her pockets.

Francis Coventry, *Pompey the Little* (1751)

The next day, being Sunday, it rained very hard; and I must observe that the Corsicans with all their resolution are afraid of bad weather to a degree of effeminacy. I got indeed a droll but a just enough account of this from one of them: 'Sir,' said he, 'if you were as poor as a Corsican and had but one coat, so that after being wet you could not put on dry clothes, you would be afraid too.'

James Boswell, *Boswell on the Grand Tour, Italy, Corsica and France, 1765–66*

12

Behind the Scenes

Never fit the dress to the body, but train the body to
fit the dress.

Elsa Schiaparelli, *Shocking Life*

'Good heavens!' said I, 'if it be our clothes alone which fit us for society, how highly we should esteem those who make them.'

Marie Ebner von Eschenbach, The Two Countesses (1893)

EPITAPH ON A TAYLOR'S WIFE

Here lies a TAYLOR's Counter-part,
Who lov'd a YARD with all her Heart.
Her cross-legg's spouse knew what would ease her,
And often stole a YARD to please her;
Yet all his CABBAGE would not save
The loving Baggage from the Grave:
But here she Slumbers, soon forgotten,
Now dead, not valued of a button.

(Anon, 1700s)

A. E. COPPARD

From The Presser

THE FIRST BUSINESS in the tailor's workshop was to light the fire, a great fire maintained with coke. Then, to sweep the room clean of its countless fragments of cloth and cotton. Heaping these in a wooden box, the boy staggered with it across the dark passage into a smaller apartment with a window, the very symbol of gloom, looking down into a dank yard where he could see people all day long going to the privy. The room contained only a colossal pile of cloth clippings covering the whole floor, and it was his unending task to sort these into their various kinds. The pile never lessened, it seemed to grow with absorbent inexorable growth. Sometimes he could scarcely enter the door to get into the room; and that implacable mountain of rags was watered with the tears of his childish hungers and despairs. He emptied the box and returned to the workshop.

Eight or nine women came in and began their work of making trousers. A massive table stood in the middle; the women sat round three sides of the room on old empty boxes – these were less comfortable than chairs, but more convenient. The room was large and well lighted from two windows. In summer the windows were a blessing to the women, the hot fire an affliction; in winter it was otherwise. Sometimes they sweated, and sometimes they sneezed or they coughed, but they never shivered. Each woman had a pad of needles tacked to her bodice, a pair of scissors and skeins of thread in her lap, and her hands were busied with the garments of men she knew nothing about. Each had a wedding ring on her nuptial finger, the beginnings of a hump on her shoulders, and the deuce knows what emotions in her heart. They were mostly young women, but they looked old, whereas Mr Sulky and Mr Alabaster were young and looked young. It reminded Johnny of the question propounded by a famous advertisement:

> Why does a woman look old
> sooner than
> a man?

And the answer was something to do with soap.

HENRY MAYHEW
From The Unknown Mayhew

SHORTLY AFTERWARDS ONE of the porters comes to the door, and says, 'Please Miss— have you got any skirts? Mrs —'s boy has called to know if you have any.' 'Yes, wait a minute, I have one,' and gives him the skirt of the dress. He takes it down, and in an obscure corner of the hall stands Mrs—'s boy, a ragged dirty little creature, about seven years old. 'Here,' says the porter, 'take this to your mother, and tell her if she doesn't get it done by nine o'clock tomorrow morning she will get no more work from this house.' 'I shall be sure to tell her, sir,' the boy replies, taking the skirt. He goes his way with the magnificent Genoa velvet under his arm, and walks slowly along until he comes to a dirty narrow street, in the neighbourhood of Carnaby Market, Golden-square. He stops at a house, pushes open the door, for it has no fastening, and mounts to the top of the house. On the landing-place there are washing-tubs and slop-pails full of dirty water, saucepans, frying-pans, and old stumps of brooms. He makes his way through these with the 'velvet skirt', and enters a room to the left; there being four families living on this story. The garret he enters is a sort of triangular-shaped room, about twelve feet square; the window is near the ceiling. In one corner of the apartment there is a small skeleton stove; in the opposite corner stands an old broken bedstead, and in one an old rickety chair. In the middle of the room is the deal table and around this are seated seven women, dirty, thinly clad, with pale and hollow countenances, weak red-looking eyes and lean emaciated frames. The one working at the head of the table is Mrs—, the boy's mother. Her husband is dead; she is about middle age. She rises and takes the skirt from the boy and demands of him what is wanted. He answers that it is to go in at nine. 'Nine in the morning!' she exclaims. 'Why I have got six from the City to go home at eight.' 'How do you know,' inquires one of the workpeople, 'that it is the lady's fault? I daresay the lady who this dress is for knows nothing about how it is made. She pays a very high price to the French people whom you have it from.'

CHARLES KINGSLEY
From Alton Locke

THOSE WHO READ my story only for amusement, I advise to skip this chapter. Those, on the other hand, who really wish to ascertain what working men actually do suffer – to see whether their political discontent has not its roots, not merely in fanciful ambition, but in misery and slavery most real and agonising – those in whose eyes the accounts of a system, or rather barbaric absence of all system, which involves starvation, nakedness, prostitution, and long imprisonment in dungeons worse than the cells of the Inquisition, will be invested with something at least of tragic interest, may, I hope, think it worth their while to learn how the clothes which they wear are made, and listen to a few occasional statistics, which, though they may seem to the wealthy mere lists of dull figures, are to the workmen symbols of terrible physical realities – of hunger, degradation, and despair.

Well: one day our employer died. He had been one of the old sort of fashionable West-end tailors in the fast decreasing honourable trade; keeping a modest shop, hardly to be distinguished from a dwelling-house, except by his name on the window blinds. He paid good prices for work, though not as good, of course, as he had given twenty years before, and prided himself upon having all his work done at home. His workrooms, as I have said, were no elysiums; but still, as good, alas! as those of three tailors out of four. He was proud, luxurious, foppish; but he was honest and kindly enough, and did many a generous thing by men who had been long in his employ. At all events, his journeymen could live on what he paid them.

But his son, succeeding to the business, determined, like Rehoboam of old, to go ahead with the times. Fired with the great spirit of the nineteenth century – at least with that one which is vulgarly considered its especial glory – he resolved to make haste to be rich. His father had made money very slowly of late; while dozens, who had begun business long after him, had now retired to luxurious ease and suburban villas. Why should he remain in the minority? Why should he not get rich as fast as he could? Why should he stick to the old, slow-going, honourable trade? Out of some four hundred and fifty West-end tailors, there were not one hundred left who were old-fashioned and stupid enough to go on keeping down their own profits by having all their work done at home and at first-hand. Ridiculous scruples! The government knew none such. Were not the army clothes, the post-office clothes, the policemen's clothes, furnished by contractors and sweaters, who hired the work at low prices, and let it out again to journeymen at still lower ones? Why should he pay his men two shillings where the government paid them one? Were there not cheap houses even at the West-end, which had saved several thousands a year merely by reducing their workmen's wages? And if the workmen chose to take lower wages, he was not bound actually to make them a present of more than they asked for? They would go to the cheapest market for anything they wanted, and so must he. Besides, wages had really been quite exorbitant. Half his men threw each of them as much money away in gin and beer yearly, as would pay two workmen at cheap house. Why was he to be robbing his family of comforts to pay for their extravagance? And charging his customers, too, unnecessarily high prices – it was really robbing the public!

Such, I suppose, were some of the arguments which led to an official announcement, one Saturday night, that our young employer intended to enlarge his establishment, for the purpose of commencing business in the 'show-trade'; and that, emulous of Messrs Aaron, Levi, and the rest of that class, magnificent alterations were to take place in the premises, to make room for which our workrooms were to be demolished, and that for that reason – for of course it was only for that reason – all work would in future be given out, to be made up at the men's own homes.

ROBERT TRESSEL

From The Ragged Trousered Philanthropists

M R SWEATER WAS the managing director and principal shareholder of a large drapery business in which he had amassed a considerable fortune. This was not very surprising, considering that he paid none of his workpeople fair wages and many of them no wages at all. He employed a great number of girls and young women who were supposed to be learning dressmaking, mantle-making or millinery. These were all indentured apprentices, some of whom had paid premiums of from five to ten pounds. They were 'bound' for three years. For the first two years they received no wages: the third year they got a shilling or eightpence a week. At the end of the third year they usually got the sack, unless they were willing to stay on as improvers at from three shillings to four and sixpence per week.

They worked from half past eight in the morning till eight at night, with an interval of an hour for dinner, and at half past four they ceased work for fifteen minutes for tea. This was provided by the firm – half a pint for each girl, but they had to bring their own milk and sugar and bread and butter.

Few of these girls ever learned their trades thoroughly. Some were taught to make sleeves: others cuffs or button-holes, and so on. The result was that in a short time each one became very expert and quick *at one thing*; and although their proficiency in this one thing would never enable them to earn a decent living, it enabled Mr Sweater to make money during the period of their apprenticeship, and that was all he cared about.

Occasionally a girl of intelligence and spirit would insist on the fulfilment of the terms of her indentures, and sometimes the parents would protest. If this were persisted in those girls got on better: but even these were turned to good account by the wily Sweater, who induced the best of them to remain after their time was up by paying them what appeared – by contrast with the other girls' money – good wages, sometimes even seven or eight shillings a week! and liberal promises of future advancement. These girls then became a sort of reserve who could be called up to crush any manifestation of discontent on the part of the leading hands.

The greater number of the girls, however, submitted tamely to the conditions imposed upon them. They were too young to realize the wrong that was being done them. As for their parents, it never occurred to them to doubt the sincerity of so good a man as Mr Sweater, who was always prominent in every good and charitable work.

At the expiration of a girl's apprenticeship, if the parents complained of her want of proficiency, the pious Sweater would attribute it to idleness or incapacity, and as the people were generally poor he seldom or never had any trouble with them. This was how he fulfilled the unctuous promise made to the confiding parents at the time the girl was handed over to his tender mercy – that he would 'make a woman of her'.

This method of obtaining labour by false pretences and without payment, which enabled him to produce costly articles for a mere fraction of the price for which they were eventually sold, was adopted in other departments of his business. He procured shop assistants of both sexes on the same terms. A youth was indentured, usually for five years, to be 'Made a Man of' and 'Turned out fit to take a Position in any House'. If possible, a premium, five, ten, or twenty pounds – according to their circumstances – would be extracted from the parents. For the first three years, no wages: after that, perhaps two or three shillings a week.

At the end of the five years the work of 'Making a Man of him' would be completed. Mr Sweater would then congratulate him and assure him that he was qualified to assume a 'position' in any House but regret that there was no longer any room for him in *his*. Business was so bad. Still, if the Man wished he might stay on until he secured a better 'position' and, as a matter of generosity, although he did not really need the man's services, he would pay him ten shillings per week!

Provided he was not addicted to drinking, smoking, gambling on the Stock Exchange, or going to theatres, the young man's future was thus assured. Even if he were unsuccessful in his efforts to obtain another position he could save a portion of his salary and eventually commence business on his own account.

However, the branch of Mr Sweater's business to which it is desired to especially direct the reader's attention was the Homeworkers Department. He employed a large number of women making ladies' blouses, fancy aprons and children's pinafores. Most of these articles were disposed of wholesale in London and elsewhere, but some were retailed at 'Sweaters' Emporium' in Mugsborough and at the firm's other retail establishments throughout the country. Many of the women workers were widows with children, who were glad to obtain any employment that did not take them away from their homes and families.

The blouses were paid for at the rate of from two shillings to five shillings a dozen, the women having to provide her own machine and cotton, besides calling for and delivering the work. These poor women were able to clear from six to eight shillings a week: and to earn even that they had to work almost incessantly for fourteen or sixteen hours a day. There was no time for cooking and very little to cook, for they lived principally on bread and margarine and tea. Their homes were squalid, their children half-starved and raggedly clothed in grotesque garments hastily fashioned out of the cast-off clothes of charitable neighbours.

But it was not in vain that these women toiled every weary day until exhaustion compelled them to cease. It was not in vain that they passed their cheerless lives bending with aching shoulders over the thankless work that barely brought them bread. It was not in vain that they and their children went famished and in rags, for after all, the principal object of their labour was accomplished: the Good Cause was advanced. Mr Sweater waxed rich and increased in goods and respectability.

Of course, none of those women were *compelled* to engage in that glorious cause. No one is compelled to accept any particular set of conditions in a free country like this. Mr Trafaim – the manager of Sweater's Homework Department – always put the matter before them in the plainest, fairest possible way. There was the work: that was the figure! And those who didn't like it could leave it. There was no compulsion.

Sometimes some perverse creature belonging to that numerous class who are too lazy to work *did* leave it! But as the manager said, there were plenty of others who were only too glad to take it. In fact, such was the enthusiasm amongst these women – especially such of them as had little children to provide for – and such was their zeal for the Cause, that some of them have been known to positively beg to be allowed to work!

By these and similar means Adam Sweater had contrived to lay up for himself a large amount of treasure upon earth, besides attaining undoubted respectability; for that he was respectable no one questioned. He went to chapel twice every Sunday, his obese figure arrayed in costly apparel, consisting – with other things – of grey trousers, a long garment called a frock-coat, a tall silk hat, a quantity of jewellery and a morocco-bound gilt-edged Bible. He was an official of some sort of the Shining Light Chapel. His name appeared in nearly every published list of charitable subscriptions. No starving wretch had ever appealed to him in vain for a penny soup ticket.

THOMAS HOOD
Song of the Shirt

With fingers weary and worn,
With eyelids heavy and red,
A woman sat in unwomanly rags,
Plying her needle and thread –
Stitch! stitch! stitch!
In poverty, hunger and dirt,
And still with a voice of dolorous pitch
She sang the 'Song of the Shirt'.

'Work! work! work!
While the cock is crowing aloof!
And work – work – work,
Till the stars shine through the roof!
It's O! to be a slave
Along with the barbarous Turk,
Where woman has never a soul to save,
If this is Christian work.

'Work – work – work
Till the brain begins to swim;
Work – work – work
Till the eyes are heavy and dim!
Seam and gusset and band,
Band and gusset and seam,
Till over the buttons I fall asleep,
And sew them on in a dream!

'O men, with sisters dear!
O men, with mothers and wives!
It is not linen you're wearing out,
But human creatures' lives!
Stitch – stitch – stitch,
In poverty, hunger and dirt,
Sewing at once, with a double thread,
A shroud as well as a shirt.

'But why do I talk of Death,
That phantom of grisly bone?
I hardly fear his terrible shape,
It seems so like my own,
It seems so like my own,
Because of the fasts I keep;
Oh God, that bread should be so dear,
And flesh and blood so cheap!

'Work – work – work!
My labour never flags;
And what are its wages? A bed of straw,
A crust of bread – and rags.
That shatter'd roof – and this naked floor –
A table – a broken chair –
And a wall so blank, my shadow I thank
For sometimes falling there!

'Work – work – work!
From weary chime to chime,
Work – work – work –
As prisoners work for crime!
Band and gusset and seam,
Seam and gusset and band,
Till the heart is sick and the brain benumb'd,
As well as the weary hand.

'Work – work – work
In the dull December light,
And work – work – work
When the weather is warm and bright;
While underneath the eaves
The brooding swallows cling
As if to show me their sunny backs
And twit me with the spring.

'Oh! but to breathe the breath
Of the cowslip and primrose sweet –
With the sky above my head,
And the grass beneath my feet;
For only one short hour
To feel as I used to feel,
Before I knew the woes of want
And the walk that costs a meal!

'Oh, but for one short hour!
A respite however brief;
No blessed leisure for love or hope,
But only time for grief!

A little weeping would ease my heart,
But in their briny bed
My tears must stop, for every drop
Hinders needle and thread!'

With fingers weary and worn,
With eyelids heavy and red,
A woman sat in unwomanly rags
Plying her needle and thread –
Stitch! stitch! stitch!
In poverty, hunger and dirt,
And still with a voice of dolorous pitch,
Would that its tone could reach the rich!
She sang this 'Song of the Shirt'.

(1843)

MRS PEEL

From Life's Enchanted Cup

THE LIFE OF our work girls interested me. They began work at 8.30 and left off at 6 o'clock. In those days there was no fixed scale of wages. Head milliners in the great houses were well paid. We paid ours £4 a week, and our second hand 25/-. The rank and file earned from 8/- to 16/- a week, and the little apprentices who made the head linings, picked up the special long pins which strew the floors of all millinery workrooms, and learned what they should, received half-a-crown a week. Some of our girls travelled to London by work-men's trains and sat in waiting-rooms, reading their novelettes until the workroom was open. It was not surprising that by 11 o'clock they needed food. In many workrooms no morning break was permitted and the girls would pro-duce food from their pockets and try to eat it unobserved, with the result that material might be spoiled.

The girls were obliged to go out in the dinner hour in order that the rooms should be aired, in conformity with the orders of the Home Office. A printed list of Home Office Regulations hung in each room and women inspectors might demand entrance at any moment to see that they were not ignored.

Accordingly, girls who could not afford to go to a restaurant ate their meal where they could. We finally decided that an apprentice should make 11 o'clock tea and the girls should be allowed a ten minutes' break at 11 o'clock to go down to the kitchen and drink it. It took Miss Brown all her time to see that the break did not extend to fifteen or twenty minutes. We also arranged that our staff should have the use of a kitchen and a couple of gas rings, which enabled them to eat their midday meal in comfort.

Our workers were generally very gay; they would sing at their work, and chatter like a cage full of birds. The word of the head milliner was law, and any conversation not approved by her was brought to an abrupt end.

One might have thought that girls living under such conditions would have resented customers who bought hats costing as much as eight and ten guineas, for that was not an unusual price when fashionable women wore afternoon hats on which there might be half-a-dozen feathers or a lancer plume, that is, a feather as much, perhaps, as a yard in length, on to each frond of which another frond was knotted. On the contrary, the girls enjoyed making these expensive hats and went short of food so that they might copy for themselves these costly models.

I had not long been in the millinery business before I began to realise how deteriorating to the moral sense is a passion for costly clothes, both to the women who buy them, to the girls who make them, and to the women who sell them. Many a girl dreamed not of a husband who she would love and who would love her, but of a rich husband who could provide the garments for which she yearned. Then when it became evident that a rich husband was unlikely to come her way, perhaps a well-to-do lover might take his place. Considering the small wage which they earned, the squalid homes in which they lived, and the fact that the small wage they earned left them dependent on their admirers for their amusements, it was surprising that so many of these girls did, as they expressed it, 'keep on the straight'.

As for our customers, many of them were absolutely hypnotised by new clothes; have them they must. If a husband could not pay, someone else would. If their moral sense did not permit this, they would actually ask to hire hats or promise that if we would lend them one for some special occasion they would introduce a new client. The *vendeuses* in their turn in order to sell their wares would descend to all kinds of trickery and blandishment. I who loved 'good' clothes so well could understand all these points of view and did not succeed in deciding how such a state of affairs could be altered unless by passing a sumptuary law and putting all women into uniform.

GEORGE AUGUSTUS SALA
From America Revisited

M ODISTES AND COUTURIÈRES – French to the backbone – I mean to the stay-lace and the back hair, abound in the French quarter. 'Céline' hangs out her sign in connection with 'robes'. 'Alphonsine' proclaims the Parisian elegance of her 'dentelles et fleurs artificielles'. 'Pauline' announces that she has a 'magasin de blanc'; and 'Léopoldine' simply says, on a pretty *pancarte*, 'chapeaux'. Chapeaux! Word of mystery and dread. Bonnets are bonnets in New Orleans. I have been to the fountain head. I have obtained information from a leader of fashion on his most momentous of points; and I am sorrowfully enabled to state that nothing fashionably wearable in the shape of a bonnet can be purchased in the Crescent City for a smaller sum than thirty-seven dollars, say seven guineas sterling. A handsome 'Gainsborough' hat, fully trimmed, will cost from forty to fifty dollars; and in this eminently 'dressy' city the ladies come down in Gainsborough hats and feathers to the late dinner at the hotels. On the whole, I am inclined to think that the most inexpensive female travelling companion that a tourist in the United States could positively take with him would be a Black Nun of one of the barefooted orders. Those black robes and veils are so very becoming. But then nuns, black or white, and barefooted or otherwise, do not marry. It is not, I apprehend, from the 'little people of the skies' in the French quarter that the grand visiting bonnets are procured. In Canal-street, nearly opposite the Grand Opera House, where M. Maurice Grau's French Opera Troupe, with Capoul as primo tenore, have lately been performing, I have noticed a magasin of austerely splendid aspect. It has but two modestly-sized windows, in which are displayed, with studied carelessness, some parcels of rich tissues, some loosely floating lace, and a dainty fan and trailing feather or two. In the background I see some lace curtains and wire gauze blinds, with the single word 'Olympe', inscribed in golden letters. Is Olympe the High Priestess of the Temple of Visiting Bonnets? I know not; nor knowing, would I dare to say. Guarda e passa. I would as soon think of calling on the Sibyl, and asking her the price of one of her Books, as of paying a visit to the mysterious Olympe.

(On New Orleans, 1882)

I have been told he had on a cut velvet coat of cinnamon colour, lined with a pink satten, embroidered all over with gold; his waistcoat, which was cloth of silver, was embroidered with gold likewise. I cannot be particular as to the rest of his dress; but it was all in the French fashion, for Bellarmine (that was his name) was just arrived from Paris . . . 'Yes, madam; this coat, I assure you, was made at Paris, and I defy the best English taylor even to imitate it. There is not one of them can cut, madam; they can't cut. If you observe how this coat is turned, and this sleeve: a clumsy English rascal can do nothing like it. Pray, how do you like my liveries? . . . All French, I assure you, except for the greatcoats; I never trust anything more than a greatcoat to an Englishman.'

Henry Fielding, *The Adventures of Joseph Andrews*

CHARLES CAVERS

From Hades! The Ladies!

THERE ARE MANY kinds come about this shop of mine, but to-day I think of two sorts.

They are heavy, dignified.

They wear handsome coats, usually black.

They wear well-ornamented hats.

Their skirts are long; one does not see their feet; they move slowly; they have dignity, solidity, substantiality.

They can smile, but they do it infrequently.

Their greatest charm, when they charm at all, is that they can be gracious.

These I call the Dames.

The others are quite sprightly.

They affect colours as well as black; they have waists as well as hips; they have smart hats and pursue fashions.

They move quickly; they cannot be deceived as to what is or what is not fashionable.

They know.

They have an exact idea of who I am and they put me completely in my place.

They are the Madams.

These are two of the sorts who frequent my place of business, who fill me with profound satisfaction when I remember how I have kept out of the temptations which have been laid before me to enter into the wedded state.

To be beholden to women for a livelihood is bad enough, but to be beholden to women for domestic happiness, that is intolerable.

It is five P.M., and I make the resolution that I will dine heavily and heartily to-night, alone, and thank God that I am a bachelor, knowing women only in matters external.

LADY DUFF GORDON ('LUCILE')
From Discretions and Indiscretions

I WAS PARTICULARLY ANXIOUS to have a department for beautiful underclothes, as I hated the thought of my creations being worn over the ugly nun's veiling or linen-cum-Swiss embroidery which was all that the really virtuous woman of those days permitted herself . . . So I started making underclothes as delicate as cobwebs and as beautifully tinted as flowers, and half the women of London flocked to see them, though they had not the courage to buy them at first.

It seems so silly now that we have just got over wearing skirts above our knees and showing backbone below the waist to think that those demure little morning dresses and diaphanous tea-gowns I made were once considered by many people 'too daring', but they were . . . I took it as a compliment, for in those days virtue was too often expressed by dowdiness, and I had no use for the dull, stiff, boned-bodice brigade. I had a message for the women I dressed. I was the first dressmaker to bring joy and romance into clothes. I was a pioneer. I loosed upon a startled London, a London of flannel underclothes, woollen stockings and voluminous petticoats, a cascade of chiffons, of draperies as lovely as those of Ancient Greece, of softly-rounded breasts (I brought in the brassière in opposition to the hideous corset of the time, which was distorting women's figures) and draped skirts which opened to reveal slender legs.

ALICE WALKER
From The Color Purple

I SIT IN THE dining room making pants after pants. I got pants now in every color and size under the sun. Since us started making pants down home, I ain't been able to stop. I change the cloth, I change the print, I change the waist, I change the pocket. I change the hem, I change the fullness of the leg. I make so many pants Shug tease me. I didn't know what I was starting, she say, laughing. Pants all over her chairs, hanging all in front of the china closet. Newspaper patterns and cloth all over the table and the floor. She come home, kiss me, step over all the mess. Say, before she leave again, How much money you think you need *this* week?

Then finally one day I made the perfect pair of pants. For my sugar, naturally. They soft dark blue jersey with teeny patches of red. But what make them so good is, they totally comfortable. Cause Shug eat a lot of junk on the road, and drink, her stomach bloat. So the pants can be let out without messing up the shape. Because she have to pack her stuff and fight wrinkles, these pants are soft, hardly wrinkle at all, and the little figures in the cloth always look perky and bright. And they full round the ankle so if she want to sing in 'em and wear 'em sort of like a long dress, she can. Plus, once Shug put them on, she knock your eyes out.

Miss Celie, she say. You is a wonder to behold.

I duck my head. She run round the house looking at herself in mirrors. No matter how she look, she look good.

You know how it is when you don't have nothing to do, I say, when she brag to Grady and Squeak bout her pants. I sit here thinking bout how to make a living and before I know it I'm off on another pair pants.

By now Squeak see a pair *she* like. Oh, Miss Celie, she say. Can I try on those?

She put on a pair the color of sunset. Orangish with a little grayish fleck. She come back out looking just fine. Grady look at her like he could eat her up.

Shug finger the pieces of cloth I got hanging on everything. It all soft, flowing, rich and catch the light. This a far cry from that stiff army shit us started with, she say. You ought to make up a special pair to thank and show Jack.

What she say that for. The next week I'm in and out of stores spending more of Shug's money. I sit looking out cross the yard trying to see in my mind what a pair of pants for Jack would look like. Jack is tall and kind and don't hardly say anything. Love children. Respect his wife, Odessa, and all Odessa amazon sisters. Anything she want to take on, he right there. Never talking much, though. That's the main thing. And then I remember one time he touch me. And it felt like his fingers had eyes. Felt like he knew me all over, but he just touch my arm up near the shoulder.

I start to make pants for Jack. They have to be camel. And soft and strong. And they have to have big pockets so he can keep a lot of children's things. Marbles and string and pennies and rocks. And they have to be washable and they have to fit closer round the leg than Shug's so he can run if he need to snatch a child out the way of something. And they have to be something he can lay back in when he hold Odessa in front of the fire. And . . .

I dream and dream and dream over Jack's pants. And cut and sew. And finish them. And send them off.

Next thing I hear, Odessa want a pair.

Then Shug want two more pair just like the first. Then everybody in her band want some. Then orders start to come in from everywhere Shug sing. Pretty soon I'm swamp.

One day when Shug come home, I say, You know, I love doing this, but I got to git out and make a living pretty soon. Look like this just holding me back.

She laugh. Let's us put a few advertisements in the paper, she say. And let's us raise your prices a hefty notch. And let's us just go ahead and give you this dining room for your factory and git you some more women in here to cut and sew, while you sit back and design. You making your living, Celie, she say. Girl, you on your way.

End of November 1834

I have made up the old black gown (which was dyed puce for me at Dumfries) with my own hands; it looks twenty percent better than when it was new; and I shall get no other this winter. I am now turning my pelisse. I went yesterday to a milliner's to buy a bonnet: an old, very ugly lady, upwards of seventy, I am sure, was bargaining about a cloak at the same place; it was a fine affair of satin and velvet; but she declared repeatedly that 'it had no air', and for her part she could not put on such a thing. My bonnet, I flatter myself has an air; a little brown feather nods over the front of it, and the crown points like a sugar loaf! The diameter of the fashionable ladies at present is about three yards; their bustles (false bottoms) are the size of an ordinary sheep's fleece. The very servant girls wear bustles: Eliza Miles told me a maid of theirs went out one Sunday with three kitchen dusters pinned on as a substitute . . .

Jane Welsh Carlyle, *Letters*

BERYL BAINBRIDGE
From The Dressmaker

H E CLOSED HIS eyes again, and soon Nellie sat down at the sewing machine and spun the wheel, pressing the treadle up and down rapidly, running material under the stabbing needle, settling into the rhythm of it, in her element. As long as he could remember, Nellie had played the machine, for that's how he thought of it. Like the great organ at the Palladium cinema before the war, rising up out of the floor and the organist with his head bowed, riddled with coloured lights, swaying on his seat in time to the opening number. Nellie sat down with just such a flourish, almost as if she expected a storm of applause to break out behind her back. And it was her instrument, the black Singer with the hand-painted yellow flowers. She had been apprenticed when she was twelve to a woman who lived next door to Emmanuel Church School: hand sewing, basting, cutting cloth, learning her trade. When she was thirteen Uncle Wilf gave her a silver thimble. She wasn't like some, plying her needle for the sake of the money, though that was important: it was the security the dressmaking gave her – a feeling that she knew something, that she was skilled, handling her materials with knowledge; she wasn't a flibbitygibbet like some she could mention. For all that she lifted the tailor's dummy out from its position under the stairs coquettishly, holding it in her arms like a dancing partner, circling the armholes with chalk, stroking the material down over the stuffed breast, standing back to admire her work with her mouth clamped full of little pins, tape measure about her neck.

ALEXANDER POPE

From The Rape of the Lock

And now unveil'd, the toilet stands display'd,
Each silver vase in mystic order laid.
First robed in white, the nymph intent adores,
With head uncover'd, the cosmetic powers.
A heavenly image in the glass appears,
To that she bends, to that her eyes she rears;
The inferior priestess, at her altar's side,
Trembling, begins the sacred rites of pride.
Unnumber'd treasures ope at once, and here
The various offerings of the world appear;
From each she nicely culls with curious toil,
And decks the goddess with the glittering spoil.
This casket India's glowing gems unlocks,
And all Arabia breathes from yonder box.
The tortoise here and elephant unite,
Transform'd to combs, the speckled and the white,
Here files of pins extend their shining rows,
Puffs, powders, patches, bibles, billet-doux,
Now awful beauty puts on all its arms,
The fair each moment rises in her charms,
Repairs her smiles, awakens every grace,
And calls forth all the wonders of her face;
Sees by degrees a purer blush arise,
And kenner lightnings quicken in her eyes.
The busy sylphs surround their darling care:
These set the head, and those divide the hair;
Some fold the sleeve, whilst others plait the gown:
And Betty's praised for labours not her own.

MAEVE BINCHY
From Circle of Friends

'WHAT DO YOU think?' Benny looked anxiously at Clodagh. 'It's a gorgeous bit of stuff. A pity to cut it up.'

'You've seen people going to these places. Will it look all right?'

'When I'm through with it and you, it will be a sensation.'

Benny looked doubtfully at Clodagh's own outfit, which was a white smock over a mauve polo-necked jumper and what looked like mauve tights. It was very far ahead for anywhere, let alone Knockglen.

'We'll cut the bodice well . . . well down like this.' Benny stood in her slip. Eve sat companionably on a radiator smoking and giving comments.

Clodagh made a gesture with the black velvet top which implied a startlingly low neckline.

'Cut it where?' Benny screamed. Clodagh gestured again. 'That's what I thought you said. I'd fall into my dinner, for God's sake.'

'Presumably you'll be wearing some kind of undergarment to prevent this.' 'I'll be wearing a bra made of surgical steel . . .'

'Yes, and we must push your bosom right up and in like this.' Clodagh made a grab at her and Benny gave a yell. 'I haven't had as much fun in years,' Eve said.

'Tell her, Eve. Tell her Mother's paying for this. She won't let me out like the whore of Babylon.'

'It's a dance, isn't it?' asked Clodagh. 'It's not a function to put forward the cause of your canonisation or anything, is it?'

'Clodagh, you're right off your head. I can't. Even if I had the courage.'

'Right. We'll give you a modesty vest.'

'A what?' 'We'll cut the thing the way it should be cut and mould you into it. Then I'll make a bit of pleated linen or something and a couple of fasteners and we can tell your Mother that this is what you'll be wearing. You can take it out as soon as you are outside the city limits of Knockglen.'

Clodagh fiddled and draped and pinned.

'Put your shoulders back, Benny,' she ordered. 'Stick your chest out.'

'Jesus, Mary and Joseph. I look like the prow of a ship,' said Benny in alarm. 'I know. Isn't it great?'

'Fellows love the prows of ships,' Eve said.' They're always saying it.' 'Shut up, Eve Malone. I'll stick the scissors in you.'

'You will not. Those are my expensive pinking shears. Now isn't that something?' Clodagh looked pleased. Even in its rough and ready state they could see what she had in mind for Benny. And it looked very good indeed.

'The Wise Woman wouldn't let her mother near the fittings for this dress,' Eve said sagely.

'They'll be climbing all over you in this,' Clodagh said happily as she began to unpin it.

'Wouldn't that be fantastic?' Benny said, smiling delightedly at her reflection in the mirror.

> *Norfolk*:
> It doth appear; for, upon these taxations,
> The clothiers all, not able to maintain
> The many of them 'longing, have put off
> The spinsters, carders, fullers, weavers, who,
> Unfit for other life, compell'd by hunger
> And lack of other means, in desperate manner
> Daring the event to the teeth, are all in uproar,
> And danger serves among them.
>   *King*:   Taxation!
> Wherein? and what taxation? My lord cardinal,
> You that are blamed for it alike with us,
> Know you of this taxation?

William Shakespeare, *King Henry VIII*

GEORGE ORWELL
From Down and Out in Paris and London

The clothes were a coat, once dark brown, a pair of black dungaree trousers, a scarf and a cloth cap; I had kept my own shirt, socks and boots and I had a comb and razor in my pocket. It gives one a very strange feeling to be wearing such clothes. I had worn bad enough things before, but not at all like these, they were not merely dirty and shapeless, they had – how is one to express it? – a gracelessness, a patina of antique filth, quite different from mere shabbiness. They were the sort of clothes you see on a bootlace seller, or a tramp.

My new clothes had put me instantly into a new world. Everybody's demeanour seemed to have changed abruptly. I helped a hawker pick up a barrow that he had upset. 'Thanks, mate,' he said with a grin. No one had called me mate before in my life – it was the clothes that had done it. For the first time I noticed too how the attitude of women varies with a man's clothes. When a badly dressed man passes them they shudder away from him with a quite frank movement of disgust, as though he were a dead cat. Clothes are powerful things.

RICHARD CHURCH
Snobs

I like a snob. I mean a mender of shoes,
A man who knows good leather when he feels it
With half-tanned thumb; who takes a shoe and peels it
Neatly from worn sole, no matter whose,
Whether a dancing lady's, or a farmer's
Mud-caked field boots, or a schoolboy's wrecks,
Or admiral's, for dustless quarter-decks,
Or champagne slippers worn by famous charmers.

I take my shoes with reverence for repair,
And like to linger to discuss the job,
Leaning across the counter for awhile
To hear about man's character and style
Betrayed in well-worn leather, sculptured there.
By daily usage. Yes, I like a snob.

RIFLEMAN HARRIS
From Recollections

THE SHOES AND boots of our party were now mostly either destroyed or useless to us, from foul roads and long miles, and many of the men were entirely barefooted, with knapsacks and accoutrements altogether in a dilapidated state. The officers were also, for the most part, in as miserable a plight. They were pallid, way-worn, their feet bleeding, and their faces overgrown with beards of many days' growth. What a contrast did our corps display, even at this period of the retreat, to my remembrance of them on the morning their dashing appearance captivated my fancy in Ireland! Many of the poor fellows, now near sinking with fatigue, reeled as if in a state of drunkenness, and altogether I thought we looked the ghosts of our former selves; still we held on resolutely: our officers behaved nobly; and Craufurd was not to be daunted by long miles, fatigue, or foul weather. Many a man in that retreat caught courage from his stern eye and gallant bearing. Indeed, I do not think the world ever saw a more perfect soldier than General Craufurd. It might be on the night following the disaster I have just narrated that we came to a halt for about a couple of hours in a small village, and together with several others, I sought shelter in the stable of a sort of farmhouse, the first roof I saw near. Here, however, we found nothing to refresh ourselves with by way of food, but some raw potatoes lying in a heap in one of the empty stalls, and which, for want of better rations, we made a meal of, before we threw ourselves down upon the stones with which the place was paved. Meanwhile, others of the men, together with two or three of our officers, more fortunate than ourselves, had possession of the rooms of the adjoining building, where they found at least a fire to warm themselves. Lieutenant Hill had a black servant with him in this retreat, a youth he had brought with him from Monte Video, where, I heard, the Rifles had found him tied to a gun they had captured there. This lad came and aroused me as I lay in the mule-stable, and desired me to speak with his master in the adjoining room. I found the Lieutenant seated in a chair by the fire when I entered. He was one of the few amongst us who rejoiced in the possession of a tolerably decent pair of boots, and he had sent for me to put a few stitches in them, in order to keep them from flying to pieces. I was so utterly wearied that I at first refused to have anything to do with them; but the officer, taking off his boots, insisted upon my getting out my wax threads and mending them; and himself and servant, thrusting me into the chair he arose from, put the boots into my hands, got out my shoemaking implements, and held me up as I attempted to cobble up the boots. It was, however, in vain that I tried to do my best towards the Lieutenant's boots. After a few stitches I fell asleep as I worked, the awl and wax-ends falling to the ground. I remember there were two officers present at the time, Lieutenants Molloy and Keppel, the latter of whom soon afterwards fell dead from fatigue during this retreat. At the present time, however, they all saw it was in vain to urge me to mend Lieutenant Hill's boots. He therefore put them on again with a woeful face and a curse, and dismissed me to my repose. Our rest was not, however, of long duration. The French were upon our trail, and before long we were up and hurrying onwards again.

(1809)

'A milliner and dressmaker admitted to the private apartments of the Queen, to the stupefaction of all who held by etiquette, Rose Bertin became a historic personage. Her influence destroys our old industries by completing the revolution commenced by the Pompadour and Du Barry, substituting for the solid magnificence of old fashions a light, frivolous, and fantastic style. At one time we see the Queen, and after her all our reigning beauties, affecting extreme simplicity, and borrowing the light white dresses of their lady's-maids; now we find them swathed in theatrical costumes, with immense crests of feathers. They raise upon their heads a gigantic scaffolding of gauze, flowers, and feathers, so that, according to the caricatures of the period, a woman's head was in the middle of her body, and society had the appearance of an extravagant fancy ball.

'The *salons* laugh at Fashion, but obey it. The workshops clamour that the Austrian is ruining the manufacturers of Lyons – our beautiful silk trade – to enrich the lawn factories of Brabanzon and the subjects of her brother, Joseph II.'

Henri Martin, *Histoire de France*

CHARLES DICKENS
The Man Milliner

'YOU SURELY KNOW the Rue de la Paix, the Street of Peace, so called because it commemorates war under the form of a column – there resides somewhere in it an Englishman who enjoys considerably greater popularity in the world of furbelows than any London preacher whatsoever. It must be avowed that this Anglais has created a novel art – the art of squeezing in a woman at the waist with a precision hitherto unknown. He possesses the inspiration of handling the scissors, and the genius of sloping out. He knows to a thread the exact point where the stuff ought to fit tight, and where it ought to fit loosely. At first sight he distinguishes in the figure of a lady what ought to be displayed and what concealed. Destiny set him from all eternity to discover the law of crinoline and the curve of the petticoat. In other aspects a perfect gentleman, always fresh shaved, always frizzled. Black coat, white cravat, the batiste shirt-cuffs fastened at the wrists with golden buttons, he officiates with all the gravity of a diplomatist who holds the fate of the world locked up in a drawer of his brain. When he tries a dress on one of the living dolls of the Chaussee d'Antin, it is with profound attention that he touches, pricks, and sounds it, marking with chalk the difficult fold. From time to time he draws back, in order to judge better of his work from a distance; he looks through his hand, closed into the shape of an eyeglass, and resumes with inspired fingers the modelling of the drapery on the person of the patient. Sometimes he plants a flower here, and ties a bow of ribbon at its side, to test the general harmony of the toilette.

Meanwhile, the modern Eve, in process of formation, resigned and motionless, silently allows her moulder to accomplish his creation. At last, when he has handled the taffety like clay, and arranged it according to his beau-ideal, he goes and takes his place, with his head thrown back, on a sofa at the further end of the room, whence he commands the manoeuvre with a wand of office.

'To the right, Madame.' The client performs a quarter of a revolution.

'To the left.' The patient turns in the opposite direction.

'In front.' Madame faces the artist.

'Behind.' She turns her back.

When all is over, he dismisses her with a lordly gesture: 'That will do, Madame.'

The Paris elegantes, marvelling at the delightful ways of their milliner in pantaloons, came to the conclusion that a man who made a robe so well ought finally to put it in place himself, and ought to stamp it with the mark of his lion's claw. Consequently, whenever there is a ball at Court, or at the Hotel de Ville, or an evening party of ceremony at the Palais Royal or the Luxembourg, at about ten o'clock at night you will see a long line of carriages drawn up before the house of the foreign ladies' tailor, with their melancholy coachman buried in their wraps. Their mistresses mount the staircase of the Temple de la Toilette; as they enter, they each receive a ticket in the order of their arrival, and are shown into a waiting room. As they can only appear one by one in the presence of the pontiff of the skirt, the last comers have sometimes to wait a long while. By a delicate attention, the master of the mansion does his best to solace as far as possible the fatigue of the ante-chamber. A buffet liberally supplied offers the consolation of meats and pastry. The ethereal petites maitresses of the Paris Salons lay in a stock of strength for the polka, by eating pate de foie gras at discretion, and washing it down with Malmsey Madeira. Thus refreshed at the expense of the establishment, they intrepidly confront the operations of the toilet. He looks, he inspects, gives a finishing touch, sticks in a pin, arranges a flower, and Madame has realised the prototype of elegance. The master gets rid of them one after the other, turning them off hand rapidly.

Nevertheless, like all great artists, this son of Albion has his caprices. He will clothe and criticise, doubtless, any woman, but he prefers ample women. He believes that those do most honour to his talent, putting it more plainly in evidence. For them he reserves all the attentions and all the ingenious flatteries of his profession. As to beauties who are reduced to the meagre volume which is rigorously indispensable to escape being a ghost, he consents to dress them, certainly – but without enthusiasm, solely as a duty to conscience.

There is not the slightest intention here to cast disfavour on the talent of the English artist, and still less on his personal character: he has a profession which he exercises. He is engaged in a commercial undertaking, and he endeavours to attract customers: there is no harm in that, for it makes all the difference to him between prosperity and ruin. But what are we to think of the customers, the aristocracy of the Exchange, virtuous, but sufficiently forgetful of themselves and their husbands to discuss with a man milliner at night the perilous problem of the height of a dress?

Published in *All the Year Round* (1867)

From the present distance in time it would seem improbable that any fashionable woman should go especially to Hull for her clothes; but so it was . . . The mode had originated with the daughters of Mrs Arthur Wilson and Mrs Charles Wilson – afterwards Lady Nunburnholme – who, coming from that district, had startled London a few years before with their good looks and their dashing clothes, and had soon made the reputation of the local dressmaker whom they were said to patronise. I remember, though I cannot be certain of the year, accompanying my mother and her cousin, Lady Westmorland, by train from Scarborough to Hull, and then being taken to see Madame Clapham, who was fitting them for the dresses they had ordered for a Court Ball. Lady Westmorland, a famous beauty, bought some of her clothes, it is true, in Paris, but as yet very few women – apart from the American contingent who thereby gained an unfair advantage over the rest – obtained them there. And though within a few years every woman who could afford to do so was following the American example, at present Hull was the rage.

Osbert Sitwell, *Left Hand, Right Hand*

EVELYN WAUGH
From Labels

THE FICTION OF Paris, conceived by Hollywood and the popular imagination, seems yearly to impose its identity more and more as the real city of Richelieu and Napoleon and Verlaine fades into the distance. This fictitious city expresses itself in dress parades, studios, and night clubs.

The first of these, because it is modern and commercialized, seems to me by far the most interesting. There is an inscrutable world, of which one occasionally catches a tantalizing glimpse or reflection, behind the industry of making women's clothes, which seems to promise, to anyone happy enough to penetrate into that close society, a rich and almost virgin literary soil. The high diplomacy of the *couturiers*; the espionage of the *copyistes*; the wicked senators' wives who smuggle their maids into the mannequin shows; the secrets and intrigues and betrayals in the *ateliers*; the simple private lives of mannequins and *vendeuses*; the genius who lives in an attic and conceives robes he will never see for beautiful women he will never meet; the great designer who steals his ideas; the life of the frock as its character is shaped and modified and enriched by the impact of each personality through whose mind it passes; its eventual emergence into reality – what a world to sack!

As Christian Dior, that most modest of men, said to me, 'No *one* person can change fashion – a big fashion change *imposes itself*.'

> Carmel Snow, *The World of Carmel Snow*

COLETTE

From The Master

MOREOVER, THE MASTER shows an almost exaggerated, I was going to write: squeamish, discretion. It is with a distant, seemingly magnetic, index finger that he commands his client's revolutions. She turns, takes a step forward, and stops, mesmerised – he does not even graze the material of the dress. Perhaps this extreme reserve is not an affectation at all. Around us I hear an exclusively feminine hum; in the warm, dry air I breathe in mixed perfumes, and that of my friend Valentine, décolleté, is fresh and strong – and I think of a confession from my corset maker, who flees her apartment at night and goes out, sick to her stomach, to have her dinner at a restaurant. 'After all those fittings, Madame, I can't bear to eat at home. It smells too strongly of women at the end of the day, it ruins my appetite.'

This is the first time I've come here with my friend Valentine, who, of course, has her dresses made by a 'master couturier'. I study the 'master', who returns the compliment. He busies himself with Valentine, but I am the one he wants to impress. He takes his time with her, he ignores his other impatient subjects – he poses, not quite knowing whether what I am making of him is a flattering portrait or a caricature . . .

He's a rather small man, well dressed, neither young nor old. His jacket is dark, his tie severe. Nothing aggressive about his clothes or his shoes, no jewellery. One doesn't think of looking for what there's too much of, but rather for what's missing. He's missing . . . a little of everything: three inches in height, as much in width, and then one would like more decisiveness in the nose, a more adventurous chin. He's arrogant without being authoritative, and his ferrety gaze deliberately loses all its expression when it fixes on something. I wonder why it is he seems disguised, from head to foot: his face looks as if it doesn't belong to him.

'A hole,' repeats Valentine devoutly, 'yes, a hole . . .'

She nervously fingers the small lace fichu pinned to her shoulders, crumpling it in her hand over the by-now-famous 'hole', high on the waist, beneath the breast. The rest of the dress is a close-fitting shift, in a singular shade of mauve, which turns blue when the folds of transparent silk are gathered. There is also a small sprinkling of long pearls at the bottom of the tunic, and some sort of ragged piece of material, without any definite purpose, which trails off to the side onto the carpet. It is an 'important' dinner dress.

'Wait! Why didn't I think of it sooner?'

The master steals off with a malicious little hop and reappears, preciously cradling what he needed to fill in the hole: a green flower, made of knitted wool, from which hangs a ludicrous cluster of blue cherries, made of knitted wool, topped by three black leaves – made of knitted wool.

'There!'

He plants the thing in the hollow of the décolleté bodice, and quickly pulls away his hand, like a cat that has burned its paw, and laughs an odious, theatrical laugh.

I look in the triple mirror at my friend Valentine. She has not batted an eyelash and, with the tips of her fingers, pushes up the knitted object, the horror, which is a disgrace to the mauve dress. Without hiding the sickness I feel, I also look at the master, who winks and leans his head to the side like a satisfied painter: I detest fools . . .

One after the other, in the dreary elegance of the white salon, the models dance the steps to the 'mermaid on her tail fin' and the 'upright serpent'. They progress with difficulty, knees joined and bound, and cut through the air as though it were heavy water, helping themselves along with their hands, which paddle the air at hip level. These are lovely creatures, whose every deformity has its grace: they no longer have any rumps – the curve is gone from the small of their backs accentuating their length: where does the stomach begin? Where are the breasts hiding?

A sign from the master hurries them on or holds them back. Now and then I move involuntarily toward a particular dress, pink and alive like a glittering skin, toward this one, in a savage blue colour which blots out everything around it, toward that one made of black velvet, deep and thick as a pelt.

But something holds my arm back and dampens my pleasure: every dress has its ludicrous flaw, the imbecilic and bizarre detail, the toad thrown there like a signature by the despotic and wicked dressmaker. I see knitted flowers on moonlight gauze and unseemly little white horsehair fringe on royal Alençon lace. A delicate train hangs from a tapestry cabbage: a sheath of black plush, slender, curvacious, with a satanic elegance, tapes off, prisoner of the heaviest foundation of white cloth, twisted into a double skirt; a Greek tunic, pure white, moves forward, barred at the knees by a row of little taffeta flounces with chenille borders; finally, a spiral skirt of green Empire faille, tied up in all directions with Tom Thumb trimmings, unleashes my indignation.

'Monsieur,' I say to the dressmaker, 'Monsieur, will you please just look at that! Surely you must know how ugly that is. It's not simply a matter of bad taste; in every one of these dresses there is an intention: take any one of them, take this one here, which wipes the floor with this little square tail of gold linen embroidered with thick white cotton! Why, *why* do you do it?'

My unexpected vehemence makes the master stop short, and his beady eyes meet mine for a long moment. He hesitates; he lets me catch his true and mediocre face, the face of a small shopkeeper who had a hard time starting out – he hesitates between his urge to deceive me and a sudden need for confession, for cynicism . . .

'Would you please tell me, Monsieur, just me, why you do this?'

He smiles a loathesome, confidential smile, he looks around him, as if he wished we were alone: will he betray his appetite for domination, claim revenge for his past as an impoverished clerk, confess the disgusted misogyny that comes from dealing with too many females, the pleasure he takes in making them ugly, in humiliating them, in subjecting them to his half-crazed fantasies, in 'branding' them . . .

He hesitates, he doesn't dare, and, finally, turning his eyes away from mine: 'Just to see . . .' he says.

WILLIAM GERHARDIE

From Of Mortal Love

SHE, HOWEVER, DID not implement her own argument, but instead, guided by Jim, answered an advertisement applying for a young woman dress designer with ideas. Dinah stressed in her letter that she was prolific in ideas. Walter insisted, in the teeth of Dinah's discretion, on her saying she was very beautiful; and to her letter she received no reply.

Then she fell back on another idea. When she lived with Aunt Flora at Cambridge she had taken lessons in drawing and sketching, and her teacher had prophesied eventual success. She believed she could do fashion drawings for the newspapers, and she followed up one or two introductions to editors, who approved her initial efforts, with reservations. They counselled her to resume her lessons so as to sharpen her outlines, which tended to get rather blurred, with a view to selling her fashion drawings eventually to some publication other than their own. After a serious consultation with Jim, it was decided that Dinah should take these lessons, and Jim put up the money, which he could ill afford. The lessons did not, as expected, lead to employment. But when Dinah had had a great many lessons, her teacher, learning in the course of casual conversation that Dinah had both designed and made the dress she was wearing, remarked: 'Now why don't you –?' And wrinkling her brows: 'I'll give you a letter to the editress of *Venus*. I know she badly needs somebody to make a model for their film-star competition.'

The editress of *Venus*, agreeably impressed by Dinah's appearance, noticed her white string belt, and quickly asked where she could get one like it. When Dinah said she had made it herself, the idea having occurred to her while seeing a twisted rope on a packing case, the editress of *Venus* said it would be a splendid idea to make this belt the feature of a new competition. Of every development, every hitch, every step on her ladder of success or depression, Dinah kept Walter informed. They met every day and she used the time between her business appointments to ring him up from a call-box; and her first question was always: 'Have you been good? Have you been a good boy? Has no other woman been to see you while I've been designing a belt?'

NANCY MITFORD
From Love in a Cold Climate

I REMEMBER THAT MY mother, during one of her rare visits to England, brought me a little jacket in scarlet cloth from Schiaparelli. It seemed to me quite plain and uninteresting except for the label in its lining, and I longed to put this on the outside so that people would know where it came from. I was wearing it, instead of a cardigan, in my house when Cedric happened to call, and the first thing he said was,

'Aha! So now we dress at Schiaparelli, I see! Whatever next?'

'Cedric! How can you tell?'

'My dear, one can always tell. Things have a signature, if you use your eyes, and mine seem to be trained over a greater range of objects than yours, Schiaparelli – Reboux – Fabergé – Viollet-le-Duc – I can tell at a glance, literally a glance.'

Madam Frances's clothes were extremely feminine; she drew heavily on lace and ribbons and specialized in pastel shades. She exploded that false theory of the Theda Bara school that men are seduced by girls who dress in red or black. Frances knew as well as Ziegfeld that men's desire is more quickly provoked by the colors worn by little girls when they, as little boys, experienced the first thrill of romantic love. The one occasion when I dared John's resentment and ordered a dress from Frances, I told her I wanted a more sophisticated shade than baby blue or pink. She had an instant solution: 'I've got it, dear! A nice sexy beige.'

Anita Loos, *A Girl Like I*

Lucien of Reboux's is a famous Paris figure. To have your hats fitted by her means you are supremely chic. To be seen walking across the showroom with Lucien's arm lightly laid around your waist means that you almost amount to royalty in the realm of fashion.

Winifred Boulter, *Night and Day*

What impresses me in these big dressmaking houses is the love, care and grace with which the women work.

Three or four old women, who used to embroider theatre costumes for Gaby Deslys and Ida Rubinstein, have a real genius which will die with them. I saw dresses this morning in the farmyard at Rochecorbon where I am shooting. They were hanging in the sun, side by side, like Bluebeard's wives, only lifeless. They lacked their souls, and the soul of a dress is a body.

Jean Cocteau, *Diary Of a Film*

Chanel had the spirit of a Till Eulenspiegel. In coping with her one could never be sure whether her mischief-making was deliberate or unconscious.

Edna Woolman Chase, *Always in Vogue*

The party was distinctly sticky. Frantically searching around for something to say, I mentioned that Mrs George Keppel had given me a Chanel necklace as a Christmas present. At once I was made to describe it. No, said Mademoiselle Chanel. It had certainly not come from her. She would never dream of having anything like *that* on sale. And the conversation dropped with a bang.

Loelia, Duchess of Westminster, *Grace and Favour*

Chanel's personality, like her designs, was something of a paradox, a mingling of the masculine and the intensely feminine . . . She seldom saw one of her creations after it was made. Her work was always completely impersonal.

Cecil Beaton, *The Glass of Fashion*

'Look at them,' she said, 'stupid sheep! Fashion editors come in here with all their airs and what do they do? – doze through half of the collection. Oh, yes, I can see them in the mirrors from my place on the stairs! Then they come up and say to me, "*Chere* Coco – marvellous – marvellous!" and go away with no idea what real fashion is.'

Coco Chanel, quoted by Bettina Ballard, *In My Fashion*

Her beauty secrets have a higher aim: the keeping of the moral line . . . We are happy to see, advancing over the marshes where our pride has been somewhat stagnant, the marvellous little head of a black swan. It belongs to Mademoiselle Chanel who, fully as much as the poets, scorns frivolity and foible.

Jean Cocteau, '100 years of the American Female', in *Harper's Bazaar*

With a black pullover and ten rows of pearls she revolutionised fashion.

Christian Dior on Chanel, *Talking About Fashion*

Minor arts can be defined as those whose expressive potentialities are limited. A tender bullfight is as inconceivable as a hilarious *caneton a la presse* or (if the glossy magazines will excuse me) a soul-searing stole: whereas a poem, a novel or a string quartet can have all these attributes. What can be done to sear the soul with yards of tulle is done, of course, in Paris. There is a definite appeal to the spirit, as well as to the eye and ear, in the sussurant creations of Christian Dior.

Kenneth Tynan, *Persona Grata*

Have you heard about the New Look? You pad your hips & squeeze your waist & skirts are to the ankle it is bliss. So then you feel romantic like Mme Greffulhe & people shout ordures at you from vans becuase for some reason it creates class feeling in a way no sables could.

Nancy Mitford, *Letters*

That is where Dior shone . . . His clothes, while wearable, gave women the feeling of being charmingly costumed; there was a faintly romantic flavour about them.

Edna Woolman Chase, *Always in Vogue*

CHRISTIAN DIOR
From Christian Dior and I

L E PATRON (AS Christian Dior is always called within the precints of 30, avenue Montaigne) came into the room.

An affectionate murmur of relief from the assembled company followed him to his chair. He smiled, shook several hands, kissed several cheeks, took up his baton, and settled down. He too was wearing a white smock. Now everything seemed simple; there were exactly the right number of chairs and people, and each one of the spectators occupied a place which he or she felt was his own. At last a tall boy in working clothes lifted the white curtain and announced:

'*Un modèle, Monsieur!*'

As if in response, another voice declaimed the words:

'San Francisco!'

And a mannequin appeared. She advanced, walked around the room with that elegant balanced movement so completely unlike a soldier's march and came to a standstill. As this was the opening number, I felt that it would probably be of comparatively minor importance, in the nature of a curtain-raiser, but at the same time prophetic of the new line. I tried to make out what the line was going to be.

Christian Dior said softly: 'It needs a different hat, something altogether more striking. Now what exactly, I wonder?'

Now that my attention was directed toward it, I found that I had not even noticed before that there was a hat. Immobile in the center of the salon, the mannequin gazed into space at a point which, according to experts, is about at the roots of the spectators' hairline. At the same time, the guardian of the jewels, the two keepers of the hats and a fourth assistant sprang to life. The first fastened on an earring, the second and third wreathed round her head a mass of black taffeta on a foundation of canvas, and a vaporous veil. Under the impact of these simultaneous attacks the mannequin blinked. Finally somebody placed the finished piece on top of her head. There were murmurs of approval saluting this collective effort. But it was still not good enough.

From his seat, Christian Dior observed: 'The flower should be larger.'

Transl. Antonia Fraser

When a woman wearing Balenciaga entered a room, no other woman existed.

Diana Vreeland, *Yves Saint Laurent*

My husband once asked him to come to his rescue in doing up a Dior dress with thirty tiny buttons up the back, and Balenciaga kept muttering as he buttoned me up, 'But Christian is mad, mad!'

Bettina Ballard on Balenciaga, *In My Fashion*

If Dior is the Watteau of dressmaking – full of nuances, chic, delicate and timely – then Balenciaga is fashion's Picasso.

Cecil Beaton, *The Glass of Fashion*

Recently in Spain I asked him if he had any drastic new changes in mind for his coming collection and he looked surprised. 'Changes?' he asked. 'Why, I never change my clothes.'

Bettina Ballard on Balenciaga, *In My Fashion*

Follow Yves down the garden path. There's always a pot of gold at the end.

Diana Vreeland, *Yves Saint Laurent*

He still has that husky Welsh mannequin, Bronwen Pugh, who drags a coat down a runway as if she had just killed it and were taking it home to her mate.

Eugenia Sheppard, *The New York Herald Tribune*,
reporting a show at the house of Balmain.

It was while I was with Robert Piguet that I learned how to 'omit' . . . Piguet knew that elegance can be found only in simplicity.

Christian Dior, *Talking About Fashion*

Freddie Grisewood asked me about mini skirts and I told him that Norman Hartnell had one day said to me that he thought they were a mistake on the whole as most women had knees 'like rock cakes, dear'.

Ailsa Garland, *Lion's Share*

13

The Moralist's Cry

What's more insufferable than your well-heeled
female?

Juvenal, Satire VI

Diogenes being at Olympia, saw at that celebrated festival some young men of
Rhodes, arrayed most magnificently. Smiling, he exclaimed, 'This is pride.'
Afterwards meeting with some Lacedemonians in a mean and sordid dress, he
said, 'And this also is pride.'

Percy Anecdotes (1823)

MARY WOLLSTONECRAFT
From A Vindication of the Rights of Woman

I ONCE KNEW A weak woman of fashion, who was more than commonly proud
of her delicacy and sensibility. She thought a distinguishing taste and puny
appetite the height of all human perfection, and acted accordingly. I have seen
this weak sophisticated being neglect all the duties of life, yet recline with self-
complacency on a sofa, and boast of her want of appetite as a proof of delicacy
that extended to, or, perhaps, arose from, her exquisite sensibility; for it is difficult to render intelligible such ridiculous jargon. Yet, at the moment, I have seen
her insult a worthy old gentlewoman, whom unexpected misfortunes had made
dependent on her ostentatious bounty, and who, in better days, had claims on
her gratitude. Is it possible that a human creature could have become such a weak
and depraved being, if, like the Sybarites, dissolved in luxury, everything like
virtue had not been worn away, or never impressed by precept, a poor substitute, it is true, for cultivation of mind, though it serves as a fence against vice?

Such a woman is not a more irrational monster than some of the Roman emper-
ors, who were depraved by lawless power. Yet, since kings have been more under
the restraint of law, and the curb, however weak, of honour, the records of history are not filled with such unnatural instances of folly and cruelty, nor does
the despotism that kills virtue and genius in the bud, hover over Europe with
that destructive blast which desolates Turkey, and renders the men, as well as
the soil, unfruitful.

Women are everywhere in this deplorable state; for, in order to preserve their innocence, as ignorance is courteously termed, truth is hidden from them . . .

From Isaiah, Chapter 3

16   Moreover the LORD saith, Because the daughters of Zion are haughty, and walk with stretched forth necks and wanton eyes, walking and mincing *as* they go, and making a tinkling with their feet:

17   Therefore the LORD will smite with a scab the crown of the head of the daughters of Zion, and the LORD will discover their secret parts.

18   In that day the LORD will take away the bravery of *their* tinkling ornaments *about their feet*, and *their* cauls, and *their* round tires like the moon,

19   The chains, and the bracelets, and the mufflers,

20   The bonnets, and the ornaments of the legs, and the headbands, and the tablets, and the earrings,

21   The rings, and nose jewels,

22   The changeable suits of apparel, and the mantles, and the wimples, and the crisping pins,

23   The glasses, and the fine linen, and the hoods, and the vails.

24   And it shall come to pass, *that* instead of sweet smell there shall be stink; and instead of a girdle a rent; and instead of wet set hair baldness; and instead of a stomacher a girding of sackcloth; *and* burning instead of beauty.

25   Thy men shall fall by the sword, and thy mighty in the war.

26   And her gates shall lament and mourn; and she *being* desolate shall sit upon the ground.

When I see one of these fine creatures sailing along in her tawdry robes of silk and gauze, frilled, flounced and firbelowed, with her false locks, her false jewels, her paint, her patches and perfumes, I cant help looking upon her as the vilest piece of sophistication that art ever produced.

Tobias Smollett, *Travels Through France and Italy* (1766)

It seems to me that as long as paint a la Ninon Enclos, soap–bubbles of Venus, hair–oil of Athens, and exaggerated fashions are sought by the 'ladies', as this paper reports, and as long as there are men who dodge the ban upon the coming fashion of tying shoes with laces, which threatens to ruin buckle–makers, by wearing a buckle on one foot and a shoe–lace on the other, so as not to cause too precipitate a change – so long there will be family estates on the market.

The Diary of Sophie V. La Roche

Had we been born needing petticoats and breeches, there is no doubt but Nature would have armed that which she hath left to the batteries of seasons and fury of weathers with some thicker skin or hide, as she hath done our finger ends and the soles of our feet. Why seems this hard to be believed? Between my fashion of apparel and that of one of my country-clowns, I find much more difference between him and me than between his fashion and that of a man who is clothed but with his bare skin.

Michel de Montaigne, *Essays*. Transl. John Florio

In truth, whatever is worth doing at all is worth doing well; and nothing can be done well without attention: I therefore carry the necessity of attention down to the lowest things, even to dancing and dress. Custom has made dancing sometimes necessary for a young man; therefore mind it while you learn it, that you may learn to do it well, and not be ridiculous, though in a ridiculous act. Dress is of the same nature: you must dress: therefore attend to it; not in order to rival or to excel a fop in it, but in order to avoid singularity, and consequently ridicule. Take great care always to be dressed like the reasonable people of your own age, in the place where you are; whose dress is never spoken of one way or another, as either too negligent or too much studied.

Lord Chesterfield, *Letters To His Son*

'Is this be-powder'd, be-curl'd, be-hoop'd mad woman my daughter?'

Henry Fielding, *Miss Lucy in Town*

France is the general reservoir from which all the absurdities of false taste, luxury and extravagance have overflowed the different Kingdoms and States of Europe.

Tobias Smollett, *Travels Through France & Italy*

I have lost much of the faith I once had in the commonsense and even in the personal delicacy of the present race of average Englishwomen by seeing how they will allow their dresses to sweep the streets.

John Ruskin, *Sesame and the Lilies*

There is no such thing as a moral dress . . . It's people who are moral or immoral.

Jennie Jerome Churchill, *Daily Chronicle* (1921)

Imagine if one of our forefathers were alive again and should see one of those his gay daughters walk in Cheapside before him . . . Sure he could not but stand amazed to think what new creature the times had yielded since he lived.

Bishop Hall, *Characters of Virtues and Vices* (1608)

INSTRUCTIONS TO LADIES:
Should you have the misfortune to possess a good natural complexion use every endeavour to destroy it with rouge etc . . . in summer dress as you please but in winter always appear as nearly a nudity as possible.

The Spirit of the Public Journal (Anon, 1809)

Sweet hearting matches are very often made up at these parties. It's quite disgusting to a modist eye to see the way the young ladies dress to atract the notice of the gentlemen. They are nearly naked to the waist, only just a little bit of dress hanging on the shoulder, the breasts are quite exposed except a little bit comeing up to hide the nipples. Plenty of false haire and teeth and paint. If a person wish to see the ways of the world, they must be a gentleman's servant, then they mite see it to perfection.

Diary of William Taylor, footman (1837)

What business have rouge and paint on a Christian face?

Saint Jerome, quoted in Lecky, *History of European Morals*

JOHN DONNE
From Paradoxes and Problemes

'FOULNESSE IS LOTHSOME: can that be so which helpes it?. . . What thou lovest in her *face* is *colour*, and *painting* gives that, but thou hatest it, not because it is, but because thou knowest it. Foole, whom ignorance makes happy: the Starres, the Sonne, the Skye whom thou admirest, also have no colour, but are faire, because they seeme to bee coloured: If this seeming will not satisfy thee in her, thou hast good assurance of her *colour*, when thou seest her *lay* it on. If her *face* bee *painted* on a Boord or Wall, thou wilt love it, and the Boord, and the Wall: Canst thou loath it then when it speakes, smiles, and kisses, because it is *painted*? Are wee not more delighted with seeing Birds, Fruites, and Beasts *painted* than wee are with Naturalls? And doe wee not with pleasure behold the *painted* shape of Monsters and Divels, whom true, wee durst not regard? Wee repaire the ruines of our houses, but first cold tempests warnes us of it, and bytes us through it: wee mend the wracke and staines of our Apparell, but first our eyes, and other bodies are offended: but by this providence of women, this is prevented. If in *kissing* or *breathing* upon her, the *painting* fall off, thou art angry; wilt thou be so, if it sticke on? Thou didst love her; if thou beginnest to hate her, then 'tis because she is not *painted*. If thou wilt say now, thou didst hate her before, thou didst hate her and love her together, bee constant in something, and love her who shewes her great love to thee, in taking this paines to seeme lovely to thee.'

The Gipsy Laddie

It was late in the night when the Squire came home
Enquiring for his lady.
His servant made a sure reply:
She's gone with the gipsum Davy
   Rattle tum a gipsum gipsum
   Rattle tum a gipsum Davy.

O go catch up my milk-white steed,
The black one's not so speedy,
I'll ride all night till broad daylight,
Or overtake my lady.

He rode and he rode till he came to the town,
He rode till he came to Barley.
The tears came rolling down his cheeks,
And then he spied his lady.

It's come go back, my dearest dear,
Come go back, my honey;
It's come go back, my dearest dear,
And you never shall lack for money.

I won't go back, my dearest dear,
I won't go back, my honey;
For I wouldn't give a kiss from gipsum's lips
For you and all your money.

It's go pull off those snow-white gloves,
A-made of Spanish leather,
And give to me your lily-white hand,
And bid farewell for ever.

It's she pulled off those snow-white gloves,
A-made of Spanish leather,
And gave to him her lily-white hand,
And bade farewell for ever.

She soon ran through her gay clothing,
Her velvet shoes and stockings;
Her gold ring off her finger's gone,
And the gold plate off her bosom.

O once I had a house and land,
Feather-bed and money;
But now I've come to an old straw pad
With the gipsies dancing round me.

Anon

JAMES DAY
Meditation on the Pride of Women's Apparel

See how some borrow'd off-cast attire,
Can puff up pamper'd clay and dirty mire:
Tell me, whence hadst thy cloaths that make thee fine,
Was't not the silly sheep's before 'twas thine?
Doth not the silk-worm, and the oxe's hide,
Serve to maintain thee in thy cheefest pride?
Do'st not thou often with those featheres vàile
Thy face, with which the ostridge hides her taile?
What art thou proud of, then? me thinks 'tis fit
Thou shouldst be humble for the wearing it:
Tell me, proud madam; thou that art so nise,
How were thy parents clad in Paradise?

At first they wore the armour of defence,
And were compleatly wrapt in innocence:
Had they not sin'd, they ne're had beene dismaid,
Nor needed not the fig-tree's leavy ayde!
  Whatever state, O Lord, thou place me in,
  Let me not glory in th' effect of sin.

(1637)

I am annoyed by the foolish absurdity of the present mode of dress.

The Life and Times of Hannah More (1856)

How can one be good and fashionable too?

Mary Jane Holmes, *The Cameron Pride* (1867)

Style never immortalised anybody.

Alan Bennett, *The Madness of George III*

COPYRIGHT ACKNOWLEDGEMENTS

The author and publisher wish to thank the following for permission to reproduce copyright extracts.

The Young Visiters by Daisy Ashford, (Chatto & Windus 1919) copyright © Daisy Ashford 1919, by permission of Howard Watson, Random House Ltd London.

Autobiography by Enid Bagnold, published by William Heinemann Ltd. Reproduction by permission Reed Consumer Books and The Enid Bagnold Trustees.

The Dressmaker by Beryl Bainbridge, by permission of Gerald Duckworth and Company Ltd.

In My Fashion by Bettina Ballard, copyright © Bettina Ballard. Permission by A.M. Heath.

Excerpt from *The L-Shaped Room* by Lynne Reid Banks, published by Chatto & Windus Ltd. Copyright © Lynne Reid Banks, 1960, by permission of John Johnson (Authors' Agent) Limited and Howard Watson, Random House Ltd London.

Talking It Over by Julian Barnes, published by Cape/Picador reprinted by permission of the Peters Fraser & Dunlop Group Ltd, and Howard Watson, Random House Ltd, London.

The Human Element by Stan Barstow, copyright © Stan Barstow. Reproduced by permission of The Agency (London) Ltd.

A Kind of Loving by Stan Barstow. Published by Michael Joseph Ltd 1960. Copyright © Stan Barstow 1960. Reproduced by permission of Michael Joseph Ltd and Doubleday, a division of Bantam Doubleday Dell Publishing Group, Inc.

The Glass of Fashion by Cecil Beaton, by kind permission of Rupert Crew Limited.

Persona Grata by Cecil Beaton and Kenneth Tynan, (originally published by Allan Wingate) by kind permission of Rupert Crew Ltd.

Zuleika Dobson by Max Beerbohm, originally published by William

Heinemann Ltd. By permission of Reed Consumer Books.

The Madness of George III by Alan Bennett, published by Faber and Faber, reprinted by permission of the Peters Fraser & Dunlop Group Ltd.

Miss Mapp by E.F. Benson. Permission by A.P. Watt Ltd on behalf of K.S.P. McDowall and the Literary Executors of the E.F. Benson Estate, and HarperCollins Publishers, New York. Copyright 1923 by George H. Doran Co. Copyright renewed 1952 by Kenneth Stewart Patrick McDowall.

First Childhood by Lord Berners. By kind permission of the Trustees of the Berners Estate.

Circle of Friends by Maeve Binchy, published by Hodder & Stoughton Ltd. Reprinted by permission of the publisher.

Night and Day by Winifred Boulter. Reprinted by Chatto & Windus, by permission of Howard Watson, Random House Ltd. London.

The Day it Rained Forever by Ray Bradbury. Short stories originally published in England by Hart-Davis Ltd, 1959. Copyright © Ray Bradbury. Reprinted by kind permission of the author.

Room at the Top by John Braine, published by Eyre & Spottiswode. Permission granted by David Higham Associates Limited.

The excerpt from *Testament of Youth* by Vera Brittain is included with the permission of Paul Berry, her literary executor, and Victor Gollancz, publishers, together with Virago Press.

Angelo's Passion by Christopher Burns. Copyright © 1988. First published by Martin Secker & Warburg. Permission granted by Sheil Land Associates Ltd.

Augustus Carp Esq by Himself Being the Autobiography of a Really Good Man, published by Boydell & Brewer. By permission of David Higham Associates.

Wise Children by Angela Carter, published by Chatto & Windus. Copyright © Angela Carter 1991. Reproduced by permission of the Estate of Angela Carter c/o Rogers, Coleridge & White Ltd, 20 Powis Mews, London W11 1JN.

We Danced All Night by Barbara Cartland. Reproduced by permission of Robson Books.

Wild Swans by Jung Chang, published by HarperCollins Publishers Limited. Permission granted by HarperCollins Publishers Ltd.

'Snobs' from *Collected Poems* by Richard Church. By kind permission of the Estate of Richard Church c/o Laurence Pollinger Limited.

Harper's Bazaar: 100 Years of the American Female, Coco Chanel by Jean Cocteau, published by Random House, Inc 1967. Copyright © Jean Cocteau 1967. By permission of Random House, Inc. New York.

The Big Sleep by Raymond Chandler. Reprinted by permission of Alfred A. Knopf.

& Nicolson and Peters Fraser & Dunlop Group Ltd.

Rebecca by Daphne du Maurier. Reproduced with permission of Curtis Brown Ltd, London on behalf of the Estate of Daphne du Maurier. Copyright © 1938 by Daphne du Maurier Browning.

Espirit de Corps by Lawrence Durrell. Reproduced with permission of Curtis Brown Ltd.

American Psycho by Bret Easton Ellis. Copyright © 1991 by Bret Easton Ellis. Reprinted by permission of Vintage Books, A Division of Random House Inc. New York, and Howard Watson, Random House Ltd London.

The Horse in the Furrow by George Ewart Evans, by permission of Faber and Faber Ltd.

A Nursery in the Nineties by Eleanor Farjeon, first published by Victor Gollancz, 1935. Reproduced by permission of David Higham Associates.

Casino Royale by Ian Fleming. Reproduced by permission of Glidrose Publications. First published by Jonathan Cape. US copyright renewed 1981. © Glidrose Productions Ltd 1953.

A Child in the Forest by Winifred Foley. Reproduced by kind permission of the author.

The Fashionable Mind by Kennedy Fraser. Reprinted by permission of Alfred A. Knopf.

Flowers for Mrs Harris by Paul Gallico. Reproduced by permission of Harold Ober Associates, New York.

Lion's Share by Ailsa Garland published by Michael Joseph Ltd, 1970. Copyright © Ailsa Garland, 1970. Reproduced by permission of Michael Joseph Ltd.

Our Lady of the Flowers and *Querelle of Brest* by Jean Genet, originally published by Anthony Blond, by permission of Howard Watson, Random House Ltd. London.

Of Mortal Love by William Gerhardie. Copyright William Gerhardie, reproduced by permission of Curtis Brown Group Ltd, London.

Clothes by Eric Gill originally published by Jonathan Cape 1931. By permission of Howard Watson, Random House Ltd. London.

The Greengage Summer by Rumer Godden originally published by Macmillan 1958. Copyright © Rumer Godden 1958. Used by permission of Macmillan General Books; Viking Penguin, a division of Penguin Books USA Inc.; and Curtis Brown Ltd, New York.

Joyce Grenfell Requests the Pleasure by Joyce Grenfell, published by Sinclair-Stevenson. © Copyright Joyce Grenfell 1976. Reproduced by permission of Richard Scott Simon Limited and Macmillan General Books.

Midnight Cowboy by James Leo Herlihy, published in UK by Jonathan Cape

INDEX